TECHNIQUES OF FINANCIAL ANALYSIS

D0104776

TECHNIQUES OF FINANCIAL ANALYSIS

Erich A. Helfert, D.B.A.

Seventh Edition

IRWIN

Homewood, IL 60430
Boston, MA 02116

A professional version of this text is published by BUSINESS ONE IRWIN.

© RICHARD D. IRWIN, INC., 1963, 1967, 1972, 1977, 1982, 1987, and 1991

Sponsoring editor: Michael W. Junior
Project editor: Jane Lightell
Production manager: Ann Cassady
Cover Designer: David T. Jones
Compositor: Better Graphics, Inc.
Typeface: 12.5/14 Caledonia
Printer: R. R. Donnelley & Sons Company

Library of Congress Cataloging-in-Publication Data
Helfert, Erich A.
    Techniques of financial analysis / Erich A. Helfert.—7th ed.
      p.   cm.
    Includes bibliographical references and index.
    ISBN 0-256-07926-9
    1. Corporations—Finance.   2. Cash flow.   3. Financial statements.
    4. Ratio analysis.   I. Title.
    HG4026.H44   1991   90–41101
    658.15'1—dc20   CIP

Printed in the United States of America
1 2 3 4 5 6 7 8 9 0 DO 7 6 5 4 3 2 1 0

To Anne

PREFACE

For the past 27 years, six editions of this book have served to give the student, analyst, or business executive a concise, practical, usable, and up-to-date overview of the key financial analysis tools needed to understand the relationship between management decisions and financial results, interpret financial reports, develop basic financial projections, evaluate capital investment decisions, assess the implications of financing choices, and derive the value of a business or a security. The techniques and measures are clearly described and demonstrated within the context of underlying financial concepts, yet without delving into theoretical abstraction.

All analytical tools and related financial concepts are discussed from a *decision-making* standpoint, that is, they are linked to the three basic *types of decisions* made continuously by the management of any going business: *investment, operating and financing*. The presentation of the materials is also structured around the *viewpoints* of the major parties interested in the analysis and performance of a business: *managers, owners, and creditors*. Practicality is paramount, however, and issues and concepts beyond the essentials are left to the more specialized texts and articles identified in the references. Self-study exercises and problems are provided after each chapter so the reader can practice applying the analytical tools and check the results against solutions provided in the Appendix.

The book has consistently maintained a unique appeal for both students and practitioners because of its clarity and common sense presentation. Originally an outgrowth of the compact technical briefing materials used in the M.B.A. program at the Harvard Business School, which supplement practical case study discussion with essential background, the book has been regularly updated and modified approximately every five years. This seventh edition reflects not only the latest practice in the use of the various financial techniques, but also the experience gained over six editions from the widespread use the book has enjoyed in university finance courses, graduate and undergraduate, and from hundreds of executive development seminars and in-company programs in the United States, Canada, and South America, and overseas. Translated into five foreign languages over the years, the book has transcended the confines of American business practice on which it is built, because the way in which the analytical methods are described makes them almost universally applicable.

The current edition has been restructured and updated to emphasize the logical, integrated flow of the materials beginning with an overview of the "business system" and key financial analysis concepts, all the way to the development of business valuation and the meaning of shareholder value. This revised sequence of the materials was tested in numerous executive development courses over the past several years. The first five chapters form an integrated set, based on the initial conceptual overview of the business system, its decisional context, and its relationship to financial statements and analytical tools in Chapter 1. The specific coverage of analytical methods begins with funds flow analysis, moves on to financial performance analysis, and financial projections, and culminates in a discussion of the financial dynamics useful in modeling financial conditions. The last four chapters deal with more specialized topics such as investment analysis, the cost of capital, financing choices, and business valuation. The final chapter on valuation was updated and expanded to take into account current trends in mergers and acquisitions. The three appendixes were also updated, and for the first time the solutions to all problems were included in Appendix III, making the book truly self-contained.

The restructuring and revision of this edition has left intact, however, the book's primary focus on the doable and practical—an "executive briefing" concept—and on building the reader's basic ability to grasp financial relationships and issues. As before, the book only presupposes that the user has some familiarity with basic accounting concepts.

I would again like to express my appreciation to my former colleagues at the Harvard Business School for the opportunity to develop the original concept of the book. My thanks also go to Lawrence R. Rosen and to my business associates and my colleagues at universities and in executive development programs here and abroad, too numerous to mention individually, for their continued extensive use of the book and for the many expressions of interest and constructive suggestions that have supported the book's evolution. I am also grateful to James A. Kennelley of Columbia University and to Richard Kolasheski of the University of Maryland for their many helpful suggestions for improving and upgrading the seventh edition of this text. Finally, I continue to be most gratified by the positive responses from so many individual users, past and current, who have found the book helpful in their studies and in their professions.

Erich A. Helfert

CONTENTS

Business. *Valuing Business Cash Flows. Value in Restructuring and Combinations. Managing for Shareholder Value.* Key Issues.

A NOTE
FROM THE EDITOR

Over the past 27 years, thousands of managers and managers-in-training have read *Techniques of Financial Analysis*. For most, it was their first exposure to understanding the relationship between finance concepts and daily decisions. It remains, for many, a valuable reference called upon for day-to-day performance.

Frequently, I talk with readers proclaiming the value of this great resource. Most recently my colleague Mike Allison, the Business Manager for our editorial group here, confessed, "When I was in manufacturing, I would refer to *(Techniques of Financial Analysis)* two or three times a week. I still do!"

I am confident you will also utilize this great resource for years to come.

Michael W. Junior

INTRODUCTION

When a student, analyst, or business executive is dealing with a financial problem or wishes to understand a financial issue related to business investment, operations, or financing, a variety of analytical techniques—and sometimes rules of thumb—are needed to generate meaningful answers. Experience has shown again and again that having a proper perspective for the problem or issue to be analyzed is as important as the selection of the appropriate tools for the analysis. This book, therefore, not only provides the key financial tools in general use but also explains how and where they are applied. Moreover, the first chapter provides a broad conceptual context for both the financial dimensions of business management and the nature of financial statements, data, and processes underlying financial analysis techniques.

While the tools and techniques covered in this book are discussed and demonstrated in detail, the user must not be tempted to view them as *ends* in themselves. It is simply not

1

enough to master the techniques! Financial analysis is both an analytical and judgmental process that helps answer questions that have been properly posed, and therefore it is a *means* to an end. We cannot stress enough that financial analysis is an aid that allows those responsible for results to make sound decisions.

Apart from specific analytical answers, the "solutions" to financial problems and issues depend significantly on the points of view of the parties involved, on the relative importance of the issue, and on the nature and reliability of the information available. In each situation the objective of the analysis must be clearly stated before pencil is put to paper or computer keys are touched; otherwise the process becomes wasteful "number crunching."

Management has been defined as "the art of asking significant questions"; the same applies to financial analysis, which should be targeted toward finding meaningful answers within the context of these significant questions, whether the results are fully quantifiable or not. In fact, the qualitative judgments involved in finding answers to financial issues can often count just as heavily as the technical results, and the analytical task is not complete until these aspects have been carefully spelled out and weighed.

The degree of precision and refinement to which any financial analysis is carried also depends on each situation. Given the uncertain nature of many of the estimates used, it is often preferable to develop ranges of potential outcomes rather than precise "answers." At the same time, it would be wasteful to further refine answers that clearly suggest the choice of particular alternatives—there is no need to belabor the obvious! Also, common sense dictates that most of the effort should be directed at areas where the likely payoff from additional analysis is large—to match the amount of energy expended with the significance of the results.

The following points are a suggested checklist for review and consideration *before* a financial analysis task is started. It will be helpful to the person actually doing the work as well as to the manager who may have assigned the question or project to an associate:

1. What is the exact nature and scope of the issue to be analyzed? Has the problem and its relative importance been clearly spelled out, including the alternatives to be considered?

2. Which specific factors, relationships, and trends are likely to be helpful in analyzing the issue? What is the order of their importance, and in what sequence should they be addressed?

3. Are there possible ways to obtain a quick ballpark estimate of the likely result, to help decide what the critical data and steps might be?

4. How reliable are the available data, and how is this uncertainty likely to affect the range of results? What confirmation might be possible?

5. How precise an answer is necessary in relation to the importance of the problem itself? Is additional refinement going to be worth the effort?

6. What limitations are inherent in the tools to be applied, and how are these likely to affect the range of results? Are the tools appropriate to the problem?

7. How important are qualitative judgments in the context of the problem, and what is the order of their significance? Which analytical steps might be obviated by such considerations?

Only after you have thought through these questions should specific analytical work on a problem proceed. The relatively small amount of effort expended on taking this critical step at the start will pay off in more focused and meaningful work. In effect, we are talking about a rational approach to problem solving—applied to financial analysis. In the end, this is what effective support of decision making in investment, operations, and financing is all about.

1 BUSINESS AS A FINANCIAL SYSTEM

This introductory chapter builds a *conceptual foundation* for discussing the analytical tools and financial concepts presented throughout the book. The perspective given here is one of viewing business—any business—as an interrelated *system of financial resource movements* that are activated by *management decisions,* large and small. This fundamental overview will give the reader a consistent context in which to understand both the purpose and nature of the analytical methods and to help assess the meaning as well as the shortcomings of analytical data used and the results obtained. This demonstration of the *dynamic nature of business*—and its expression in financial terms—serves as an introduction to financial modeling and should also encourage the reader to visualize the judgmental aspects of financial analysis beyond mere technical methodology. Another conceptual overview introduces the nature of *financial statements* and their relationship to business decisions, followed by a review of the *objectives of financial processes* as a backdrop for the use of analytical data and techniques discussed throughout this book.

THE DECISIONAL CONTEXT

The operation and performance of a business depends on many individual or collective *decisions* that are continually made by its management team. Every one of these decisions ultimately causes a *financial impact*, for better or worse, on the condition and the periodic results of the business. In essence, the process of managing involves a series of economic choices that activates movements of financial resources connected with the business.

For example, hiring an employee will result in a future series of salary or wage payments, while selling merchandise on credit releases goods from inventory and creates a documented obligation by the customer to remit payment 30 or 60 days hence. Similarly, the purchase of a new manufacturing facility will bring about a potentially complex set of financial obligations to be met, while successful negotiation of a line of credit with a lender will cause an inflow of funds into the business, to be repaid in future periods.

Some of the decisions management makes are major, such as investment in a new facility, raising large amounts of debt, or adding a new line of products or services. Most other decisions are part of the day-to-day process in which every functional area of a business is managed. The combined effect of all decisions can be observed periodically when the performance of the business is judged through various financial statements and special analyses.

Fundamentally, management makes decisions on behalf of the owners of the business to *deploy various resources for expected economic gain*. In this context, all business decisions can be grouped into three basic areas: (1) the *investment* of resources, (2) the *operation* of the business through the use of these resources, and (3) the proper mix of *financing,* which provides the funding of these resources.

Today's business world is one of infinite variety—enterprises of all sizes engage in areas such as manufacturing, trade, finance, and myriad services, with widely different legal and organizational structures. Common to all, however, is this basic theme of management: *Planned commitments of resources for the purpose of creating, over time, economic value sufficient to recover all resources employed and to earn a margin of profit in addition.*

Over the long run, therefore, the result of management's resource deployments should be a *net improvement in the economic position of the owners*—including their ability to make further resource commitments. This net improvement (i.e., the creation of additional "shareholder value") should raise the value of the business as judged by the securities markets if the stock is traded publicly, or it should be reflected in the value offered by potential buyers of the business. If no such value increment is achieved, the economic viability of the business is in question.

The basic task—and also the challenge—of financial analysis is to develop a reasonably consistent and meaningful set of data and relationships, abstracted from the combined results of management decisions on investments, operations, and financing for the purpose of judging the financial condition and outlook for the business in terms of economic performance and value.

THE BUSINESS SYSTEM

When management operates a business, the daily decisions made impact the financial resources of the business in one way or another in a *dynamic interrelationship.* As we said earlier, all management decisions cause resource movements of various kinds. From now on we will use the term *fund flows* to characterize these movements. *Funds* is a common financial term denoting resources, whether committed by the business in the form of cash balances, receivables, inventories, and plant and equipment, or obtained by the business in the form of loans, vendor credit, bonds, or shareholder capital. Management decisions cause changes in the magnitude and pattern of funds flows, both in funds committed (uses) and in funds obtained (sources), with the objective of enhancing shareholder value over time. As we will see later in this chapter and again in Chapter 2, there are formal ways of tracking and analyzing funds flow patterns to assist a manager or analyst in judging the results and prospects of a business.

Let us now take a conceptual view of how a business operates and demonstrate, with the help of a simplified systems diagram, the basic funds pattern and the key relationships by decisional area. With it we will also establish a first overview of key financial analysis measures and key business strategies as they relate to the business system and to management decisions. Every one of these measures and concepts will, of course, be discussed in greater depth in the appropriate chapters of this book.

Figure 1–1 presents a flow chart containing all major elements necessary to understand the broad funds patterns of a typical business. The boxes and arrows are arranged to show a closed system of funds flows, all interrelated with each other and organized in three sections: *investment, operations,* and *financing.* The key analytical areas are identified by major decisional segment on the left side of the flow diagram, while the key strategies are similarly listed on the right side. The top segment represents the two components of business investment, that is, the *investment base* already in place and the addition of *new investments.* The center segment illustrates the operational interplay of three basic elements: *price, volume of product or services,* and *fixed plus variable costs.* The bottom segment represents the basic financing decisions for a business in two parts. The first is the disposition of the *operating profit* achieved for a period, which normally is divided between *dividends* paid to owners, *interest* paid to lenders,

Figure 1-1
The Business System—an Overview

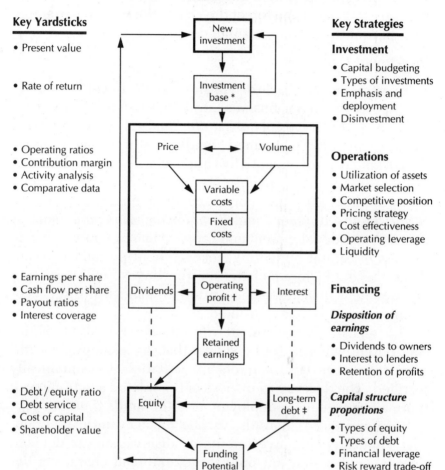

Key Yardsticks

- Present value

- Rate of return

- Operating ratios
- Contribution margin
- Activity analysis
- Comparative data

- Earnings per share
- Cash flow per share
- Payout ratios
- Interest coverage

- Debt / equity ratio
- Debt service
- Cost of capital
- Shareholder value

Key Strategies

Investment

- Capital budgeting
- Types of investments
- Emphasis and deployment
- Disinvestment

Operations

- Utilization of assets
- Market selection
- Competitive position
- Pricing strategy
- Cost effectiveness
- Operating leverage
- Liquidity

Financing

Disposition of earnings

- Dividends to owners
- Interest to lenders
- Retention of profits

Capital structure proportions

- Types of equity
- Types of debt
- Financial leverage
- Risk reward trade-off

* Assumes that an amount equal to depreciation is continuously reinvested here, in order to maintain all existing facilities in good order.

† Assumes that legally required income taxes have been paid after deducting interest, and operating profit is shown here net of such taxes.

‡ Assumes a continuous rollover of debt (refinancing), that is, there is no reduction in debt levels from repayments, as new funds are raised to cover these.

and *retained earnings* kept in the business. The second deals with the key aspects of a company's long-term capital sources. It reflects the split between *ownership equity* (augmented by retained earnings) and *long-term debt* held by outsiders. The decisions in the last segment jointly affect the *funding potential* for investment which, as the arrow indictes, supports the *new investments* at the top of the chart. We will now examine each part of the system in some detail.

Investment Decisions

Investment is the basic driving force of the business system. It supports the major business strategies developed by management and involves plans *(capital budgets)* for committing existing or newly obtained funds to three main areas: (1) *working capital* (essentially cash balances, receivables due from customers, and inventories, less trade credit obtained from suppliers and other normal current obligations), (2) *new facilities and equipment,* and (3) *major spending plans* (such as research and development and promotional programs). In the process of capital budgeting, management periodically validates the deployment of the existing investment base and chooses new investments in order to achieve desired economic returns for the shareholders.

The opposite of investment, *disinvestment,* is also a significant option when it can be shown that, for example, a withdrawal from current markets or activities is economically justified. The decision to dispose of the related assets allows a more advantageous redeployment of the funds thus freed.

It is important to note the various linkages in the diagram. They indicate that investments or disinvestments decided upon should match not only the operational characteristics and needs of the business, but also the financial policies management deems acceptable. For example, the selection of current and potential markets, a strategic choice, will affect how and where new facilities will be deployed. The characteristics of these markets, such as an outlook for rapid growth, might require significant future investments, which could be constrained by the company's funding potential under current financial policies.

The yardsticks helpful in the selection of new investments and disinvestments are generally based on *present value* concepts. These will be discussed in greater detail in Chapter 6.

The yardsticks for measuring the effectiveness with which the existing investment base is employed basically use *rate of return* concepts. These will be discussed specifically in Chapter 3.

Whether investments involve plant and equipment, various physical resources such as mineral deposits, intangibles such as proprietary technology, deployment of human resources, incremental working capital, and other outlays, investment commitments are the operational "trigger" for action in almost every kind of business.

Conduct of Operations

Here key strategies and decisions involve the *effective utilization* of the funds invested in serving *selected markets* and the task of setting appropriate *pricing and service* policies that are competitive in filling the customers' needs. These choices invariably involve economic trade-offs in which management must balance the impact of competitive price and other actions on sales volume and on the profitability of products or services. At the same time all operations of the business must be made and maintained *cost effective* to achieve competitive success.

Such results depend in part on understanding and exploiting *operating leverage*, that is, the effect on the company's profitability of the level and proportion of *fixed (period) costs* committed to the operations, versus the amount and nature of *variable (direct) costs* incurred in manufacturing, service, or trading operations. This concept will be expanded in Chapter 5. Management must also be careful to manage operating funds in ways that maintain the ability to meet current obligations *(liquidity)*. The interplay of all these forces and decisions results in the net *operating profit* for a period.

The key yardsticks in this segment include a variety of operating ratios that measure the effectiveness with which funds are employed, as well as specific expense and profit indicators. Also, there are measures for the relative profit contribution margin of different products and services and a whole variety of comparative operating data and statistics against which to compare the cost-effectiveness of particular operations. All of these measures will be discussed in more detail in Chapters 3 and 4.

Financing Decisions

This segment represents the various choices available to management to fund the investments and operations of the business over the long term. Two key areas of strategies and decisions are identified, the *disposition of profits* and the shaping of the company's *capital structure*. Normally this set of decisions is made at the highest levels of management and endorsed by the board of directors of a corporation.

Disposition of profits involves the basic three-way split of net profit after taxes between owners, lenders, and reinvestment in the business. Each element is affected by current or past management decisions and policies. The payment of *dividends* to owners is at the discretion of the board of directors of a corporation. Here the critical choice is the relative amount of dividends paid out, which directly affects the possible use of profit for reinvestment and growth. The payment of *interest* to lenders is a matter of contractual obligation. The amount of interest payments incurred relative to operating profit, however, is a direct function of management policies and actions regarding the use of debt: the higher the proportion of debt in the capital structure, the greater will be the demand for profit dollars to be used as interest expense, and the greater will also be the risk exposure of the company. *Retained earnings* are the residual profits for the period, after payment of interest and dividends and after providing for applicable income taxes. Combined with any new funds provided by investors and lenders, retained earnings expand the funding potential for additional investment and growth.

Key measures in the area of earnings disposition are *net earnings* and *cash flows* on a per share basis, indicators of the ability to compensate both lenders and owners, and specific ratios measuring *dividend payout, coverage of interest,* and *coverage of total debt service* requirements. These are discussed in Chapter 3.

Capital structure planning and strategy involves selecting and balancing the relative proportions of funds obtained from *ownership* sources and long-term *debt* obligations, which, after taking into account *business risk* and *debt service* requirements, should result in an acceptable level of overall profitability. Numerous types of equity can be employed as ownership funding, and the choices of debt instruments are similarly varied (as discussed in Chapter 8).

The key concept in the choice of funding methods is the impact of *financial leverage* (as discussed in Chapter 5). In essence, financial leverage can be defined as prudent use of funds obtained from fixed cost debt obligations in financing investment opportunities with potential earnings higher than the cost of the interest. A positive difference between earnings and cost will enhance ownership equity and thus shareholder value, just as earnings lower than the interest cost will penalize ownership equity and value. Management decisions here amount to a conscious economic trade-off between risk and reward expectations.

Key measures in the area of capital structure strategy include ratios measuring the *return on equity* and various *debt service coverage* ratios (as discussed in Chapter 3), ratios for relative levels of *debt and equity* (as discussed in Chapter 5), measures of the *cost of* various forms of *capital* (as discussed in Chapters 7 and 8), and *shareholder value concepts* (as discussed in Chapter 9).

Internal Assumptions

Our very simplified model of the business system contains three key assumptions as stated in the footnotes. First, *depreciation* expense is not recognized as such, because we have assumed that an amount *equal* to the annual depreciation write-off made against operating profit will be automatically *reinvested* each year in the investment base in order to maintain the productive capacity of the business, but without providing any incremental profits. This is the reason why Figure 1-1 shows operating profit as the ultimate operating result. The assumption reflects a very common rule of thumb in financial analysis that an ongoing operation needs to spend about the amount of depreciation to keep facilities in proper repair. If management planned not to do this, any uncommitted depreciation funds would have to be added to the operating profit and would become available for new investment. (Chapter 2 discusses the funds aspects of depreciation.)

Second, we assume that all statutory income taxes for every period have been calculated, paid, and subtracted in arriving at *operating profit* and that all appropriate deductions have been taken in the process, including the interest expense recognized in the system diagram.

Third, we assume that the amount of existing *long-term debt* outstanding remains unchanged; that is, there is no provision made for paying off this debt as long as the business is operating and growing. Instead, a continuous *rollover* of debt is assumed; that is, new financing is arranged as repayments of existing debt become due. This is a way of maintaining the relative proportion of funding from debt and equity sources over time. Normally, as the amount of owners' equity grows with every period of profitable operations, management will likely wish to match, in proportion, the incremental retained earnings with an incremental amount of new debt—unless management decides that a change in policy is appropriate for a variety of reasons. Under the latter conditions, specific assumptions would have to be made about the pattern of repayments planned, which would, of course, change the relative proportions of debt and equity outstanding over time.

Interrelationships of Key Strategic Areas

It should be obvious by now that our concept of the basic business system forces us to recognize and deal with the dynamic interrelationships of the key management strategies, policies, and decisions and the basic funds movements caused by them. Consistency among these variables is an important aspect of the long-term success of a company. For example, it would be ineffective for a company to set aggressive objectives for its operations while at the same time restricting itself to a set of rigid and conservative financial policies. Similarly, paying out high levels of current operating profit as dividends while maintaining a restrictive debt policy would clash with an objective of holding market share in a rapidly expanding business. Under such circumstances adequate funds for new investment would simply not be available.

The basis for successful management is a consistent set of business strategies, investment objectives, operating goals, and financial policies that will reinforce each other rather than conflict. Our simplified systems diagram has provided a way to recognize these interrelationships in an initial broad context of decisions and funds flows.

THE NATURE OF FINANCIAL STATEMENTS

In order to apply our insights gained from the conceptual overview, we must now look for information that will allow the manager or analyst to track the condition and results of a business and assist in understanding the funds flow patterns in more specific terms. The process of financial analysis involves reviewing a great variety of formal or informal data relevant to the specific purpose of the analysis. Some of the data are common to most types of financial analysis, while others provide specialized information.

The most common form in which basic financial information about a business is available publicly—unless a company is privately held—is a set of financial statements issued under guidelines of the public accounting profession and under the supervision of the Securities and Exchange Commission, where applicable. The set of statements usually contains *balance sheets* as of given dates, *operating statements* for given periods, and *funds flow statements* for the same periods. A special statement highlighting the *changes in owners' equity* on the balance sheet is commonly provided as well.

Since financial statements are the basis for most analytical efforts pertaining to a business, we must first understand their nature, coverage, and limitations before we can use the data and observations derived from these statements for our analytical judgments. Financial statements, which are prepared according to commonly accepted accounting principles, do reflect the effects of past and current decisions made by management. They involve considerable ambiguity, however. Financial statements are governed by financial accounting rules that attempt to consistently and fairly account for every business transaction using the principle of historical costs at the time of transaction and the principle of matching revenues and costs through accrual and allocation. These rules by their very nature leave the results, particularly the economic impact, open to some interpretation.

The Balance Sheet

The balance sheet as of *any given date* describes the categories and amounts of *assets* employed by the business (i.e., the funds committed) and the offsetting *liabilities* incurred to lenders and owners (i.e., the funds obtained). Also called the *statement of financial condition*, or *statement of financial position*, it must always balance because the total assets invested in the business at any point in time, by definition, are matched precisely by the liabilities and owners' equity supporting these assets.

The major categories of assets, or uses of funds, are: *(a)* *current assets*, items that turn over in the normal course of business within a relatively short period of time, such as cash, marketable securities, accounts receivable, and inventories. *(b) fixed assets*, such as land, mineral resources, buildings, machinery, vehicles, and so forth, all of which are used over the long term, and *(c) other assets*, such as deposits, patents, and various intangibles like goodwill.

Major sources of funds are: *(a) current liabilities*, which are obligations to vendors, tax authorities, employees, and lenders due within one year, *(b) long-term liabilities*, a variety of debt instruments repayable beyond one year, such as mortgages and bonds, and *(c) owners' equity*, which represents the funds contributed by various classes of owners of the business as well as accumulated earnings retained in the business.

Balance sheets are *static* in that, like a snapshot, they reflect conditions on the date of their preparation. They are also *cumulative* in that they represent the effects of all decisions and transactions that have taken place and have been accounted for up to the date of preparation.

Financial accounting rules require that all transactions be recorded at cost when incurred, and retroactive adjustments to recorded values are made only in very limited circumstances. As a consequence, balance sheets, being cumulative, display assets and liabilities acquired or incurred at different times. Because the current economic value of assets can change, particularly in the case of longer-lived items such as buildings and machinery, or resources such as land and minerals, the costs stated on the balance sheet may not reflect true values. Moreover, changes in the value of the currency in which the transactions are recorded can, over time, distort the balance sheet. Finally, a number of relatively recent rules require the estimation and recording of contingent liabilities arising from a variety of future obligations such as pensions and health care costs, further introducing a series of value judgments.

The accounting profession, through its Financial Accounting Standards Board, has expended a great deal of effort to resolve these and other issues affecting the meaning of the balance sheet, but with only partial success. The standards continue to evolve, and a manager or analyst must therefore make interpretive judgments when reviewing and analyzing this statement. We will discuss the most important of these issues specifically as we examine analytical techniques in later chapters.

In our decisional context of investment, operations, and financing, the balance sheet can be viewed as a cumulative listing of the impact of investment and financing decisions, while the *net* effect of operations in the form of periodic profit

Figure 1–2
Balance Sheet in Decisional Context

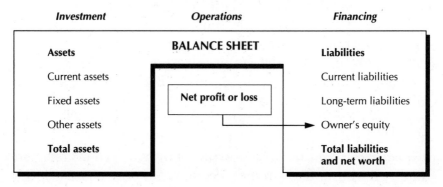

or loss is reflected in the ownership equity account. Figure 1–2 is a simple conceptual picture of the balance sheet as it relates to the three areas of management decisions.

The major categories normally found on the balance sheet are listed. However, this is a simplification. In actual practice, the analyst encounters a large variety of detailed asset, liability, and net worth accounts because balance sheets reflect the unique nature of a given company and the business it is in. But the actual accounts can always be grouped into the basic categories listed.

As an example of the balance sheet of a major corporation, Figure 1–3 shows the consolidated balance sheet for December 31, 1989, and December 31, 1988, of TRW Inc., as published in its 1989 Annual Report, but presented here without accompanying notes. TRW Inc. is an international company headquartered in Cleveland, Ohio. It focuses on products and services with a high technology or engineering content to the space and defense, automotive, and information systems markets, in which the company typically holds leading positions. Founded in 1901, the company employs about 74,000 people in 21 countries and ranks 62nd in sales in the 1989 Fortune 500 listing. We will use TRW's published financial statements as

Figure 1-3
TRW INC. AND SUBSIDIARIES
Consolidated Balance Sheets at December 31
($ millions)

Assets	1989	1988
Current assets:		
Cash and cash equivalents	$ 114	$ 127
Accounts receivable	1,431	1,286
Inventories	480	419
Prepaid expenses	67	60
Deferred income taxes	203	213
Total current assets	2,295	2,105
Property, plant and equipment at cost	4,127	3,733
Less: Allowances for depreciation and amortization	(2,173)	(1,940)
Total property, plant and equipment—net	1,954	1,793
Intangible assets:		
Intangibles arising from acquisitions	534	328
Capitalized data files and other intangibles	319	84
Less: Accumulated amortization	(94)	(55)
Total intangible assets—net	759	357
Other assets	251	187
Total assets	$5,259	$4,442
Liabilities and Shareholders' Investment		
Current liabilities:		
Short-term debt	$ 459	$ 96
Accrued compensation	304	281
Trade accounts payable	456	461
Other accruals	443	443
Dividends payable	26	29
Income taxes	72	62
Current portion of long-term debt	34	24
Total current liabilities	1,794	1,396
Long-term liabilities	155	173
Long-term debt	1,063	863
Deferred income taxes	462	426
Minority interests in subsidiaries	36	18
Shareholders' investment:		
Serial preference stock II (involuntary liquidation		
$15 million and $18 million)	1	1
Common stock (shares outstanding 60.6 million and 60.2 million) . .	38	38
Other capital	194	191
Retained earnings	1,516	1,358
Cumulative translation adjustments	48	34
Treasury shares—cost in excess of par value	(48)	(56)
Total shareholders' investment	$1,749	$1,566
Total liabilities and shareholders' investment	$5,259	$4,442

Adapted from 1989 TRW Inc. Annual Report.

examples in Chapters 2 and 3 and demonstrate the use of analytical techniques on the data contained in them.

The Operating Statement

The operating statement reflects the effect of management's operating decisions on business performance and the resulting profit or loss for the owners of the business *over a clearly specified period of time*. The profit or loss calculated in the statement increases or decreases owners' equity on the balance sheet. The operating statement is thus a necessary adjunct to the balance sheet in explaining the major component of change in owners' equity, and it provides essential performance assessment information.

The operating statement, also referred to as the *income statement, earnings statement,* or *profit and loss statement,* displays the revenues recognized for a specific period and the costs and expenses charged against these revenues, including write-offs (i.e., depreciation and amortization of various assets) and taxes. Revenues and costs involve elements such as sales for cash or credit, purchases of goods or services for resale or manufacture, payment of wages, incurring trade credit, scheduling production for inventory, and so on. The operating statement represents the best effort of the firm's accountants to match the relevant items of revenue with the relevant items of expense.

Again, these efforts are governed by "generally accepted accounting principles." How some costs and expenses are handled involves the accountants' judgments. Among the areas subject to such judgments are the depreciation of assets being used over more periods than the one reported, the cost of goods purchased or manufactured in previous periods, and proper allocation of general expenses to a specific period. We will take up the more critical judgment areas as we apply the analysis techniques in later chapters.

When viewed in our decisional context, the operating statement in the center column of Figure 1–4 expands the details of transactions and allocations that make up one of the key

Figure 1–4
Operating Statement in Decisional Context

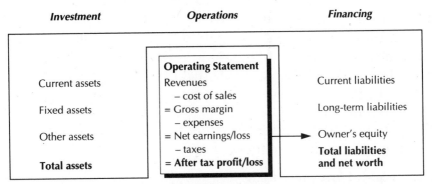

Figure 1–5
TRW INC. AND SUBSIDIARIES
Statement of Earnings
For the Years Ended December 31, 1989 and 1988
($ millions)

	1989	1988
Sales	$7,340	$6,982
Cost of sales	5,779	5,565
Gross profit	1,561	1,417
Administrative and selling expenses	780	780
Research and development expenses	256	225
Interest expense	138	130
Total expenses	1,174	1,135
Other income—net	12	138
Earnings before income taxes	399	420
Income taxes	136	159
Net earnings	$ 263	$ 261
Per share of common stock:		
Fully diluted	$4.25	$4.23
Primary	$4.31	$4.29

Adapted from TRW Inc. 1989 Annual Report.

performance elements, profit or loss. Again we are providing an actual example in Figure 1–5, the consolidated operating statement of TRW Inc. for the years ending December 31, 1989, and December 31, 1988.

The combination of a balance sheet and an operating statement will provide more basic insights than the balance sheet alone. But because the operating statement covers a period of time, while the balance sheet describes conditions at the end of a period, it is useful to have balance sheets for both the *beginning and the end* of the period covered by the operating statement.

When we use balance sheets that bracket the period under analysis, the net effects of investment, operating, and financing decisions can be related to the specific period, be it a month, quarter, year, or any other time interval represented by the operating statement.

The Funds Flow Statement

Over a period of time the profit and loss account will not be the only area affected by management's operating decisions. There will also be changes in most assets and liabilities, particularly in the accounts making up working capital, such as cash, receivables, inventories, and current payables. The statement that displays such changes in terms of funds movements is called a *funds flow statement*. It provides the basis for a *dynamic analysis* that focuses on the *changes* in financial condition resulting from the decisions made during a given period. The statement is prepared from a comparison of the beginning and ending balance sheets and is also linked to the operating statement for the period. It reflects decisions involving *uses and sources* of funds, that is, *(a)* commitments of funds to invest in assets or to repay liabilities or *(b)* raising of funds through additional borrowing or by reducing asset investments. One major source of funds, of course, is profitable operations in which revenues exceed costs and expenses. In contrast, unprofitable operations are a use of funds. The importance of the funds flow statement to the analysis of business performance should be clear.

The amount of detail in the funds flow statement can vary widely, depending on the nature of the business and the different funds movements emphasized. Basic formats used to differ just as much. Beginning with recent years, however, the Financial Accounting Standards Board required that all published funds flows statements follow a common format listing uses and sources by the familiar three decision areas: *investments, operations, and financing*. This was a recognition of the usefulness of funds flow statements in understanding more of the dynamics of the business system as discussed earlier. Figure 1–6 shows the funds flow statement in terms of our management decision context.

One of the aspects of the funds flow statement that requires some explanation is the treatment of accounting write-offs. From a funds flow standpoint, write-offs such as depreciation and amortization merely represent bookkeeping entries that *do not affect funds*. The reason is simply that the assets being amortized by these entries represent funds committed in *past* periods. Consequently, the write-off categories, insofar as they had reduced net profit, are *added back* here as a positive funds flow, thus restoring the funds from operations to their level before the write-off. Handling of this adjustment will be illustrated more specifically in Chapter 2.

Figure 1–6
Funds Flow Statement in Decisional Context

Management Decision Area

Investment	*Operations*	*Financing*
FUNDS FLOW STATEMENT		
Current assets (plus or minus)		Current liabilities (plus or minus)
Fixed assets (plus or minus)		Long-term liabilities (plus or minus)
Other assets (plus or minus)	Net profit or loss (plus or minus)	Owner's equity (plus or minus)
Total assets (plus or minus)	(Adjustments for write-offs)	Total liabilities and net worth (plus or minus)
Uses or Sources	**Sources or Uses**	**Sources or Uses**

The funds flow statement has the same inherent limitations as the balance sheet and the operating statement because it is derived from the data contained in these statements. Another limitation is the necessity of displaying the *net* change in each asset, liability, and ownership account reported, which may "bury" major individual transactions that occurred during the period and offset each other. As we said before, management decisions are made in a continuous sequence, and the balance sheets and operating statement for the period capture only their net effect. If there were material transactions, such as major investments, acquisitions, or divestitures, however, they are generally noted specifically in the company's funds flow statement.

The consolidated funds flow statement of TRW for the years ended December 31, 1889, and December 31, 1988, in Figure 1–7 shows how the various elements are listed in practice. A number of adjustments based on internally available information have been made by TRW to show more clearly the nature of funds movements during the periods covered.

The Statement of Changes in Owners' Equity

The fourth financial statement commonly provided by a business is an analysis of the main *changes during a specific period* in the owners' capital accounts, or net worth. We know from the earlier discussion that one of these changes is the profit or loss for the period, as displayed in the operating statement. But other management decisions may have affected owners' equity. For example, many corporations, including TRW, pay dividends on a quarterly basis. Such dividends are normally paid in cash, reducing both the cash balance and owners' equity. Another decision may be to provide additional capital through sale of common stock. A third area may involve write-offs or adjustments of asset values connected with disposition of assets or business combinations. A fourth area involves the complex adjustments related to the exchange of foreign currencies by companies doing business internationally. The net change in owners' equity may thus be

Figure 1–7
TRW INC. AND SUBSIDIARIES
Statement of Cash Flows
For the Years Ended December 31, 1989 and 1988
($ millions)

	1989	1988
Operating Activities:		
Net earnings	$263	$261
Adjustments to reconcile net earnings to net cash provided by operating activities:		
Depreciation and amortization	400	349
Restructuring	(59)	(106)
Foreign currency exchange losses	29	54
Equity in unremitted losses (earnings) of affiliated companies	3	(3)
Dividends received from affiliated companies	—	31
Deferred income taxes	15	(180)
Other—net	3	18
Changes in assets and liabilities, net of effects of businesses acquired or sold:		
Accounts receivable	(96)	(132)
Inventories and prepaid expenses	(47)	(42)
Accounts payable and other accruals	(4)	74
Other—net	(14)	19
Net cash provided by operating activities	493	343
Investing Activities:		
Capital expenditures	(452)	(417)
Proceeds from divestitures	28	453
Acquisitions, net of cash acquired	(448)	(10)
Investments in other assets	(67)	(47)
Proceeds from sales of property, plant and equipment	14	10
Other—net	(14)	(41)
Net cash used in investing activities	(939)	(52)
Financing Activities:		
Increase (decrease) in short-term debt	450	(179)
Proceeds from debt in excess of 90 days	259	82
Principal repayments in excess of 90 days	(156)	(82)
Dividends paid	(105)	(99)
Other—net	7	15
Net cash provided by (used in) financing activities	455	(263)
Effect of exchange rate changes on cash	(22)	(46)
Increase (decrease) in cash and cash equivalents	(13)	(18)
Cash and cash equivalents at beginning of year	127	145
Cash and cash equivalents at end of year	$114	$127

Adapted from TRW Inc. 1989 Annual Report.

selectively split into its major components to highlight the impact of these decisions. Figure 1–8 provides a conceptual view of the statement.

The limitations of this special analytical statement largely depend on how much the issuing company chooses to disclose beyond what is legally required. Unless a company decides to provide specific information related to ownership accounts, the analyst may find it difficult to reconstruct the components of financial change from published data alone. Viewed in our context of performance assessment, the statement of changes in owners' equity thus can be clearly recognized as subsidiary information that helps us understand the financing sector of the balance sheet.

Again TRW's consolidated statement of changes in owners' (shareholders') equity for the years ended December 31, 1989, and December 31, 1988, is given as an actual example in Figure 1–9. The format used displays the principal changes very clearly.

Figure 1–8
Statement of Changes in Owners' Equity in Decisional Context

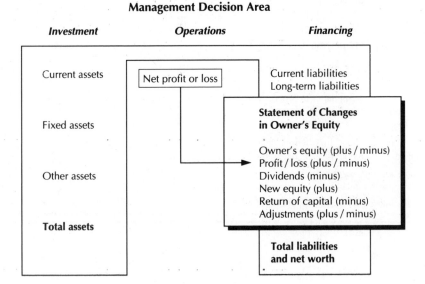

Management Decision Area

Figure 1–9
TRW INC. AND SUBSIDIARIES
Statement of Changes in Shareholders' Investment
For the Years Ended December 31, 1989 and 1988
($ millions)

	1989 Shares	Dollars	1988 Shares	Dollars
Serial Preference Stock II:				
Series 1:				
Balance at January 1 and				
December 31	.1	$ —	.1	$ —
Series 3:				
Balance at January 1 and				
December 31	.2	1	.2	1
Common Stock:				
Balance at January 1	60.2	38	59.7	37
Sale of stock and other	.4	—	.5	1
Balance at December 31	60.6	38	60.2	38
Other Capital:				
Balance at January 1		191		190
Sale of stock and other		3		1
Balance at December 31		194		191
Retained Earnings:				
Balance at January 1		1,358		1201
Net earnings		263		261
Redemption of shareholder				
purchase rights		—		(3)
Dividends declared:				
Preference stock:		(1)		(1)
Common stock ($1.72 and $1.66				
per share)		(104)		(100)
Balance at December 31		1,516		1,358
Cumulative Translation Adjustments:				
Balance at January 1		34		58
Translation adjustments		14		(24)
Balance at December 31		48		34
Treasury Shares—Cost in Excess of Par Value:				
Balance at January 1		(56)		(70)
Purchase of shares		(3)		(2)
Sold under stock options		11		16
Balance at December 31		(48)		(56)
Total shareholders' investment		$1,749		$1,566

Adapted from TRW Inc. 1989 Annual Report.

In this portion of the chapter we have provided an overview of the nature and relationships of the four major financial statements as the background for analysis of the results of management decisions and their impact on funds movements. Our decisional framework can help us visualize the coverage and relationship of the four financial statements.

Note that the generalized overview in Figure 1–10 displays not only what the four statements cover in terms of key information but also how they are related, being derived from the same basic information. The dotted line indicates the impact of accounting write-offs.

To summarize, the *balance sheet* describes the financial condition of a business at a point in time. It shows the cumulative effect of previous decisions and includes the profits or losses for preceding periods. The *operating statement* matches revenues and expenses for a specific period, including write-offs and allocations. It provides more detail about the elements making up the aftertax net profit and loss that was recorded in arriving at the owners' equity on the balance sheet. In contrast to the two previous statements, the *funds flow statement* is a dynamic look in that it highlights the *net changes* in assets, liabilities, and ownership accounts over a specific period. It allows the analyst to see the pattern of funds uses and sources that resulted from management's decisions concerning investments, operations, and financing. The statement recognizes and corrects for the fact that write-offs and amortization of assets acquired in the past are bookkeeping entries and do not affect funds. Finally the *statement of changes in owners' equity* gives more details concerning the change in ownership accounts as recorded on the beginning and ending balance sheets.

Within the limitations of accounting rules and accountants' judgments, financial statements are an effort to reflect, with reasonable consistency, all business transactions that, over time, result in a net improvement or worsening of the economic value of owners' equity. We have seen decisions and

Figure 1–10
Generalized Overview of Financial Statements

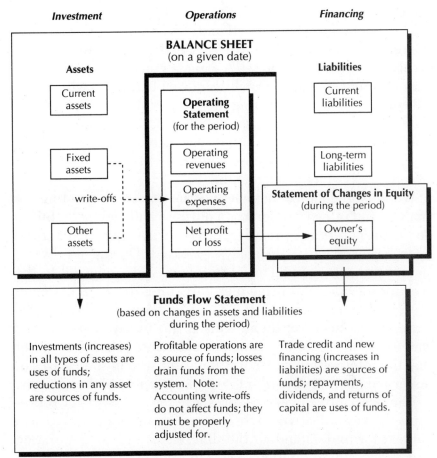

Management Decision Area

Investment	*Operations*	*Financing*

BALANCE SHEET
(on a given date)

Assets — Liabilities

- Current assets
- Fixed assets
- write-offs
- Other assets

Operating Statement
(for the period)
- Operating revenues
- Operating expenses
- Net profit or loss

- Current liabilities
- Long-term liabilities

Statement of Changes in Equity
(during the period)
- Owner's equity

Funds Flow Statement
(based on changes in assets and liabilities during the period)

Investments (increases) in all types of assets are uses of funds; reductions in any asset are sources of funds.

Profitable operations are a source of funds; losses drain funds from the system. Note: Accounting write-offs do not affect funds; they must be properly adjusted for.

Trade credit and new financing (increases in liabilities) are sources of funds; repayments, dividends, and returns of capital are uses of funds.

transactions as an interlinked series of movements of funds that are summarized on the financial statements.

As we will discuss in the ensuing chapters, the manager or analyst must review these statements, carefully interpret their meaning, and apply standard techniques as well as explicit judgments in evaluating the financial and economic performance of the company under review.

THE CONTEXT OF FINANCIAL ANALYSIS

Having explored the broad background of the business system and the nature of financial statements, it will be useful to provide one more context that allows us to put the materials of the book into proper perspective. It will reinforce a number of the references we have made earlier to the judgmental aspects involved in financial analysis. A manager or analyst performing various kinds of financial analysis normally does so with a specific purpose in mind. During the process of analysis, financial statements, special analyses, data bases, and other information sources are used to derive reasonable judgments about past, current, and prospective conditions of a business and the effectiveness of its management.

We must recognize that not only the person performing the analysis and interpretation has a purpose and viewpoint but so do the preparers and providers of the various types of data and information on which the analysis is based. During our discussion of the nature of financial statements, we referred to the accounting rules and principles governing the compilation of these documents and to the need to allow for the specific biases introduced by them. This is not to say that financial statements are right or wrong in an absolute sense, but rather that the information may have to be adjusted in some cases or discarded in others in order to suit the purpose of the analysis.

The descriptive overview presented in Figure 1–11 represents the key objectives of three major financial processes, as a context for understanding the differences in data generation and analytical orientation. The table identifies *financial accounting, financial analysis*, and *managerial economics* as processes whose objectives differ, but which frequently have to draw on each other for information and data. We must consider the orientation and focus of these processes when information is shared between them or exchanged for use by any one of them. Our ultimate aim is to analyze and judge business problems, company performance, and shareholder value in *economic* terms, which requires careful adjustment of data and analyses that were prepared with different objectives in mind.

Figure 1-11
The Different Objectives of Financial Processes

Financial Accounting	Financial Analysis	Managerial Economics
Profit determination	**Financial information**	**Activity economics**
• Revenue recognition	• Adjustment process	• Task analysis
• Expense recognition	• Trend analysis	• Economic allocation
• Cost allocation	• Profit projection	• Contribution analysis
• Profit definition	• Cash flow projection	• Trade-off determination
Value determination	**Comparative data**	**Resource effectiveness**
• Historical costs	• Industry analysis	• Investment base
• Conservatism	• Competitor analysis	• Capital investments
• Equity determination	• Economic conditions	• Capital divestments
• Contingency recognition	• Adjustment areas	• Human resources
Tax determination	**Market analysis**	**Shareholder value**
• Legal data requirements	• Share price patterns	• Cash flow patterns
• Income; expense timing	• Market trends	• Cost of capital
• Tax management issues	• Value drivers	• Investor expectations
• Statement adjustments	• Market models	• Risk/reward trade-off

When we speak of financial analysis within the scope of this book, our main emphasis is on the objectives of the middle column, titled *financial analysis*, but we include portions of the right column, *managerial economics*, because the two areas are related. A large portion of the materials we employ, however, are originated on the left, by *financial accounting*, and some are obtained from the right, from internal data bases on which managerial economics depends.

As we already implied earlier, there are three major objectives in **financial accounting** as governed by professional standards and SEC regulations: *(a) profit determination, (b) value determination*, and *(c) tax determination*.

The data gathering and analysis in the first area focuses on recognizing when revenue is earned during a period and when matching expenses are to be recognized. A clear distinction is drawn between the recording of a revenue or expense transaction and the actual receipt or disbursement of cash, which may lag the recognition of the revenue or expense item by days or months. Similarly, costs incurred in the past may be allocated to current or future periods with the objective of determining a profit figure that matches only "recognized" revenue and expense elements. This has significant implications for funds flow analysis, as we will see.

The process of *value determination* rests on the principle of *historical costs,* a *conservative* concept that uses transaction evidence as the value criterion. When economic values of assets change, adjustments in these recorded values are made for reductions only, in readily identifiable areas such as accounts receivable that have become uncollectible, or inventories where the market value has declined below cost. Increases are recognized only when assets are sold, not while they are being held. The residual value of a business, that is, its recorded ownership *equity* (book value), therefore, may over time bear little resemblance to the market value (economic value) of the equity. In addition, the growing emphasis on recording *contingencies* of all kinds introduces a bias in value because only potential liabilities are established, but not potential gains. As we mentioned before, long-term pension and benefit obligations are recognized, as are potential liabilities arising from all types of operational, legal, and contractual issues.

Meanwhile, appreciation of assets like land, buildings, natural resources, technological advances, and so forth, is left unrecognized until they are disposed of. As the wave of takeovers in the eighties demonstrated, careful analysis of the target companies' balance sheets uncovered massive amounts of unrecorded potential gain that was realized in the eventual breakup of the acquired companies.

Tax determination is governed by the *legal requirements* of the current tax code, which often involves modified principles of income and expense recognition, including disallowance of certain costs and expenses. Tax rules tend to speed up the *timing* of revenue recognition versus financial accounting rules and also to spread out expense recognition. The rules are clearly intended to enhance current tax receipts. Differences between financial accounting for reporting purposes and tax accounting give rise to *tax management issues* in companies and industries where the amounts involved are significant enough to affect actual decisions on investments, operations, and financing.

From the standpoint of financial analysis, the important question has to do with the effect of tax accounting on the financial statements used for analysis. As we will see, the amount of taxes actually paid versus the amount shown on the operating statement can differ materially, and the *adjustments* made on the balance sheet to compensate for this situation may indicate significant funds movements.

Financial analysis in this context has three objectives, *(a)* the interpretation of *financial information*, *(b)* the use of *comparative data*, and *(c)* analysis of *financial markets*.

The first area essentially involves judgmental interpretation of the financial statements and other financial data about a company for purposes of assessing and projecting its performance and value. The key judgments focus on the *adjustment process*, in which data reported under accounting principles are modified or converted into information that permits economic and funds flow judgments to be made. It is rare that the financial data as generally provided can be used in their exact form to derive analytical judgments. Applying the various ratios and relationships discussed in Chapter 2, for example, often leads to questions and actual adjustments during the process of analysis. *Trend analysis* uses various series of adjusted past data to look for and analyze significant changes in magnitudes and ratio relationships over time and becomes one of the bases of *profit projection*. Finally, the ultimate adjustment leads to an analysis of the *cash flows* generated by the business and the *projection* of these cash flows as an indicator of economic performance and value.

Comparative data are an essential part of financial analysis as they help put judgments about a particular company or business in perspective. By implication, all judgments made about performance and value are relative to the standards and perceptions of the analyst; comparable data assist in confirming these judgments. *Industry analysis* involves the selection of relevant groupings of companies and compiling appropriate data and ratios (sometimes available in data bases) against which to measure the company being studied. The important issue here again is the need to interpret and adjust the financial data so that they match the data used for the original company. *Competitor analysis* applies the same process to individual companies that compete directly with the business. *Economic conditions* are brought into the analysis as a backdrop for explaining past variations and as a guide to projecting future performance and value.

Market analysis involves study and projection of the *pattern of share prices* of the company and its competitors relative to stock *market trends*. It is here that financial analysis becomes a bridge between published financial statements reporting accounting performance and market trends reflecting the economic value of a company. The analyst focuses on the *value drivers* behind the market value of the shares, which are basic economic variables like cash flow generated and relative cost effectiveness of the business. *Market models* range from simple relationships of key variables and share price to complex computer simulations, in an effort to determine the current and potential shareholder value created by the business.

Managerial economics encompasses three basic objectives (a) establishing *activity economics*, (b) determining *resource effectiveness*, and (c) calculating *shareholder value*. All three areas are focused on economic insights that will allow management to make decisions enhancing shareholder value. In that sense the orientation of managerial economics is very closely allied to the basic purpose of financial analysis as we define it here—in fact, the third objective directly supports the ultimate question asked by financial analysis. Consequently, the book addresses the most important areas of objectives two and three.

Activity economics is a summary term defining analyses that establish economically relevant data for any operational aspect of a business. *Task analysis* amounts to determining the true economic cost of a task, such as the series of steps required to provide a service, or the phases of a manufacturing process. It goes beyond cost accounting principles that often fall short of proper *economic allocation* of jointly used resources or do not include all aspects of the task. *Contribution analysis* refers to measuring the difference between the revenues created and the economic costs involved in a line of business or a particular product or service. Economic contribution data assist management in choosing which combination of activities will create the most economic value. The choices always call for economic trade-offs based on economic data—not accounting information. A new field of analysis called "activity-based accounting" is gaining acceptance as a means of gathering data relevant to this purpose.

Resource effectiveness addresses the question of how well, from an economic standpoint, the resources employed by a business are being utilized or will be utilized in the future. This includes measuring the returns from the existing *investment base* in place, the justification of new *capital investments* or *capital divestments,* and the returns from *human resources*. As we mentioned earlier, these questions will be discussed in Chapters 2 and 6, and the need for considering an economic basis for these judgments will be highlighted.

Shareholder value, the ultimate goal of management, is based on a combination of past and projected *cash flow patterns,* the *cost of capital* of the particular company, and the *expectations of investors* for this type of business. In essence, shareholder value becomes an expression of the *risk/reward trade-off* underlying any investment in the equity of a company. It will be discussed in detail in Chapters 7 and 9.

SUMMARY

In this chapter we have provided a conceptual overview of the *business system* as a dynamic interrelationship of funds flows activated by management decisions. We recognized three basic *decision areas:* investment, operations, and financing. The systems view demonstrated how the decisions in each area were affected by key strategies and policies and how consistency was essential to run the system for the ultimate goal, enhancing *shareholder value*. The overview also provided a first look at major *areas of financial and economic analysis* and how it related to management strategies and decisions.

A second conceptual overview introduced the major *financial statements* commonly prepared by companies and their relationship both to each other and to the three decisional areas defined earlier. We also gave a first indication how the origin, rationale, and limitations of financial statements affect the potential for analyzing *performance and value*.

The third conceptual discussion reinforced the *context* within which *financial analysis* takes place and provided an overview of the various objectives of analysis and data preparation. This was done to highlight the need to build a bridge between *accounting-oriented data* and the ultimate objective of financial analysis, judging business performance and shareholder value in *economic terms*. Adjustment areas were suggested as prerequisites for developing useful information, and the analyst's *judgmental role* was emphasized.

The chapter serves as a *contextual preview* of the various analytical concepts explored in the remainder of the book. It is intended to reinforce the point that financial analysis is not a freestanding activity or an end in itself, but rather an effort to understand and judge the characteristics and performance of a highly interrelated system of financial relationships.

SELECTED REFERENCES

Deschamps, B., and D. Mehta. *Chief Financial Officer: Strategy Formulation and Implementation*. New York: John Wiley & Sons, 1988.

Johnson, H. Thomas, and Robert S. Kaplan. *Relevance Lost: The Rise and Fall of Management Accounting*. Boston, Mass.: Harvard Business School Press, 1987.

Porter, Michael E. *Competitive Advantage: Creating and Sustaining Superior Performance*. New York: The Free Press, 1985.

Rappaport, Alfred. *Creating Shareholder Value*. New York: The Free Press, 1986.

Vancil, Richard F., and Benjamin R. Makela, eds. *The CFO Handbook*. Homewood, Ill.: Dow Jones-Irwin, 1986.

2   MANAGING
       OPERATING
       FUNDS

This chapter deals with the key issues surrounding the *flow of funds* through a business, that is, the management of the funds required to operate any business. Given the conceptual overview presented in Chapter 1, we are beginning the discussion of analytical techniques with this subject. It is critically important to understand the specific funds movements caused in the business system by daily management decisions on investment, operations, and financing. Management decisions, in one form or another, affect the company's ability to pay its bills, obtain credit from suppliers and lenders, extend credit to its customers, and maintain a level of operations that matches the demand for the company's products or services, supported by appropriate investments. Every decision has a monetary impact on the ongoing *cycle* of uses or sources of funds. It is management's job to maintain an appropriate balance between the inflows and outflows of funds at all times and to allow for any *changes* in operations, caused by management decisions or by outside influences, that may affect these flows.

Managing operating funds properly is critical to successful business performance. New businesses often find that balancing operating funds needs and sources is a struggle for plain survival. Yet, well-established companies likewise must devote much management time and effort to operational financing. As we shall see, proper management of operating funds requires an understanding of the *systems impact* of investment, operating, and financing decisions. It further requires insight into the effect of *different operating patterns* on funds uses and sources. Funds flows are affected differently depending on the nature of a company's operations, which may have a level, growing, or declining pattern. Finally, one must be aware that short-term *working capital management* is *not independent* of the longer-term financial structure with which the business is funded. Funds sources and uses arise as a matter of course during operations that may also affect long-term investments and long-term capital sources. It is for this reason that the chapter focuses on the broader issue of *operating funds management*, which *includes* the specific needs for working capital, but is not *limited* by the common definition of working capital as the *net* of current assets and liabilities.

In Chapter 3 we will examine a variety of performance measures drawn from financial statements, which we know to be periodic summaries of financial condition and operating results. As we shall see, these summaries often *mask peaks and valleys* of funds movements—critical financing needs, for example—because these took place *during* the period covered by the statements. Yet managing a business is an *ongoing* day-to-day process.

In this chapter, we will examine specifically how *funds* constantly *cycle* through a business, what the *implications* of these movements are, and how to identify the critical financial variables that must be weighed in making daily operating decisions. We will demonstrate the funds impact of *variability of operations* in different forms, and discuss key *accounting issues*, such as *inventory costing* and methods of *depreciation*. We will then return to the preparation and interpretation of *funds flow statements*, using our example of TRW's 1989 and 1988 performance, and examine the major types of analytical steps needed to make funds flow statements meaningful.

FUNDS FLOW CYCLES

Businesses vary widely in orientation, size, structure, and products or services, but they all experience *operating funds cycles* in their own fashion. Even a solitary ice cream vendor selling cones for cash has to provide an inventory on wheels, which is slowly converted into cash as the day progresses. He invested his own cash at the beginning of the day to purchase the ice cream from his supplier and hopes to recoup it with a markup for profit at the end of the day. The initial decision to commit his own cash to inventory can be displayed as shown in Figure 2–1, which recognizes the three decisional contexts discussed in Chapter 1.

If our vendor was short of cash, he may even have signed an IOU at the supplier's, promising to pay for the inventory once he has sold it, using the day's receipts as funding. This situation would modify the picture, as is shown in Figure 2–2. Here the creditor's funds effectively supplant the owners' funds, if only for a single day.

Figure 2–1
Ice Cream Vendor
Initial Cash Investment to Start the Day

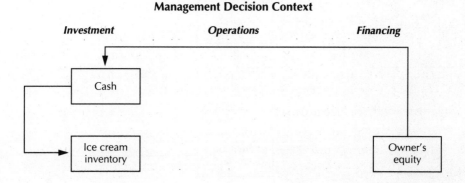

Figure 2–2
Ice Cream Vendor
Initial Use of Credit to Start the Day

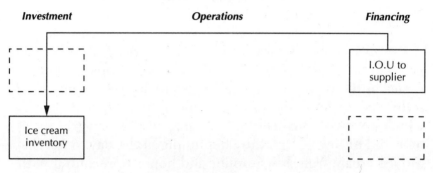

In any event, the vendor's funds cycle is a short one. An initial investment in inventory, funded with his own cash or with supplier credit, is followed by cash sales during the day. These receipts build up his cash balance for the succeeding day's operations. We have shown the first day of the self-funding situation in Figure 2–3, where cash on hand is built up by the sales receipts, inventory is drawn down during the day,

Figure 2–3
Ice Cream Vendor
Profitable Operations during the Day

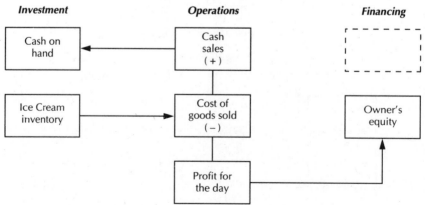

and where the difference between sales revenue and the cost of the ice cream sold represents the profit, which increases ownership equity.

The next morning our vendor will either use the cash collected to replenish his inventory or pay off the supplier so that he will be extended credit for the next cycle. Any profit above the cost of the goods sold will be his to keep—or to invest in inventory for another day.

In Figure 2-4 we have shown the funds movements involved for the initial supplier credit situation. If the vendor wanted to operate on the second day, he would have cash to purchase only some of the necessary inventory, that is, up to the amount of the profit he made. He would have to decide whether to ask for renewed credit or whether to supply the remaining funds from his own resources.

The funds cycles of larger and more structured businesses differ only in complexity, not in concept. Even for the largest conglomerate the ultimate form of settlement of a transaction is *cash*. Meanwhile, however, the operational funds cycle involves a great variety of partially offsetting credit extensions,

Figure 2-4
Ice Cream Vendor
Repayment of Credit after Profitable Day

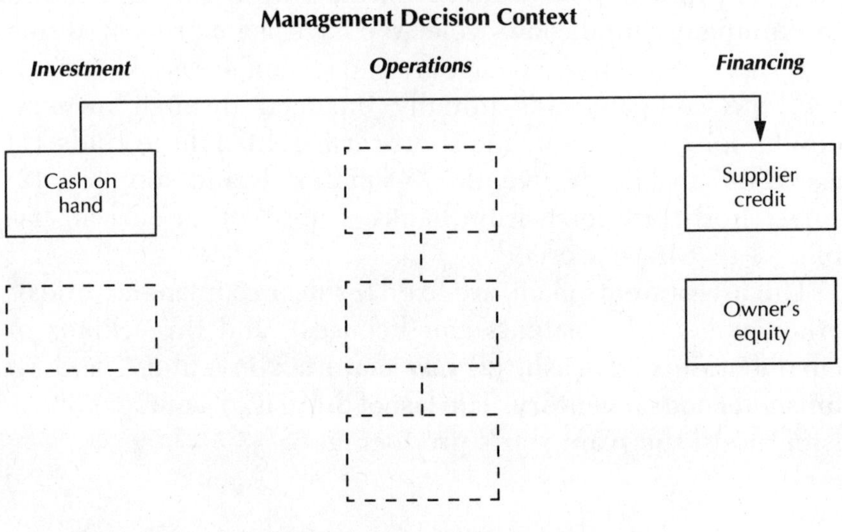

Management Decision Context

changes in inventories, transformation of assets, and so forth, that *precede* the cash collections or payments. In essence, the funds cycle arises because of a series of *lags* in the *timing* of business transactions. Our ice cream vendor has a lag of a few hours between the buildup of his inventory and its ultimate conversion into cash through many small transactions. A large manufacturer may have a lag of months between the time a product is made in the factory and the ultimate collection of the selling price from customers who purchased on credit. Management must always plan for and find *financing for the funds tieds up* because of these lags.

To illustrate the nature of the concept, we will explore in some detail the funds cycle of a simplified *manufacturing* operation and the funds cycle for *selling* the products. We have separated the two processes for purposes of discussion, even though the funds cycles are *intertwined* in an ongoing business that both produces and sells products. The sales cycle *alone*, of course, applies to any retail, wholesale, or trading operation purchasing goods for resale.

The Funds Cycle for Manufacturing

For purposes of illustration, we will assume that the Widget Manufacturing Company has just begun operations and is going to produce widgets for eventual sale. Figure 2–5 shows the company's funds flow cycle. We have again presented this in terms of the three management decision areas. As we can see, the company was initially financed through owners' equity, long-term debt, and short-term debt of three kinds: (1) accounts payable due vendors of materials and supplies, (2) some short-term loans from banks, and (3) other current liabilities that have accrued.

The investments made are fixed assets (i.e., plant facilities), other assets (i.e., patents and licenses), and three kinds of current assets: (1) cash, (2) raw materials inventory, and (3) finished goods inventory. The last of these is, of course, nonexistent until the plant starts producing.

Figure 2–5
Funds Flow Cycle For Manufacturing

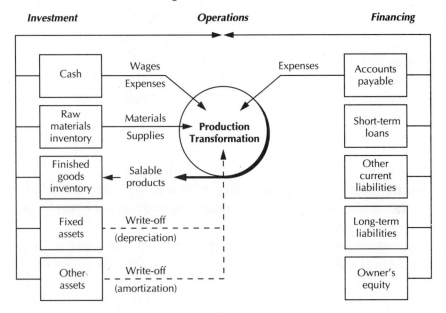

We can assume that long-term debt and owners' equity are the logical sources for funds for the plant and equipment, matching the long-term commitment involved, while the short-term loan most likely provided the ready cash needed to start operations. Materials and supplies were bought on credit from the vendors.

As production begins, a basic *transformation* process takes place. Some of the available cash is used to pay weekly wages and various ongoing expenses. Materials and supplies are withdrawn from inventory to be used in manufacture. Some operating inputs, like power and fuel oil, are obtained on credit and are temporarily financed through accounts payable. Depreciation for the use of the plant and equipment is charged against the transformation process through an accounting write-off, and licenses are similarly amortized. As widgets are finished on the factory floor, they are moved into the warehouse and are reflected in the finished goods inventory account.

In the *absence* of any widget *sales*, the production process continuously transforms cash, raw materials, and some trade credit into a growing buildup of finished goods inventory. A fraction of the original cost of fixed and other assets is also transformed into finished goods—even though no funds are moved—by means of an *accounting write-off* which affects the books only.

What are the financial implications of this transformation? From the time the business was originally set up, the operational funds flow has only affected the *working capital* accounts. Cash and raw materials, which were *sources* of funds, have been drawn down. An additional source has been found in trade credit, and not to be overlooked is the temporary funding employees provide over their respective pay periods until their paychecks are cashed. The major *use* of the funds has been to build up finished goods inventory. Unless the company can eventually turn these finished goods into *cash* through sale to its customers, the continued inventory buildup will drain the cash reserves and the raw material stores. These would have to be replenished by new infusions of credit or owners' equity—or both. Adding to the cash drain is the obligation to begin, at some point, repayment of accounts payable for trade credit incurred, on the usual terms of 30 or 45 days from the invoice date.

From a funds flow standpoint, several *timing lags* are significant in our example. First, a *supply* of raw materials sufficient for several days of operation has to be kept on hand to ensure uninterrupted manufacturing. Next there is a *physical* lag in the number of days required to produce a widget, which involves buildup of an inventory or work in process, that is, widgets in various stages of completion. Last, a sufficient number of widgets must be produced and kept at all times in finished goods inventory to support an ongoing sales effort.

The *total* of these lags has to be financed through funds provided by owners and creditors on a continuous basis.

Offsetting this funds use, but only in part, is the length of time over which *credit* is extended by the company's suppliers. This is a favorable lag because purchases of raw material and supplies, as well as certain other expenses will be financed by the vendors for 30 or 45 days, or for whatever length of time is common practice in the industry. With ongoing operations, *new* credit will continue to be extended as repayments are made. As already mentioned, another significant favorable lag is the temporary funding provided by the employees of the company whose wages are paid periodically, thereby in effect extending credit to their employer for a week, two weeks, or even a month, depending on the payroll pattern. Such funding is recognized among the current liabilities as accrued wages. Other accruals, such as taxes owed, will similarly provide temporary funds.

As we observed before, however, the buildup of finished goods in the warehouse cannot go on indefinitely, and at some point *sales revenues* will be essential to replenish the cash needed for settling the company's obligations as they become due. Thus, we must examine the funds implications of the selling process to complete the picture.

The Funds Cycle for Sales

The funds flows connected with selling the widgets produced can similarly be examined in terms of our decisional framework, as shown in Figure 2–6. Operations now include the main accounts in the operating statement: *sales, cost of goods sold, selling expenses,* and *net income*.

The selling cycle is based on another major lag, which results from the extension of credit to the company's customers. If the widgets were sold for cash, collection would, of course, be instantaneous. With the extension of normal trade credit, however, the company has to *await* the collection of *accounts receivable* after 30, 45, or whatever number of days is usual in

Figure 2–6
Funds Flow Cycle For Sales

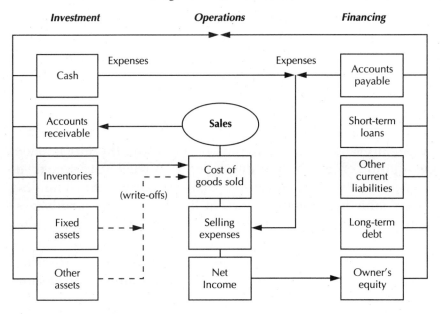

the industry. This lag, like the ones in production, has to be financed *continuously* because for any given volume of sales, an equivalent value of 30, 40, or 50 days' worth of sales will be outstanding. As collection takes place, *new* credit will be extended to customers—just as was the case with the vendors supplying the company itself.

Cost of goods sold is the value of the widgets withdrawn from finished goods inventory, each of which represents a share of the labor, raw material, overhead, and other costs expended in its manufacture. *Selling expenses,* which consist of the salaries of the sales force, the marketing support staff, and advertising and promotional costs will be paid partly in cash, partly with funds obtained from creditors. After these costs and expenses have been subtracted from sales revenue, the resulting *net income,* subject to taxes to be paid, will increase the owners' equity.

What are the funds flow implications of this picture? First of all, assuming that the company is maintaining a *level* volume of sales and manufacturing operations, management must plan for *continuous* long-term commitment of funds invested in *working capital,* as well as for obtaining the funds necessary for investment *expenditures* on fixed and other assets supporting operations, and finally allow for *repayment* of debt. Sufficient funds have to be committed for storing raw materials and work in process to carry on production for finished goods to support smooth sales and deliveries and for accounts receivable to permit proper credit extension to customers. Finally, a minimum level of cash must be maintained for punctual payment of currently due obligations.

The sources of this financing will come only in part from *accounts payable,* which can support a portion of raw materials, supplies, and ongoing operating expenses in line with the normal number of days' credit extended by the suppliers. The difference between the amount of funds continually tied up in inventories and receivables and the funds provided by current accounts payable must come from sources that are relatively permanent, such as *long-term debt* and *owners' equity.*

The dynamics of the system are such that the requirement for working capital funds is *constant* as long as the business operates on a *sustained* level. As we shall see, however, the amount of this requirement will change when operating conditions themselves change.

VARIABILITY OF FUNDS FLOWS

So far we have assumed that our company, after start-up, has reached a fairly steady level of operations. Under these conditions, the funds cycle is also *stable.* Unless there are significant changes in operating conditions or in the marketplace, the financing needed to support operations will remain a function of effective *inventory management,* sound customer credit *management,* and the prudent use of *supplier credit,* as well as reliable relations with other *lenders,* such as banks. Clearly, any worsening in collections from customers or tightening of credit terms extended by suppliers or lenders will increase the continuous financing needed.

Rarely does a company enjoy the steady state that has made financing so predictable in our example. In reality, several major external and internal factors can affect a business. Major external forces include *seasonal* variations and *cyclical* movements in the economy, which go beyond the impact of actions taken by the company's competitors. Major internal forces, among others, encompass management's ability to seize opportunities for *growth* or its inability to stem a *decline* in the company's volume of operations. Each of these conditions has its own particular implications in terms of funds flows, and we will illustrate the most important of these.

Seasonal Variations

A fairly large number of industries experience distinct seasonal operating patterns, that is, specific months or weeks of high sales, followed by an often dramatic decline in demand. These ups and downs repeat themselves quite predictably. Examples are most common in retailing operations, many of which are geared to special holiday periods or specific customer segments with seasonal style or gift requirements. Producers of seasonal items, like snowmobiles or bathing suits, will experience high fluctuations in demand. Another seasonal pattern impacts canneries that process specific crops or other seasonal foods.

Common to all seasonal businesses is a funds cycle with *large swings* over a *short period* of a year or less. The financial implications for management are quite obvious. During the low point of demand, ongoing operations have to be supported with funds from internal or external sources (unless the business can be shut down, as are some seasonal resorts). In most cases, inventories are gradually built up, either through production or through purchase from suppliers. As was the case in our simple example earlier, funds for this will have to come from credit, loans, and even owner's equity. Once the selling activity begins, growing amounts of receivables due from customers on normal credit terms have to be funded by the company. It is not until the first receivables are collected that *cash* starts flowing back into the business. The financial lags are usually such that collection of the receivables from peak sales will occur well *after* the peak of funding requirements has occurred.

As a result, management must make several critical decisions, among them the size of the buildup of inventories relative to anticipated demand, the level of operating and other expenditures during the operating cycle, and the nature of the funding to finance the bulge in requirements. Allowances must be made for contingencies such as lower-than-expected demand or prices, or both, delays in collections from customers, or the time involved in arranging for short- term financing with banks and other lenders. Otherwise the business could find itself strapped because its own financial obligations must be met before collections are made.

In Chapter 3 we will discuss applying turnover relationships and the aging of receivables as a means of judging the effectiveness of asset use by management. Under highly seasonal conditions such relationships are unstable because lags and surges in the accounts during the period spanned by financial statements make ratio comparisons difficult. A more direct evaluation of a seasonal business is possible through a month-to-month (or week-to-week) analysis of funds changes and a careful assessment of changes in the funds cycle of the company from peak to peak or trough to trough, instead of comparing quarterly or year-end financial statements.

Cyclical Variations

A variant of the seasonal cycle is the *cyclical pattern of funds movements* that involves external changes impacting the company over several years. However, these general economic variations and specific industry cycles are long-term and *not* as regular and predictable as seasonal variations. The economic swings that affect a business or industry tend to bring *many more variables* to play, such as changes in raw materials prices and availability, competitive conditions in the marketplace, capital investment needs, and so forth. Nevertheless, the principles we observed in dealing with the seasonal pattern apply here as well.

Funds lags during a cyclical upturn or downturn tend to be *magnified* by the lag in decision making as management tries to gage, from its day to day experience, whether the economy is undergoing a long-term change. For example, a sudden *downturn* in housing construction will leave many producers and wholesalers of building materials with inventories in excess of slumping demand. As sales decrease and the prices of lumber, plywood, and other commodities fall, management is faced with a funding crisis. Ongoing production operations will transform raw material into products that cannot be sold; thus, production must be curtailed. Lower volume and prices will decrease the eventual cash flow from current sales, while collections from past higher sales are going to run out.

A cyclical downturn brings several management challenges: management must *recognize*—with reasonable confidence— that a turning point has indeed arrived, then proceed to *manage inventories* by curtailing purchases and production, and *reduce ongoing costs* wherever possible. Careful management of *credit*, both extended and received, is another vital aspect.

In a cyclical *upswing*, lags in decision making may result in insufficient inventories and production as sales volume surges. To compensate, extra shifts or outside purchases may be used at times, even though the costs incurred may be higher than normal and affect profitability. Growing sales will also raise the amount of credit extended to customers. Thus, a cyclical boom will likely require the infusion of *additional capital* to provide the increased working capital needed and to finance increased physical operations. The latter may involve additional investment in plant and facilities.

Overall it may be said that a cyclical upswing will usually require an increase in medium-to long-term financing to support added levels of working capital and other financial requirements, while a downswing will first result in rising inventories—until management can adjust its operations— and then begin to release cash, which can be used to repay credit obligations. This condition will hold only if working capital and production levels are carefully managed downward, however.

Growth/Decline Variations

It should be clear now that a business that continues to *grow successfully* must also continually increase its funding of working capital and other expenditures, and these funds will be *permanently* tied up. Consider the following rules of thumb: If the business sells on 30-day credit, the value of each incremental layer of sales will be added to accounts receivable for 30 days and must be funded. Similarly, if the business turns over its inventory nine times per year, the value of the incremental cost of the goods sold will have to be added to inventories for 40 days (360 ÷ 9).

Offsetting this additional use of funds, but *only in part*, will be the increase in accounts payable and other minor accruals as sources. The credit extension by the company's vendors will amount to an equivalent value of the additional purchases for 30 days, if that is the usual credit pattern. But because the required investment in accounts receivable and inventories is normally much more than *twice* the credit from payables and accruals, it is clear that successful *growth* means the *extensive funding* of additional working capital. To this need must be *added* the funds required for expansion of physical facilities.

What should also be clear is that in a successful company this funds use is *permanent and growing* and must be financed over the *long term* through the use of owners' equity and long-term debt—quite unlike the case of the seasonal business. Normally, reinvestment of profits is not a sufficient source because in a fastgrowth business the contribution from the profit margin may be far outweighed by these funding demands. We will demonstrate this in greater detail in Chapter 5.

A business that *declines* in volume and is managed to undergo such shrinkage efficiently can in fact become a strong *generator of cash*. Here the opposite of the growth situation prevails. As sales decline, management should deliberately adjust operations and inventories to the lower levels, thus *releasing* the funds that had been tied up in receivables and inventories and forgoing the smaller change in vendor credit. If this is done properly, the situation is analogous to that of the seasonal business, except that the release of funds will be much *slower*. If the decline is *not* managed properly, however, the specter of inventory markdowns, operating inefficiencies, and emergency actions will negatively affect the release of funds.

Basically, the ability to release funds depends on the careful removal of layers of activity that no longer need to be supported. A proportional shrinkage of receivables and inventories, partly offset by declining payables, becomes the major potential cash source, apart from the disposal of other assets no longer needed.

In summary, variability in funds flows results from *external* conditions or *management actions*, or both. A business operating in a steady state has a *permanent* stock of working capital as well as properties, facilities, equipment, and other assets. As a general rule of thumb the amount of funds tied up in current assets far exceeds trade credit sources and normal short-term borrowings. Thus the introduction of any significant *variability* in the level of operations can cause major shifts in a company's financial condition from changes in *working capital* alone. In addition, funding for other needs, such as capital investments and major spending programs, must be superimposed on this pattern. In Chapter 4 we will discuss these issues in the context of the techniques of forecasting funds requirements.

Generalized Funds Flow Model

At this point it is useful once again to examine the overall relationships of funds movements in a generalized framework. The diagram is applicable to any business, large or small. In Figure 2–7 we have added flow lines that show the potential funds *movements* and the *linkages* between the main accounts

Figure 2–7
Generalized Funds Flow Diagram

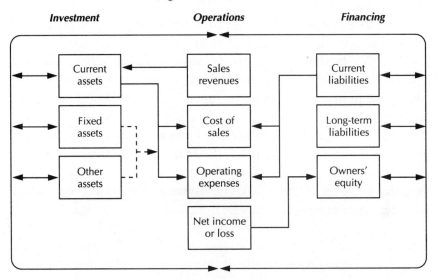

Management Decision Context

Investment	Operations	Financing

Current assets	Sales revenues	Current liabilities
Fixed assets	Cost of sales	Long-term liabilities
Other assets	Operating expenses	Owners' equity
	Net income or loss	

Investments (increases) in all types of assets are uses of funds; reductions in assets are sources of funds.

Profitable operations are a source of funds; losses drain funds from the system. **Note:** Accounting write-offs do **not** affect funds and must be adjusted for.

Trade credit and new financing (increases in liabilities) are sources of funds; repayments, dividends and returns of capital are uses of funds.

of the balance sheet and operating statement. A summary of *sources* and *uses* in terms of our management decision context is given at the bottom of the diagram.

This representation will be a useful reference when we discuss some of the more technical aspects of constructing funds flow statements in the last section of this chapter.

FUNDS FLOW STATEMENT REFINEMENTS

Having provided the basic concepts of how funds flow through a business, we are now ready to examine the *construction* of actual funds flow statements. Companies that are publicly held and publish regular financial statements are required to provide a statement of funds flows along with balance sheets and operating statements. Where such statements are not readily available, however, or in situations where the analyst wishes to project future funds movements, it is necessary to understand the basic principles and adjustments required to develop meaningul funds flow statements.

For the remainder of this chapter we will therefore go through the process of developing a funds flow statement, show the major steps involved, and discuss the key accounting aspects, such as write-offs and other noncash adjustments, that have to be considered when transforming the accounting information on the financial statements into the funds flow pattern we are interested in. For this purpose, we will again use the 1989 and 1988 TRW Inc. balance sheets and operating statements shown in Chapter 1 as Figures 1–3 and 1–5. We will work back from these statements to develop a derived funds flow statement, which we can compare to the one published by TRW. As we will see, some of the adjustments must be based on our own assumptions because we do not have available the detailed records of the company. Our version of the funds flow statement will approximate, but not be identical to, the key funds figures shown in TRW's statement.

We will begin with a look at the straightforward funds movements taken directly from *differences* in balance sheet items. Then we will examine in greater detail three commonly encountered refinements in funds flow analysis. These areas of refinement—*adjustments to retained earnings (owners' equity), adjustments to net income,* and *adjustments to net fixed assets*—will give us greater insight into the results of management decisions in our three key areas of investments, operations, and financing. TRW's consolidated balance sheets and consolidated income statements are reproduced below as Figures 2–8 and 2–9, and supplementary notes from TRW's 1989 annual report explaining the key accounting policies followed by TRW are shown in Figure 2–10.

To develop a funds flow statement, the *changes* in the accounts of the beginning and ending balance sheets for the period of analysis must be classified as *uses* and *sources*. We

Figure 2–8
TRW INC. AND SUBSIDIARIES
Consolidated Balance Sheets at December 31
($ millions)

Assets	1989	1988	Change
Current assets:			
Cash and cash equivalents	$ 114	$ 127	− 13
Accounts receivable	1,431	1,286	+145
Inventories	480	419	+ 61
Prepaid expenses	67	60	+ 7
Deferred income taxes	203	213	− 10
Total current assets	2,295	2,105	+190
Property, plant, and equipment at cost	4,127	3,733	+394
Less: Allowances for depreciation and amortization . . .	(2,173)	(1,940)	+233
Total property, plant, and equipment	1,954	1,793	+161
Intangible assets:			
Intangibles arising from acquisitions	534	328	+206
Capitalized data files and other	319	84	+235
Less: Accumulated amortization	(94)	(55)	+ 39
Total intangible assets—net	759	357	+402
Other assets	251	187	+ 64
Total assets	$5,259	$4,442	+817
Liabilities and Shareholders' Investment			
Current liabilities:			
Short-term debt	$ 459	$ 96	+363
Accrued compensation	304	281	+ 23
Trade accounts payable	456	461	− 5
Other accruals	443	443	–0–
Dividends payable	26	29	− 3
Income taxes	72	62	+ 10
Current portion of long-term debt	34	24	+ 10
Total current liabilities	1,794	1,396	+398
Long-term liabilities	155	173	− 18
Long-term debt	1,063	863	+200
Deferred income taxes	462	426	+ 36
Minority interests in subsidiaries	36	18	+ 18
Shareholders' investment:			
Serial preference stock II	1	1	–0–
Common stock	38	38	–0–
Other capital	194	191	+ 3
Retained earnings	1,516	1,358	+158
Cumulative translation adjustments	48	34	+ 14
Treasury shares—cost in excess of par	(48)	(56)	+ 8
Total shareholders' investment	1,749	1,566	+183
Total liabilities and shareholders' investment	$5,259	$4,442	+817

Figure 2-9
TRW INC. AND SUBSIDIARIES
Statement of Earnings
For the Years Ended December 31, 1989 and 1988
($ millions)

	1989	1988
Sales	$7,340	$6,982
Cost of sales	5,779	5,565
Gross profit	1,561	1,417
Administrative and selling expenses	780	780
Research and development expenses	256	225
Interest expense	138	130
Total expenses	1,174	1,135
Other income—net	12	138
Earnings before income taxes	399	420
Income taxes	136	159
Net earnings	$263	$261
Per share of common stock:		
Fully diluted earnings	$4.25	$4.23
Primary earnings	$4.31	$4.29
Depreciation of property, plant and equipment	$349	$324
Amortization of intangibles, other assets	51	25
Dividends paid	105	99

have done this in Figure 2–11, where increases and decreases in assets and liabilities are assigned to the appropriate categories, following the rules we developed earlier.

However, some of these balance sheet categories are too broad for our purpose. As a result, several of the funds flows are not specifically delineated. First of all, *net profit* from operations is not recognized as such, but is encompassed in the change in retained earnings. Next, although we know that *dividends* were paid, these are also reflected in the net change in retained earnings. We know that *depreciation and amortization* were sizable, but at this point they are buried in the changes in net plant and equipment and in intangible assets. Also, we know that there were significant investments in facilities as well as acquisitions of other smaller companies. What we can observe from the simple statement in Figure 2–11 is an

Figure 2-10
TRW INC. AND SUBSIDIARIES
Notes to Financial Statements, 1989 Annual Report
Summary of Accounting Policies

Principles of consolidation—The financial statements include the accounts of the company and its subsidiaries except for an insurance subsidiary. The wholly-owned insurance subsidiary and investments in affiliated companies, which are not significant individually or in the aggregate, are accounted for by the equity method.

Long-term contracts—The percentage of completion (cost-to-cost) method is used to estimate sales under fixed-price and fixed-price incentive contracts. Sales under cost-reimbursement contracts are recorded as costs are incurred. Fees based on cost, award fees, and incentive fees are included in sales at the time such amounts are reasonably estimable.

Accounts receivable—Accounts receivable at December 31, 1989 and 1988, included $656 million and $652 million, respectively, related to long-term contracts, of which $394 million and $355 million, respectively, were unbilled. Unbilled costs, fees, and claims represent revenues earned and billable in the following month as well as revenues earned but not billable under terms of the contracts. Substantially all of such amounts will be billed during the following year. Retainage receivables and receivables subject to negotiation were not significant.

Inventories—Inventories are stated at the lower of cost or market. At December 31, 1989 and 1988, inventories valued using the last-in, first-out (LIFO) method were $91 million and $95 million, respectively. Inventories not valued by the LIFO method are principally on the first-in, first-out (FIFO) method. Had the cost of all inventories been determined by the FIFO method, which approximates current cost, inventories at both December 31, 1989 and 1988, would have been greater by $70 million. Inventories applicable to long-term contracts were not significant.

Depreciation—Depreciation is computed using the straight-line method for the majority of the company's depreciable assets. The remaining assets are depreciated using accelerated methods.

Intangible assets—Intangible assets are stated on the basis of cost. Intangibles arising from acquisitions prior to 1971 ($75 million) are not being amortized because there is no indication of diminished value. Intangibles arising from acquisitions after 1970 are being amortized by the straight-line method principally over 40-year periods. Capitalized data files are amortized by the straight-line method over periods not exceeding 15 years.

Post-employment benefits—TRW provides health care and life insurance benefits for a majority of its retired employees, principally those located in the United States and Canada. Retirees in certain other countries are provided similar benefits by plans sponsored by their governments. Generally, the company recognizes the costs of providing these benefits as they are paid. The costs of providing post-employment benefits at ongoing operations were $15 million in 1989, $12 million in 1988, and $10 million in 1987. The costs of post-employment benefits for divested businesses are charged to previously established reserves.

Income taxes—Deferred income taxes arise from timing differences between income tax and financial reporting and principally relate to income recognition on long-term contracts, depreciation, and certain accruals. Deferred income taxes have not been provided on undistributed earnings of certain subsidiaries whose earnings are considered to be permanently reinvested. As substantial foreign tax credits would be available to off-set United States income taxes on future remittances of such undistributed earnings, the additional taxes payable would not be significant.

Earnings per share—Fully diluted earnings per share is computed based on the weighted average number of shares of common stock outstanding during each year, including common stock equivalents (stock options) and assuming the conversion of the Serial Preference Stock II—Series 1 and 3. Primary earnings per share is computed based on the weighted average number of shares of common stock outstanding during each year, including common stock equivalents.

Reclassifications—Certain prior year amounts have been reclassified to conform to the 1989 presentation.

Figure 2–11
TRW INC. AND SUBSIDIARIES
Statement of Balance Sheet Changes
For the Year Ended December 31, 1989
($ millions)

Sources:

Decrease in cash and cash equivalents	$ 13
Decrease in deferred income tax assets	10
Increase in short-term debt	363
Increase in accrued compensation	23
Increase in income taxes owed	10
Increase in current portion of long-term debt	10
Increase in long-term debt	200
Increase in deferred income tax liabilities	36
Increase in minority interests	18
Increase in other capital	3
Increase in retained earnings	158
Increase in cumulative translation adjustments	14
Decrease in treasury shares	8
	$866

Uses:

Increase in accounts receivable	145
Increase in inventories	61
Increase in prepaid expenses	7
Increase in net property, plant and equipment	161
Increase in net tangible assets	402
Increase in other assets	64
Decrease in trade accounts payable	5
Decrease in dividends payable	3
Decrease in long-term liabilities	18
	$866

indication of the broad financial implications of year-over-year growth in TRW. The major *funds uses* were (1) in net intangible assets, which suggests the recording of goodwill from acquisitions made, (2) in net plant and equipment, and (3) in working capital items, especially accounts receivable and inventories. The key *net funds sources* were (1) increases in both short-term and long-term debt and (2) the net increase in retained earnings as a result of profit for the period less dividends paid. Although we do, at this point, have a certain amount of insight into TRW's sources and uses of funds, we can further refine our analysis of the company's funds flow pattern by making a series of adjustments, using what information is available to us at this point.

Adjustments to Retained Earnings

The net change in *retained earnings* usually contains at least two elements of interest. The first is *net profit or loss* from operations which is, of course, reflected on the operating statement. The second is the amount of cash *dividends paid* to the various classes of shareholders. Both normally represent major funds movements that should be shown separately, one as a source and the other as a use. Often certain *adjustments* have been made to the retained earnings account, however. These may include changes in balance sheet reserves, value adjustments in selected accounts, goodwill adjustments, and currency translation adjustments. Such adjustments should be highlighted if they are significant.

In the case of TRW we know from the operating statement that net profit (income) for 1989 was $263 million. This amount must have been added to the retained earnings account. The operating statement also indicated that cash dividends paid were $105 million, which was subtracted. The net of these two figures is $158 million, exactly as shown in Figure 2–11. This suggests that no other adjustments were made in the account in 1989.

We can verify this by referring to the company's statement of changes in ownership equity. An abbreviated version of TRW's 1989 statement of changes in shareholders' investment, earlier presented in Chapter 1, is shown below in Figure 2–12. In the section on retained earnings we learn that in the prior year there had been an adjustment for redemption of shareholder purchase rights, but no such effect took place in 1989. We can therefore separate the net change in retained earnings into its two main components, as we have done in Figure 2–13, which also contains the remaining adjustments still to be discussed.

Figure 2–12
TRW INC. AND SUBSIDIARIES
Abbreviated Statement of Changes in Shareholders' Investment
For the Years Ended December 31, 1989 and 1988
($ millions)

	1989	1988
Serial Preference Stock II:	$ 1	$ 1
Common Stock	38	38
Other Capital:		
Balance at January 1	191	190
Sale of stock and other	3	1
Balance at December 31	194	191
Retained Earnings:		
Balance at January 1	1,358	1,201
Net earnings	263	261
Redemption of shareholder purchase rights	—	(3)
Dividends declared:		
Preference stock	(1)	(1)
Common stock ($1.72 and $1.66 per share)	(104)	(100)
Balance at December 31	1,516	1,358
Cumulative Translation Adjustments:		
Balance at January 1	34	58
Translation adjustments	14	(24)
Balance at December 31	48	34
Treasury Shares—Cost in Excess of Par Value:		
Balance at January 1	(56)	(70)
Purchase of shares	(3)	(2)
Sold under stock options	11	16
Balance at December 31	(48)	(56)
Total shareholders' investment	$1,749	$1,566

Some additional comments will be useful here. Had the company made significant bookkeeping adjustments during the period on balance sheet accounts and reflected these changes in retained earnings, the analyst could choose to, in effect, cancel out the amounts involved by adjusting both accounts to their preadjustment level. Whether to do this "reversing" is a matter of judgment and depends on what the funds flow statement is used for. Unless the amounts involved

Figure 2–13
TRW INC. AND SUBSIDIARIES
Derived Funds Flow Statement
For the Year Ended December 31, 1989
($ millions)

Funds from Operations:	Sources	Uses
Net income	$ 263	
Depreciation (nonfunds item)	349	
Amortization (nonfunds item)	51	
Deferred income taxes (net)	46	
Increase in current liabilities (payables, accruals, taxes, long-term debt due)	35	
Increase in current assets (cash, receivables, inventories, prepaids)	—	200
Total operational funds flows	744	200
Net funds from operations	544	
Funds for Investment:		
Capital investments (adjusted for depreciation of $349)		510
Investment in intangible assets (adjusted for amortization of $51)		453
Investment in other assets		64
Total funds for investment		1,027
Funds from Financing:		
Increase in short-term debt	$ 363	
Increase in long-term debt	200	
Decrease in long-term liabilities	—	18
Increase in minority interests	18	
Increase in other capital	3	
Decrease in treasury shares	8	
Currency translation adjustments	14	
Dividends paid	—	105
Total financing funds flows	606	123
Net funds from financing	483	
Totals	$1,027	$1,027

are truly significant, the extra refinement is probably not worth the effort.

Another item, stock dividends, which some companies pay in lieu of or in addition to cash dividends, can be handled similarly. Strictly speaking, stock dividends involve no change in economic value. They simply increase the number of shares outstanding slightly without affecting the stated value of the total owners' equity. It is important that such refinements do not divert us from the key purpose of the analysis, which is to gage the *effect on funds* of *major management decisions* made during the period.

Adjustments to Net Income

As we know, net income is derived after a number of book-keeping *write-offs* have been taken, the largest of which normally is depreciation. Another write-off is the amortization of patents, licenses, and other intangible assets arising in the normal course of business or from acquisitions, while a third is used to reflect the depletion of mineral deposits and standing timber. We remember that such write-offs reflect the apportionment of *past expenditures* and therefore do not involve current funds movements. Any write-offs of significance should be recognized as such and must be *added back* to income (thereby cancelled out) in the funds flow statement.

This practice, however, results in a common misconception of viewing depreciation and amortization as *actual* sources of funds. We must remember that depreciation and amortization as such do *not create any funds*—they are only accounting entries that reduce reported income. They do, of course, affect the amount of *income taxes* paid, but this positive funds effect has already been recognized in the amount of income taxes that was deducted before arriving at net income.

One factor to remember while adjusting for depreciation and amortization is that a *corresponding* adjustment should be made in the asset accounts from which they arose. We recall that depreciation charges for a period are recorded as a *reduction* in net fixed assets through the vehicle of accumulated depreciation. Amortization is normally charged directly against the asset account being written off, but may also be accumulated like depreciation. When we show depreciation and amortization as funds "sources," we are in effect increasing net income. But we must also *restore* the same amount to the relevant asset account. Otherwise our funds flows will not balance. (We will return to the specifics of this adjustment in the next section.)

In TRW's case, depreciation and amortization were shown at the bottom of the operating statement as $349 million and $51 million respectively, and these amounts should be listed in Figure 2-13 after net income as funds sources, because their addition in effect restores net income to its pre-write-off level. The respective asset accounts should also be adjusted accordingly.

Deferred taxes are another major funds flow element that affects net income. As we discussed earlier, deferred taxes arise because some revenues and expenses, particularly depreciation, are timed differently for tax purposes than for financial reporting purposes. Taxes *paid* may be lower than taxes *provided for* on the income statement. The amount of the difference is shown as a liability on the balance sheet. Reported income therefore does *not* reflect the funds benefit from the lower taxes actually remitted. We should show any increase in deferred taxes as a *source* in our funds flow statement, in effect adding it to reported net income.

Deferred taxes can also arise from timing differences in the recognition of revenue from installment contracts or projects that are billed on a percentage of completion basis. Here the opposite effect can occur because a company may have to report revenue—and thus income—for tax purposes sooner than it is recognized for accounting purposes. In effect, this amounts to a prepayment of taxes, and the difference will be recorded on the balance sheet as a deferred tax *asset*. Any increase in a deferred tax asset amounts to a use of funds—the opposite of an increase in deferred tax liabilities, as we would expect. Over time, this asset will change, just like deferred tax liabilities, as differences between tax reporting and accounting requirements increase or decrease. Because timing differences are due to the changing requirements of the Internal Revenue Code, future modifications in the tax laws may significantly affect the deferred tax concept.

For purposes of our funds flow statement we can take changes in deferred taxes directly from the balance sheet, and there is no need to make any further adjustments. Some analysts prefer to net out the changes in deferred tax assets and liabilities and show a single amount on the statement. In 1989 TRW's deferred tax liabilities rose by $36 million, while deferred income tax assets fell by $10 million. Both should be reflected as sources in conjunction with the reported net income of $263 million, and, accordingly, the total of $46 million is shown in Figure 2-13.

Other elements in the net income picture will sometimes result from adjustments of assets and liabilities on the balance sheet. Normally these amounts are not significant enough to warrant special attention. If they are substantial, the analyst can again choose to reverse them to keep the funds flow analysis "pure." The relevance of any particular item to the purpose of the analysis must be the overriding factor in this decision.

Finally, net income is often affected by gains and losses from the sale of capital assets. This will be discussed in detail in the next section.

Adjustments to Net Fixed Assets

The change in net fixed assets—*property, plant, and equipment*—results from shifts in a variety of funds and nonfunds flow items. It is made up of changes in the gross fixed assets account and changes in accumulated depreciation. Nonrecurring asset adjustments from retirement of various fixed assets often also have an effect. In most cases, funds flow analysis is more meaningful when at least the major elements of the net change in fixed assets are recognized. Normally the funds flow pattern behind the change in net fixed assets is significant enough to warrant this special attention. At the same time, fixed assets effects are among the more difficult aspects of financial analysis to understand. This is partly because fixed assets represent the *net* of an asset and a reserve account. Another part of the problem is the mystique surrounding depreciation and asset write-offs.

The easiest approach to the subject is to lay out the components of the fixed asset account and to observe the relevance of the figures. Then we can look for additional information in other parts of the published statements. Some of this information may be available only to the insider, however. In such cases we must make do with reasonable assumptions.

In our TRW example, the balance sheet in Figure 2–8 provides the following information:

	12-31-89	12-31-88	Change
Property, plant and equipment at cost	$4,127	$3,733	+$394
Less: Accumulated depreciation and amortization . . .	2,173	1,940	+ 233
Net property, plant and equipment	$1,954	$1,793	+$161

Our basic task is to identify the relevant *individual* funds sources and uses that in combination amounted to the *net use* (net increase) of $161 million shown. Quite obviously, there was an increase of $394 million in gross property, plant, and equipment, which must have been due to new investments (a use). At the same time, accumulated depreciation rose by $233 million, which is largely due to current write-offs (a source, as we discussed before).

In some cases, this coarse breakdown of sources and uses is sufficient, and many analysts will let the matter rest here. Yet we already know, for instance, that *actual* depreciation for the period as shown on TRW's operating statement was $349 million, far *more* than the change in accumulated depreciation. There must have been other elements affecting the picture. As a result, depending on the depth of analysis desired, the following questions arise:

1. What are the relevant elements of funds flow in the *accumulated depreciation* account, one of which was the reported amount of depreciation for the year?

2. What was the *total* amount of *new investment* in plant, equipment and rental machines—a major aspect of the management decision process?

3. Were there any divestitures and asset retirements (i.e., reduction in gross plant and equipment) that significantly affected the company's funds flow?

These questions are interrelated and can be handled at two levels of complexity. The *simpler* approach is to assume that normally the amount of depreciation taken for the year ($349 million in the case of TRW) will *equal* the amount by which accumulated depreciation has increased. If this in fact is *not* the case, as we discovered in our example, then there must have been some reduction in the accumulated depreciation account which, for simplicity, we can assume to represent the *abandonment* of *fully depreciated* assets during the period.[1] We thereby imply that no proceeds at all were received. This simple but often adequate approach also eliminates the problem of having to deal with any gains or losses on the *sale* of capital items. The adjustments involved in this simpler level of analysis modify our funds flow layout as follows:

	(1) 12-31-88	(2) Additions	(3) Deductions	(4) 12-31-89	(5) Change
Gross property, etc.	$3,733	+$510*	−$116†	$4,127	+$394
Less: Accumulated depreciation	1,940	+ 349	− 116‡	2,173	+ 233
Net property, etc.	$1,793	$161	–0–	$1,954	+$161

*Derived figure.
†Must be same as in accumulated depreciation if fully depreciated assets were abandoned.
‡Assumed figure in order to balance the change in the account.

Because we must reconcile the data with the *net* changes in the accounts on the balance sheet, our simple assumption has given us the necessary data to complete the funds flow analysis. We recognize the actual depreciation write-off of $349 million as a source (column 2) and accept the *derived* amount of $510 million as the new capital investment, a use. The process relies on an *assumed* write-off of $116 million of fully depreciated assets, which, under normal accounting practice, equally reduces *both* the asset *and* the accumulated depreciation accounts (column 3). This practice is observed in our analysis. We are ignoring possible tax implications that would tend

---

[1] Fully depreciated assets, when scrapped, are removed by an accounting entry that credits (reduces) assets by the amount of the recorded value and debits (reduces) accumulated depreciation by the same amount.

to confuse the issue, but do little to improve the accuracy of our analysis.

From a funds flow point of view we now have all the elements needed to identify and separate the sources and uses behind the change in the net plant and equipment account as reflected in Figure 2–11:

Source: Depreciation for the period	$349
Use: New investment	510
Adjusted net use	$161

It is obvious that our relatively simple adjustment of the net balances in the two accounts has improved our assessment of one of the most important management decisions: the amount of *new fixed asset investment*. Our original version in Figure 2–11 reflected only a fraction of this sizable commitment for future growth.

We can now assemble a modified funds flow statement from the information displayed earlier in Figure 2–11, which is improved by the adjustments we have made in owners' equity, net income, and plant and equipment. In Figure 2–13, we have arranged the derived TRW funds flow data in terms of our three familiar areas of management decision—operations, investment, and financing—to provide a picture of the effect of TRW management decisions in 1989. We can see that operational decisions resulted in a net funds source of $544 million, which is net of an increase in working capital of $165 million (a $200 million increase in current assets and a $35 million increase in current liabilities).

Funds required for investment in total amounted to $1,027 million, which included our derived capital investment figure of $510 million, as well as a sizable investment in intangible assets. Since we chose to show the amortization of the latter as part of operational funds flows, an offsetting increase of $51 million had to be made to approximate the gross investment in intangibles. These intangibles arose from the acquisition and divestiture activities of TRW during 1989, the biggest single element of which was the acquisition of the Chilton Corporation, whose nationwide credit data files on consumers represent a valuable asset added to the information services sector of TRW.

Funds flows from financing decisions were most significant in the area of short-term borrowing, with new long-term debt and dividend payments being the next largest items.

Yet we are *still* short of a fully accurate picture because we made one simplifying assumption—that *fully depreciated* assets were abandoned and written off. A check of the company's annual report reveals that actual 1989 capital outlays for property, plant, and equipment were $452 million, while the acquisitions made in 1989 amounted to $448 million. We further learn that proceeds from divestitures were $28 million, while proceeds from sales of property, plant, and equipment were $14 million. We are quite close on the acquisition estimate, if only because of the large intangible asset component, but in any case it is not possible without detailed internal records to reconstruct the exact nature of the transactions.

If we were interested in reconciling our analysis with the added bit of information on capital expenditures—that is, the fact that some assets were sold—we must follow a second, *more complex* level of analysis. In effect we have to dig more deeply and try to understand the accounting adjustments that were probably made in the fixed asset accounts. Our simple assumption used for Figure 2–12 about fully depreciated assets left out the possibility of receiving any proceeds or recognizing gains or losses from the disposition of property and other fixed assets. Normally the amounts involved are relatively minor, as is proportionately true in the example of TRW (only about a 3 percent adjustment is necessary).

If there are any *proceeds* from assets sold—and this can be ascertained through examination of published financial data for most larger companies—there must have been three effects on the company's statements. First, the write-off in the gross property account and in the accumulated depreciation must have *differed* by the amount of any remaining *book value* of the assets disposed of. This expectation slightly complicates our basic data.

Second, any gain or loss resulting from cash proceeds being larger or smaller than the remaining book value would have affected *net income*. If such gains or losses were material, they would be reflected in the operating statement. For purposes of funds flow analysis, net income can therefore be split into operating earnings as one source and the reported *gain or loss* as another source or use.

Third, proceeds received from disposition of the asset will have been buried in the *cash* account. Yet, if these proceeds had differed substantially from the book value of the assets, they should be recognized as a source, that is, if they were material. Unless there is a specific indication in the operating statement about gains or losses, we simply *assume* that the *proceeds* received exactly *matched* the remaining *book value*. Consequently, the reduction in gross plant and equipment this represents must have been a cash *source* for the period.

When we compare TRW's actual statement, reproduced again in Figure 2–14 to our derived statement in Figure 2–13, we find that, apart from differences in presentation, many of the figures we have developed are reflected there as well. The items on which the statements disagree all require more detailed knowledge than is normally available in published statements. Adjustments for the costs of restructuring, the accounting for acquisitions and dispositions, the treatment of working capital changes shown net of the effects of businesses acquired or sold, and details in the financing section of TRW's funds flow statement reflect information that was not available to us. Also, a number of minor funds movements are netted out. In broad terms, however, our derived statement reasonably approaches the overall magnitude of funds movements in the three decision areas.

To summarize, in this section we constructed a funds flow statement that goes beyond simply listing the changes readily observable from a comparison of beginning and ending balance sheet accounts. We achieved this by making informed

Figure 2–14
TRW INC. AND SUBSIDIARIES
Statement of Cash Flows
For the Years Ended December 31, 1989 and 1988
($ millions)

Operating Activities:	1989	1988
Net earnings	$263	$261
Adjustments to reconcile net earnings to net cash provided by operating activities:		
Depreciation and amortization	400	349
Restructuring	(59)	(106)
Foreign currency exchange losses	29	54
Equity in unremitted losses (earnings) of affiliated companies	3	(3)
Dividends received from affiliated companies	—	31
Deferred income taxes	15	(180)
Other—net	3	18
Changes in assets and liabilities, net of effects of businesses acquired or sold:		
Accounts receivable	(96)	(132)
Inventories and prepaid expenses	(47)	(42)
Accounts payable and other accruals	(4)	74
Other—net	(14)	19
Net cash provided by operating activities	493	343
Investing Activities:		
Capital expenditures	(452)	(417)
Proceeds from divestitures	28	453
Acquisitions, net of cash acquired	(448)	(10)
Investments in other assets	(67)	(47)
Proceeds from sales of property, plant, and equipment	14	10
Other—net	(14)	(41)
Net cash used in investing activities	(939)	(52)
Financing Activities:		
Increase (decrease) in short-term debt	450	(179)
Proceeds from debt in excess of 90 days	259	82
Principal repayments in excess of 90 days	(156)	(82)
Dividends paid	(105)	(99)
Other—net	7	15
Net cash provided by (used in) financing activities	455	(263)
Effect of exchange rate changes on cash	(22)	(46)
Increase (decrease) in cash and cash equivalents	(13)	(18)
Cash and cash equivalents at beginning of year	127	145
Cash and cash equivalents at end of year	$114	$127

adjustments in several of the accounts. The *purpose* of the refinements was to highlight significant results that reflect management decisions involving investments, operations, and financing. If a funds flow statement is not made available as a matter of course, the analyst can *approximate* the statement an insider could prepare by going through the adjustment process demonstrated. We must usually examine three areas in more depth: the components of the change in *owners' equity*, the elements in *net income*, particularly those relating to accounting write-offs, and the various components of change in the *fixed asset* accounts and related accumulated depreciation. Under most conditions the analyst will be able to come close enough to the actual figures to be able to construct a funds flow statement that is meaningful in format and content.

SUMMARY

In this chapter we demonstrated the funds flow cycle involved in any business, large or small, and its implication for management. We began with a simple illustration of basic funds movements, and then discussed *operating funds cycles* from a manufacturing and sales standpoint. We observed the nature and behavior of *working capital* and highlighted the impact of *variability of operations* and demonstrated the effect of *funds lags* on the nature and duration of financing required to support a business. The insights gained included the need to consider the *permanence* of basic working capital requirements, the financial drain of even successful *growth*, and the potential funds release from *decline* in volume.

Several key questions arise as funds movements are analyzed. Most relate to the *types of funds commitments* (uses) made compared to the *sources of funds available*. Have enough long-term funds been provided to fund ongoing growth in working capital and fixed asset expansion? Are most sources of funds temporary loans and credit extension? Is the business counting on *profits* to fund peaks of need that may *exceed* such expectations? In essence, funds flow analysis is a broad-brush *dynamic* view of the financial management of the business that relates *changes* in conditions to the key financial *implications* by reconstructing the major funds transactions during the period. The techniques are simple, requiring only basic accounting knowledge to provide this *extra dimension* in assessing balance sheets and operating statements.

SELECTED REFERENCES

Anthony, Robert N., and James S. Reece. *Accounting Principles.* 6th ed. Homewood, Ill.: Richard D. Irwin, 1988.

Brealey, Richard, and Stewart Myers. *Principles of Corporate Finance.* 3rd ed. New York: McGraw-Hill, 1988.

Garrison, Raymond H. *Managerial Accounting: Concepts for Planning Control, Decision Making,* 5th ed. Homewood, Ill.: Richard D. Irwin, 1988.

Ross, Stephen; Randolph Westerfield; and Jeffrey Jaffe. *Corporate Finance.* 2nd ed. Homewood, Ill.: Richard D. Irwin, 1990.

Seitz, Neil. *Financial Analysis: A Programmed Approach.* 3rd ed. Reston, Va.: Reston Publishing, 1984.

Vancil, Richard F. and Benjamin R. Makela, eds. *The CFO Handbook.* Homewood, Ill.: Dow Jones-Irwin, 1986.

Van Horne, James C. *Financial Management and Policy.* 8th ed. Englewood Cliffs, N.J.: Prentice-Hall, 1989.

Weston, J. Fred, and Thomas E. Copeland. *Managerial Finance.* 9th ed. Hinsdale, Ill.: Dryden Press, 1989.

SELF-STUDY EXERCISES AND PROBLEMS

(Solutions in Appendix III)

1. Develop a funds flow statement from the balance sheets and income statements of the CBA Company (on pages 73 and 74) for the year 1990. Make appropriate assumptions and comment on the results.

CBA COMPANY
Balance Sheets
December 31, 1989, and 1990

Assets	1989	1990
Current assets:		
Cash	$ 39,700	$ 27,500
Marketable securities	1,000	11,000
Accounts receivable (net)	81,500	72,700
Inventories	181,300	242,000
Total current assets	303,500	353,200
Fixed assets:		
Land	112,000	112,000
Plant and equipment (net)	445,200	464,800
Total fixed assets	557,200	576,800
Other assets	13,300	21,500
Total assets	$874,000	$951,500
Liabilities and Net Worth		
Current liabilities:		
Accounts payable	$ 71,200	$ 83,000
Notes payable	50,000	140,000
Accrued expenses	33,400	36,300
Total current liabilities	154,600	259,300
Long-term debt:		
Mortgage payable	106,000	90,800
Net worth:		
Common stock	225,000	230,000
Earned surplus	388,400	371,400
Total net worth	613,400	601,400
Total liabilities and net worth	$874,000	$951,500

CBA COMPANY
Operating Statements for 1989 and 1990

	1989	1990
Net sales	$1,133,400	$1,147,700
Cost of goods sold*	740,500	813,300
Gross margin	392,900	334,400
Expenses:		
Selling expense	172,500	227,000
General and administrative	65,500	71,800
Other expenses	22,200	25,000
Interest on debt	9,700	14,300
Total expenses	269,900	338,100
Profit (loss) before taxes	123,000	(3,700)
Federal income tax	56,600	(1,700)
Net income (loss)†	$ 66,400	$ (2,000)

*Includes depreciation of $31,500 for 1989 and $32,200 for 1990.
†Dividends paid were $30,000 for 1989 and $15,000 for 1990.

2. Work the following exercises:

   a. The following data about the ABC Company's operations and conditions for the year 1990 are available from a variety of sources:

Depreciation for 1990	$ 21,400
Net loss for 1990	14,100
Common dividends paid	12,000
Amortization of goodwill, patents	15,000
Inventory adjustment—write-down	24,000
Investments in fixed assets	57,500
Loss from abandonment of equipment	4,000
Balance of earned surplus, 12–31–89	167,300

   Which of the items above affect earned surplus during 1990 (the only surplus account of the company), and what is the balance of earned surplus as of December 31? Which of the items above are funds sources, and which are funds uses? Can depreciation be considered a funds flow item if the operating results are negative? What would be different if the $4,000 loss from abandonment had been a gain from sale of assets instead? Discuss.

   b. The following items, among others, appear on the funds flow statement of DEF Company for the year 1990:

Outlays for properties and fixed assets	$1,250,500
Profit from operations after taxes	917,000
Funds from depreciation	1,613,000

The only other information readily available is as follows:

Gross property and fixed assets, 12–31–89 . . . . $8,431,500
Gross property and fixed assets, 12–31–90 8,430,000
Accumulated depreciation, 12–31–90 3,874,000

Determine the change in the *net* properties and fixed assets accounts from this information, and spell out your assumptions. How significant would be the likely effect on the results if you used some possible alternative assumptions? Discuss.

c. The XYZ Company experienced the transactions and changes listed below, among many others, during 1990, and these affected its balance sheet as follows:

Fixed assets recorded at $110,000 were sold for $45,000 (gain reflected in net income.)

Accumulated depreciation on these specific assets was $81,000.

Accumulated depreciation for the company as a whole decreased by $5,000 during 1990.

Total depreciation charged during 1990 was $78,500.

Balance of gross fixed assets was as follows: 12–31–89, $823,700, and 12–31–90, $947,300.

From this information, determine the amount of new investment in fixed assets for 1990 which should be shown in the funds flow statement. What was the amount of change in the *net* fixed assets account during 1990? Which other items shown above or derived from these should be shown on the funds flow statement? What assumptions are necessary? Discuss.

3. Develop a funds flow statement from the balance sheets, income statements, and earned surplus statements of the FED Company, shown below, for the year 1990. Make appropriate assumptions and comment on the results. If you net out changes in working capital accounts into one figure, will significant information be obscured? Will it be helpful to assign uses and sources to key management decision areas? Discuss.

Other data: (1) sold fully depreciated machinery for $4,000, (2) issued $20,000 of common stock ($1 par) to reduce note payable, and (3) issued $4,000 of preferred stock to outsiders.

FED COMPANY
Balance Sheets, December 31, 1989, and 1990
($000)

Assets	1989	1990	Change
Current assets:			
Cash	$ 12	$-0-	− $12
Marketable securities	18	-0-	− 18
Accounts receivable (net)	68	73	+ 5
Notes receivable	30	50	+ 20
Inventories	131	138	+ 7
Total current assets	259	261	+ 2
Fixed assets:			
Land	25	25	-0-
Plant and equipment	268	283	+ 15
Less: Accumulated depreciation	157	160	+ 3
Net plant and equipment	111	123	+ 12
Total fixed assets	136	148	+ 12
Other assets:			
Prepaid expenses	12	14	+ 2
Patents, organization expense	30	27	− 3
Total other assets	42	41	− 1
Total assets	$437	$450	+$13

Liabilities and Net Worth

	1989	1990	Change
Current liabilities:			
Bank overdraft	$-0-	$ 4	+$ 4
Accounts payable	73	97	+ 24
Notes payable	100	70	− 30
Accrued expenses	13	22	+ 9
Total current liabilities	186	193	+ 7
Long-term liabilities:			
Secured notes payable	40	20	− 20
Net Worth:			
Deferred income taxes	25	27	+ 2
Preferred stock	35	39	+ 4
Capital surplus	90	109	+ 19
Earned surplus	51	51	-0-
Common stock	10	11	+ 1
Total net worth	211	237	+ 26
Total liabilities and net worth	$437	$450	+$13

FED COMPANY
Operating Statement for 1989 and 1990
($000)

	1989	1990
Sales	$1,115	$1,237
Cost of goods sold:		
Material	312	345
Labor	274	341
Depreciation	24	26
Overhead	158	210
Cost of goods sold	768	922
Gross profit	347	315
Expenses:		
Selling and administrative expense	268	297
Interest on debt	9	7
Total expenses	277	304
Profit before taxes	70	11
Income taxes	32	5
Net income	$ 38	$ 6

FED COMPANY
Statement of Earned Surplus for 1990
($000)

Balance 12-31-89			$51
Additions:			
Net income from 1990 operations		$6	
Gain from sale of fixed assets		4	10
			61
Deductions:			
Preferred dividends		2	
Common dividends		5	
Patent, other amortization		3	10
Balance, 12-31-90			$51

4. The ZYX Company, a vegetable packing plant, operates on a highly seasonal basis, which affects its financial results during various parts of its fiscal year and forces a financial planning effort in tune with these fluctuating requirements. From the nine quarterly balance sheets shown in the table, which cover two fiscal years of the ZYX Company, develop a funds flow analysis that will appropriately reflect the funds requirements and sources as balanced by company management.

Data you may need in addition to that shown in the table on the next page include (1) purchases of machinery, $48,000 in April 1990 and $50,000 in April 1991; (2) depreciation charged at $6,000 per quarter through April 1990, at $7,000 through April 1991, and at $8,000 through July 1991; and (3) dividends paid at $15,000 per quarter through October 1990 and at $18,000 per quarter through July 1991.

Comment on the various alternative ways this analysis can be developed, and state your reasons for the choices you made. What are your key findings?

ZYX COMPANY
Balance Sheets by Fiscal Quarters
July 31, 1989, to July 31, 1991
($000)

	1989		1990				1991		
Assets	7-31	10-31	1-31	4-30	7-31	10-31	1-31	4-30	7-31
Cash	$ 21	$ 30	$ 74	$ 91	$ 7	$ 28	$ 90	$103	$ 16
Accounts receivable	114	247	319	128	141	293	388	151	103
Inventories	231	417	315	131	271	467	351	98	310
Net plant and equipment	239	233	227	269	262	255	248	291	283
Other assets	15	16	16	15	15	14	18	18	17
Total assets	$620	$943	$951	$634	$696	$1,057	$1,095	$661	$729
Liabilities and Net Worth									
Accounts payable	$ 68	$297	$121	$103	$ 79	$ 314	$ 188	$ 97	$ 84
Notes payable	35	126	294	—	63	178	342	—	80
Mortgage payable	80	80	75	75	70	70	65	65	60
Preferred stock	100	100	100	100	100	100	100	100	100
Common stock	100	100	100	100	125	125	125	125	125
Earned Surplus	237	240	261	256	259	270	275	274	280
Total liabilities and net worth	$620	$943	$951	$634	$696	$1,057	$1,095	$661	$729

3 ASSESSMENT OF
BUSINESS
PERFORMANCE

As we already established in the preceding chapters, the performance of a business is the result of many individual decisions made continually by its management. To assess business performance, therefore, involves analyzing the cumulative financial and economic effects of these decisions and judging the results through the use of comparative measures. In Chapter 2 we developed a broad understanding of the nature of the funds flows that are fundamental to any business and are the consequence of various types of management decisions. In this chapter we will discuss the *analysis of business performance* on the basis of *published financial data* as reflected in the financial statements prepared according to generally accepted accounting principles. These are the most common data available for the purpose. Financial statements are the periodic "score cards" that track the results of business investment, operations, and financing. Our focus will be on *key financial relationships and indicators* that allow the analyst to assess past performance and also to project assumed future results, and we will point out their meaning as well as the limitations inherent in them.

Ratio Analysis and Performance

Many analytical techniques, including those involving a variety of financial ratios, are available for performance assessment. However, the reader should be reminded that different techniques are appropriate for different purposes. Before any analysis is undertaken, the analyst must clearly define the *viewpoint* taken, the *objectives* of the analysis, and the potential *standards* of comparison. In financial analysis there is often a temptation "to run all the numbers"—yet normally only a few relationships will yield the information and insights the analyst really needs. A ratio can relate any magnitude to any other, such as net profit to total assets or current liabilities to current assets—the choices are limited only by the analyst's imagination.

The actual *usefulness* of any particular ratio, however, is strictly governed by the specific *objectives* of the analysis. Moreover, ratios are not absolute criteria: meaningful ratios serve best to point out *changes* in financial conditions or operating performance and help illustrate the trends and patterns of such changes which, in turn, may indicate to the analyst the risks and opportunities for the business under review.

A further caution should be noted here. Performance assessment based on financial statements deals with *past* data and conditions from which it may be difficult to extrapolate future expectations. Yet we must remember that only the *future* can be affected by decisions made as a result of any financial analysis—the past is gone.

No attempt to assess business performance can provide firm answers. Any insights gained are *relative* because business and operating conditions vary so much from company to company and from industry to industry. Comparisons and standards based on past performance are especially difficult in large, multibusiness companies and conglomerates, where specific information by individual line of business is normally limited. Accounting adjustments of various types present further complications. To deal with all of these apsects is far beyond the scope of this book. Nevertheless, the analyst must keep these cautions in mind when dealing with the available numerical data that necessarily reflect the effects of all of these conditions.

In this section we will discuss and characterize the key ratios and measures commonly applied in financial analysis of business performance. Only the most important techniques will be dealt with. Our discussion will be developed around the major viewpoints that can be taken in performing financial performance analysis, and we will cover the usefulness of the different measures for each viewpoint.

Many different individuals and groups are interested in the success or failure of a given business. The most important are owners (investors), managers, lenders and creditors, employees, labor organizations, government agencies, and society in general ("the public"). These groups differ in their view of business results and performance and will often go beyond financial data to include broader and more intangible values in their assessments.

Closest to the business from a day-to-day standpoint but also responsible for long-range performance is the *management* of the organization—whether professional managers or owner/managers. Managers are responsible and accountable for operating efficiency, current and long-term profitability, and the effective deployment of capital, human effort, and other resources. Next are the various *owners* of the business, who are especially interested in the current and long-term profitability of their equity investment. They expect growing earnings and dividends, which will bring about growth in the economic value of their "stake." Then there are the providers of "other people's money," *lenders and creditors* who extend funds to the business for various lengths of time. They are mainly concerned about the reliability of the interest payments due them, about the ability of the business to repay the principal, and about the availability of specific residual asset values that give them a margin of protection against their risk. Other groups such as *government, labor,* and *society,* have specific objectives of their own—the reliability of tax payments, the ability to pay wages, stability of employment, or the financial wherewithal to meet various social and environmental obligations, for instance.

We will develop the ensuing discussion of business performance measures and tests around the first three viewpoints, that is, *management, owners,* and *lenders.* These viewpoints are, of course, interdependent and differ mainly in their emphasis. The reader should keep in mind that some of the measures are, of course, also applicable to the viewpoints of the other groups mentioned. In Figure 3–1 below, the principal areas of financial performance of interest to the three groups are shown along with the ratios and measures relevant

Figure 3–1
Financial Performance Measures by Area and Viewpoint

Management	*Owners*	*Lenders*
Operational analysis	**Profitability**	**Liquidity**
Gross margin	Return on total net worth	Current Ratio
Profit margin	Return on common equity	Acid test
Operating expense analysis	Earnings per share	Quick sale value
Contribution analysis	Cash flow per share	Cash flow patterns
Operating leverage	Share price appreciation	
	Total shareholder return	
	Shareholder value analysis	
Resource management	**Disposition of earnings**	**Financial leverage**
Asset turnover	Dividends per share	Debt to assets
Working capital management	Dividend yield	Debt to capitalization
Inventory turnover	Payout/retention	Debt to equity
Accounts receivable patterns	Dividend coverage	Risk/reward tradeoff
Accounts payable patterns		
Human resource effectiveness		
Profitability	**Market indicators**	**Debt service**
Return on assets (after taxes)	Price/earnings ratio	Interest coverage
Return before interest and taxes	Market to book value	Interest and principal
Return on current value basis	Relative price movements	coverage
	Cash flow multiples	Cash flow analysis

to these areas. We will follow the sequence of measures shown in the table and discuss each subgrouping within the three broad viewpoints.

Management's Point of View

As mentioned before, management has a dual interest in the analysis of financial performance—to assess the efficiency and profitability of operations and to judge how effectively the business resources are being used. The assessment of operations is largely based on an analysis of the operating (income) statement, while the effectiveness of resource use is usually measured by a review of both the balance sheet and the income statement.

For purposes of illustration we will again use appropriate information from the sample statements of TRW Inc. for 1989 and 1988, which were reproduced in Chapter 1 as Figures 1–3 and 1–5. Slightly abbreviated versions of TRW's balance sheet and operating statement are shown on pages 86 and 87 (Figures 3–2 and 3–3), and we will use this information for the remainder of this chapter. For added convenience we have also expressed the various items on the operating statement as a percent of sales.

Operational Analysis.   For the business as a whole or any of its subdivisions, an assessment of operations is generally performed through a "common numbers" or percentage analysis of the operating statement. The ratios are usually based on *net sales,* that is, gross sales revenues after any returns and allowances. Use of net sales as the base provides a reasonable standard for measurement, which is particularly useful when tracking progress over a series of past periods or when making comparisons between different companies.

The ratios derived are used both to judge the relative *magnitude* of selected key elements and to determine any *trends* towards improving or declining performance. During the analysis we must keep in mind the type of industry involved and its particular characteristics, as well as the individual trends and special conditions of the company being studied.

Figure 3–2
TRW INC. AND SUBSIDIARIES
Consolidated Balance Sheets at December 31
($ millions)

Assets	1989	1988
Current Assets:		
Cash and cash equivalents	$ 114	$ 127
Accounts receivable	1,431	1,286
Inventories	480	419
Prepaid expenses	67	60
Deferred income taxes	203	213
Total current assets	2,295	2,105
Property, plant, and equipment at cost	4,127	3,733
Less: Allowances for depreciation and amortization	(2,173)	(1,940)
Property, plant, and equipment—net	1,954	1,793
Intangible assets:		
Intangibles arising from acquisitions	534	328
Capitalized data files and other intangibles	319	84
Less: Accumulated amortization	(94)	(55)
Total intangible assets—net	759	357
Other assets	251	187
Total assets	$5,259	$4,442

Liabilities and Shareholders' Investment		
Current liabilities:		
Short-term debt	459	96
Accrued compensation	304	281
Trade accounts payable	456	461
Other accruals	443	443
Dividends payable	26	29
Income taxes	72	62
Current portion of long-term debt	34	24
Total current liabilities	1,794	1,396
Long-term liabilities	155	173
Long-term debt	1,063	863
Deferred income taxes	462	426
Minority interests in subsidiaries	36	18
Shareholders' investment:		
Serial preference stock II	1	1
Common stock (60.6 and 60.2 million shares)	38	38
Other capital	194	191
Retained earnings	1,516	1,358
Cumulative translation adjustments	48	34
Treasury shares—cost in excess of par value	(48)	(56)
Total shareholders' investment	1,749	1,566
Total liabilities and shareholders' investment	$5,259	$4,442

Figure 3–3
TRW INC. AND SUBSIDIARIES
Statement of Earnings
For the Years Ended December 31, 1989 and 1988
($ millions)

	1989	Percent of Sales	1988	Percent of Sales
Sales	$7,340	100.0%	$6,982	100.0%
Cost of sales	5,779	78.7	5,565	79.7
Gross profit	1,561	21.3%	1,417	20.3%
Administrative and selling expenses	780	10.6	780	11.1
Research and development expenses	256	3.5	225	3.2
Interest expense	138	1.9	130	1.9
Total expenses	1,174	16.0%	1,135	16.2%
Other income—net	12	0.1	138	1.9
Earnings before income taxes	399	5.4	420	6.0
Income taxes	136	1.8	159	2.3
Net earnings	$263	3.6%	$261	3.7%
Per share of common stock:				
Fully diluted	$4.25		$4.23	
Primary	$4.31		$4.29	

For example, the gross margin of a jewelry store with slow turnover of merchandise and high markups will be far greater (50 percent is not uncommon) than that of a supermarket, which depends for its success on low margins and high volume (gross margins of 10 to 15 percent are typical). In fact, comparison of a particular company's ratios to those of similar companies in its industry *over a number of time periods* will provide the best clues as to whether the company's performance is improving or worsening. Many published annual overviews of company and industry performance use such ranking approaches, such as the annual Fortune 500, and individual companies usually develop their own comparisons with the performance of relevant competitors. It is also often useful to depict graphically a series of performance data over time, a process now easily achieved with the growing capabilities of electronic spreadsheets.

Gross Margin and Cost of Goods Sold Analysis. One of the most common ratios in operational analysis is the calculation of cost of goods sold (cost of sales) as a percentage of net sales. This ratio indicates the magnitude of the cost of goods purchased or manufactured, or the cost of services provided, in relation to the margin left over for operating expenses and profit. The ratios calculated from our sample statements appear as follows:

$$\text{Cost of goods sold} = \frac{\$5,779}{\$7,340} = 78.7\% \ (1988: 79.7\%)$$

$$\text{Gross margin} = \frac{\$1,561}{\$7,340} = 21.3\% \ (1988: 20.3\%)$$

The cost of goods sold of 78.7 percent and the gross margin of 21.3 percent indicate the margin of "raw profit" from operations. Remember that gross margin reflects the relationship of prices, volume, and costs. Any change in gross margin can involve a combination of changes in the selling price of the product and in the level of manufacturing costs if the product was made by the company, as well as a change in the product mix of the business. In a trading or service organization, gross margin can be affected by the price charged for the product or service provided and the prices paid for the merchandise purchased on the outside, or for services provided from internal or external resources. Volume of operations can be significant if, for example, a manufacturing company has high fixed costs (see Chapter 5 for a discussion of operating leverage) or a trading company has less buying power and economies of scale than a large competitor.

In the case of TRW the cost of goods sold and the gross margin shown in the Annual Report represented a *combination* of the three major product lines, that is, the income statement consolidated Space and Defense, Automotive, and Information Systems. We note an improvement of one percentage point over the prior year. For a more detailed insight, it would be desirable to calculate the gross margin for the individual areas, if this information were available. The company provided in its Annual Report a selective breakdown, by major product line, of sales, operating profit, identifiable assets, depreciation and amortization, and capital expenditures, which allows some overall comparisons but would have to be supplemented by internal information for a detailed ratio analysis.

There are particular complications in the analysis of manufacturing companies because the nature of the cost accounting system determines the specific costing of products for inventory and for current sale. Significant differences can exist between the apparent cost performance of companies using standard full cost systems and those using direct costing (in the latter case, fixed manufacturing costs are not allocated to individual products but charged as a block against operations). The charges for a period of operations can be greatly affected by the choice of accounting methods. Inflation, which affects the prices of both cost inputs and goods or services sold, or currency fluctuations in the case of international businesses, further distort the picture. We will take up some of these issues later in this chapter.

Any major change in a company's cost of goods sold or gross margin over a relevant period of time would call for further analysis to identify the cause. The relevance of the time period depends on the nature of the business; for example, many businesses have normal seasonal fluctuations, while others are affected by longer-term business cycles. Thus, the ratio serves as a signal rather than an absolute measure, as is the case with most of the measures discussed.

Profit Margin. The relationship of reported net profit after taxes (net income) to sales indicates management's ability to operate the business with sufficient success not only to recover the cost of the merchandise or services, the expenses of operating the business (including depreciation), and the cost of borrowed funds, but also to leave a margin of reasonable compensation to the owners for putting their capital at risk. The ratio of net profit (income) to sales (total revenue) essentially expresses the cost/price effectiveness of the operation.

As we will demonstrate later, a more significant ratio for this purpose is the relationship of profit to the capital employed in producing it.

The calculation of the net profit (net earnings) ratio is simple, as the figures from our TRW example show:

$$\text{Profit margin} = \frac{\$263}{\$7,340} = 3.6\% \ (1988: 3.7\%)$$

A variation of this ratio uses net profit *before* interest and taxes. This result represents the operating profit before any compensation is paid to debt holders. It is also the profit before the calculation of federal and state income taxes, which are often based on modified sets of deductible expenses and accounting write-offs. The use of this ratio rests on the assumption that it provides a "purer" view of operating effectiveness, undistorted by financing patterns and tax calculations. Called earnings before interest and taxes (EBIT), this pretax, preinterest income would be:

$$\text{Profit margin} = \frac{\$399 + \$138}{\$7,340} = 7.3\% \ (1988: 7.9\%)$$

There is a sound argument, however, for considering income taxes, however calculated, as an ongoing business expense. The formula can therefore be modified by using profit *after* taxes but *before* interest—again, to focus on operating efficiency by leaving out any compensation to the various holders of capital. In terms of the figures we are using this would be:

$$\text{Profit margin} = \frac{\$263 + (1 - .341)138}{\$7,340} = 4.8\% \ (1988: 4.9\%)$$

For convenience in making the adjustment to aftertax profit, we assume that the interest paid during the period was fully tax deductible, and we simply add back the *aftertax* cost of interest, which is pretax interest times one minus the tax rate, employing either the effective (average) tax rate paid (34.1 percent in TRW's case) or, ideally, the marginal (highest bracket) corporate tax rate for the firm in question. The choice of tax rates depends on the complexity of the company's taxation pattern. Because TRW operates worldwide and therefore is subject to a variety of taxes, we are forced to rely on the effective overall rate paid, which happened to be quite close to the marginal corporate tax rate prevailing in the United States in 1989. Chapter 7 contains a specific discussion of the cost of debt and the nature of the necessary adjustments.

We note in Figure 3–3 that TRW had significant "other income," particularly in 1988, amounting then to $138 million before taxes, or about 10 percent of gross profit. Because this income was largely due to restructuring activities, it can be argued that this item is extraordinary and should be disregarded for the purpose of the ratios we just covered. As a rule, if there are unusual or nonrecurring income and expense elements not directly related to ongoing operations, the analyst should adjust the ratios by excluding such items when measuring operating effectiveness. The adjustment is done on the same basis as for interest; that is, the net effect of revenue or expense items must be calculated if aftertax comparisons are desired. In TRW's case the year-to-year comparison would improve, as the 1988 ratios would be lowered somewhat by the adjustment.

Operating Expense Analysis.   Various expense categories are routinely related to net sales. These comparisons include such items as administrative expense, selling and promotional expenses, and many others typical of particular businesses and industries. The general formula used to calculate this expense ratio is:

$$\text{Expense ratio} = \frac{\text{Various expense items}}{\text{Net sales}} = \text{Percent}$$

There are a few expense categories shown in the abbreviated operating statement of TRW and the ratio to sales was calculated for each in Figure 3–3. In practice, a *greater* breakdown is often desirable. Many trade associations collect extensive financial data from their members and compile published statistics on expense ratios, as well as on most of the other ratios discussed in this chapter. These publications help provide standards of comparison and the basis for trend analysis. References to such information sources are listed at the end of the chapter and also in Appendix II. To make the comparisons reasonable, great care is often taken to categorize the businesses within the industry by size and other characteristics, in an effort to reduce the degree of error introduced by large-scale averaging. Even without such data, a skilled analyst will scan the revenue and expense categories on an income statement as a matter of course to see if any of them seem out of line with the particular company's experience.

Contribution Analysis. This type of analysis has been used mainly for internal management, although it is increasingly applied in broader financial analysis. The process involves relating net sales to the "contribution margin" of individual product groups or of the total business. The calculations require a very selective analysis or estimate of the fixed and variable costs and expenses of the business and take into account the effect of operating leverage. (See Chapter 5.) Only directly variable costs are subtracted from net sales to show the contribution of operations toward fixed costs and profits for the period. This is calculated as follows:

Contribution to fixed cost and profit =
$$\frac{\text{Net sales} - \text{Direct costs (i.e., variable costs)}}{\text{Net sales}} = \text{Percent}$$

Significant differences can exist in the contribution margins of different industries, due to varying needs for capital investment and resultant cost-volume conditions. Even within a company, various lines of products or services may contribute quite differently to fixed costs and profits, and there has been a great deal of development of so-called *activity-based accounting* systems that serve as the basis for an economic assessment of the relative contribution of various lines of profit, thereby going beyond the limitations of existing cost accounting systems.

Contribution margins are useful as a broad tool in judging the risk characteristics of a business, that is, the amount of leeway management enjoys in pricing its products and services and in its ability to control costs and expenses under different economic conditions. Analysis of break-even conditions and of pricing strategies as they relate to volume achieved become important in this context. Chapter 5 contains a more extensive discussion of these points.

Resource Management.   Here we are interested in judging the effectiveness with which management has employed the *assets* entrusted to it by the owners of the business. When examining a balance sheet, an analyst will draw company-specific conclusions about the nature of the assets employed, looking at relative proportions and judging whether the company has a viable asset base. Clues, such as high accumulated depreciation relative to recorded property, plant, and equipment, may suggest aging facilities in need of upgrading, or a significant jump in cash balances may suggest excess funds. In a more overall sense, a few ratios are used to judge trends in resource utilization. The ratios essentially involve *turnover* relationships and express, in various forms, the relative amount of capital used to support the volume of business transacted.

Asset Turnover.   The most commonly used ratios relate *net sales to gross assets* or *net sales to net assets*. The measure indicates the size of the recorded asset commitment required to support a particular level of sales or, conversely, the sales dollars generated by each dollar of assets. While simple to calculate, overall asset turnover is a crude measure at best, because the balance sheets of most well-established companies list a whole variety of assets at the widely differing cost levels of past periods. These recorded values often have little relation to current economic values, and the distortions grow with any significant change in the level of inflation or with the appreciation of assets such as real estate. It is this discrepancy in values that often attracts corporate raiders intent on realizing true economic values through a breakup of the company and selective disposal, as we will discuss in Chapter 9.

Another distortion is caused by a company's mix of product lines where most manufacturing activities are asset intensive, while others (like services or wholesaling) need relatively fewer assets to support the volume of revenues generated. Again, wherever possible, a breakdown of total financial data into major product lines should be attempted. Basically, the turnover ratio is another of several clues that, in combination, can indicate favorable or unfavorable performance.

If gross assets are used for the purpose, the calculation for TRW appears as follows:

$$\frac{\text{Net sales}}{\text{Gross assets}} = \frac{\$7,340}{\$5,259} = 1.40 \; (1988: 1.57)$$

or

$$\frac{\text{Gross assets}}{\text{Net sales}} = \frac{\$5,259}{\$7,340} = 0.72 \; (1988: 0.64)$$

If net assets (*total assets* less *current liabilities*, which equals the *capitalization* of the business) are used, the calculations are either:

$$\frac{\text{Net sales}}{\text{Net assets}} = \frac{\$7,340}{\$5,259 - \$1,794} = 2.12 \; (1988: 2.29)$$

or

$$\frac{\text{Net assets}}{\text{Net sales}} = \frac{\$3,465}{\$7,340} = 0.47 \; (1988: 0.44)$$

The difference between the two sets of calculations lies in the choice of the asset total—that is, whether to use gross assets or net assets. Using net assets eliminates current liabilities from the total. The assumption is that current liabilities, which are mostly operational (accounts payable, current taxes due, current repayments of short-term debt, and accrued obligations), are available to the business as a matter of course. Therefore the amount of assets employed in the business is effectively *reduced* through these ongoing operational credit relationships. Such reasoning is especially important for trading firms, where the size of accounts payable to suppliers is quite significant in the total balance sheet.

Working Capital Management. Among the assets of a company, the key working capital accounts—*inventories* and *accounts receivable*—are usually given special attention. The ratios used to analyze these categories attempt to establish the relative effectiveness with which inventories and receivables are managed. They aid the analyst in detecting signs of deterioration in value or excessive accumulation of inventories and receivables. The amounts in these accounts stated on the balance sheet are generally related to the single best indicator of activity, such as sales or cost of sales (cost of goods sold), on the assumption that a reasonably close relationship exists.

Inventories cannot be judged precisely, short of an actual count, verification, and appraisal of value. Because an outside analyst can rarely do this, the next best step is to relate the recorded inventory to net sales or to cost of goods sold to see whether there is a shift in the relationship over a period of time. Normally *average* inventory values are used to make this calculation (the average of beginning and ending inventories). At times it is also desirable to use only *ending* inventories, especially in the case of rapidly growing firms where inventories are being built up to support steeply rising sales. Furthermore, it is necessary to closely observe the method of inventory costing employed by the company—such as last-in, first-out (LIFO), first-in, first-out (FIFO), average costing, and so forth—and any changes made during the time span covered by the analysis. (We will discuss inventory costing and other accounting issues later in this chapter.)

While the simple relationship of sales and inventories will often suffice as a broad measure of performance, it is usually more precise to relate inventories to *cost of goods sold*, because only then will *both* factors be stated on a comparable basis. The use of the net *sales* figure introduces a distortion, in that recorded sales include a markup that is not included in the stated cost of the inventories. The difference in the two methods of calculation is reflected in the equation below:

$$\frac{\text{Average inventory}}{\text{Net sales}} = \frac{.5(\$419 + \$480)}{\$7,340} = 6.1\% \ (1988: 6.4\%)$$

or

$$\frac{\text{Average inventory}}{\text{Cost of sales}} = \frac{\$450}{\$5,779} = 7.8\% \ (1988: 8.1\%)$$

In the sample calculations we have employed *total* TRW sales and cost of goods and services. The fact that there are three major product lines suggests that a more refined analysis may be desirable. Inventories essentially relate to manufactured products, which in TRW's case would be the space and defense and automotive businesses but not necessarily the information systems and services line. If the latter were more significant than its current share of less than 10 percent in sales volume, it would be useful to develop separate ratios, if detailed inventory information were available. As we will see later, the line of business breakdown furnished by TRW does not provide this information—as is usual with most published financial reports.

When we deal with any manufacturing company, we must also be particularly aware of the problem of accounting measurements—so often encountered when using other analytical methods—because the stated value of inventories can be seriously affected by the specific cost accounting system employed.

In assessing the effectiveness of inventory management, the *number of times* inventory has *turned over* during the period of analysis is more commonly used in working capital analyses. The TRW figures appear as follows:

$$\frac{\text{Net Sales}}{\text{Average inventory}} = \frac{\$7,340}{\$450} = 16.3 \text{ times} \ (1988: 15.4 \text{ times})$$

or

$$\frac{\text{Cost of sales}}{\text{Average inventory}} = \frac{\$5,779}{\$450} = 12.8 \text{ times} \ (1988: 12.3 \text{ times})$$

These calculations reflect the frequency with which the inventory was turned over during the operating period. In

TRW's case, turnover improved due to a combination of inventory management and change in the mix of products, partly due to its restructuring and acquisition activities. Generally speaking, the higher the turnover number the better, because low inventories often suggest a minimal risk of unsalable goods and indicate efficient use of capital. Yet inventory turnover figures that are well above industry practice may signal the potential for inventory shortages, resultant poor customer service, and thus the risk of suffering a competitive disadvantage. The final judgment depends on the specific circumstances.

The analysis of *accounts receivable* again is based on *net sales*. Here, the question arises of whether accounts receivable outstanding at the end of the period closely approximate the amount of credit sales we would expect to remain uncollected under prevailing credit terms. For example, a business selling with terms of net/30 would normally expect to show as accounts receivable the recorded sales of the prior month. If 40 or 50 days' sales were reflected on its balance sheet, this could mean that some customers had difficulty paying or were abusing their credit privileges, or that some sales had to be made on extended terms.

An exact analysis of accounts receivable can only be made by examining the *aging* of the individual accounts recorded on the company's books. Aging involves classifying accounts receivable into brackets of days outstanding—10 days, 20 days, 30 days, 40 days, and so on—and relating this pattern to the credit terms applicable in the business. Because this type of analysis requires access to inside information, financial analysts assessing the business from the outside must be satisfied with the relatively crude overall approach of restating accounts receivable in terms of *daily sales*. This is done as follows, and TRW again shows an improvement over 1988:

$$\frac{\text{Net sales}}{\text{Days in the year}} = \frac{\$7{,}340}{360} = \$20.39 \text{ million/day (1988: \$19.39 million)}$$

and

$$\frac{\text{Accounts receivable}}{\text{Sales per day}} = \frac{\$1{,}431}{\$20.4} = 70.1 \text{ days (1988: 66.3 days)}$$

A complication arises when a company's sales are normally made to different types of customers under varying terms or when the sales are made partly for cash and partly on account. If at all possible, cash and credit sales should be differentiated. If no detailed information is available on this aspect and on the terms of sale used, the rough average shown above must suffice to provide a broad indication of trends.

A similar process can be applied to judge a company's performance with regard to *accounts payable*. The analysis is a little more complicated because accounts payable should be specifically related to the *purchases* made during the operating period. Normally such information is not readily available to the outside analyst, except in the case of trading companies, where the amount of purchases can be readily deduced by adding the change from beginning to ending inventories to the cost of goods sold for the period. In a manufacturing company, purchases of goods and services are buried in the cost-of-goods-sold account and in the inventories at the end of the operating period. A very crude approximation can be made in such cases by relating accounts payable to the average daily use of raw materials, if this expense element can be identified from the available information.

In most cases, we can follow the approach used for analyzing accounts receivable, if it is possible to approximate the average *daily purchases* for the period. The number of days of accounts payable is then directly related to the normal credit terms under which the company makes purchases, and serious deviations from that norm can be spotted.

Proper management of accounts payable involves paying within the terms, but not sooner, yet taking discounts whenever offered for early payment, such as 2 percent if paid in 10 days versus the full amount due in 30 days. Credit rating agencies can be a source of information to the analyst because they will express an opinion on the timeliness with which a company is meeting its credit obligations, including accounts payable.

Human resource effectiveness has been gaining increased attention in recent years. Ratios used in measuring this complex area go beyond purely financial relationships such as sales per employee or profit per employee. Many are based on carefully developed statistics on output data, such as various productivity assessments and on managing human resources, such as employment, training, and development costs, and the whole complex of compensation and benefits administration.

Profitability.   Here the issue is the effectiveness with which management has employed both the *total assets* and the *net assets* as recorded on the balance sheet. The effectiveness is judged by relating *net profit*—defined in a variety of ways— to the *assets* utilized in generating the profit. The relationship is one of the more telling analyses, although again the nature and timing of the *stated values* on the balance sheet will tend to distort the results.

Return on Assets.   The easiest form of profitability analysis is to relate reported *net profit* (*net income*) to the *total assets* on the balance sheet. *Net assets* (total assets less current liabilities), which are equivalent to the total long-term sources on the balance sheet, may also be used, using the argument mentioned earlier that operating liabilities are available essentially without cost to support a portion of the current assets. The net assets are also called the *capitalization* of the company, representing the portion of the total assets supported by equity and long-term debt. In both cases it is also possible to use average assets for the period, instead of ending balances. The calculations for both forms of return on assets (ending balance) appear as follows:

$$\frac{\text{Net profit}}{\text{Assets}} = \frac{\$263}{\$5,259} = 5.0\% \; (1988: 5.9\%)$$

or

$$\frac{\text{Net profit}}{\text{Net assets (capitalization)}} = \frac{\$263}{\$5,259 - 1,794} = 7.5\% \; (1988: 8.6\%)$$

While either ratio is an indicator of overall profitability, the results can be seriously distorted by nonrecurring gains and losses, changes in the company's capital structure (the proportion of interest-bearing long-term debt to owners' equity), by significant restructuring and acquisitions and by changes in the federal income tax regulations applicable for the period analyzed. It is usually desirable to make further adjustments if some of these conditions prevail.

EBIT Return on Assets. As we stated before, net profit (net income, or net earnings) is the final operating result after interest and taxes are deducted. It is therefore affected by the proportion of debt in the capital structure and the resultant interest charges. A somewhat more meaningful result can be obtained if we eliminate *both* interest and taxes from the profit figure. (EBIT, earnings before interest and taxes, was mentioned earlier.) Moreover, it will generally be useful to eliminate any significant unusual or nonrecurring income and expense items. The revised ratio expresses the *gross earnings power* of the capital employed in the business independent of the pattern of financing that provided the capital and independent of changes in the tax laws. The calculation, based on average assets, is as follows:

$$\frac{\text{Net profit* before interest and taxes (EBIT)}}{\text{Average assets}} = \frac{\$525}{\$4,850} = 10.8\%$$
$$(1988: 9.3\%)$$

or

$$\frac{\text{Net profit* before interest and taxes (EBIT)}}{\text{Average net assets (capitalization)}} = \frac{\$525}{\$3,256} = 16.1\%$$
$$(1988: 13.9\%)$$

If we accept the argument that income taxes are a normal part of doing business, this result can be modified by using net profit before interest but *after* taxes. We can again employ the simple adjustment shown earlier to add back to net profit the aftertax cost of interest and the aftertax effect of any nonrecurring income and expense items. If there is reason to believe that actual income taxes paid were modified for any reason and thus that the effective tax rate paid does not reflect normal

---

*Before "other income—net."

conditions, we should use the marginal income tax rate to calculate the net effect of interest and other items added back. In this example we have used the marginal tax rate of 34 percent, applied to interest and other income. The calculations are as follows:

$$\frac{\text{Net profit* after taxes, before interest}}{\text{Average assets}} = \frac{\$346}{\$4,850} = 7.1\% \ (1988: 5.8\%)$$

or

$$\frac{\text{Net profit* after taxes, before interest}}{\text{Average net assets (capitalization)}} = \frac{\$346}{\$3,256} = 10.6\% \ (1988: 8.6\%)$$

Note that the results of the last two sets of more refined calculations show a significant increase in TRW's overall effectiveness of asset utilization, in contrast to the first calculation that was based on net profit alone. Again, it would be useful to break down these results into major product lines, but in most cases there is not enough information to make all the adjustments from published data.

Another refinement used at times is the relationship of profit, defined in the various ways we have described, to the net assets of the business restated on a *current value basis*. This requires a series of very specific assumptions about the true economic value of various assets or business segments of a company, and it is employed particularly by analysts developing a case for the takeover of a company that may be underperforming on this basis.

In summary, the various ratios available for judging a business from the point of view of management deal with the effectiveness of operations, the effectiveness of capital deployment, and the profitability achieved on the assets deployed. These measures are all affected to some degree by uncertainties involving accounting and valuation methods, but together they can provide reasonable clues to a firm's performance and also suggest areas for further analysis.

---

*Before "other income—net."

We now turn to the second of the three viewpoints relevant in analyzing performance, that of the owners of a business. These are the investors to whom management is responsible and accountable. So far, we have not mentioned the owners directly, even though it should be quite clear that management, in the timing, execution, and appraisal of the results of operations, must be fully cognizant of, and responsive to, the owners' viewpoint and expectations, just as it must be alert to the lenders' viewpoint and criteria.

Owners' Point of View

The key interest of the owners of a business—the shareholders in the case of a corporation—is *profitability*. In this context, profitability means the returns achieved through the efforts of management on the funds invested by the owners. The owners are also interested in the *disposition* of earnings that belong to them, that is, how much is reinvested in the business versus how much is paid out to them as dividends. Finally, they are concerned about the effect of business results on the *market value* of their investment, especially in the case of publicly traded stock. The key concepts related to this last aspect are taken up in detail in Chapters 7 and 9, and we will only make brief reference to them here.

Profitability. The relationship of profits earned to the shareholders' stated investment is watched closely by the financial community. Analysts track several key measures that express the company's performance in relation to the owners' stake. Two of these, *return on net worth* and *return on common equity*, address the profitability of the total ownership investment, while the third, *earnings per share*, measures the proportional participation of each unit of investment in corporate earnings for the period.

Return on Net Worth. The most common ratio used for measuring the return on the owners' investment is the relationship of *net profit* to *net worth* (equity, or shareholders' investment). In performing this calculation, we do not have to make any adjustments in net profit because this figure has already been properly reduced by the interest charges, if any, paid to creditors and lenders. Therefore, net income for purposes of this calculation is the *residual* result of operations and belongs totally to the holders of common or preferred equity shares. Within the shareholder group, only those holding *common* shares have a claim on the residual after obligatory preferred dividends have been paid.

The relationship is calculated as follows:

$$\frac{\text{Net profit}}{\text{Net worth (equity)}} = \frac{\$263}{\$1,749} = 15.0\% \ (1988: \ 16.7\%)$$

Here we have used the *ending* shareholders' investment in the calculation for TRW. It is quite common, however, to use the *average* equity for this calculation, on the assumption that profitable operations build up shareholders' equity *during* the year and that therefore the annual profit should be related to the midpoint of this buildup. In fact, TRW used this method to calculate the ratio published in its annual report:

$$\frac{\text{Net profit}}{\text{Average net worth}} = \frac{\$263}{.5 \ (\$1,566 + \$1,749)} = 15.9\% \ (1988: \ 17.5\%)$$

A possible distortion must be mentioned here. Frequently, questions arise about the way a particular liability account on the balance sheet, *deferred taxes*, should be handled in this analysis. As we mentioned before, this account shows the accumulated difference between the accounting treatment and the tax treatment of a variety of revenue and expense elements. Essentially it represents tax payments deferred due to a *timing difference* in recognizing tax deductions allowable under prevailing Internal Revenue rules. In effect, a liability is recorded against the time that this accumulated tax benefit might begin to be "recaptured" by the Internal Revenue Service. This would happen if the company stopped investing in depreciable assets or if future tax laws eliminated accelerated depreciation or if recognition of income differences changed, as happened in 1989 with installment contracts under revised Internal Revenue rules, which particularly affects the space and defense sector of TRW.

Some analysts argue that deferred income taxes are, in effect, owners' equity set aside against future higher tax levels. Others argue that they represent a form of long-term debt. Because there is no consensus on the analytical treatment, deferred income taxes often are not included in *any* of the ratio calculations. Given that this accumulation on the liability side of the balance sheet can be quite large, material differences can result from an inclusion of deferred taxes as owners' equity or long-term debt.

Return on Common Equity. A somewhat more refined version of the calculation of return on owners' investment is based on earnings accruing to the holders of *common* shares *only*, if there are several types of stock outstanding, such as preferred stock in different forms. The net profit figure employed for analysis is first reduced by dividends paid to holders of preferred shares and by other obligatory payments, such as distributions to holders of minority interests. Net worth is likewise reduced by the amount of preferred equity and any minority elements, to yield the common equity figure. TRW, in effect, has only common stock outstanding, since its Serial Preference Stock II is reflected at the very nominal value of $1.0 million. Thus we will merely show the formula for the calculation because the results will be the same as before:

$$\frac{\text{Net profit to common}}{\text{Average common equity}} = \text{Percent}$$

Return on common equity is a widely published statistic. Rankings of companies and industry sectors are compiled by major business magazines and rating agencies. Return on common equity is closely watched by stock market analysts and, in turn, by management and the board of directors. The accuracy of recorded values and earnings calculations is an issue in these ratios as well, however, and adjustments may be necessary if the analyst is aware of major inconsistencies.

Earnings per Share. The analysis of earnings from the owners' point of view centers on *earnings per share* in the case of a corporation. This ratio simply involves dividing net profit to common stock by the average number of shares of common stock outstanding:

$$\frac{\text{Net profit to common}}{\text{Average number of shares outstanding}} = \text{Earnings per share}$$

Earnings per share is a measure to which both management and shareholders pay a great deal of attention. It is widely used in the valuation of common stock and is often the basis for setting specific corporate objectives and goals as part of strategic planning. Chapter 8 contains more background on the uses and limitations of this measure. Normally the analyst does not have to calculate earnings per share because the result is readily announced by corporations large and small. In TRW's case, earnings per share were reported as $4.31 for 1989 ($4.29 for the previous year) in the TRW Inc. 1989 annual report (see Figure 3–3). Earnings per share are available on both an annual and a quarterly basis and are a matter of record whenever a company's shares are publicly traded.

A recent requirement by the Financial Accounting Standards Board and the Securities and Exchange Commission calls for the calculation of earnings per share on two basis: The first is the so-called *primary earnings per share*, which uses average shares actually outstanding during the period. The second basis makes the assumption that all shares *potentially* outstanding be counted in addition to actual shares outstanding, that is, shares that would result from the conversion of preferred and debt securities that are convertible into common shares under various provisions, and shares from options by employees and others not yet exercised. The result is referred to as *fully diluted* earnings per share and reflects the reduction in earnings per share that would result from any "overhang" of such potential shares—putting the investment community on notice that such a dilutive effect is possible. In TRW's case, the potential dilution is quite minor, as fully diluted earnings per share amount to $4.25 versus primary earnings per share of $4.31 ($4.23 versus $4.29 in 1988).

Even though the earnings per share figure is one of the most readily available statistics reported by publicly held corporations, some complications exist nevertheless. Apart from possible unusual elements in the quarterly and annual net profit pattern, the number of shares outstanding varies during the year in many companies, either because of newly issued shares (new stock offerings, stock dividends paid, options exercised, etc.), or because outstanding old shares are retired (purchase of treasury stock). Therefore the *average* number of shares outstanding during the year is commonly used in this calculation. Moreover, any significant change in the number of shares outstanding (such as would be caused by a stock split, for example) requires retroactive adjustments in past data to ensure comparability.

A great deal of interest among analysts focuses on *past* earnings per share, both quarterly and annual. *Future* projections are frequently made on the basis of past earnings. Fluctuations and trends in actual performance are compared to the projections and watched closely for indications of strength or weakness. Again, great caution is advised in interpreting these data. Allowances must be made for unusual elements both in the earnings figure and in the number of common shares outstanding.

Cash Flow per Share. A calculation to approximate the cash flow per share is frequently used as a rough measure of the company's ability to pay *cash dividends*. The cash flow per share ratio is an effort to simulate the operating funds flow on a per share basis. It is developed from a *net profit* figure to which operating *write-offs* such as depreciation, amortization, and depletion have been added back. We recall from our earlier discussion of the funds flow statement that such accounting write-offs do not represent a movement of funds. Therefore, adding back these bookkeeping entries restates the net profit in a form that approximates the funds generated by operations. The calculation parallels the earnings per share ratio:

$$\frac{\text{Net profit to common plus write-offs}}{\text{Average number of shares outstanding}} = \text{Cash flow per share}$$

In the case of TRW, we know that depreciation and amortization amounted to $349 million and $51 million respectively. The average number of shares outstanding was given in the Annual Report as $60.8 million for purposes of calculating primary earnings per share. Write-offs thus amounted to $6.58 per share, which when added to the primary earnings per share of $4.31, results in a cash flow per share of $10.89. Cash flow per share is used to indicate the potential availability of cash for dividends and various other disbursements. Because the use of funds in a business is largely at the discretion of management, however, the figure is at best only a crude indication of the potential to pay dividends. A more extensive analysis of funds flows is required to judge the pattern of sources and uses, as we demonstrated in Chapter 2.

Share Price Appreciation. Apart from current earnings generated for the shareholders, there is an expectation by investors of the appreciation of the value of the common shares in the stock market over time. The main driver for this appreciation is the creation of additional economic value—that is, the generation of more positive cash flows than outlays in the long run through the combined effect of investment, operating, and financing decisions. We will discuss the shareholder value creation more fully in Chapter 9, but suffice it to say here that the analyst will look for movement in the share prices that at least match and hopefully outperform the trend in the stock market as a whole and the trend of particular business segments as expressed in relevant composites of the share price trends of selected companies.

Total Shareholder Return. The return to investors holding shares in a company will be a combination of share price appreciation (or decline) and cash dividends received over appropriate time periods selected for analysis. Since only part of the earnings belonging to shareholders are paid out in the form of dividends, the relevant positive inflow to the shareholder is the stream of dividends received, not the announced earnings per share. The full economic benefit received by the shareholder is the sum of this stream of dividends and the change in the price of the stock. Such calculations for published companies are routinely available in investor services publications. (See Appendix II.)

This concept is closely related to shareholder value analysis, which will be discussed in Chapter 9.

Disposition of Earnings. The periodic separation of earnings (net profit) into dividends paid and earnings retained is closely watched by shareholders and the financial community because the retained residual builds up the owners' equity recorded on the balance sheet and is a source of funds for management's use. Thus, earnings are either *reinvested* in the business to support further growth or are *paid out* in part or full as dividends. Cash dividends are the most common form of payment, although stock dividends are also frequently used. In the latter case no cash is involved. Instead, additional fractional shares are issued to each holder of record. If there is a normal cash dividend paid as well, stock dividends result in fractionally higher cash dividends, of course.

Dividends per Share. Dividends are generally declared publicly on a *per share basis* by a corporation's board of directors, who are the elected representatives of the shareholders, and no calculation is necessary. Dividend policy is the prerogative of the board, which has legal authority to set payments at any level it deems appropriate. Because the market value of common stock is in part influenced by dividends paid and anticipated, the board generally deals with this periodic decision very carefully. TRW Inc. paid dividends of $1.72 per share in 1989 and $1.63 in 1988.

Dividend Yield. Annual dividends per share can be related to current or average *share prices* to derive the dividend yield:

$$\frac{\text{Annual dividend per share}}{\text{Average market price per share}} = \text{Dividend yield}$$

This is a measure of the return on the owners' investment from cash dividends. In the case of TRW, the 52-week range of stock prices from January 1989 to December 1989 was 49⅞ to 41¼, with an average of approximately 45½. The dividend yield at $1.72 per share thus amounts to 3.8 percent. The ratio falls short as a basis for comparision with other companies, however, because dividend policies differ widely. As we stated above, the total economic return normally enjoyed by the shareholder is a *combination* of dividends and market appreciation of the stock.

Payout/Retention.   A ratio commonly used in connection with dividend policy is the so-called *payout ratio*, which represents the proportion of earnings paid out to the shareholders in the form of cash during any given year:

$$\frac{\text{Cash dividends per share}}{\text{Earnings per share}} = \frac{\$1.72}{\$4.31} = 39.9\% \ (1988: 38.0\%)$$

Because most boards of directors tend to favor paying a fairly stable dividend per share, adjusted only gradually, the payout ratio of a company may fluctuate widely in the short run in response to swings in earnings performance. Over a period of several years, however, the payout ratio can often be used to indicate the tendency of directors to reinvest funds in the business versus paying out earnings to the shareholders. There are no firm standards for this ratio, but the relationship is significant in characterizing the "style" of the corporation. High-growth companies tend to pay out relatively low proportions of earnings because they prefer to reinvest earnings to support profitable growth. Stable or moderate-growth companies tend to pay out larger proportions. Some companies pay no cash dividends at all or provide stock dividends in the form of additional shares. Many more factors must, of course, be considered in making judgments in this area, and the reader is directed to the references at the end of this chapter for further insight into both concepts and practices.

Dividend Coverage.   Owners are also interested in the degree to which their dividends are *covered* by earnings and cash flow. Furthermore, they are concerned about the degree to which the proportion of debt in the capital structure and its associated interest and repayment requirements will affect management's ability to achieve reasonably stable and growing earnings and to pay dividends commensurate with the owners' expectations. A variety of coverage ratios can be calculated, but they hardly differ from the ones we will take up in the discussion of the lenders' point of view.

Market Indicators. We will only briefly mention two ratios that are commonly used as indicators of stock market values, the *price/earnings ratio* and the *market to book ratio*. The subject of market valuation will be covered in detail in Chapters 6 and 8.

Price/Earnings Ratio. The simple relationship between current or expected *earnings per share* and the current *market price* of the stock is often quoted by both management and owners. The ratio is also called the *earnings multiple*, and it is used to indicate how the stock market is judging the company's earnings performance and prospects. The calculation is quite straightforward and relates current market prices of common shares to the most recent available earnings per share on an annual basis:

$$\frac{\text{Market price per share}}{\text{Earnings per share}} = \text{Earnings multiple (price/earnings ratio)}$$

The result is a simple factor. If fully diluted earnings differ significantly from primary earnings per share, the calculation can be done on both bases. The earnings multiple is used quite commonly as a rough rule of thumb in valuing companies for purposes of acquisition. Earnings multiplies vary widely by industry and by company and are, in effect, a simple overall approximation of the market's current judgment of industry and company risk versus past and prospective earnings performance. They are tracked by various investor services and related to total market averages as well as average price earnings multiples for selected industry groups, to be able to assess the relative performance of a particular company.

The reverse of the earnings per share formula is the so-called *earnings yield*, which relates earnings per share to the market price. Although it is sometimes used to express the current yield the owner enjoys, the measure can be misleading because earnings are not normally paid out in full as dividends. Thus, the earnings yield cannot be compared to, for example, the yield on a bond where interest payments are contractual, because as we already know, the economic return to the shareholder is a combination of the dividends received and the appreciation of the stock.

Market to Book Ratio.   This indicator relates *current market value* on a per share basis to the *book value* of owners' equity as stated on the balance sheet, also on a per share basis. TRW's December 31, 1989, book value per share was $28.60, while the average market value for 1989 was almost 60 percent higher. The market to book ratio leaves much to be desired as a measure of performance for many of the reasons mentioned in earlier discussions of other ratios. In addition, while in a given company the relationship between stated balance sheet values and market values may be favorable, the ratio does not truly help the analyst judge what comparable expectations should be for other firms. Thus the measure can only be a beginning step in the appraisal of long-term performance and outlook.

Relative Price Movements.   While the typical investor is interested in the absolute change in the value of the shares held, the insights from the relative performance of the stock to the market as a whole and appropriate averages for specific industries can be useful to assess the trend of a particular company. These movements can be expressed in absolute dollar terms or in several of the ratios mentioned above. In view of the growing importance of cash flow thinking, fuelled by the acquisition and leveraged buyout boom of the 1980s, services like Value Line chart company *cash flow multiples* as an additional indicator of relative price movements.

In summary, the ratios pertinent to the owners' view of a company's performance are measures of the *return* owners have *earned* on their stake and the *cash* rewards they received in the form of *dividends*. These results depend on the earning power of the company and on management policies and decisions regarding the use of financial leverage and reinvestment. Ultimately, these affect the economic value of the owners' capital commitment, as reflected in stock market prices. The concepts and issues are taken up in more detail in Chapter 9.

Lenders' Point of View

While the main orientation of management and owners is toward the business as a going concern, the lender of necessity has to be of two minds. Lenders have an interest in funding the needs of a successful business that will perform as expected. At the same time, they must consider the possible negative consequences of default and liquidation. Sharing none of the rewards of success other than receiving regular payments of interest and principal, the lender must carefully assess the risk of recovering the original funds extended, particularly if they have been provided for a long period of time. Part of this assessment must be the ultimate value of the lender's claim in case of serious difficulty.

The claims of a general creditor rank behind federal tax obligations, accrued wages, and the claims of secured creditors who lend against a specific asset, such as a building or equipment. Thus, caution dictates looking for a margin of safety in the assets held by the company, a "cushion" against default. Several ratios are used to assess this protection by testing the *liquidity* of the business. Another set of ratios tests the relative debt exposure, or *leverage* of the business, in order to weigh the position of lenders versus owners. Finally, there are coverage ratios relating to the company's ability to provide *debt service* from funds generated by ongoing operations.

Liquidity.   One way to test the degree of protection afforded lenders focuses on the short-term credit extended to a business for funding operations. It involves the *liquid assets* of a business, that is, those current assets that can readily be converted into cash, on the assumption that these would form a ready cushion against default.

Current Ratio.   The ratio most commonly used to appraise the debt exposure represented on the balance sheet is the current ratio. This relates *current assets* to *current liabilities* in an attempt to show the safety of current debtholders' claims in case of default. The calculation is shown using TRW's relevant totals from Figure 3–2:

$$\frac{\text{Current assets}}{\text{Current liabilities}} = \frac{\$2,295}{\$1,794} = 1.28{:}1 \ (1988{:}\ 1.51{:}1)$$

Presumably the larger this ratio, the better the position of the debt holders. From the lenders' point of view, a higher ratio would certainly appear to provide a cushion against drastic losses of value in case of business failure. A large excess of current assets over current liabilities seems to help protect claims, should inventories have to be liquidated at a forced sale and should accounts receivable involve sizable collection problems. Seen from another angle, however, an excessively high current ratio might signal slack management practices. It could indicate idle cash balances, inventory levels that have become excessive when compared to current needs, and poor credit management that results in overextended accounts receivable. At the same time, the business might not be making full use of its current borrowing power.

A very common rule of thumb is the belief that a current ratio of 2:1 is "about right" for most businesses, because this ratio appears to permit a shrinkage of up to 50 percent in the value of current assets while still providing enough cushion to cover all current liabilities. The problem with this concept is that the current ratio measures an essentially *static* condition and assesses a business as if it were on the brink of liquidation. The ratio does not reflect a going concern, which should be the top priority of management. The lender or creditor looking for future business with a successful client should bear this in mind. Note that TRW's year-to-year decline in the ratio was brought about by a significant one-time increase in short-term debt in 1989, which as a temporary measure should cast no negative implications on the creditworthiness of the company.

Acid Test.   An even more stringent test, although again on a static basis, is the acid test or *quick ratio*, which is calculated using only a *portion* of current assets—cash, marketable securities, and accounts receivable—which are then related to current liabilities as follows:

$$\frac{\text{Cash + Marketable securities + Receivables}}{\text{Current liabilities}} = \frac{\$114 + \$1,431}{\$1,794} = .86{:}1$$

(1988: 1.01:1)

The key concept here is to test the *collectibility* of current liabilities in the case of a real crisis, on the assumption that inventories would have no value at all. As drastic tests of the ability to pay in the face of disaster, both the current ratio and acid test are helpful. From an operational standpoint, however, it is better to analyze a business in terms of the expected total future *cash flow pattern*. The proportion of current assets to current liabilities normally covers only a small part of this total.

Quick Sale Value. Another stringent test that can be applied to the business as a whole by testing through a series of assumptions what cash value the various assets of the company would bring in a hurried sale. Again, this is a liquidation point of view that does not allow for the ongoing cash flow patterns.

Financial Leverage. As we will discuss in greater detail in Chapters 5 and 8, successful use of debt enhances earnings for the owners of the business because returns earned on these funds over and above the interest paid belong to the owners and thus increase owners' equity. From the lenders' viewpoint, however, when earnings do not exceed or even fall short of the interest cost, fixed interest and principal commitments must still be met. The owners through their management must fulfill these claims, which might then severely affect owners' equity. The positive *and* negative effects of leverage increase with the proportion of debt in a business. The risk exposure of the providers of debt grows, as does the risk exposure of the owners. From the lenders' point of view, a variety of ratios that deal with total debt, or long-term debt only, *in relation* to various parts of the balance sheet, are more inclusive measures of riskiness than leverage alone. The ratios measure the risk exposure of the lenders in relation to the available asset values against which all claims are held.

Debt to Assets.   The first and broadest test is the proportion of *total debt*, both current and long-term, to *total assets*, which is calculated as follows:

$$\frac{\text{Total debt}}{\text{Total assets}} = \frac{\$3,474^*}{\$5,259} = 66.0\% \ (1988\colon 64.3\%)$$

This ratio describes the proportion of "other people's money" to the total claims against the assets of the business. The higher the ratio, the greater the likely risk for the lender. It is not necessarily a true test of the ability of the business to cover its debts, however, because as we have already observed, the asset amounts recorded on the balance sheet are not necessarily indicative of current economic values, or even liquidation values. Nor does the ratio give any clues as to likely earnings fluctuations that might affect current interest and principal payments.

Debt to Capitalization.   A more refined version of the debt proportion analysis involves the ratio of *long-term debt* to *capitalization*. The latter is again defined as the sum of the long-term claims against the business, both debt and owners' equity, but does not include short-term (current) liabilities. This total also corresponds to net assets, unless some adjustments were made, such as ignoring deferred taxes. The calculation appears as follows, when deferred taxes are included:

$$\frac{\text{Long-term debt}}{\text{Capitalization (net assets)}} = \frac{\$1,680}{\$3,465} = 48.5\% \ (1988\colon 48.0\%)$$

If deferred taxes are excluded from debt, the ratio changes to 35.2 percent and 34.0 percent respectively.

A great deal of emphasis is placed on this particular ratio, carefully defined for any particular company, because many lending agreements of both publicly held and private corporations contain covenants regulating maximum debt exposure expressed in terms of debt to capitalization proportions. As we shall see later, however, there is growing emphasis on a more relevant aspect of debt exposure, namely, the ability to *service*

---

*Includes deferred income tax liabilities.

the debt from ongoing funds flows, a much more dynamic view of lender relationships.

Debt to Equity. A third version of the analysis of debt proportions involves the ratio of *total debt,* normally the sum of current liabilities and all types of long-term debt, to total *owners' equity,* or *net worth.* The debt to equity ratio is an attempt to show, in another format, the relative proportions of lenders' claims to ownership claims and is used as a measure of debt exposure. It is expressed as either a percentage or as a proportion, and in the example shown the figures again were taken from TRW's balance sheet in Figure 3–2:

$$\frac{\text{Total debt}}{\text{Net worth (equity)*}} = \frac{\$3,474}{\$1,785} = 194.6\% \ (1988: 180.4\%)$$

If deferred taxes are considered equity, the result becomes 134.0 percent and 121.0 percent respectively. In preparing this ratio, as in some earlier instances, the question of deferred income taxes is often sidestepped by leaving this long-term claim out of the capitalization figure altogether. We have included it here and shown the results for the two different definitions of deferred taxes. One specific refinement of this formula uses only *long-term debt,* as related to *net worth,* while another refinement adjusts the calculation to express *long-term debt* as a proportion of total *capitalization less long-term debt,* which implicitly considers the effect of deferred taxes if they are not ignored. For this illustration we have considered deferred taxes as part of the capitalization, but not specifically as debt or equity.

$$\frac{\text{Long-term debt}}{\text{Net worth (equity)*}} = \frac{\$1,218}{\$1,785} = 68.2\% \ (1988: 65.4\%)$$

or

$$\frac{\text{Long-term debt}}{\text{Capitalization } - \text{ Long term debt}} = \frac{\$1,218}{\$3,465 - 1,218} = 54.2\% \ (1988: 51.5\%)$$

---

*Includes minority interests.

The various formats of these relationships imply the care with which the ground rules must be defined for any particular analysis and for the covenants governing specific lending agreements. They only hint at the risk/reward trade-off implicit in the use of debt, which will be discussed in more detail in Chapters 7 and 9.

Debt Service. Regardless of the specific choice from among the several ratios we just discussed, debt proportion analysis is in essence *static* and does not take into account the operating dynamics and economic values of the business. The analysis is totally derived from the balance sheet, which in itself is a static snapshot of the financial condition of the business at a single point in time.

Nonetheless, the relative ease with which these ratios are calculated probably accounts for their popularity. Such ratios are useful as indicators of trends when they are applied over a long period time. However, they still do not get at the heart of an analysis of creditworthiness, which involves a company's ability to pay both interest and principal on schedule as contractually agreed upon, that is, to service its debt.

Interest Coverage. One very frequently encountered ratio reflecting a company's debt service uses the relationship of *net profit (earnings) before interest and taxes* (EBIT) to the amount of the *interest payments* for the period. This ratio is developed with the expectation that annual operating earnings can be considered a basic source of funds for debt service and that any significant change in this relationship might signal difficulties. Major earnings fluctuations are one type of risk considered. No hard and fast standards for the ratio itself exist; rather, the prospective debtholders often require covenants in the loan agreement spelling out the number of times the business is expected to cover its debt service obligations. The ratio is simple to calculate, and we can employ the EBIT figure developed for TRW earlier in the management section:

$$\frac{\text{Net profit before interest and taxes (EBIT)}}{\text{Interest expense}} = \frac{\$525}{\$138} = 3.8 \text{ times}$$

$$(1988: 3.2 \text{ times})$$

The specifics are based on judgment, often involving a detailed analysis of a company's past, current, and prospective conditions.

Interest and Principal Coverage. A somewhat more refined analysis of debt coverage relates the *net profit* of the business, *before interest and taxes,* to the sum of current *interest and principal repayments,* in an attempt to indicate the company's ability to service its debt. A problem arises with this particular analysis because interest payments are tax deductible, while principal repayments are not. Thus we must be on guard to think about these figures on a *comparable* basis. One correction used involves converting the principal repayments into an equivalent pretax amount. This is done by dividing the principal repayment by the factor one minus the effective tax rate. The resulting calculation appears as follows, if we take as repayments the $156 million in principal (due in over 90 days) TRW paid in 1989, as indicated in the funds flow statement in its Annual Report:

$$\frac{\text{Net profit before interest and taxes (EBIT)}}{\text{Interest} + \dfrac{\text{Principal repayments}}{(1 - \text{tax rate})}} = \frac{\$525}{\$138 + \dfrac{\$156}{(1 - .341)}}$$

$$= \frac{\$525}{\$138 + \$237} = 1.4 \text{ times}$$

Another format uses operating cash flow (net profit after taxes plus write-offs), taken from Figure 3–3, to which aftertax interest has been added back. This is then compared to the sum of aftertax interest and principal repayment, and the calculation for 1989 appears as follows:

$$\frac{\text{Operating cash flow} + \text{Interest} (1 - \text{tax rate})}{\text{Interest} (1 - \text{tax rate}) + \text{Principal repayments}} =$$

$$\frac{\$663^* + \$138\,(.659)}{\$138(.659) + \$156} = \frac{\$754}{\$247} = 3.0 \text{ times}$$

Cash Flow Analysis. Determination of a company's ability to meet its debt obligations is most meaningful when a review

---

*$263 + $349 + $51

of past profit and cash flow patterns is made over a long enough period of time to indicate the major operational and cyclical fluctuations that are normal for the company and its industry. This may involve financial statements covering several years or several seasonal swings, as appropriate, in an attempt to identify characteristic high and low points in earnings and funds needs. The pattern of past conditions can then be projected into the future to see what margin of safety remains to cover interest, principal repayments, and other fixed payments, such as major lease obligations. These techniques will be discussed in Chapter 4.

If a business is subject to sizable fluctuations in aftertax cash flow, lenders may be reluctant to extend credit when the debt service cannot be covered several times at the low point in the operational pattern. In contrast, a very stable business would encounter less stringent coverage demands. The type of *dynamic* analysis involved is a form of financial modeling that can be greatly enhanced both in scope and in the number of possible alternative conditions explored by using electronic spreadsheets.

RATIOS AS A SYSTEM

The ratios discussed in this chapter have many elements in common, as they are derived from key components of the same financial statements. In fact, they are often interrelated and can be viewed as a system. Thus their usefulness lies in the analyst's ability to turn a series of ratios into a dynamic display, highlighting the elements that are the important *levers* used by management to affect operating performance. In internal analysis, many companies employ systems of ratios and standards that segregate into their components the series of decisions affecting operating performance, overall returns, and shareholder expectations. DuPont was one of the first to do so. Many years ago that company published a chart showing the effects and interrelationships of decisions in these areas, the first "model" of the business.

We will demonstrate the relationships between the ratios discussed using two key parameters segregated into their elements: *return on assets*, which is of major importance for judging management performance, and *return on equity*, which serves as the key measure from the owners' viewpoint. We will leave aside the refinements applicable to each to concentrate on the *linkages*. As will be demonstrated, it is possible to model the performance of a given company by expanding and relating these ratios. Needless to say, careful attention must be paid to the exact definition of the elements entering into the ratios for a particular company to achieve internal consistency.

Elements of Return on Assets

The basic formula for return on assets (ROA) was:

$$\text{Return on assets} = \frac{\text{Net profit}}{\text{Assets}}$$

We also know that net profit was related to asset turnover and also to sales. Thus, it is possible to restate the formula as follows:

$$\text{Return on assets (ROA)} = \frac{\text{Net profit}}{\text{Sales}} \times \frac{\text{Sales}}{\text{Assets}}$$

Note that the element of sales cancels out in the second formula, resulting in the original expression. But we can further expand the relationship by substituting more elements in the basic equation:

$$\text{ROA} = \frac{(\text{Gross margin} - \text{expenses})(1 - \text{tax rate})}{\text{Price} \times \text{Volume}}$$
$$\times \frac{\text{Price} \times \text{Volume}}{\text{Fixed} + \text{Current} + \text{Other assets}}$$

We can see that the relationships expressed here serve as a simple model of key *decision levers* management can employ to improve return on assets. For example, *gross margin* improvement is important, as is *expense* control. *Price/volume* relationships are canceled out, but are important in arriving at gross margin, as we know. (The first bracket could have been expanded to include this element.) *Asset management* is very important because the return on assets will rise if fewer assets are employed, and all the measures of effective management of working capital apply. Minimizing *taxes* within the legal options available will also improve the return.

Elements of Return on Equity

A similar approach can be taken with the basic formula for return on owners' equity:

$$\text{Return on equity} = \frac{\text{Net profit}}{\text{Equity}}$$

If we use some of the known relationships to expand the expression, the following formula emerges:

$$\text{Return on equity} = \frac{\text{Net profit}}{\text{Assets}} \times \frac{\text{Assets}}{\text{Equity}}$$

Note that in effect the formula states that return on equity (ROE) consists of two elements: the net profit on assets and the degree of leverage or debt capital in the business. "Assets to equity" is a way of describing this proportion.

We can expand the formula even more to include components of the return on assets:

$$\text{ROE} = \frac{\text{Net profit}}{\text{Sales}} \times \frac{\text{Sales}}{\text{Assets}} \times \frac{\text{Assets}}{\text{Assets} - \text{Liabilities}}$$

Now we can again look for the key decision levers that management should use to raise the return on owners' equity. As before, improving profitability of sales (operations) comes first, combined with effective use of assets that generate sales. The added factor is the boosting effect given by debt in the capital structure. The greater the liabilities, the greater the improvement in return on equity—assuming, of course, that the business is profitable to begin with. Using other people's money is helpful until the risk of default on debt service in a down cycle becomes significant. The analyst can use this simple framework to test the impact on return of one or more changed conditions and to test how sensitive the result is to the magnitude of change introduced.

We will return to the subject of business modeling again in Chapters 4 and 5.

ACCOUNTING ISSUES

The impact of accounting practices and decisions on the management of funds was briefly mentioned in Chapter 1, where accounting write-offs and deferred taxes were identified as aspects to be considered. At this point it will be useful to refine our understanding of these issues a little further because possible alternative treatments of these matters at times signifcantly affect the assessment of operations as well as the patterns of funds flows. A review of the key choices available to management in the areas of *inventory costing* and *depreciation methods* may help the reader in forming his or her own judgments when faced with interpreting financial statements and funds flows. We will also briefly mention the *effects of inflation*, although no satisfactory methods of dealing with that issue have been established so far.

Inventory Costing

One accounting challenge present at all times is the proper allocation of a portion of the costs accumulated in the inventory account to the actual goods being sold. We can visualize *layers of cost* built up over time in the inventory account, which correspond to the physical movement of raw materials, work in process, and finished goods into storage. The accountant wants to *match revenues and expenses* in keeping track of the inventory account, yet from a physical standpoint, it is just as possible to ship the oldest unit on hand as it is to ship the most recent arrival. The warehouse supervisor can even pick the goods at random.

If unit costs never changed, matching costs to revenues would not be a problem because the accountant would simply track the number of units shipped and multiply them by the unchanged unit cost, regardless of the actual physical choices made by the warehouse supervisor. In real life, however, several problems arise. A manufacturing company may experience fluctuations that affect the *unit cost* of the products inventoried. This effectively results in *different layers of cost* recorded in the finished goods inventory account. Further, the *prices* of raw materials and other inputs may be positively or negatively influenced by supply and demand. The materials inventory account will therefore reflect different layers of cost. Most cost accounting systems allow for variances to the extent they are predictable, but larger swings do affect costs that are charged to periodic operating statements. Finally, there is the impact of *general inflation*—or, more rarely, *deflation*. The impact of inflation on inventories generally is a steady rise in the cost of the more recent additions, resulting in successive layers of escalating costs.

The accountant is therefore faced with a real problem in the effort to match costs and revenues. If unit costs are growing significantly from period to period, deciding *which* costs to charge against the revenues for a period can have significant effects on the financial statements. If the more "logical" method of removing the oldest units first is used, the oldest— and presumably lowest—unit costs will be charged against current revenues. Depending on how quickly the inventory turns over, such costs may *lag current* conditions by months and even years. Therefore, under rising price levels, first-in, first-out inventory costing (FIFO), causes the profit on the income statement to be *higher* than it would be if current unit costs had been charged. At the same time, the balance sheet will reflect inventory values that are reasonably current, because the oldest, lowest cost units are being removed. Under conditions of falling prices, the opposite effects are encountered, of course.

If last-in, first-out costing (LIFO) is used as prices rise, the income statement will be charged with current costs and thus reflect lower but more realistic profits. The balance sheet, however, will show inventory values that in time will be highly *understated* because only the oldest and lowest layers of cost remain.

We could argue that the choice of methods does not really matter because one of the financial statements will be distorted in *either* case. The question then simply becomes whether more realistic balance sheet values or more realistic reported profits are preferred. There is a significant *funds aspect* involved, however. The choice of methods affects the amount of *income taxes paid* for the period. The higher earnings under FIFO are taxed as income from operations, even though they contain a profit made from old inventories. Therefore, one criterion in making the choice is the difference in tax payments, which *does* affect the company's funds. LIFO is preferable from this standpoint, even though with continued inflation inventory values stated on the balance sheet will become more and more obsolete. Yet surprisingly, FIFO has remained a very common form of inventory costing, despite the fact that it can lead to a funds drain from higher tax payments. Apparently the higher reported *income* under FIFO costing is attractive enough to many managements to outweigh the actual tax disadvantage.

In contrast to other permissible choices of accounting methods for tax purposes, current federal tax laws do *not* allow the use of one inventory costing method for *tax calculation* and another for *bookkeeping and reporting*. Thus, the ideal combination of LIFO for tax purposes and FIFO for reporting earnings cannot be employed. In fact, many firms employ an averaging method for inventory costing, or a combination of methods.

Trading firms, retailers, and companies experiencing significant fluctuations in the current values of inventories often adjust inventory values, usually at year-end, using the conservative method of restating inventories at cost or market value, whichever is lower, and writing off the difference against current profits. Such periodic adjustments tend to *reduce* stated values, not raise them, and allow the company to reflect the negative effects of changed conditions so as not to overstate inventory values. Under inflationary conditions this practice does not, of course, assist in resolving the inventory costing issues we have just discussed.

Depreciation Methods

Depreciation is based on the accountant's desire to reflect as a charge against current operations some appropriate fraction of the original cost of assets employed in producing revenues. Because physical assets other than land deteriorate with use and eventually wear out, the accounting challenge is to establish an appropriate period of time over which portions of the cost of the asset are charged against revenues. Moreover, the accountant has to decide on the pattern of the depreciation write-off, that is, level, declining, or variable depreciation. Another issue involves estimating any salvage value that may be realized at the end of an asset's useful life. Only the difference between asset cost and such salvage value is normally depreciated.

A similar rationale is applied to intangible assets such as patents and licenses, which are *amortized* and charged against operations over an appropriate period of years and to specialized assets such as mineral deposits and timber, on which *depletion* allowances are calculated.

In the case of physical assets, the depreciation write-off is shown as a charge in the operating statement and is accumulated on the balance sheet as an offset to the fixed assets involved, in an account called *accumulated depreciation* or *reserve for depreciation*. Thus, over time, the original asset value stated on the balance sheet is reduced as periodic charges are made against operations. For performance assessment, the significance of depreciation write-offs is in the *appropriateness* of the charges in light of the nature of the assets and industry conditions, and thus depreciation's impact on *profits* and *balance sheet values*. The significance for purposes of *funds* management is the *tax impact* of depreciation. Under normal circumstances depreciation is a tax-deductible expense, even though it is only an accounting allocation of past expenditures. The highest depreciation write-off legally possible will normally be taken by management to minimize the cash outlay for taxes, unless operating profits are insufficient over the taxable period (including tax adjustments like operating loss carry-back and carry-forward, which permit making use of losses to reduce the taxes of profitable periods) to take full advantage of the deductions.

The choice of depreciation methods is made easier by the provision in the current tax laws allowing the use of *one* method for bookkeeping and reporting purposes and *another* for income tax calculation. Recall that this was not possible for inventory valuation. Thus a company can enjoy the best aspects of both depreciation concepts: slower depreciation for reporting higher profits and faster depreciation for paying lower taxes.

The difference between the taxes actually paid versus what would be due had the book profit been taxed is accumulated on the balance sheet as a liability, *deferred taxes*, or as an asset, *deferred tax assets* as we discussed earlier. The liability will keep growing if a company continually adds to its depreciable assets and consistently uses faster write-offs for tax purposes. If the company stops growing or changes its depreciation policies, actual tax payments in future periods will increase and the differences will begin to reduce the deferred taxes account. There is no current consensus on how to treat this often significant amount in the calculation of performance assessment measures.

What are the most common *choices* for depreciation write-offs? Historically, accounting practice favored *straight-line depreciation*. This is determined by dividing the cost of the asset (less the estimated salvage value) by its expected life. For example, an asset costing $10,000, with a salvage value of $400 and a six-year life would be depreciated at the annual rate of $1,600 (one sixth, or 16⅔ percent of $9,600). A variant of this method is *unit depreciation,* in which the allocation is based on the total number of units estimated to be produced over the life of the asset, and the annual depreciation is based on the number of units produced in that year.

Because many types of assets, such as automobiles, lose more of their value in early years, and also because allowing faster write-offs provides an incentive to reduce current income taxes, several methods of *accelerated depreciation* were developed over time. The two most common methods will be mentioned here.

Double-declining balance depreciation is calculated by using twice the annual rate of straight-line depreciation (33⅓ percent for a six-year life), multiplying the full original cost of the asset for the first year with this factor and the declining balance for each successive year. In other words, in our example one third of the remaining balance would be depreciated in each year (see Figure 3–4). The last year's depreciation is the remaining balance, and any salvage value is recognized by reducing the amount charged in the *final* year.

Sum-of-year-digits depreciation is calculated by adding the digits for all the years of the asset's life (1 + 2 + 3, etc.). The total is the denominator in a fraction. (For a six-year life this sum would be 21: 1 + 2 + 3 + 4 + 5 + 6.) The numerators represent each year of useful life, in *reverse* order. (In our example, the fractions are 6/21, 5/21, 4/21, 3/21, 2/21, and 1/21). In a given year, the depreciation write-off is the asset's original cost (less salvage value) multiplied by the fraction for that year.

The depreciation methods permitted under prevailing Internal Revenue codes have changed frequently, especially during the 1980s. Under the 1986 revision of the tax code, the IRS lengthened the lives over which various classes of depreciable assets can be written off. Six asset classes were established for personal property, with lives of 3, 5, 7, 10, 15, and 20 years. For real property (e.g., buildings), two classes of 27.5 and 31.5 years were defined, which must be depreciated straight-line. The IRS stipulated the double-declining balance method for assets with up to 10 years of life, and a variation of this method, the 150 percent declining balance method, for

128

Figure 3–4
Comparative Annual Depreciation Patterns
($10,000 asset with six-year life and $400 salvage value)

	Straight-Line Method	Double-Declining Balance Method*	150 Percent Declining Balance Method*†	Sum-of-Years Digits Method
Year one:	$1,600	$3,333	$2,500	$2,743
Year two:	1,600	2,222	1,875	2,286
Year three:	1,600	1,482	1,407	1,829
Year four:	1,600	988	1,406	1,371
Year five:	1,600	658	1,406	914
Year six:	1,600	917	1,006	457
Total:	$9,600	$9,600	$9,600	$9,600

*Year six is shown net of salvage value of $400.
†Switch to straight line in year four; required for 15- and 20-year IRS asset classes.

assets with a 15- and 20-year life. In either case, a switch to straight-line depreciation in the latter years is permitted, when this becomes advantageous. These methods must be used if a company chooses to use accelerated depreciation for *tax* purposes, while *any* other method can be employed for bookkeeping and reporting. The specifics of the tax regulations applicable at the time of the analysis are best examined in the detailed materials provided by the Internal Revenue Service.

The different patterns of depreciation resulting from the use of the various methods are shown in Figure 3–4.

The Impact of Inflation

The extreme inflationary conditions in the United States beginning in the early 1970s resulted in significant distortions in many of the calculations we discussed. Many other countries have, of course, had to deal with far more insidious levels of inflation for much longer periods of time. In the United States, the accounting profession and the Securities and Exchange Commission have expended much effort in developing new ways to account for and disclose the impact of changes in prices of goods and services and of fluctuating exchange rates due in part to inflation. However, the intricacies and arguments abundant in this difficult area are beyond the scope of this book. We are only mentioning a few of the basic mechanisms commonly employed to deal with price level changes where this is necessary to understand the impact on financial analysis. Thus Chapters 2, 4, and 9 refer to essential price level adjustments pertaining to the subjects of operating funds management, projections, and valuation. Appendix 1 contains a discussion of the basic concepts underlying the inflation phenomenon.

In performance analysis, the main problem associated with inflation is the use of *historical costing* as a generally accepted accounting principle. The original cost of assets utilized in and charged to operations is reflected on the balance sheet. Depreciation and amortization reflect past values, which are often lower than current values. Financial statements of particularly heavily capitalized industries with long-lived depreciable assets and physical resources tend to reflect overstated profits and taxes and understated asset values. This raises the issue of comparability of companies of different ages and certainly of comparability of whole industries. Even short-term fluctuations in values will affect companies with high inventory turnover such as wholesalers.

Another area of distortion affects the *viewpoint of the lender*. In inflationary times, the declining value of currency will affect borrowing/lending relationships because eventual repayment will be made in less valuable dollars. Thus, the lender would be at a disadvantage unless the interest rate contracted for is high enough to offset this risk. The dramatic rise in the 1970s and subsequent fall in the 1980s of short- and long-term interest rates in response to growing and waning inflationary pressures will remain in the memories of long-term lenders in particular.

Among the many methods used to deal with price level changes are replacement cost accounting, new forms of inventory valuation, and partial or full periodic restatement of financial reports. In fact, inflation has turned the deceptively simple accounting principle of matching costs and revenues into an economic and intellectual challenge. As yet, there are no consistent ways of appraising the difference between this type of recast statement and the original accounting statements.

SUMMARY

In this chapter, we discussed essential aspects of the main *financial statements* as a basis for appraising business performance. With this background, we demonstrated that the assessment of performance is made meaningful when seen from the *points of view* of the key groups interested in the company's success.

We chose to concentrate on the particular viewpoints of three groups—*management, owners, and lenders*—which are essential to the functioning of the business. The insights of these groups are used and expanded by others for their own particular needs. All three groups are concerned about the success of the business, each from its own standpoint.

It is management's prime duty to bring about stability, growth, and reliable earnings performance with the investment entrusted to it by the owners. We found that within the wide range of ratios displayed, the crucial test is the *economic return* on the *capital* employed in the business and its attendant effect on the *value of the ownership* stake. We also found that the ratios are *linked* by their common information base, and many are directly connected through the common use of certain elements. They are best interpreted when the business is viewed as a system of interdependent conditions responding to the decisions of management. To this end, modeling and computer simulation are increasingly accepted and meaningful, because many individual ratios are, by their nature, only *static* tests that cannot do justice to the dynamics of a business.

Shortcomings in the analysis relate to the limitations of the *accounting principles* commonly used, and further distortions are introduced through *price-level changes* stemming from inflation, currency fluctuations, and economic changes. No definitive ways of compensating for these problems have as yet been found to make financial analyses comparable and economically meaningful. As a result, the analyst must use *judgment* at all times.

SELECTED REFERENCES

Anthony, Robert N., and James S. Reece. *Accounting: Text and Cases.* 6th ed. Homewood Ill.: Richard D. Irwin, 1988.

Bernstein, Leopold A. *Financial Statement Analysis: Theory, Application, and Interpretation.* 3rd ed. Homewood, Ill.: Richard D. Irwin, 1983.

Brealey, Richard, and Stewart Myers. *Principles of Corporate Finance.* 3rd ed. New York: McGraw-Hill, 1988.

Fraser, Lyn M. *Understanding Financial Statements: Through the Maze of a Corporate Annual Report.* Reston, Va.: Reston Publishing, 1985.

Ross, Stephen; Randolph Westerfield, and Jeffrey Jaffe. *Corporate Finance.* 2nd ed. Homewood, Ill.: Richard D. Irwin, 1990.

Van Horne, James C. *Financial Management and Policy.* 8th ed. Englewood Cliffs, N.J.: Prentice-Hall, 1989.

Weston, J. Fred, and Thomas E. Copeland. *Managerial Finance.* 9th ed. Hinsdale, Ill.: Dryden Press, 1989.

Robert Morris Associates. *Annual Statement Studies.*

Dun & Bradstreet. *Industry Norms and Key Business Ratios.*

Troy, Leo. *Almanac of Business and Industrial Financial Ratios.* Englewood Cliffs, N.J.: Prentice-Hall.

SELF-STUDY EXERCISES AND PROBLEMS
(Solutions Provided in Appendix III)

1. Work the following exercises:
   a. A company has achieved a 1990 net profit, which represents 11.4 percent of net sales. What is the company's return on net worth if

asset turnover is 1.34 and the capitalization is 67 percent of total assets? How would a faster asset turnover affect the result?

b. A company's gross margin on sales for 1990 is 31.4 percent. Total cost of goods sold amounted to $4,391,300, and net profit was 9.7 percent of sales. What are the company's total assets if the ratio of sales to assets is 82.7 percent? What is the return on capitalization if current liabilities are 21 percent of total assets?

c. What is the change in a company's current ratio of 2.2:1 (current assets are $573,100) if the following actions are taken individually? Also, how does each item affect working capital?
   The company:
   1. Pays $67,500 of accounts payable with cash.
   2. Collects $33,000 in notes receivable.
   3. Purchases merchandise worth $41,300 on account.
   4. Pays dividends of $60,000, of which $42,000 had been shown as accrued (an unpaid current liability).
   5. Sells machine for $80,000, on which book value is $90,000 and accumulated depreciation is $112,000.
   6. Sells merchandise on account which cost $73,500. Gross margin is 33 percent.
   7. Writes off $20,000 from inventory as scrap and amortizes $15,000 of goodwill.

d. From the following data calculate the outstanding days' receivables and payables for a company, using the methods shown in the chapter. What is the inventory turnover, calculated in different ways? Discuss your assumptions.

Sales for three months	$437,500
Cost of sales	298,400
Purchases	143,500
Beginning inventory	382,200
Ending inventory	227,300
Accounts receivable	156,800
Accounts payable	69,300
Normal sales terms	2/10,n/30
Normal purchase terms	n/45

2. From the following financial statements of the ABC Company for 1989 and 1990, prepare the ratios and measures discussed in this chapter.
   a. Ratios from the viewpoint of management.
   b. Ratios from the viewpoint of owners.
   c. Ratios from the viewpoint of lenders.
   Comment on the changes shown between the two years, and discuss the significance of the results from the three points of view. Indicate which additional kinds of comparison you would like to make for this company, a manufacturer of electronics, and the type of information you would need.

ABC COMPANY
Balance Sheets
December 31, 1989 and 1990
($ millions)

Assets	1989	1990
Current assets:		
Cash	$ 82.7	$110.9
Accounts receivable (net)	92.6	146.2
Inventories	88.8	129.5
Prepaid expenses	2.8	6.2
Advances from government	5.3	2.8
Total current assets	272.2	395.6
Property, plant, and equipment	215.2	283.4
Less: Accumulated depreciation	101.2	119.6
Net property	114.0	163.8
Other assets	3.1	4.2
Total assets	$389.3	$563.6

Liabilities and Net Worth		
Current liabilities:		
Accounts payable	$ 43.4	$ 62.9
Accrued income tax	36.7	44.0
Accrued pension and profit sharing	27.1	38.4
Other accruals	21.9	31.2
Current portion of long-term debt	2.1	—
Total current liabilities	131.2	176.5
Debentures (9% due 1993)	—	94.0
Other long-term debt	7.8	4.1
Deferred income tax	5.2	7.6
Common stock ($1 par)	10.1	10.2
Paid-in surplus	25.1	27.2
Earned surplus	209.9	244.0
Total liabilities and net worth	$389.3	$563.6

ABC COMPANY
Operating Statements for 1989 and 1990
($ millions)

Assets	1989	1990
Net sales	$655.1	$872.7
Cost of goods and services*	460.9	616.1
Gross profit	194.2	256.6
Selling, general, and administrative expenses	98.3	125.2
Employee profit sharing and retirement	26.9	38.7
	125.2	163.9
Operating profit	69.0	92.7
Other income	1.1	1.8
	70.1	94.5
Interest paid	1.0	7.4
	69.1	87.1
Provision for income taxes	31.8	40.1
Net profit†	$ 37.3	$ 47.0
*Depreciation and amortization	$28.2	$38.5
†Common dividends paid	5.5	6.0

3. Select a major manufacturing company, a retailing firm, a public utility, a bank, and a transportation firm. From an information source like Value Line, Moody's, or Standard & Poor's, develop a historical analysis of key measures you consider significant to appraise the effectiveness of management, the return to the owners, and the position of the lenders. Develop significant industry comparisons and comment on the relative position of your chosen company. Also comment on some of the assumptions and choices you have to make on the selection of specific accounts and data to work the analytical techniques.

4 PROJECTION OF FINANCIAL REQUIREMENTS

Up to this point we have discussed the appraisal of performance and the management of operating funds in the context of *past* decisions involving investments, operations, and financing. This chapter brings a shift in emphasis to a *forward look,* that is *forecasting* likely future conditions, a critically important task in managing any business. We will discuss the key concepts and techniques of *projecting operating performance* and the expected *financial requirements* with which to support future operations. Such projections normally involve alternative plans developed for different conditions.

The projection of financial requirements is only *part* of the business planning process with which management positions the company's future activities relative to the expected economic, competitive, technical, and social environment. When business plans are developed, they are usually structured around specific goals and objectives cooperatively set by the organization and its subgroups. The plans normally spell out strategies and actions for achieving desired short-term, intermediate, and long-term results. These, in turn, are quantified in financial terms, in the form of *projected financial statements (pro forma statements)* and a variety of *operational budgets*. Often detailed *cash budgets* and *funds flow statements* are included to provide greater insight into the funds implications of the projected activities. The concepts and techniques discussed in Chapters 2 and 3 are, as we will see, necessary tools with which to quantify projected conditions.

The scope of this book allows us to focus only on the *major* methods and formats of financial projection. We cannot explicitly take into account the broader strategic planning framework through which the future direction of the company should be explored before any financial quantification can become fully meaningful. At the same time, financial projection techniques by themselves can be useful simulations of the likely results of broad assumptions about a variety of future conditions. The ease with which pro forma financial statements can be developed makes them attractive as approximations from which refinements are possible with additional information and insights, as alternatives for action are narrowed down.

The use of planning models and computer-generated spreadsheets has grown explosively in the 1980s, as has the availability of a large selection of software packages offering financial simulation and projection capabilities. While these commercial offerings differ in their specific orientation and degree of sophistication, they are built around the very concepts we will be discussing in this chapter. Computer speed and multiple tracking capabilities have eliminated much of the drudgery of tracing investment, operational, and financing assumptions through the financial framework of a business. Yet the analyst must *first understand* and be comfortable with the basic *financial techniques and relationships* embodied in the computer models in order to take advantage of the capabilities of the available software. Therefore this book focuses not on how to use spreadsheets, but on the financial techniques themselves.

The main techniques of financial projection fall into three categories: *pro forma financial statements, cash budgets, and operating budgets*. Pro forma statements, as the name implies, are projected financial statements embodying a set of assumptions about a company's future performance and funding requirements. Cash budgets are detailed projections of the specific incidence of cash moving in and out of the business. Operating budgets are detailed projections of departmental revenue and/or expense patterns, and they are *subsidiary* to both pro forma statements and cash flow statements. All three categories involve an organized arrangement of financial and economic data for the purpose of assessing future performance and funds requirements. As we will see, the three methodologies are also closely *interrelated*. This interrelationship can be exploited to achieve consistent financial forecasts. We will also examine basic *financial modeling* and the use of *sensitivity analysis* for testing the impact of changes in critical assumptions underlying the financial projections.

PRO FORMA FINANCIAL STATEMENTS

The most comprehensive look at the likely future financial performance of a company can be obtained by developing a set of pro forma statements. These statements are merely an *operating statement* and a *balance sheet* extended into the future. The pro forma operating statement represents an *"operational plan"* for the business as a whole, while the pro forma balance sheet reflects the anticipated *cumulative* impact of assumed future decisions on the *financial condition* of the business at a selected point in time. Both statements are prepared by taking the most readily available estimates of future activity and projecting, account by account, the assumed results and conditions. A third statement, a pro forma *funds flow statement*, adds further insight by displaying the various funds movements expected during the forecast period.

Pro forma projections can be done at any level of detail desired. In summarized form, these statements are one of the most widely used ways of quickly making estimates. They are particularly favored by bank loan officers, who must assess the creditworthiness of the client company from a total financial standpoint. Detailed plans are not needed to construct complete pro forma statements, even though the results of a formal planning process would increase the degree of precision. Instead, selected *ratios* can be used to produce statements that are entirely satisfactory, particularly as a first look. As we will demonstrate, an important aspect of pro forma analysis is the ability to find the *funds requirements* necessary for the company as of the date the pro forma balance sheet is prepared.

To show how pro forma statements are developed, we will use the example of ficticious manufacturing company called XYZ Corporation. The company makes and sells three different products, has a seasonal pattern with the low point occurring in December, and is currently profitable. The most recent actual results available are for the third quarter of 1990. These statements are the initial set of data that allow us to project ahead. But we can also ask management for additional information as needed. The pro forma projection is to be made for the last quarter of 1990, and the objective is to determine both the level of profit for the quarter and the amount of additional funds that will be needed as of the end of the year.

Pro Forma Income Statement

We begin the process with the *pro forma operating statement* for XYZ Corporation. The operating statement is normally prepared first because the amount of aftertax profit developed there must also be reflected in the pro forma balance sheet as a change in retained earnings. The starting point for the operating statement, as shown on the first line in Figure 4–1 on pages 140–41 is a projection of the unit and dollar volume of *sales*. These can be estimated in a variety of ways, ranging from trend-line projection to detailed departmental sales forecasts by individual product, built up from field estimates. In the absence of any other information we may, of course, make our own "guesstimates" based on past overall results. In the case of XYZ Corporation, we know that a seasonal pattern exists and that sales can be expected to decline in the last quarter.

In Figure 4–1 we have shown the actual operating statement for the third quarter of 1990 as a base for our analysis. Dollar amounts are given for key revenue and cost elements, as well as a breakdown into percent of sales, or "common numbers." The series of assumptions we must make will use the third quarter experience as a guide, as we have been assured that the quarterly pattern over the years has been reasonably stable.

Company statistics from past years suggest that during the fourth quarter an 18 to 20 percent drop in sales volume from the third quarter is normal. We will take the midpoint of this range as a beginning assumption. After calculating a 19 percent drop in *unit* volume, we make the further assumption that both *prices* and *product mix* will remain unchanged. It is possible, of course, to make different assumptions about volume, prices, and mix in order to reflect specific insights or to test the impact of "what if" questions. In our case an inquiry to sales management will confirm that the set of assumptions about sales matches their own forecast.

Next we turn to *cost of goods sold*. The actual third-quarter operating statement provides details on the main components—*labor, materials, overhead,* and *delivery*—in cost of goods sold. We can calculate the proportion of cost that each of these elements represents and assume that the same proportions will hold during the fourth quarter. But we must also remember that the last quarter is the company's seasonal low point, and we can assume that some inefficiencies are likely to raise overall production costs as operations slow. Without more data we can assume a rise of something like one percentage point in the ratio of cost of goods sold to sales as a quick way

Figure 4-1
XYZ CORPORATION
Pro Forma Income Statement
For the Quarter Ended December 31, 1990
($000)

	Actual Quarter Ended 9-30-90		Pro Forma* Quarter Ended 12-31-90		Assumptions and Sources of Information
Units sold	137,000		111,000		Last quarter is seasonal low; past data show 18 to 20 percent decline from third quarter.
Net sales	$12,650	100.0%	$10,250	100.0%	Projected 19 percent lower volume with same price and mix.
Cost of goods sold:					
Labor	2,210		1,810		21.5% of cost of goods as before.
Materials	2,045		1,680		20.0% of cost of goods as before.
Overhead	5,685		4,660		55.5% of cost of goods as before.
Delivery	305		250		3.0% of cost of goods as before.
Cost of goods sold . . .	10,245	81.0	8,400	82.0	Increase of 1 percentage point to simulate operating inefficiencies.
Gross margin	2,405	19.0	1,850	18.0	

Expenses:

Selling expense	875	6.9	825	8.0	Assume drop of $50, to show lower activity.
General and administrative expenses	585	4.6	600	5.9	Assume slight increase for year-end costs.
Total expenses	1,460	11.5	1,425	13.9	
Operating profit	945	7.5	425	4.1	Shows effect of less efficient operations.
Interest	190	1.5	175	1.7	Based on outstanding debt.
Profit before taxes	755	6.0	250	2.4	
Income taxes	272	2.2	90	0.9	Projected at 36%.
Net income	483	3.8	160	1.5	
Dividends	100	0.8	-0-	-0-	No payment of dividends scheduled.
Retained earnings	383	3.0%	160	1.5%	Carried to balance sheet.
Depreciation added back	575		600		From *fixed asset records* (assume tax and book depreciation are the same).
Cash flow after dividends	$ 958		$ 760		Rough measure of cash from operations (should add back any dividends to reflect operations only).

* All projections are rounded off.

to allow for the seasonal distortion. The dollar penalty of this assumption is a reduction in gross margin of 1 percent of $10,250,000 or $102,500. Other levels of cost of goods sold could, of course, be tested. Note that cost of goods sold and gross margin can be estimated *directly* without the detailed cost breakdown (labor, materials, etc.) given in the third-quarter operating statement.

The main *expense* categories can be estimated by again examining the actual statement for the third quarter. The figures provided there might simply be accepted as our projection. *Selling expense* is shown as $875,000. Given that the fourth quarter has lower sales activity, we can assume a small decrease, such as $50,000. A reduction fully proportional to the 19 percent drop in volume would not be realistic, however, given that many of the costs, such as salaries of marketing personnel, are essentially fixed in the near term. *Administrative expense* is rounded off a little higher for purposes of our projection because of expected nonrecurring year-end expenses. Note that both expense elements now represent a higher proportion of sales than was true for the actual prior quarter. If the analyst believes that this result seems out of line, it may, of course, be modified. Even if historical patterns were available in great detail, we must remember that the projection deals with the future and that the purpose of the exercise is to make the most realistic assumptions possible. The estimates will *remain* assumptions, however, until actual experience supersedes them.

As a result of our assumptions, the fourth quarter *operating profit* falls by over half a million dollars, and the aftertax profit ratio drops to less than half of its former level. This is due mostly to the 19 percent drop in sales volume and the associated loss in profit contribution. This reduction represents $2.4 million of sales, which with a normal cost of goods sold of 81 percent, would have contributed $456,000. Moreover, we assumed certain inefficiencies in operations and only a partial ability to reduce what are mostly fixed expenses. As we stated before, the analyst can examine this result and judge its appropriateness.

Interest is charged according to the provisions of the out-standing debt, and this information can be provided by the financial officer. The operating statement will be completed once we calculate *income taxes* (assumed here at an effective rate of 36 percent) to arrive at *net income*. We note that the amount of net income has dropped significantly in response to the slowdown in operations. A further assumption needs to be made about dividends to arrive at retained earnings for the period, which have to be reflected in the pro forma balance sheet. In XYZ's case, no dividends have been declared, ac-cording to the financial officer. As a last step we have added back the *depreciation* for the period to approximate the *cash flow from operations*. This is a quick estimate that we will review in the context of all other expected funds movements.

Pro Forma Balance Sheet

Armed with the data about expected operations, we can now develop the *pro forma balance sheet*, which is illustrated in Figure 4–2. Again we must make specific assumptions about each account on the statement, working from the actual bal-ance sheet at the beginning of the forecast period and addi-tional information we can obtain from management. We have relative freedom to make and vary our estimates, except that there *must* be *consistency* between the assumptions affecting *both* the operating statement and the balance sheet. The ob-jective is not accounting precision, of course, but rather to develop an indication of approximate funds needs three months hence and of the overall financial condition of the company at that time.

We begin the calculations with the first account, *cash*, and make the assumption that three months hence the company would need to keep only the minimum working balance in its bank accounts. The information source for this figure ($1,250,000) again is the financial officer. In the absence of such specific data we could assume a level of cash that is com-mon among companies of this size. As we will see later, the desired amount of cash on hand will affect the amount of funds the company may have to borrow. We must not forget that any

Figure 4-2
XYZ CORPORATION
Pro Forma Balance Sheet as of December 31, 1990
($000)

	Actual 9–30–90	Change	Pro Forma 12–31–90	Assumptions and Sources of Information
Assets				
Current assets:				
Cash	$ 1,450	– 200	$ 1,250	Cash set at estimated minimum balance.
Accounts receivable	4,250	–1,200	3,050	Represents 30 days' sales (from December sales projection).
Raw materials	1,500	–0–	1,500	Safety level; requirements purchased as needed.
Finished goods	4,050	– 750	3,300	Reduced production by 19 percent.
Total current assets	11,250	–2,150	9,100	Drop reflects seasonal pattern.
Fixed assets:				
Land	2,500	–0–	2,500	No change assumed.
Plant and equipment	20,800	–1,500	19,300	Sale of machines with original cost of $1,500 and accumulated depreciation of $950.
Less: Accumulated depreciation	8,350	– 350	8,000	Depreciation for period $600, per income statement, less reduction of $950 from sale of machines.
Net plant and equipment	12,450	–1,150	11,300	
Total fixed assets	14,950	–1,150	13,800	
Other assets	1,250	–0–	1,250	No change assumed.
Total assets	$27,450	–3,300	$24,150	

Liabilities and Net Worth

Current liabilities:

Accounts payable	$ 1,120	− 410	$ 710	45 days' purchases (from November/December purchase estimates).
Notes payable	3,000	−1,500	1,500	Repayment as scheduled.
Due contractor	3,400	−2,900	500	From payment schedule.
Accruals	1,250	− 310	940	Tax payments (−$400) and tax accrual (+$90).
Total current liabilities	8,770	−5,120	3,650	Reflects heavy current repayments of obligations.
Long-term liabilities	8,500	−0−	8,500	No change.
Common stock	4,250	+ 250	4,500	Sale of stock under option.
Retained earnings	5,930	+ 160	6,090	Retained earnings per income statement (no payment of dividends).
Total liabilities and net worth	$27,450	−4,710	22,740	
Funds required		+1,410	1,410	"Plug" figure representing financing need as of 12–31–90, the same as in Figure 4–4.
		−3,300	$24,150	

145

cash balance maintained as an ongoing requirement on the balance sheet represents an *investment* like any other.

Next we turn to *accounts receivable*. If the company sells its products on terms of net 30, it can expect to have at least 30 days' sales outstanding—more, if some of its customers are late in paying. On the December 31 balance sheet the figure would represent the sales of the whole month of December. We do not have the exact December sales estimate, however, because our pro forma operating statement shows sales for the last *three* months *combined*. In the absence of specific *monthly* sales estimates we could assume that one third of the projected quarterly sales would be outstanding at the end of the quarter. In our case that would be one third of the $10,250,000 in Figure 4–1, or $3,417,000. But we learn after some discussion with sales management that in view of the *seasonal low* in December, the company's sales force projects the month's sales at only $3,050,000. This amount thus becomes the 30 days of sales we can assume to be outstanding in the form of accounts receivable at the end of the year.

Raw material inventory can be projected by using monthly withdrawal and purchase patterns, information that the company would be able to provide. Manufacturing management informs us that for reasons of continuity, they like to keep on hand at all times $1,500,000 worth of raw materials, and thus frequent purchases are made as required to maintain that level.

Finished goods inventory is likely to decline in response to lower sales and production activity, and we have calculated a 19 percent reduction. If we considered this an optimistic assumption because of the precision required in adjusting production exactly to the seasonal low, a higher amount can, of course, be specified. The consequence would be a *lesser* amount of *funds released* from declining inventories as operations slow down.

When we add up all our changes in the *current asset accounts*, we find that the total is projected to decline by over $2 million, releasing these funds for other uses. Such a pattern reflects the normal funds flow expectations from seasonal operations, as was discussed in Chapter 2.

Fixed assets are affected by several events. While *land* remains unchanged, we are told that some machines will be sold during the last quarter. Their original cost was $1.5 million, against which $950,000 of depreciation has been accumulated. They are to be sold for book value, which involves no taxable gain or loss. To reflect the transaction, the plant and equipment account on our pro forma balance sheet must be reduced by the original cost, while accumulated depreciation must be reduced by the $950,000 of past write-offs recorded there. We also know from the pro forma operating statement that normal depreciation for the period will be $600,000. This amount has to become an addition to the accumulated depreciation account. As a net result of the two changes, accumulated depreciation will decline by $350,000. *Other assets* are assumed to be unchanged.

On the liability side, *accounts payable* are assumed to decline in response to lower activity in the last quarter. We are told that payables are mostly related to purchases of raw material. We could approximate accounts payable, which have terms of net 45, by assuming that about one half of the 90-day raw materials use indicated on the pro forma operating statement would be outstanding ($840,000). But we have additional inside information on the actual level of *purchases* scheduled, and our assumption can be refined to show all of December's purchases ($460,000) plus one-half of November's ($250,000) as total accounts payable outstanding at year end ($710,000).

Other current liabilities must be analyzed in terms of specific payment schedules. We are informed that *notes payable* carry a provision for repayment of $1.5 million during the quarter. The account *due contractor* requires XYZ Corporation to make a payment of almost $3 million owed on past construction that has become due this period. *Accruals* largely involve income tax and other tax obligations. We already know from the pro forma operating statement that tax accruals projected for the quarter will be $90,000. We are also told that the company must make an estimated tax payment of $400,000 during the quarter. These two items will net out to a reduction in accruals of $310,000. Note that total current liabilities are estimated to be reduced by about $5.1 million, a significant *use of funds* over the forecast period.

Long-term liabilities are assumed to remain unchanged, while the recorded value of *common stock* is expected to increase by $250,000 as stock options are exercised. Finally, *retained earnings* will increase by the net profit (income) of $160,000 calculated on the pro forma operating statement.

When the results are added up, the pro forma balance sheet *will not balance*. This is not surprising inasmuch as we did not use double-entry bookkeeping to balance our calculations. Instead, we made a variety of *independent* assumptions about many of the accounts, taking care only to be *consistent* with the related projections in the pro forma *operating statement*. Having done so, and given that we are reasonably satisfied with our assumptions, the *balancing figure* required to equalize assets and liabilities represents either the *funds need* or the *excess funds* of the company on the pro forma balance sheet date.

This "plug" figure, as it is often called, serves as a quick estimate of what additional indebtedness the company will face on the date of the statement or what uncommitted funds it will have at its disposal. The plug will *not* indicate, however, the peaks and valleys in funds requirements that may have occurred *during* each month of the quarter. These could be found by generating *intermediate* balance sheets more frequently than every 90 days. In other words, we could find any major fluctuations in funds conditions by taking financial "snapshots" in more closely spaced intervals. As we will see shortly, the cash budget is a more direct way of tracing the ups and downs of funds requirements within the forecast period. Before turning to the cash budget, however, we will briefly discuss the further interpretation of balance sheet changes by means of funds flow analysis.

Pro Forma Funds Flow Statement

As we observed in Figure 4–2, some very significant changes took place between the beginning and ending balance sheets of the forecast period. A *pro forma funds flow statement* will help us to highlight the funds movements reflected in these changes and their impact on the company's financial condition. Using the techniques discussed in Chapter 2, we can take the changes in the balance sheet and selected information from the operating statement to construct the pro forma funds flow analysis shown in Figure 4–3. Under the prevailing practice we have divided the funds flows into funds from operations, funds for investment, and funds from financ-

Figure 4–3
XYZ CORPORATION
Pro Forma Funds Flow Statement
For the Quarter Ended December 31, 1990

	Sources	Uses
Funds from operations		
Net income	$ 160	$ —
Depreciation (noncash charge)	600	—
Working capital changes		
Decrease in cash	200	—
Decrease in receivables	1,200	—
Decrease in finished goods	750	—
Decrease in payables	—	410
Decrease in accrued taxes	—	310
Totals	2,910	720
Net funds from operations	2,190	
Funds from investments		
Proceeds from sale of machinery	550	—
Funds for financing		
Repayment of notes	—	1,500
Repayment of construction loan	—	2,900
Proceeds from stock option	250	—
Totals	250	4,400
Net funds for financing		4,150
Funding requirement as of 12/31/90	1,410	—
	$4,150	$4,150

ing. From the data displayed, it becomes quite obvious that the reduced *operations* are expected to release a significant net amount of working capital, $1.43 million, of which $1.2 million comes from reduced accounts receivable alone. This is in addition to the cash flow from operations (i.e., net income plus depreciation of $0.76 million), for a total of $2,190,000.

The net sources from operations are outweighed by significant funds needs for financing, however. To meet various financial obligations currently due, $4.4 million is scheduled for repayment. The $1.5 million notes payable represents repayment of a *seasonal* funds need, which is made possible by the significant release of *working capital* as the seasonal low approaches.

The sale of machinery and the proceeds from the exercise of stock options assist somewhat in this, but the funding gap remaining is still $1.41 million. It should be clear by now that if we make any *changes* in the various assumptions behind the pro forma projections, the size of the funding gap will be directly affected. In fact, it is often very helpful to test the sensitivity of the projected conditions to changes in key assumptions, such as sales volume, collection patterns, and major cost deviations.

Funding stresses *during* the forecast period still have not been dealt with, however. These occur because the gradual *release* of operating funds caused by the seasonal slowdown during the quarter will *lag the decline in volume*. Thus the exact scheduling of the repayments within the three-month period could cause significant shortfalls. If all repayments came due in *October*, for example, the funding gap would be much *higher during that month* than the pro forma statements suggest for the end of December. As we will see, only a detailed cash budget will reveal such hidden fluctuations.

To summarize, pro forma statements are a convenient and relatively simple way of projecting *expectations* about a company's performance. To create these statements requires maintaining *consistent* assumptions between the operating statement and the balance sheet, but otherwise a great degree of *subjective judgment* is involved. The balancing element in the pro forma balance sheet is the *funds need* or *funds excess* resulting from the conditions assumed. This *plug* will vary as assumptions are changed. Pro forma funds flow statements help highlight the funds movements implied by changes in the balance sheet. Pro forma analysis is *limited* by the *static* nature of the balance sheet that shows funds needs only at a specific point in time and not their ebb and flow. A more dynamic *intraperiod* analysis requires either generating several short-term pro forma statements at key decision points or making the budgetary forecast embodied in the cash budget.

CASH BUDGETS

Cash budgets, or *cash flow statements,* are very specific month-by-month or even week-by-week planning vehicles normally prepared by the financial staff of a company. They focus exclusively on the specific *incidence* of cash receipts and payments. The financial manager who uses a cash budget is very interested in observing the *changing levels* of the cash account, which must be maintained at a level sufficient to allow timely payments of obligations as they become due. As a consequence, the financial manager must plan *cash activity* to reflect in very specific detail the *timing* of the inflows and outflows of cash in response to planned operational and invest-ment activities.

As we will see, cash budgets again show the level of funds needs or excesses. The level at the *end of the period* will exactly *match* the level shown on the *pro forma balance sheet* if the cash budget was prepared using the *same* basic assump-tions employed in generating the pro forma statements.

Cash budgeting, in principle, is quite simple. It is similar to personal budgeting, where bills due are matched with receipts from paychecks, dividend checks, bank interest payments, and so on. This matching is necessary to determine funds requirements as they affect the cash balance available for pay-ment. The cash balance will probably fluctuate from day to day, week to week, or month to month. If a company's collections from credit sales tend to lag for weeks while wages and purchases must be paid currently, serious cash shortages can occur. (The reader will recall the discussion in Chapter 2, where the concept of lags was explored in relation to funds flows.) Similarly, cash payments for nonrecurring items, such as outlays for capital equipment, may cause temporary funding problems that must be met. Given what it covers, the cash budget is the ultimate expression of funds flow analysis because in the end *all funds movements have a cash effect*.

In preparing a cash budget, a *time schedule* of estimated receipts and payments of cash must be laid out. This schedule shows, period by period, the net effect of projected activity on the cash balance. The selection of the time *intervals* covered by the cash budget depends on the nature of the business and the trade terms under which it operates. If daily fluctuations are likely to be large, as in the banking business, day-to-day projections will be necessary. In other cases, weekly, monthly, or even quarterly projections will suffice.

Let us now turn to the data of XYZ Corporation and prepare a *monthly* cash budget for the last quarter of 1990. This will increase our understanding of the funds flow picture beyond that provided by the pro forma analysis alone. In Figure 4–4 on pages 154–55 we have presented some of the basic data of the company's operations regarding sales, production, and purchases. We show two months of actual activities *prior* to the forecast period because due to the credit terms of sales and purchases, the *cash lag* from these past months will influence the three months being projected.

The lag effect can be clearly demonstrated in the first of the *cash receipts*, collection of receivables. On the assumption that the company's customers will continue to remit within the 30-day terms, cash receipts for any month should be the sales made in the *prior* month. In contrast, if there were a *60-day* collection period, collections would represent the sales made *two* months earlier. Thus, any expected change in customer behavior or in the credit terms themselves must be reflected in a different receipts pattern. It is often helpful to draw a scale of time periods on which the days, weeks, or months of dollar *sales* are first recorded when they occur. Using this scale, any assumed collection experience can be simulated by "staggering" (that is, delaying) the dollar *receipts* according to the appropriate number of days. For example, a schedule of sales and collections on 30-day credit would appear as follows:

	January	February	March	April	May	June
Credit sales	$25,000	$30,000	$40,000	$42,000	$35,000	$30,000
Collections	(Dec. sales)	25,000	30,000	40,000	42,000	35,000

The *proceeds* from the exercise of stock options and from the sale of used machinery have been budgeted in their respective months of incidence. The *total* cash receipts for each month show a declining pattern that lags the declining sales, but this is moderated somewhat by the nonoperating proceeds from options and sale of used machinery.

As we turn to the disbursements, we encounter another lag in payments for purchases made on credit. Under XYZ's normal credit terms of 45 days we can assume that the company's payments will lag by 45 days. Consequently, purchases made in the second half of August and the first half of September will be paid for in October, with a similar pattern repeating itself in November and December. In other words, one month's worth of purchases staggered by 45 days will be paid in a given month. Again, a time scale with 15-day intervals will help illustrate this payment pattern.

Inasmuch as the last quarter of 1990 is projected in a *declining pattern* to December's seasonal low in sales and manufacturing activities, the staggered timing due to credit terms shifts somewhat higher cash receipts as well as payments into a period of low operating activity. Funds are *released* in the process, as we would expect when we recall the discussion of changes in operations and their funds impact in Chapter 2. This funds result matches what we observed in the totals provided by the pro forma analysis. Had there instead been a *rising* volume of operation, more cash would have become tied up in working capital, and additional funds would be required. In that case the cash budget would have reflected the lag effect of the lower activities of the earlier months. It should be appar-

Figure 4-4
XYZ CORPORATION
Sample Cash Budget for the Quarter Ended December 31, 1990
($000)

	August	September	October	November	December	Total for Quarter
Basic data:						
Unit sales	48,000	46,000	42,000	36,000	33,000	111,000
Unit production	50,000	50,000	35,000	34,000	31,000	100,000
Change in inventory	+2,000	+4,000	−7,000	−2,000	−2,000	−11,000
Sales volume (on credit)	$4,450	$4,250	$3,850	$3,350	$3,050	$10,250
Purchases (on credit)	760	740	520	500	460	1,480
Cash receipts:						
Collection of receivables—prior month's sales; normal terms of 30 days assumed			$4,250	$3,850	$3,350	$11,450
Proceeds from sale of stock options			-0-	250	-0-	250
Proceeds from sale of used machines at book value (original cost, $1,500)			-0-	-0-	550	550
Total cash receipts			4,250	4,100	3,900	12,250

Cash disbursements:

Payment for purchases*	750	630	510	1,890
Production payroll (from operating budget)	560	545	500	1,605
Manufacturing expenses (from operating budget)	1,265	1,260	1,235	3,760
Selling and delivery expenses (from sales budget)	350	345	335	1,030
General overhead expenses (from administrative budget)	200	200	200	600
Interest payment on debt	-0-	-0-	175	175
Principal payment on note payable	1,500	-0-	-0-	1,500
Federal tax payment	400	-0-	-0-	400
Payments on construction of new plant	-0-	2,000	900	2,900
Total cash disbursements	5,025	4,980	3,855	13,860
Net cash receipts (disbursements)	(775)	(880)	45	$(1,610)
Cumulative net cash flow	$ (775)	$(1,655)	$(1,610)	

Analysis of cash requirements:

Beginning cash balance	$1,450	$ 675	(205)	$ 1,450
Net cash receipts (disbursements)	(775)	(880)	45	(1,610)
Ending cash balance	675	(205)	(160)	(160)
Minimum cash balance	1,250	1,250	1,250	1,250
Cash requirements	$ 575	$1,455	$1,410	$ 1,410

* Normal terms of 45 days assumed. Payments therefore represent one month's purchases prior to last 1.5 months (e.g., half of August and half of September paid during October).

ent by now that there is a critical need for careful cash budgeting in a business where operating levels and payments swing widely.

Other cash disbursements, (*payroll, manufacturing expenses, selling and delivery, and general overhead*) are shown without lags, on the assumption that payments for these expenses and obligations are to be made within the month they are incurred. This assumption could be slightly incorrect in the case of payroll disbursements and certain manufacturing expenses. Such items could indeed lag by one or two weeks. How precisely these lags are dealt with is a function of the relative importance of the cash flow problems they represent.

Production-related payments, such as payroll and manufacturing expenses, are based on the declining pattern of *production* shown in the basic data section of Figure 4–4, which also reflects a gradual inventory reduction. Yet, in the pro forma operating statement for the period, cost of goods sold are normally based on the pattern of *selling* activities for ease of projection. Thus, the pro forma statement and the more detailed cash budget may differ because the assumptions concerning sales and production are different. To ensure complete consistency, it is therefore necessary to determine carefully whether the pattern of production is projected on a different basis than the pattern of sales.

As an example of such a potential difference, it is entirely possible that the seasonal low could be used by management to build up inventories in advance of the expected resurgence of sales. If that were so, the inventory assumption for the pro forma balance sheet would have to be adjusted upwards to show the build-up of inventories and the resultant additional funds need. The cash budget, in turn, would have to reflect the higher expenditures involved in producing for inventory. Recognizing differences in production and selling patterns is a key to refining the projection of company performance and to making cash budgeting results consistent with the pro forma statements.

The final result of our cash budget is a picture of the monthly cash effect of the operating plans on which it is based and the net funds needs or excesses each month. Note that the funds need at the end of December ($1,410,000) exactly matches the indication we received from the pro forma statements because the same assumptions were used throughout.

To summarize, cash budgets lay out in specific detail the *exact timing incidence* of cash receipts and disbursements. Like household budgets, they allow us to watch for *peaks and valleys* in cash availability and to schedule additional financing or repayments as needed. Unlike pro forma statements, which are limited to the beginning and end of a specific period, cash budgets can be drawn up for as many *intervals* as desired *within* a period to simulate the fluctuations in cash flow. Given the *same assumptions* in terms of the volume of production and sales and the handling of receipts, payments, credit, and so forth, the cash budget and pro forma statements will agree in terms of the funds needs or excesses at the *end* of the period covered.

OPERATING BUDGETS

The pro forma statements and cash budget we prepared for XYZ Corporation provide an *overall view* of the company's future performance. But in any sizable company, a hierarchy of more specific *operating budgets* are normally prepared. Operating budgets are essentially internal documents. As expressions of ongoing operations, such budgets are linked closely to the organizational structure of the company and to the type of performance measurement used by the particular company. These budgets are part of the planning process we mentioned earlier and are very useful as a background for pro forma and cash flow projections when a higher degree of detail and accuracy is desired.

Most managements structure their companies into manageable parts, for each of which an executive or manager is held responsible. The structure may be by *functions*, that is, sales, production, purchasing, and so on. In other cases, the organization may be composed of a set of smaller *profit centers*, each of which is expected to make a profit contribution to total

company performance. Even though there are countless variations of organizational structure, the principles of budgeting
and financial projection are straightforward and commonly applicable. Projection of operating results must take a form that
reflects the *scope* of the business unit involved. It must be
related to the elements *controllable* by the responsible manager and should be the basis on which the manager's *performance* is measured. These criteria obviously require that
operating budgets be carefully designed to fit the particular
unit's conditions and the management style of the company as
a whole. This means that there is a great deal of difference in
the approaches taken by various companies, even within the
same industry, and there may be differences within the same
company in terms of operating budgets for different organizational units. A growing body of literature has recognized the
criteria and impact of what is called *responsibility accounting*
within a given organization.

For purposes of our discussion a few illustrations of basic
operational budgeting will suffice. Among the various internal
operating budgets routinely prepared by XYZ Corporation are
the *annual sales budget by quarters* and *a quarterly factory
budget*. The sales budget is designed to show the sales unit's
projected contribution to total corporate profits, while the
factory budget reflects expected output and the total costs
incurred in producing the forecast volume. There are many
other types of profit and expense budgets, but we will limit our
discussion to these two, showing how they are used to provide
background information for the financial analyst preparing and
analyzing pro forma statements and cash budgets.

Sales Budget

As is shown in Figure 4–5, the sales manager must first
project the level of *unit sales* expected in the market territories
served. The projection is made by major product line. Most
likely this forecast will be built up from the individual judgments of the persons closest to current and potential customers. Economic conditions will likely be factored in, as will the

Figure 4–5
XYZ CORPORATION
Sample Quarterly Sales Budget
Year Ended December 31, 1990

	First	Second	Third	Fourth	Total
			Quarter		
Basic data:					
Unit sales (number of units):					
Product A	2,700	2,900	3,000	2,800	11,400
Product B	8,000	8,500	10,000	8,000	34,500
Product C	17,500	18,500	21,000	16,000	73,000
Price level (per unit):					
Product A . . . . $	145	$ 145	$ 150	$ 150	—
Product B	92	92	95	95	—
Product C	74	74	74	74	—
Number of salespersons	25	25	25	26	—
Operating budget ($000):					
Sales revenue . . . . $	2,423	$ 2,572	$ 2,954	$ 2,364	$10,313
Less: returns, allowances	25	26	28	24	103
Net sales	2,398	2,546	2,926	2,340	10,210
Cost of goods sold	1,916	2,051	2,322	1,868	8,157
Margin before delivery	482	495	604	472	2,053
Delivery expense	56	60	68	54	238
Gross margin	426	435	536	418	1,815
Selling expense (controllable):					
Salespersons'					
compensation	94	94	94	98	380
Travel and entertainment	32	32	32	33	129
Sales support costs	23	23	26	24	96
Total selling expenses . . .	149	149	152	155	605
Gross contribution	277	286	384	263	1,210
Departmental period costs	18	18	18	18	72
Net contribution	259	268	366	245	1,138
Corporate support (transferred):					
Staff support	23	25	25	27	100
Advertising	50	50	75	50	225
General overhead	63	63	63	63	252
Total corporate					
support	136	138	163	140	577
Profit contribution					
(before taxes) . . . . $	123	$ 130	$ 203	$ 105	$ 561

marketing strategies XYZ Corporation and its competitors are likely to follow.

Next, the *price levels* for each product must be estimated. Prices commonly are a function of three factors: industry pricing practices, the competitive environment, and the cost effectiveness of the company's manufacturing operations. Once price is established, *the sales revenue* can be calculated. Then the *cost of goods sold* for the products transferred internally or possibly purchased on the outside must be determined. The difference between the revenue and cost is the *margin before delivery* achieved by the sales unit. Next are the projected *delivery costs* to the customers, if these are borne by the company. Controllable *selling expenses* include *compensation* to sales personnel, *travel and entertainment*, and *sales support costs*.

The result is *gross contribution* from selling activities, which must be reduced by estimated *departmental period costs* (costs like rent, managers' salary, and other items that do not vary with short-term fluctuations in volume) to arrive at the *net contribution* provided by the department. After deducting allocated *corporate support costs*, which are staff support, advertising, and general overhead, the *profit contribution* for the period is established. In making all of these estimates, the sales manager can use past relationships and selected ratios, tempered by his or her judgment concerning changes in future conditions.

In our example, both basic data and dollar elements are broken down by quarters and estimated for the full year 1990. There is nothing unique about the format we have selected here, because many different arrangements of such information are possible to suit any specific organization. Generally, a company prescribes the format for its managers to follow in preparing projected activity budgets, both to maintain a degree of uniformity and to lessen the accounting problem of consolidating the projections when preparing overall financial forecasts. From the standpoint of financial projection, the sales and contribution data in our example are the raw material that goes into the total operating plan of the company.

Factory Budget

The sales budget we just discussed is basically a projection of *profit contribution*. However, companies also must forecast for operations or activities that involve only *costs* or expenses. An example of this type of projection, a cost budget for a factory, is shown in Figure 4–6. This time the data are given for each month. We have included three months and the total for the quarter. The period shown is the second quarter, dur-

Figure 4–6
XYZ CORPORATION
Sample Factory Budget
For the Quarter Ended June 30, 1990

	April	May	June	Total
Basic data:				
Number of shifts (5-day week)	3	3	3	3
Days worked	20	21	22	63
Hourly employees per shift	33	33	33	33
Number of machines	35	35	34	—
Unit production:				
Product A	1,000	1,050	1,100	3,150
Product B	2,400	2,510	2,640	7,550
Capacity utilization	94%	94%	96%	95%
Down time for repairs (hours)	–0–	36	–0–	36
Operating budget:				
Direct costs (controllable):*				
Manufacturing labor	$ 57,600	$ 60,500	$ 63,400	$181,500
Raw materials	53,800	56,400	59,200	169,400
Operating supplies	6,500	6,900	7,300	20,700
Repair labor and parts	7,300	12,400	6,500	26,200
Power, heat, light	4,200	4,500	4,800	13,500
Total direct costs	129,400	140,700	141,200	411,300
Period costs (controllable):				
Supervision	5,500	5,500	5,500	16,500
Support labor	28,500	28,500	28,500	85,500
Insurance, taxes	8,700	8,700	8,700	26,100
Depreciation	20,500	20,500	20,500	61,500
Total period costs	63,200	63,200	63,200	189,600
Total controllable costs	192,600	203,900	204,400	600,900
General overhead (allocated)	72,000	72,000	72,000	216,000
Total cost	$264,600	$275,900	$276,400	$816,900

* Where appropriate, unit costs can be shown.

ing which sales and production are expected to increase. Again, the amount of detail included and the presentation format are chosen to suit the particular needs and preferences of the organization. This time we selected to arrange the headings and data to show that certain cost items (both direct and period costs) are under the *control* of the local manager. (Other costs, like *allocated* general overhead, are transferred in from corporate headquarters and thus beyond the local manager's control.) This arrangement of the data will also be useful if the operating plan serves as a *control device* with which to measure the performance of the unit.

Both sales and costs budgets commonly include additional columns in which *actual* as opposed to projected figures are recorded. In addition, *variance* columns are frequently used to measure deviations from plan. We will not go into such refinements here, because our examples were only meant to show the type of internal budgeting and projection used formally or informally in most organizations preparatory to developing an overall financial forecast.

INTERRELATIONSHIP OF FINANCIAL PROJECTIONS

It should be obvious by now that the various types of projection presented in this chapter are closely related. If all three forecasts—pro forma statements, cash budgets, and operating budgets—are based on the *same* set of assumptions about receipts and collections, repayment schedules, operating rates, inventory levels, and so on, they will all precisely *fit together* in the fashion illustrated in Figure 4–7. The financial plans and the projected funds need or excess will *differ* only if different *assumptions* concerning funds flow are used, particularly in the pro forma statements on the one hand and the cash budget on the other. It is quite easy to reconcile pro forma statements and cash budgets, however, by carefully thinking through the key assumptions to be made, one by one, and by laying out formats that contain sufficient detail and background data.

Figure 4–7
Interrelationship of Financial Projections

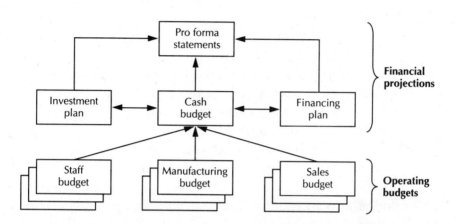

The diagram shows how the various operational budgets flow into a combined cash budget, which in turn is reinforced by specific data from the investment and financing plans (see below). The combined information supports the pro forma statements at the top of the diagram. Thus, pro forma statements are the all-encompassing expression of the expected conditions for the period ahead. As a consequence, if we choose to make pro forma statements *direct overall estimates,* as we discussed, rather than building them up from the budgets and plans of the company, they in effect will *imply specific assumptions* about *all* the other elements in the diagram.

We have not yet discussed some of the elements shown in Figure 4–7. *Staff budgets* are spending plans based on the expected cost of operating various service functions of a company. These budgets are prepared and used in the same fashion as other expense budgets.

Investment plans are projections of new outlays for land, buildings, machinery and equipment, and related incremental working capital, as well as major outlays for new products and services, expanding markets, new technology, and so forth. They may also contain plans to *divest* any of the company's fixed assets. We recall that XYZ Corporation made a minor reduction in its capital investments by selling some used machines while a recently constructed plant was in the final stages of payment, as evidenced by the amount that had become due and payable to the contractor. This facility investment was already reflected on the actual balance sheet of September 30, 1990, largely supported by long-term debt raised earlier. Only the current contractor payment was properly scheduled as a pro forma cash disbursement. The company might consider raising some additional long-term debt to fund the new facility, as operations are not providing enough cash flow to pay off the contractor liabilities.

Financing plans are schedules of proposed future additions to or reductions in indebtedness or ownership funds during the forecast period. They may involve significant expansion or restructuring of a company's capital structure, depending on the projected capital requirements. XYZ Corporation planned no specific future financing, but provisions would have to be made for financing the sizable funds need established with the pro forma analysis and to avoid having to strain its current funds as the plant is paid off.

A word about projection methodology should be added here. Any form of financial projection involves both an examination of *past* trends and specific assumptions about *future* behavior of revenues, costs, expenses, and other receipts and payments. Past trend analysis may range from simple "eyeballing" of obvious patterns to applying a variety of statistical methods to the available data in order to establish a trend line or curve as the basis for judging future conditions. The projection of key variables may start with such a trend, but the hard judgments about likely changes must override the temptation merely to extrapolate past conditions. The mathematical elegance of statistical methods should not be allowed to supplant the effort of making realistic future assumptions, both about specific company and market conditions, industry performance, and the national and world economic outlook affecting the likely financial performance of the business. The reader is directed to the references and to Appendix II for selected information on both forecasting techniques and sources of information that will assist the analyst in the technical and judgmental aspects of financial projection.

FINANCIAL MODELING AND SENSITIVITY ANALYSIS

In recent years the computer software available for financial modeling has vastly expanded the financial analyst's ability to explore the consequences of different assumptions, conditions, and plans. In principle, these software packages are no more than mathematical representations of key financial accounting relationships, ratios and formats, supported by automatic subroutines that calculate, update, and display data and results in whatever form is desired. The process is based on the *very same* steps and reasoning discussed in this chapter.

A full-fledged financial model encompasses elements such as the company's accounting procedures, depreciation schedules, tax calculations, debt service schedules, debt covenants and restrictions, inventory policies, and so on. With financial modeling and spreadsheets, the data, assumptions, and format can be "custom tailored" so that the financial analyst can reflect the specific characteristics of a given company. With the help of such a model, the analyst can calculate the projected results of conditions expected by the company. Ease of operation allows the analyst to examine several sets of assumptions and assess alternative outcomes.

The major difference between the projection techniques discussed in this chapter and the use of spreadsheets and computer models basically only involves the *degree of automation* of the process. A cash budget done by hand is essentially a model of the cash-flow pattern of the company. In constructing such a budget, the analyst must take into account corporate policies regarding accounting methods, tax reporting, and other detailed operating rules. These constraints can also be incorporated into a basic financial planning software package.

The difference is that the computer can "run" different options, while simultaneously tracking all important interrelationships much more easily and quickly than is possible when an analysis is done by hand, as is implied in Figure 4–8.

The financial modeling software available on the market is constantly evolving, and the reader should familiarize him- or herself with the latest offerings available. In scope, the modeling packages range all the way from spreadsheets with which to calculate simple condensed pro forma statements to highly sophisticated representations of a company's financial accounting system. In the latter case the generalized model is extensively refined, with the help of the company's financial staff, to reflect the company's specific situation. Some com-

Figure 4–8
Financial Modeling:
An Overview of Relationships between Inputs and Outputs

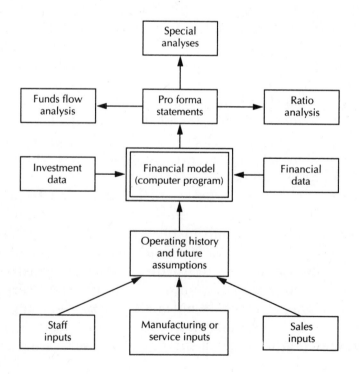

panies have developed models that not only will calculate the results of specific sets of assumptions, but also contain "optimizing routines" that select the most desirable alternative investment and financing patterns according to criteria stipulated by management. Other models include statistical projection programs that can be used for initial trending of key variables from past experience. It is clearly beyond the scope of this book to treat in detail the vast number of concepts and specialized techniques involved in the building and use of computerized financial models.

Figure 4–8 depicts a broad overview of the major relationships represented in a full-fledged model. The central element is the software program that governs the calculations and displays, with the inputs coming from various sources and the outputs grouped into our familiar categories of analysis.

Sensitivity Analysis

One of the advantages of modeling is the ability to perform *sensitivity analysis* with considerable ease. This type of analysis involves selecting a few key conditions and altering them to determine the sensitivity of the result to such changes. For example, one of the key assumptions in our pro forma analysis of XYZ Corporation was the usual seasonal pattern of an 18 to 20 percent decline in sales volume in the last quarter. If there were reason to believe that a more serious drop might occur, the analyst could estimate the dollar decline in contribution from each additional 1 percent decrease in volume. If all other conditions were to remain the same, that dollar decline would be the *lost contribution* from the units left unsold. The impact on funds needs would be traced by adjusting aftertax profits and by recognizing that there would be a change in working capital because sales levels are lower, except in inventory where the unsold units might remain. If prices were considered unstable, a series of assumptions about the effect of lower prices for one or all of the product lines could be traced. In every case the critical test would be the sensitivity of the funds need to the changes in *each* of the three months. Clearly, many other tests could be made and related to the altered result brought about by the change in a given assumption.

The key to this type of reasoning is the analyst's judgment as to which elements in the operating and financial patterns being projected are *most subject* to variability. Then the task is to simulate how sensitive the desired result is to each change. Given such a range of results, the decision maker using the analysis can judge the *riskiness* of the proposed course and adjust operating and financial policies accordingly. A computer model is *not critical* to making such sensitivity test. Even our simple pro forma statements and cash budgets can be easily modified to answer basic questions of this sort. Nonetheless, with relevant software, the analyst can examine many more possibilities and determine the impact of a far greater number of assumptions. Sensitivity tests can be performed on more than one variable *simultaneously*, and whole *scenarios* can be developed with the financial impact reflected in the output. We will return to sensitivity analysis again in later chapters.

SUMMARY

The principles of financial projection discussed in this chapter revolve around the use of *pro forma statements* and various types of *budgets*. We observed that financial projection is only *part* of the broader process of *business planning*. Financial projection can be expressed in the familiar form of financial statements and in many specifically tailored budget formats. The process is *simple* in that it represents an orderly way of sorting out the financial impact of investment, operational, and financing decisions. The process is *difficult* in that judgments about *future* conditions are fraught with uncertainty, as planning of any sort must be. It is here that the use of *sensitivity analysis*, the calculation of the impact of *alternative assumptions* can narrow the range of uncertainty. Financial projection basically is modeling of the future in the context of operational and policy constraints. To the extent that more detail and more options for future plans are desired, automation of the process with the help of computer-based *financial modeling* can yield the significant benefits of speed, accuracy, and greater insight.

SELECTED REFERENCES

Anthony, Robert N., and James S. Reece. *Accounting: Text and Cases*. 8th ed. Homewood, Ill.: Richard D. Irwin, 1988.

Murdick and Georgoff. "The Manager's Guide to Forecasting." *Harvard Business Review*, March/April 1986.

Ross, Stephen; Randolph Westerfield; and Jeffrey Jaffe. *Corporate Finance*. 2nd ed. Homewood, Ill.: Richard D. Irwin, 1990.

Seitz, Neil. *Business Forecasting on Your Personal Computer*. Reston, Va.: Reston Publishing Company, 1984.

Vancil, Richard F., and Benjamin R. Makela, eds. *The CFO Handbook*. Homewood, Ill.: Dow Jones-Irwin, 1986.

Van Horne, James C. *Financial Management and Policy*. 8th ed. Englewood Cliffs, N.J.: Prentice-Hall, 1989.

Weston, J. Fred, and Thomas E. Copeland. *Managerial Finance*. 9th ed. Hinsdale, Ill.: Dryden Press, 1989.

SELF-STUDY EXERCISES AND PROBLEMS

(Solutions are provided in Appendix III)

1. Complete the following exercises, based on these selected data about a company. Consider each exercise separately.

Total assets on 12–31–90	$2,750,000
Sales for the year 1990	9,137,000
Current assets on 12–31–90	1,315,000
Long-term debt on 12–31–90	210,000
Current ratio on 12–31–90	2.4:1
Cost of goods sold for 1990	83% of sales
Purchases during 1990	$5,316,000
Depreciation for 1990	174,000
Net profit after taxes for 1990	131,000
Taxes on income for 1990	112,000

a. Currently the company's accounts receivable outstanding are 18 days' sales. To meet competitive pressures in 1991, the company will have to extend credit to an average of 40 days' sales to maintain operations and profits at 1990 levels. No other changes are contemplated for the next year, and sales and operations are expected to continue at 1990 rates. What is the impact of this change in credit policy on corporate funds needs? Will the company have to borrow? What if credit had to be extended to 60 days? Discuss.

b. The inventory levels maintained by the company have averaged $725,000 during 1990 with little fluctuation. If turnover were to slow to seven times (average inventory in cost of goods sold) due to a switch to a consignment policy, what would the financial impact be? Assume no change in sales levels. What other changes are likely to take place, and how would these affect the company's financial stance? What if turnover rose to 11 times? Discuss.

c. Payment for purchases has been made under normal trade terms of 2/10, n/30 with discounting done as a matter of policy. Suppliers anxious for business are beginning to offer 2/15, n/45 terms, which will become universal during the coming year. What would the financial impact of this change be if the company were to follow its policy of discounting purchases? What trade-off has to be considered? Discuss.

d. If the company is planning capital expenditures of $125,000 and simultaneously is planning to pay dividends at the rate of 60 percent of net profits, what are the financial implications, assuming all other elements are unchanged?

e. If sales are expected to grow 10 percent for the following year, with all *normal* relationships under (a) through (c) unchanged, what financial considerations arise? How would the intentions of (d) look then? Discuss.

2. In September 1991, ABC Company, a manufacturing firm, was making budget plans for the 12 months beginning November 1, 1991. Projected sales volume was $4,350,000, as compared to an estimated $3,675,000 for the fiscal year ended October 31, 1991. The best estimates of the operating results for the current year are shown in the operating statement.

The projected increase in volume of operations was expected to bring improvements in efficiency, while at the same time some of the cost factors would continue to rise absolutely, in line with past trends. Following this statement are the specific working assumptions with which to plan financial results for the next year.

ABC COMPANY
Estimated Operating Statement
For the Year Ended October 31, 1991
($000)

		Amount		Percent
Net sales		$3,675		100%
Cost of goods sold:				
Labor	$919			25.0
Materials	522			14.2
Overhead	743			20.2
Depreciation	133	2,317	3.6	63.0
Gross profit		1,358		37.0
Selling expense	305			8.3
General and administrative expenses	323	628	8.8	17.1
Profit before taxes		730		19.9
Income taxes		336		9.1
Net income		$ 394		10.8%

Assumptions for fiscal year 1992.

Manufacturing labor would drop to 24 percent of direct sales because volume efficiency would more than offset higher wage rates.

Materials cost would rise to 14.5 percent of sales because some price increases would not be offset by better utilization.

Overhead costs would rise above the present level by 6 percent of the 1991 dollar amount, reflecting higher costs, and additional variable costs would be encountered at the rate of 11 percent of the incremental sales volume.

Depreciation would increase by $10,000, reflecting the addition of some production machinery.

Selling expenses would rise more proportionately, by $125,000, because additional effort would be required to increase sales volume.

General and administrative expense would drop to 8.1 percent of sales. Income taxes (federal and state) were estimated at 46 percent of pretax profits.

Develop a pro forma operating statement for the ABC Company and discuss your findings.

3. In December 1991, the DEF Company, a distributor of stationery products, was planning its financial needs for the coming year. As a first indication, the firm's management wished to have a pro forma balance

sheet as of December 31, 1992, to gage funds needs at that time. Estimated financial condition as of December 31, 1991, was reflected in this balance sheet:

DEF COMPANY
Estimated Balance Sheet,
December 31, 1991

Assets

Current assets:

Cash	$ 217,300
Receivables	361,200
Inventories (pledged as security)	912,700
Total current assets	1,491,200

Fixed assets:

Land, buildings, trucks, and fixtures	421,500
Less: Accumulated depreciation	217,300
Total fixed assets	204,200
Other assets	21,700
Total assets	$1,717,100

Liabilities and Net Worth

Current liabilities:

Accounts payable	$ 612,300
Note payable—bank	425,000
Accrued expenses	63,400
Total current liabilities	1,100,700
Term loan—properties	120,000
Capital stock	200,000
Paid-in surplus	112,000
Earned surplus	184,400
Total liabilities and net worth	$1,717,100

Operations for the ensuing year were projected using the following working assumptions to plan the financial results:

Sales were forecast at $10,450,000, with a gross margin of 8.2 percent.

Purchases were expected to total $9,725,000, with some seasonal upswings in May and August.

Accounts receivable would be based on a collection period of 12 days, while 24 days' accounts payable would be outstanding.

Depreciation was expected to be $31,400 for the year.

Term loan repayments were scheduled at $10,000, while bank notes payable would be allowed to fluctuate with seasonal needs.

Capital expenditures were scheduled at $21,000 for trucks and $36,000 for warehouse improvements.

Net profits after taxes were expected at the level of 0.19 percent of sales.

Dividends for the year were scheduled at $12,500.

Cash balances were desired at no less than $150,000.

Develop a pro forma balance sheet and discuss your findings.

4. In September 1991, the XYZ Company, a department store, was planning for cash needs during the last quarter of 1991 and the first quarter of 1992. The Christmas buying season always meant a considerable strain on finances, and the first planning step was development of a cash budget. The following data were available for this purpose:

Projected sales (half for cash, half charged on 90-day account):

October	$ 770,000	January	$650,000
November	690,000	February	580,000
December	1,010,000	March	720,000

Projected purchases (half on n/45; 40 percent on 2/10, n/30; 10 percent for cash):

October	$610,000	January	$320,000
November	535,000	February	450,000
December	290,000	March	480,000

Projected payments on purchases as of 9-30-91:

Due by October 10 (2% discount)	$ 60,000
Due by October 31 (net 45)	257,000
Due by November 15 (net 45)	113,000
Total	$430,000

Projected collections of receivables as of 9-30-91:

Due in October	$215,000
Due in November	245,000
Due in December	265,000
Total (bad debts negligible)	$725,000

Projected financial data:

Minimum cash balance required	$75,000
Beginning cash balance (October 1)	95,000
Mortgage payments (monthly)	7,000
Cash dividend due December 31	40,000
Federal taxes due January 15	20,000

Projected operations: salaries and wages average 19 percent of sales, cash operating expenses average 14 percent of sales.

Develop a monthly cash budget to show the seasonal funds requirements. Discuss your findings.

5. A newly formed space technology company, the ZYX Corporation, was in the early stages of planning for the first several months of operations. The initial capital put up by the founders and their associates amounted to 250,000 shares of $1 par value stock. Furthermore, patents estimated to be worth $50,000 were provided by two of the principals in exchange for 50,000 shares of common stock. Equipment costing $175,000 was purchased with the funds, and organization expenses of $15,000 were paid. Operations were to start February 1, 1991.

Orders already in hand amounted to $1,400,000 of electronic devices, which at an estimated monthly output of $400,000 (sales value), represented almost four months' sales. More orders were expected from contacts made. Monthly operating expenses and conditions were estimated as follows:

Manufacturing labor	$ 60,000
Rent for building	18,500
Overhead costs	76,000
Depreciation	6,000
Write-off of patents	500
Selling and administrative expenses	55,000
Purchases of materials, supplies	125,000
Sale terms	n/30
Collection experience expected	45 days
Purchase terms	n/30
Raw materials inventory level	$ 60,000
Finished goods inventory level	145,000
Prepaid expenses (average)	12,000
Accrued wages	1 week's
Accrued taxes (40% effective rate)	As incurred

If the company wanted to maintain a minimum cash balance of $40,000, what would the financial situation be after six months of operations? Develop pro forma statements and discuss the likely timing of any funds needs. How are the next six months likely to affect this picture? Discuss your findings.

6. The ABC Supermarket's management expected the next six months (January 1, 1991, through June 30, 1991) to bring a variety of cash requirements beyond the normal operational outflows. A monthly cash budget was to be developed to trace the specific funds needs. The following projections were available for the purpose:

   a. Cash sales projected:

January	$200,000	April	$200,000
February	190,000	May	230,000
March	220,000	June	220,000

b. Cost of goods sold averages 75 percent of sales.

c. Purchases closely scheduled with sales volume. Payments average a 15-day lag behind purchases. December purchases were $168,000.

d. Operating expenses projected:

   1. Salaries and wages at 12 percent of sales, paid when incurred.

   2. Other expenses at an average 9 percent of sales, paid when incurred.

   3. Rent of $3,500, paid monthly.

   4. Income tax payments of $2,000 due in January, March, and June, and $3,500 due in April.

   5. Cash receipts from sale of property at $6,000 per month due in March, April, and May.

   6. Payments on note owed local bank due as follows: $3,000 in February and $5,000 in May.

   7. Repayments of advances to principals of the firm due at $3,000 each in January, March, and May.

   8. New store fixtures of $48,000 acquired, and four payments of $12,000 each due in February, March, April, and May.

   9. Old store fixtures with a book value of $4,500 scrapped, to be written off in January.

   10. Rental income from a small concession granted on the premises to begin at $300 per month in March.

Develop a cash budget as requested and show the effect of the operations and other elements described above on the beginning cash balance of $42,500. The principals of the firm would like to keep a cash balance of not less than $20,000 at any one time. Will additional funds be required? If so, when? Discuss your findings.

7. The XYZ Company, a fast-growing manufacturing operation, found its inventories in 1991 increasing faster than growth in sales. (As additional territories and customers had been developed, production schedules were stepped up in an effort to provide excellent service levels.) Also, collections had deteriorated, and the company's receivables represented two months' sales compared to normal 30-day terms. Because both conditions caused considerable pressures on the company's finances, a change to a level production schedule was considered beginning October 1, 1991, to allow inventories to be worked off while still providing employment to the company's full-time workers. Also, more effort would be expended on collections. A six-month trial of the new policy was to be analyzed in September before implementation, and the following assumptions and data were provided:

a. Current sales and forecast:

August	$1,925,000	December	$2,450,000
September (est.)	2,050,000	January	2,625,000
October	2,175,000	February	2,750,000
November	2,300,000	March	2,850,000

b. Current purchases and forecast (terms n/45):

August	$750,000	December	$650,000
September (est.)	675,000	January	650,000
October	650,000	February	650,000
November	650,000	March	650,000

c. Collection period, current and forecast:

August 31	63 days	December 31	40 days
September 30 (est.)	60	January 31	40
October 31	50	February 28	40
November 30	50	March 31	40

d. Materials usage beginning October: $825,000 per month.

e. Wages and salaries, beginning October: $215,000 per month, paid as incurred.

f. Other manufacturing expenses, beginning October: $420,000 per month, paid as incurred.

g. Depreciation: $43,000 per month.

h. Cost of goods sold has consistently averaged 70 percent of sales.

i. Selling and administrative expenses: October and November, 15 percent of sales; December and January, 14 percent of sales; and February and March, 12 percent of sales.

j. Payments on note payable: $750,000 each in November and February.

k. Interest due in January: $300,000.

l. Dividends payable in October and January: $25,000 each.

m. Income taxes due in January: $375,000.

n. Most recent balance sheet (estimated) is shown on the next page.

From the data given, develop a cash budget for the six months ended March 31, 1992, and pro forma statements for the quarters ended December 31, 1991, and March 31, 1992. Assume income taxes to be 50 percent, do not detail cost of goods sold, and assume no changes in accounts not specifically analyzed or projected here. What funds needs arise, and when? What if the collection speedup effort were unsuccessful and receivables stayed at 60 days? Discuss your findings about the policy changes being considered.

XYZ COMPANY
Estimated Balance Sheet
For September 30, 1991
($000)

Assets

Current assets:

Cash		$ 740
Accounts and notes receivable		3,975
Inventories:		
Raw materials	$ 2,725	
Finished goods	6,420	9,145
Total current assets		13,860
Plant and equipment	12,525	
Less: Accumulated depreciation	5,315	7,210
Other assets		1,730
Total assets		$22,800

Liabilities and Net Worth

Current liabilities:

Accounts payable	$ 1,050
Notes payable	4,120
Accrued liabilities	2,875
Total current liabilities	8,045
Long-term debt	5,250
Preferred stock	1,750
Common stock	5,000
Earned surplus	2,755
Total liabilities and net worth	$22,800

5   DYNAMICS OF THE BUSINESS SYSTEM

Having covered the basic techniques of performance analysis, funds flow analysis, and projection of financial requirements in the preceding three chapters, we need to revisit the business system as a whole and discuss the key dynamic aspects of financial management and planning. In Chapter 1 we described the interrelationship of financial yardsticks and management policies in broad terms. Now we are equipped to demonstrate the dynamics of the business system by focusing on the concept of *leverage*, both as it affects *operations* and as it impacts the *financing* decisions of management. With these concepts more firmly established, we can then turn to describe and demonstrate integrated *financial growth plans*, in which we will test the financial impact of policy changes in investment, operations, and financing. This integrated view of financial analysis allows us to visualize the total business system performance and to understand the concept of *sustainable growth*. The broader concept of *shareholder value* will be dealt with extensively in Chapter 9, which represents the capstone for most financial analysis.

The reader is encouraged to review the first section of Chapter 1, which describes the business system and the key interrelationships, many of which we will test in this discussion.

LEVERAGE

Leverage, as previously mentioned, refers to the often favorable condition of having a *stable element of cost support a wide range of volume levels*. *Operating leverage* means that part of the ongoing costs of the business are fixed during significant changes in operating volume. As a consequence, profits are boosted or depressed more than proportionally for variations in volume. Similarly, *financial leverage* occurs when a company's capital structure contains obligations with fixed interest rates. The effect of this condition is similar to the case of operating leverage. Again, earnings after interest are boosted or depressed more than proportionally as operating volume fluctuates. Operating and financial leverage are one and the same in principle.

However, there are differences in the specific elements involved and in the methods of calculation of each type of leverage. *Both* operating and financial leverage can be present in any business, and their respective impact on net profit will tend to be mutually *reinforcing*.

Operating Leverage

Distinguishing between fixed and variable costs, that is, those costs that vary with time and those that vary with the level of activity, is an old idea. This distinction is the basis for *break-even analysis*. The concept of "breaking even" essentially springs from the simple question of how many units of product or service a business must sell in order to *"cover" its fixed costs*. Presumably, prices are set at a level high enough to recover all direct, that is, variable costs, and leave a margin of *contribution* towards fixed costs and profit. Once sufficient units have been sold to accumulate the amount of contribution needed to *offset fixed*, or period *costs*, the margin from any *additional* units sold will turn into pure profit—unless a new layer of fixed costs has to be added at some future point as volume increases significantly. An understanding of this principle will improve our insight into how the operational aspects of a business relate to financial planning and projections. But in a broader sense it will allow us to appreciate the *distorting effect* that significant operating leverage may exert on the measures and comparisons of financial analysis.

A word of caution must be added here. There is nothing *absolute* in the concept of fixed costs, because in the longer run every cost element becomes variable. Costs are the consequence of management decisions, and can be altered by management decisions. Therefore, the breakeven concept must be treated with a degree of flexibility.

As we mentioned, introduction of fixed costs to the operations of a business tends to *magnify* profits at higher levels of operation. This is due to the incremental *contribution* each additional unit provides over and above the strictly variable costs incurred in producing it. Depending on the *proportion* of fixed and variable costs in the company's cost structure, the total incremental contribution from the added units can result in a sizable *overall jump in profit*. Once all fixed costs have been recovered by the contributions from a sufficient minimum number of units, profits grow *proportionately faster* than the growth in volume. Unfortunately, the same effect holds for *declining* volumes of operations, which result in a *decline in profit* and acceleration of losses *disproportionate* to the rate of volume reduction. Leverage is definitely a two-edged sword!

We can establish the basic definitions needed to analyze leverage as follows:

$$\text{Profit} = \text{Total revenue} - \text{Total cost}$$
$$\text{Total revenue} = \text{Volume (quantity)} \times \text{Price}$$
$$\text{Total cost} = \text{Fixed cost} + \text{Variable cost}$$

The formal way of describing leverage conditions is quite simple. We are interested in the effect on profit (I) of changes in volume (V). The elements which bear on this are the unit price (P), unit variable costs (C), and fixed costs (F). The relationship is as follows:

$$I = VP - (VC + F)$$

This formula can be rewritten as:

$$I = V(P - C) - F$$

which illustrates that profit depends on the number of goods or services sold times the difference between unit price and unit variable cost—which is the contribution to the constant element, fixed costs. As unit volume changes, the unit contribution $(P - C)$ times the change in volume will be equal to the total change in profit. Under normal conditions the constant, fixed costs (F) will remain just that, at least in the short term. The relative changes in profit for a given change in volume will, of course, be magnified as long as the fixed element remains. Another way of stating the leverage relationships is to use profit as a percent of sales (s), one of the ratios developed in Chapter 3. Using the previous notation.

$$s = \frac{I}{VP}$$

and defining I in terms of its components, the formula becomes:

$$s = \frac{V(P - C) - F}{VP}$$

and slightly rewritten:

$$s = \left[1 - \frac{C}{P} \right] - \frac{F}{VP}$$

This indicates that the profit-to-sales ratio depends on the contribution per unit of sales, less fixed costs as a percent of sales revenue. We observe that, to the extent fixed costs are present, they cause a reduction in the profit ratio. The larger the F, the larger the reduction. A change in volume, price, or unit cost, however, will tend to have a disproportional impact on s because F is constant.

Let us examine how the process works, using some concrete examples, Figure 5–1 shows the cost/profit conditions for a simple business with relatively high fixed costs of $200,000 in relation to volume of output and variable costs per unit. The company has a maximum level of production of 1,000 units, and for simplicity we assume there is no lag between production and sales. Units sell for $750 each, and variable costs of materials, labor, and supplies amount to $250 per unit. As a consequence, each unit provides a contribution of $500 toward fixed costs and profit.

The *break-even* chart is a simple representation of the conditions just outlined. At zero volume, fixed costs amount to $200,000, and these remain level as volume is increased until full capacity has been reached. Variable costs, on the other hand, accumulate by $250 per unit as volume is increased until a level of $250,000 has been reached at capacity, for a total cost of $450,000. Revenue rises from zero in increments of $750 until total revenue has reached $750,000 at capacity.

Where the revenue and variable cost lines cross (at 400 units of output), a *break-even condition* of no profit and no loss has been reached; the total cumulative revenue of $300,000 at that point is just sufficient to offset the fixed costs of $200,000 plus the total variable costs of $100,000 (400 units at $250 each). If operations increase beyond this point, profits are generated; while at volumes less than 400 units, losses are incurred. The break-even point can be found numerically, of course, by simply dividing the total fixed costs of $200,000 by the unit contribution of $500, which results in 400 units, as we expected:

$$\text{Break-even point } (I = 0): \frac{F}{P - C} = V$$

$$\text{Zero profit} = \frac{\$200,000}{\$500} = 400 \text{ units}$$

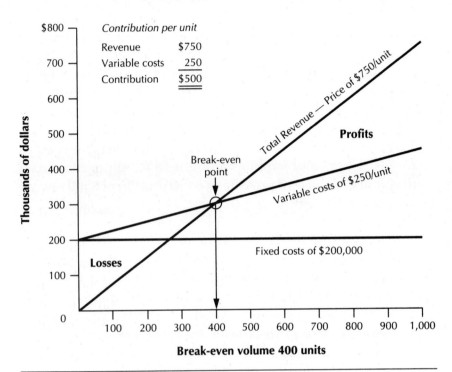

Figure 5–1
ABC CORPORATION
Simple Operating Break-Even Chart: Basic Conditions

Contribution per unit

Revenue	$750
Variable costs	250
Contribution	$500

Break-even volume 400 units

Profits and Losses as a Function of Volume Changes of 25 Percent

Volume	Increase	Profits	Increase
400	—	–0–	—
500	25%	$ 50,000	Infinite *
625	25	112,500	125%
781	25	190,500	69
976	25	288,000	51

Volume	Decrease	Losses	Increase
400	—	–0–	—
300	25%	$ 50,000	Infinite *
225	25	87,500	75%
169	25	115,500	32
127	25	136,000	18

* Infinite because the base is zero.

The most interesting aspect of the break-even chart, however, is the clear demonstration that increases and decreases in profit are *not proportional*. A series of 25 percent increases in volume above the break-even point will result in much larger percentage jumps in profit growth. The relevant figures for our example are displayed in the table under the chart. They show a gradual decline in the growth rate of profit from infinite to 51 percent. Similarly, as volume decreases below the break-even point in 25 percent decrements, the growth rate of losses goes from infinite to a modest 18 percent, as volume approaches zero. Thus, changes in operations *close* to the break-even point, whether up or down, are likely to produce *sizable* swings in earnings. Changes in operations well above or below the break-even point will cause lesser fluctuations.

We must be careful in interpreting these changes, however. As in any percentage analysis, the specific results depend on the starting point and the relative proportions of the components. In fact, operating management will generally be much more concerned about the *total* amount of change in profit than about percentage fluctuations. Moreover, it is easy to exaggerate the meaning of profit fluctuations unless they are carefully interpreted in the context of a company's total cost structure and its normal level of operations. Nevertheless, the concept should be clear—the closer to its *break-even point* a firm operates, the more dramatic will be the profit impact of volume changes. The financial analyst assessing the company's performance or making financial projections must attempt to understand where the level of its current operations is relative to normal volume and the break-even point and interpret the results of the analysis accordingly.

Furthermore, the greater the relative level of *fixed costs*, the more powerful the effect of leverage becomes. Our need to understand this aspect of the company's cost structure increases commensurately. In capital-intensive industries, such as steel, mining, forest products, and heavy manufacturing, most of the costs of production are fixed for a wide range of volumes. This condition tends to accentuate profit swings as such companies move away from break-even operations. Another example is the airline industry, which from time to time substantially increased the capacity of its flight equipment (e.g., from the 727 to the 747 jumbo jet). The fixed costs associated with owning and operating these aircraft caused sharp drops in profit for most airlines. As business and private travel rose to approach the new levels of capacity, several airlines experienced dramatic improvements in profits. In contrast, service industries, such as consulting firms, can directly influence their major cost—manpower—by adjusting the number of employees as *demand changes*. Thus, they are much less subject to the effects of the operating leverage phenomenon.

As we observed earlier, there are three main elements management can *influence* in the operating leverage relationship: *fixed costs*, *variable costs*, and *price*, all of which are in one way or another related to *volume*. We shall demonstrate the effect of changes in all three by *varying* the basic conditions in our example one by one.

Effect of Lower Fixed Costs.   If management can lower *fixed costs* through energetic reductions in overhead or using facilities more intensively, the effect can be a significant lowering of the break-even point. As a consequence, its effect of boosting profits will move to a lower level of operations. This change is shown in Figure 5–2. Note that lowering of fixed costs by one eighth has led to a corresponding reduction in break-even volume. It will now take one eighth fewer units contributing $500 each to recover the lower fixed costs. From the table we can observe that 25 percent volume changes from the reduced break-even point lead to increases or decreases in profit quite similar to our first example in Figure 5–1. Reducing fixed costs, therefore, is a very direct and effective way of lowering the break-even point to improve the firm's profit performance.

Figure 5–2
ABC CORPORATION
Simple Operating Break-Even Chart: Effect of Reducing Fixed Costs
(reduction of $25,000)

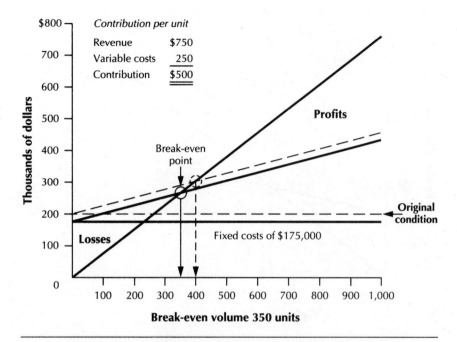

Break-even volume 350 units

Profits and Losses as a Function of Volume Changes of 25 Percent

Volume	Increase	Profits	Increase
350.........................	—	–0–	—
438.........................	25%	$ 44,000	Infinite *
547.........................	25	98,500	125%
684.........................	25	167,500	69
855.........................	25	252,000	51

Volume	Decrease	Losses	Increase
350.........................	—	–0–	—
262.........................	25%	$ 44,000	Infinite *
196.........................	25	77,000	75%
147.........................	25	101,500	32
110.........................	25	120,000	18

---

* Infinite because the base is zero.

Figure 5–3

ABC CORPORATION

Simple Operating Break-Even Chart: Effect of Reducing Variable Costs
(reduction of $25 per unit)

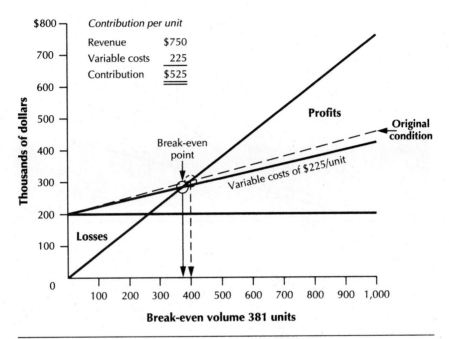

Break-even volume 381 units

Profits and Losses as a Function of Volume Changes of 25 Percent

Volume	Increase	Profits	Increase
381	—	–0–	—
476	25%	$ 49,900 *	Infinite †
595	25	112,375	125%
744	25	190,600	69
930	25	288,250	51

Volume	Decrease	Losses	Increase
381	—	–0–	—
286	25%	$ 50,150	Infinite †
215	25	87,125	75%
161	25	115,475	32
121	25	136,475	18

---

* First 25 percent change not exactly equal due to rounding.

† Infinite because the base is zero.

Effect of Lower Variable Costs.   If management is able to reduce the *variable costs* of production (direct costs)— thereby increasing the contribution per unit—the action can similarly affect profits at current levels and influence the movement of the break-even point itself. In Figure 5–3 we have shown the resulting change in the *slope* of the variable cost line, which in effect *widens* the area of profit. Loss conditions are similarly reduced. However, the change in break-even volume resulting from a 10 percent change in variable costs is *not* as dramatic as the change experienced when fixed costs were lowered by one eighth. The reason is that the reduction applies only to a small portion of the total production cost, because variable costs are relatively low in this example. (This illustrates the point we made earlier about having to consider the relative proportions in this type of analysis.) Only at the full capacity of $1,000 units does the profit impact of $25,000 correspond to the effect of the reduction of $25,000 in fixed costs in the earlier example. At lower levels of operations, lower unit volumes and the lesser impact of variable costs combine to minimize the effect. Nevertheless, the result is clearly an improvement in the break-even condition, and a profit boost is achieved earlier on the volume scale. Again, 25 percent incremental changes are tabulated to show the specific results.

Effect of Lower Prices.   Up to this point we have concentrated on *cost* effects that are largely under the control of management. In contrast, *price changes* are to a large extent dependent on the firm's competitive environment. As a result, price changes normally affect the competitive equilibrium and will directly influence the unit volume a business is able to sell. Thus it is not enough to trace the effect of raised or lowered prices on the break-even chart, but we must also anticipate the likely change in volume resulting from the price change. In other words, raising the price may more than proportionately affect the volume the company will be able to sell competitively, and the price action may actually bring about *lower total profits*. Conversely, lowering the price may more

Figure 5–4
ABC CORPORATION
Simple Operating Break-Even Chart: Effect of Reducing Price
(reduction of $50 per unit)

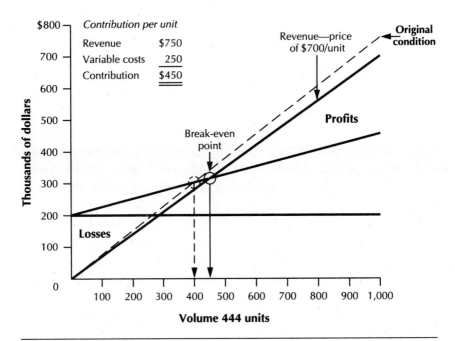

Profits and Losses as a Function of Volume Changes of 25 Percent

Volume	Increase	Profits	Increase
444	—	–0–	—
555	25%	$ 49,750 *	Infinite †
694	25	112,300	125%
867	25	190,150	69
1084	25	287,800	51

Volume	Decrease	Losses	Increase
444	—	–0–	—
333	25%	$ 50,150 *	Infinite †
249	25	87,950	75%
187	25	115,850	32
140	25	137,000	18

* First 25 percent change not exactly equal due to rounding.

† Infinite because the base is zero.

than compensate for the lost contribution per unit by boosting the total unit volume that can be sold against competition.

Figure 5–4 demonstrates the effect of lowering the price by $50 per unit, a 6.7 percent reduction. Note that this raises the required break-even volume by about 11 percent, to 444 units—in other words, the company needs to sell an additional 44 units *just to recoup* the loss in contribution of $50 from the sale of *every* unit. For example, if current volume was 800 units, with a contribution of $400,000 and a profit of $200,000, the price drop of $50 would require the sale of enough *additional* units to recover 800 times $50, or $40,000. This must be done despite a *lower* per unit contribution of $450. Consequently, 89 additional units have to be sold at the lower price—which represents a volume increase of 11 percent. Note that this requires a *more* than proportional change in unit volume (11 percent) versus change in price (6.7 percent).

Price changes affect the internal operating results, but they may have an even more pronounced and lasting impact on the competitive environment. If a more than proportional volume advantage—and therefore improved profits—can be obtained over a significant period of time after the price has been reduced, this may be a wise move. Otherwise, if price reductions can be expected to be quickly matched by other competitors, the final effect may simply be a drop in profit for everyone, because little if any shift in relative market shares would result. This is not the place to discuss the many strategic issues involved in pricing policy; the intent is merely to show the effect of this important element on the operating system and to provide a way of analyzing likely conditions.

Multiple Effects on Break-Even Conditions.   In the foregoing analysis, cost, volume, and price implications and their impact on profit were analyzed separately. In practice, the many conditions and pressures encountered by a business often affect these variables *simultaneously. Cost, volume, and price* for a single product may all be changing at the same time in subtle and often unmeasurable ways. Analysis is further complicated when *several products* are involved, as is true of

192

Figure 5–5
ABC CORPORATION
Generalized Break-Even Chart: Allowing for Changing Cost
and Revenue Conditions

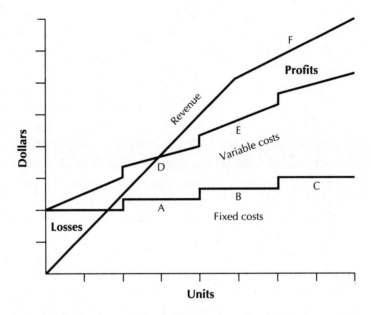

A. A new layer of fixed costs is triggered by growing volume.
B. A new shift is added, with additional requirements for overhead costs.
C. A final small increment of overhead is incurred as some operations require overtime.
D. Efficiencies in operations reduce variable unit costs.
E. The new shift causes inefficiencies and lower output, with more spoilage.
F. The last increments of output must be sold on contract at lower prices.

all major companies. In such cases, changes in the sales mix can introduce many complexities. Moreover, our simplifying assumption that production and sales are *simultaneous* does not necessarily hold true in practice; the normal lag between production and sales has a significant effect, and it must be taken into account. In a manufacturing company, sales and production can be widely out of phase. Some of the implications arising from this condition were discussed in Chapter 2, when we dealt with funds flow conditions under varying levels of operations, and in Chapter 3, when we examined the relationship of cash budgets and pro forma operating statements.

Up to this point, we have assumed that operating conditions were essentially *linear*, which allowed us to simplify our analysis of leverage and break-even conditions. A more *realistic* framework is suggested in Figure 5–5. The chart shows potential changes in both fixed and variable costs over the full range of operations. Possible changes in price-revenue developments are also reflected. In other words, changes in *all three* factors affecting operating leverage are reflected at the *same time*.

The chart further indicates that the simple straight-line relationships used in Figures 5–1 through 5–4 are normally only approximations of the "step functions" and the gradual shifts in cost and price often encountered under realistic circumstances. Inflationary distortions arising over time must also be considered. A few of the possible changes in conditions and sample reasons for these are described below the chart.

Financial Leverage

The basic fixed/variable cost relationship can also be used to examine the effect of various proportions of debt in the financial structure of a company, that is, to analyze financial leverage. A close similarity exists between operating and financial leverage in that both present an opportunity to gain from the fixed nature of certain costs in relation to increments of profit. With *financial leverage*, the advantage arises from the possibility that funds borrowed at a *fixed interest* rate can be used for investment opportunities earning a rate of return *higher than* the interest paid. The difference, of course, accrues as profit to the owners of the business. Given the ability to make investments that consistently provide returns *above* the going rate of interest, it will be to a company's advantage to engage in "trading on equity," as the concept is often called. This means borrowing as much as prudent debt management will permit and thereby boosting the return on owners' equity by the difference between the rate of return achieved and the rate of interest paid. The opposite effect will, of course, apply if the company earns returns below the rate of interest paid.

Figure 5–6 shows the leverage effect on return on equity under three conditions of return on net assets. All three curves are based on the assumption that funds can be borrowed at a low 4 percent per year *after taxes*, to dramatize the visual effect. If the normal return on the company's capitalization *before* interest and *after* taxes is 20 percent (curve A), growing proportions of debt cause a dramatic rise in return on equity. This return jumps to infinity (and with it the risk) as debt nears 100 percent—a condition not entirely unusual in recent take-overs and leveraged buyouts! Curves B and C show the lever-age effect under more modest earnings conditions. While

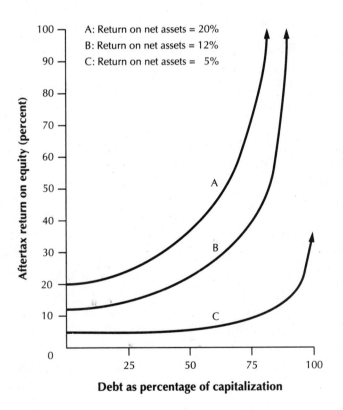

Figure 5–6
ABC CORPORATION
Return on Equity as Affected by Financial Leverage
(aftertax interest on debt is 4 percent)

somewhat lessened, the return on equity still shows sharp increases as the proportion of debt rises. As we observed before, leverage works also in the opposite direction. This is suggested by the fact that the distances between curves A, B, and C increase with higher debt levels. Should earnings drop, the plunge in return on equity can be massive.

To express the financial leverage relationships, we begin by defining the components, as we did in the case of operating leverage. Profit after taxes (I) now has to be related to equity (E) and long-term debt (D). We also single out the return on equity (R) and return on net assets (capitalization) before interest and after taxes (r), as defined in Chapter 3. Finally, the interest rate after taxes (i) must be noted.

First, we define the return on equity as

$$R = \frac{I}{E}$$

and the return on capitalization (the sum of equity and debt) as

$$r = \frac{I + Di}{E + D}$$

Using this formula we now restate profit (I) in terms of its components,

$$I = r(E + D) - Di$$

which represents the difference between the return on the total capitalization ($E + D$) and the aftertax cost of interest on outstanding debt. We then find that our first formula can be rewritten in this way:

$$R = \frac{r(E + D) - Di}{E}$$

which we can restate as

$$R = r + \frac{D}{E}(r - i)$$

This formulation highlights the leverage effect, represented by the positive expression after r, that is, the proportion of debt to equity, multiplied by the difference between the earnings power of net assets and the aftertax cost of interest. Thus, to the extent that debt is introduced into the capital structure, the return on equity is boosted as long as interest cost does not exceed earnings power.

When we apply the formula to one set of conditions that pertained in the graph of Figure 5–6, the results can be calculated as follows. Given $i = 4\%$, and $r = 12\%$, then for

1. $D = 0$, $E = \$100$ R equals 12.0%
2. $D = \$25$, $E = \$ 75$ R equals 14.7%
3. $D = \$50$, $E = \$ 50$ R equals 20.0%
4. $D = \$75$, $E = \$ 25$ R equals 36.0%

In this illustration, we have four different debt/equity ratios, ranging from no debt in the first case to a 3:1 debt/equity relationship in the fourth case. Given an aftertax cost of interest of 4 percent and the normal opportunity to earn 12 percent after taxes on net assets invested, the return on equity in the first case is also 12 percent after taxes—because no debt exists, and the total capitalization is represented by equity. As increasing amounts of debt are introduced to the capital structure, however, the return on equity is boosted considerably, because in each case the return on investment far exceeds the cost of interest paid to the debtholders. This was, of course, demonstrated in the graph of Figure 5–6. The reader is invited to work through the opposite effect, that is, interest charges in excess of the ability to earn a return on the investments made with the funds.

We are also interested in the impact of leverage on the return on net assets, or capitalization (r), which we obtain first by reworking the formula:

$$R = r + \frac{D}{E}(r - i)$$

into

$$r = \frac{RE + Di}{E + D}$$

Given $i = 4\%$, and $R = 12\%$, we can determine the *minimum* return on capitalization necessary to obtain a return on equity of 12%, for

1. $D = \quad\; 0, E = \$100$ r equals 12%
2. $D = \$25, E = \$\; 75$ r equals 10%
3. $D = \$50, E = \$\; 50$ r equals 8%
4. $D = \$75, E = \$\; 25$ r equals 6%

This is a useful way of testing the expected return from new investments. The approach simply turns the calculation around by fixing the return on equity and letting the expected return on investment vary. The calculation is straightforward. Note that the required amount of earnings on net assets, or capitalization, drops sharply as leverage is introduced, until it begins to approach the 4 percent aftertax interest cost. It will never quite reach this figure, however, because normally some small amount of equity must be maintained in the capital structure.

While it is simple to work out the mathematical relationships, the translation of these conditions into the appropriate financial strategies is much more complex. No management is completely free to vary the capital structure at will, and there are practical as well as legal and contractual constraints on any company to maintain some "normalcy" in the liability side of the balance sheet. While no absolute rules exist, the various tests of creditworthiness run the gamut of the ratios discussed in Chapter 3, particularly the measures oriented to the *lenders' point of view*. With enlightened self-interest in mind, lenders will impose upper limits on the amount of debt capital to be utilized by a potential borrower. For manufacturing companies the amount of long-term debt will normally range between 0 and 50 percent of their capitalization, while public utilities will range between 30 and 60 percent. Trading companies with highly liquid assets may have even higher debt proportions. The vast increase in leveraged buyouts during the 1980s has introduced a far higher than "normal" level of debt into the capital structures of many companies. In these cases financial leverage is used to the ultimate extent, which also vastly increases the exposure to the adverse effects of cash flow falling below expectations.

As stated before, we are interested in the effects of financial leverage on the broader area of financial planning for a company. As such, it is only one of several aspects affecting performance. In the next section, we will integrate financial leverage and the other key factors into a broader financial plan.

FINANCIAL GROWTH PLANS

Most managements aspire to successfully building ever *larger* businesses, whenever the opportunities in the marketplace permit this. Typically, common shareholders also expect *growing economic benefits* to accrue from share ownership. Thus it is not surprising that one important dimension of financial planning is continual testing of the *effects of growth on investment, operations, and financing*. The choices of financial policy open to management have different impacts on the expected results, and therefore must be tested along with the operational aspects of the plans. Management can set a variety of financial objectives and financial policies to direct and constrain the company's planning effort and the specific financial projections based on these plans. Foremost among the *financial objectives* is, of course, return on shareholders' equity. But this objective in turn is derived from specific objectives about *growth in earnings per share, growth in total profits, growth in dividends, growth in market value,* and *growth in shareholders' equity*. None of these objectives can *singly* be used as an overall standard, of course.

Foremost among the *financial policies* is the amount of financial leverage the company considers prudent, and subsidiary to it are the various measures of creditworthiness that management will wish to observe as constraints.

To demonstrate the buildup of an integrated financial plan that enables us to observe the effect of growth and its relationship to financial objectives and policies, we will begin by selecting just *one* of the objectives named above to work through a simple *conceptual model* of an hypothetical company. The format of this model is the basic *framework* that will allow us later to build a more detailed integrated financial plan. It will also serve to demonstrate the concept of *sustainable growth*.

Basic Financial Growth Model

A simple way of demonstrating the interrelated elements that affect growth in the business system is to use the objective of *growth in owners' equity*, as recorded on the balance sheet. Not only is this particular element easy to calculate, but it also indirectly encompasses the effects of profit growth and dividend payout.

Table 5–1 is such a simplified financial model that allows us to trace the several aspects affecting growth in a company, namely, leverage, profitability, earnings disposition, and financing. With its help we can demonstrate the effect *different financial policies* have on the objective of growth in owners' equity. Three cases have been worked out. The first shows an *unleveraged* company with $500,000 in equity that pays no dividends and reinvests all of its profits in operations similar to its present activities. The second case shows the same company, but in a leveraged condition with a 1:1 *debt/equity ratio*. In the third case, we take the conditions of the second case, but assume a *dividend payout* of 50 percent of earnings. All other financial conditions are assumed to remain constant.

Let us trace through the data for Case I. Given a gross return on net assets of 10 percent after taxes, the amount of net profit generated for the year is $50,000, all of which can be reinvested in the company's activities in the form of *new* investment for expansion, profit improvements, and so on. At the same time, we assume that the amount of annual depreciation is spent on maintaining the present facilities in sound operating condition. The reader will recall a similar assumption from the business system diagram in Chapter 1.

The results of Case I are a net return (after interest, which is 0 in this example) on net assets, or capitalization, of 10 percent, a return on equity of 10 percent, and therefore growth in

Table 5–1

Financial Growth Model: Three Different Policies ($000)

	Case I	Case II	Case III
Capitalization:			
Debt/equity ratio	0:1	1:1	1:1
Debt	–0–	$250	$250
Equity	$500	250	250
Net assets	$500	$500	$500
Profitability (after taxes):			
Gross return on net assets*	10%	10%	10%
Amount of profit	$50	$50	$50
Interest at 4%	–0–	10	10
Profit after interest	$50	$40	$40
Earnings disposition:			
Dividend payout	0%	0%	50%
Dividends paid	–0–	–0–	$20
Reinvestment	$50	$40	$20
Financing:			
Additional debt	–0–	$40	$20
New investment possible	$50	$80	$40
Results (in percent):			
Net return on net assets (capitalization)†	10%	8%	8%
Return on equity	10	16	16
Growth in equity‡	10	16	8

*Profits *before* interest, *after* taxes related to net assets (capitalization) as a measure of operational return on assets.

†Profits *after* interest and taxes related to net assets, as often shown in financial reports.

‡The growth in recorded equity based on earnings reinvested after payment of dividends.

equity of 10 percent. This condition holds because all profits are retained in the business for reinvestment. In Table 5–2 we have calculated three additional periods of operations for this particular company, without changing the assumptions. We can quickly observe that given stable policies and conditions, equity growth will indeed continue at 10 percent per year.

Case II differs only with regard to the use of *debt financing*. Because $250,000 has been borrowed at 4 percent after taxes, $10,000 of aftertax interest must be deducted from the amount of profit on net assets, which reduces the amount available for reinvestment to $40,000. If management wishes to maintain

Table 5-2
Financial Growth Model: Results of Three Different Policies Held Constant over Three Periods

	Case I			Case II			Case III		
	Period 1	Period 2	Period 3	Period 1	Period 2	Period 3	Period 1	Period 2	Period 3
Capitalization:									
Debt/equity ratio	0:1	0:1	0:1	1:1	1:1	1:1	1:1	1:1	1:1
Debt	-0-	-0-	-0-	$250	$290	$336.4	$250	$ 270	$291.6
Equity	$500	$550	$605	250	290	336.4	250	270	291.6
Net assets	$500	$550	$605	$500	$580	$672.8	$500	$ 540	$583.3
Profitability (after taxes):									
Gross return on net assets*	10%	10%	10%	10%	10%	10%	10%	10%	10%
Amount of profit	$ 50	$ 55	$60.5	$ 50	$58.0	$ 67.28	$ 50	$54.0	$58.32
Interest at 4%	-0-	-0-	-0-	10	11.6	13.46	10	10.8	11.66
Profit after interest	$ 50	$ 55	$60.5	$ 40	$46.4	$ 53.82	$ 40	$43.2	$46.66
Earnings disposition:									
Dividend payout	0%	0%	0%	0%	0%	0%	50%	50%	50%
Dividends paid	-0-	-0-	-0-	-0-	-0-	-0-	$ 20	$21.6	$23.33
Reinvestment	$ 50	$ 55	$60.5	$ 40	$46.4	$ 53.82	$ 20	$21.6	$23.33
Financing:									
Additional debt	-0-	-0-	-0-	$ 40	$46.4	$ 53.82	$ 20	$21.6	$23.33
New investment possible	$ 50	$ 55	$60.5	$ 80	$92.8	$107.64	$ 40	$43.2	$46.66
Results:									
Net return on net assets (capitalization)†	10%	10%	10%	8%	8%	8%	8%	8%	8%
Return on equity	10	10	10	16	16	16	16	16	16
Growth in equity‡	10	10	10	16	16	16	8	8	8
Growth in total profit (after interest)	—	10	10	—	16	16	—	8	8

*Profits *before* interest, *after* taxes related to net assets (capitalization) as a measure of operational return on assets.
†Profits *after* interest and taxes related to net assets, as often shown in financial reports.
‡The growth in recorded equity based on earnings reinvested after payment of dividends.

its policy of a 1:1 debt/equity ratio, an additional $40,000 can be borrowed. This raises the funds available for new investment to $80,000. Compared to Case I, the results have changed in several ways. Net return on capitalization has dropped to 8 percent because interest charges were introduced. As we expected, however, return on equity was boosted to 16 percent when leverage was introduced. Under these conditions, growth in equity can be similarly maintained at a level of 16 percent as long as all of the internally generated funds are reinvested in opportunities returning 10 percent, and matching amounts of debt funds are obtained and similarly invested.

In Case III, the introduction of *dividends* is the only change involved. A 50 percent payout reduces the internal funds available for reinvestment to $20,000, and also reduces the available additional debt to $20,000, under a 1:1 debt/equity ratio. Total funds for new investment have thus been reduced to $40,000. The dividend action seriously affects our assumed objective of growth in equity, which is now only half the level in Case II.

This very simple model illustrates the effects of a combination of decisions about investment, operations, earnings disposition, and financing strategy. It permits easy analysis of changes. Clearly the conditions have been oversimplified, but any refinements in the assumptions about such items as return on net assets, dividend payout ratios, and increments of additional borrowing, to name but a few, will only be variations on the basic theme expressed here.

Sustainable Growth

If growth in ownership equity were indeed considered to be the chief objective in our illustration, it would be useful to express the relationships on the basis of formulas similar to those used earlier.

In Case I, when no debt was employed and no dividends were paid, the following relationship held:

$$g = r$$

where g is growth in equity and r is the aftertax rate of return on capitalization. This formula simply expresses the fact that under these basic conditions, return on capitalization is *equal* to return on equity, and growth in equity is *equal* to return on equity.

In Case II, debt is introduced to the capital structure, and we add the leverage effect to the formula as we did before:

$$g = r + \frac{D}{E}(r - i)$$

where D is debt, E is equity, and i the interest rate after taxes. Leverage, as we discussed earlier, is a direct function of the proportion of debt in the total capital structure and the size of the margin between the return on investment and the interest cost of the funds, both after taxes. Because all earnings are reinvested, the rate of *growth* in equity must be equal to the *return* on equity—which is a combination of the return on net assets and the boost from leverage.

In Case III, the introduction of dividends slows the growth in equity because only the earnings *retained* can be reinvested. We have to adjust each of the two components of the formula to reflect this change. The factor p stands for the proportion of earnings retained as a percentage of total earnings, and the resulting formula is shown below:

$$g = rp + \frac{D}{E}(r - i)\,p$$

We now have a generalized formula for the *rate* of growth in equity that can be *sustained* by a business if *stable* conditions and policies hold. It is called the *sustainable growth formula*. If the business, over the long run, is able to invest its funds at the return indicated, if management maintains the debt/equity proportion stable and if interest costs and the dividend payout ratio do not change, then the growth in equity achieved will stabilize at the rate determined by the formula.

As we stated before, growth in equity is only one of several different types of financial objectives. Table 5–2 also shows the applicability of such modeling to another objective, this time the growth in earnings. As the last line of the "Results" section indicates, under our stable sets of policies, growth in total earnings (profit after taxes) stabilizes at the same rate as growth in equity. In fact, the formula used for growth in equity applies to this objective as well, because the profit growth depends on the same variables. As changes in policies are introduced, however, the fluctuations in year-to-year profit can be severe. The reader is invited to test the formulation, using these and other possibilities.

Similar models can be developed for the conditions affecting earnings per share, dividends per share, debt service, or any other financial area of the business. We will not attempt to go into detail about these, but rather let growth in equity and growth in earnings serve as examples. The capabilities of computer-based spreadsheets are of great assistance in these types of analysis.

Integrated Financial Plan

We can now turn to an illustration of an integrated financial plan, which in concept and format is based on the models in Tables 5–1 and 5–2. This time the focus is on taking a set of operating and financial assumptions and working them through this format. The XYZ company is considering a number of changes in its financial policies, and management wishes to study the impact of the combination of operating projections and policy modifications on its rate of growth and profitability over the next five years. The resulting integrated financial plan is shown in Table 5–3. It encompasses changes in debt/equity proportions, return on net assets, interest cost (changing as debt proportions rise), and dividend payout.

One of the key benefits of displaying the interrelationships in this way is that any obviously inconsistent conditions will show up in the results. As undesirable effects occur, the analyst can explore them with more tenable assumptions and calculate the impact of such changes. Planning frameworks of this kind are now easily obtainable either in preset form or through

Table 5-3
XYZ CORPORATION
Integrated Financial Plan:
Sample Five-Year Projection of Effect of Policy Changes
($000)

	Year 1	Year 2	Year 3	Year 4	Year 5
Capitalization:					
Debt/equity ratio	0.5:1	0.75:1	0.75:1	1:1	1:1
Debt	$300	$ 468	$ 489	$ 688	$ 728
Equity	600	624	652	688	728
Net assets	$900	$1,092	$1,141	$1,376	$1,456
Profitability (after taxes):					
Return on net assets	8%	7%	8%	8%	9%
Amount of profit	$ 72	$ 76	$ 91	$ 110	$ 131
Interest after taxes	4%	4%	4%	4.5%	4.5%
Amount of interest	$ 12	$ 19	$ 20	$ 31	$ 33
Profit after interest	$ 60	$ 57	$ 71	$ 79	$ 98
Earnings disposition:					
Dividend payout	60%	50%	50%	50%	40%
Dividends paid	$ 36	$ 29	$ 35	$ 39	$ 39
Reinvestment	$ 24	$ 28	$ 36	$ 40	$ 59
Financing and investment:					
New debt, old ratio	$ 12	$ 21	$ 27	$ 40	$ 59
New debt, revised ratio	156	–0–	172	–0–	–0–
New investment	$192	$ 49	$ 235	$ 80	$ 118
Results:					
Net return on net assets*	6.7%	5.2%	6.2%	5.7%	6.7%
Return on equity	10.0	9.1	10.9	11.5	13.4
Growth in equity	4.0	4.6	5.5	5.8	8.1
Earnings per share (100,000 shares)	$0.60	$ 0.57	$ 0.71	$ 0.79	$ 0.98
Dividends per share	0.36	0.29	0.35	0.39	0.39

*Return after taxes and interest.

readily adaptable spreadsheets for use on personal computers. Again, we stress that computing power does *not obviate the need to understand the relationships* we are demonstrating here.

XYZ Corporation has a total capitalization of $900,000 and starts with a debt/equity ratio of 0.5:1 (i.e., every dollar of equity is matched by 50 cents of long-term debt). Current return on net assets after taxes but before interest is 8 percent, which provides a profit of $72,000. Interest after taxes requires $12,000, which leaves a net profit of $60,000. With a dividend payout of 60 percent, cash dividends of $36,000 are required, which leaves a balance of $24,000 for reinvestment. Because the debt/equity ratio is to be maintained at 0.5:1, new debt of $12,000 can be incurred, supported by the increased equity.

In anticipation of major expansion plans, management has decided to *raise* its debt/equity ratio to .75:1 for Year 2. This would necessitate additional borrowing of $156,000 at the end of Year 1 *beyond* the increase of $12,000 that would be possible under the old debt/equity ratio. For simplicity, we have assumed that all changes take place at year-end.

The results for the first year show a net return on capitalization of 6.7 percent, a return on equity of 10 percent, and a growth in equity of 4 percent. Earnings per share are $0.60 and dividends per share are $0.36. The influx of new funds at the beginning of Year 2 raises the company's capitalization to well over $1.0 million.

For Year 2, the assumption about returns is *lowered* to reflect some normal inefficiencies as the new funds are invested; the overall return on net assets is 7 percent. After making proper allowance for interest payments, profits available are $57,000. A change in dividend payout to 50 percent requires only $29,000 in dividend payments, leaving $28,000 for reinvestment. Under the existing debt/equity ratio of 0.75:1 this amount is matched by $21,000 of new debt. These combined funds are added to the investment base for Year 3.

The process is repetitive as changes in policies are anticipated at the end of each year's operations. For example, we find a sizable new influx of capital in Year 4, as debt/equity proportions are changed to 1:1. Some additional interest cost is assumed, because higher rates will be charged by lenders as the capital structure becomes more leveraged and thus more risky. At the same time, however, the effectiveness of employing capital (return on net assets) has been left at 8 percent in

Years 3 and 4, but raised to 9 percent in Year 5, allowing some time for the new investments to become effective.

The results at the bottom of the table indicate some fluctuations in the net return on capitalization over the years, as either profitability or interest cost is changed. The return on equity, however, after dropping in Year 2, rises steadily to a sizable 13.4 percent in Year 5. Growth in equity jumps, after some intermediate boosts, to about double the original 4 percent rate in Year 5, that is, to 8.1 percent. Changes in total profit after interest are quite significant, as policy changes from year to year take effect. Similarly, growth in earnings per share fluctuates while dividends per share are somewhat diminished—showing little or no growth for most years.

The results obtained from using such a model raise some realistic questions. For example, it may not be prudent to change the dividend payout ratio in sizable steps as was done. We observe a drop in dividends per share of almost 20 percent in the second year. In the absence of general economic problems, the corporation's directors might be very reluctant to produce this result because a consistent dividend pattern is generally considered desirable. Therefore the dividend payout rate for Year 2 might be maintained near the original level with the purpose of avoiding a drop in dividends per share. The dividend payout percentage would be lowered only as total earnings rise sufficiently to permit paying a level or even growing dividend. At the same time, it might be useful to refine assumptions about return on net assets. We have used an overall percentage. It would be more realistic if we split the analysis into return on *existing* assets and return on *incremental* assets, taking into account the *lag* in expected returns on the new assets.

Such a refinement might be particularly useful if a company were diversifying its operations and expecting a highly *different return* from some of these new activities. More attention might also be paid to the assumption that depreciation *will be reinvested* without generating additional profits. A company that is consolidating some of its ongoing operations to free funds for redeployment in more diversified lines of business might *not be willing* to reinvest the equivalent of depreciation in old product lines.

The main purpose of this illustration is to show the overall usefulness of financial planning in the context of the business system, first introduced in Chapter 1. By observing the key results in response to a variety of different inputs, the analyst can arrive at a set of assumptions and recommendations that fairly reflect management's desires and capabilities. Many more refined formats are, of course, possible, and the process is greatly enhanced by the use of computer spreadsheets.

SUMMARY

In this chapter we have attempted to integrate some of the key concepts discussed in the earlier parts of the book into the *dynamic system framework* established in Chapter 1. We added an expanded treatment of *operating* and *financial leverage* to demonstrate the important impact of fixed cost elements on changing operating conditions. Through the use of a simplified *financial modeling* approach we demonstrated the need for *consistency* in operating and financial objectives and policies. We applied the modeling approach to the needs and policies of a company and developed an *integrated financial plan* with which we tested the impact of changes in the policies on the company's growth and performance.

In the end, the key test of financial analysis is the *viability of the methods* and results as *predictors* of future activity, which was a major point made in the earlier chapters. Often the optimal approach requires use of quite detailed and sensitive financial models of the business. Yet the outside analyst, and even insiders, will often be well served with *simplified yardsticks and models* that can sufficiently approximate solutions to planning alternatives. In this sense, the chapter draws together many of the points of earlier materials to give the reader an *overall*, albeit simplified, framework for analysis.

SELECTED REFERENCES

Anthony, Robert N., and James S. Reece. *Accounting: Text and Cases.* 8th ed. Homewood, Ill.: Richard D. Irwin, 1988.

Donaldson, Gordon. *Strategy of Financial Mobility.* Boston: Division of Research, Graduate School of Business Administration, Harvard University, 1969 (a classic).

Donaldson, Gordon. "Financial Goals and Strategic Consequences." *Harvard Business Review*, May-June 1985, p. 56.

Garrison, Raymond H. *Managerial Accounting: Concepts for Planning, Control, Decision Making*, 5th ed. Homewood, Ill.: Richard D. Irwin, 1980.

Porter, Michael E. *Competitive Strategy.* New York: Free Press, 1980.

Vancil, Richard F., and Benjamin R. Makela eds. *The CFO Handbook.* Homewood, Ill.: Dow Jones-Irwin, 1986.

Van Horne, James C. *Financial Management and Policy.* 8th ed. Englewood Cliffs, N.J.: Prentice-Hall, 1989.

Weston, J. Fred, and Thomas E. Copeland. *Managerial Finance.* 9th ed. Hinsdale, Ill.: Dryden Press, 1989.

SELF-STUDY EXERCISES AND PROBLEMS

(Solutions are provided in Appendix III)

1. The ABC Corporation, a manufacturing company, sells a product at a price of $5.50 per unit. The variable costs involved in producing and selling the product are $3.25 per unit. Total fixed costs are $360,000. Calculate the break-even point and draw an appropriate chart.

   a. Calculate and demonstrate the effect of leverage by noting the profit impact of moving from the break-even point in 20 percent volume increments and decrements.

   b. Calculate and graph separately the impact of a 50-cent drop in price, a 25-cent increase in variable cost, and an increase of $40,000 in fixed cost.

   c. Draw a graph and discuss the implications if an increase in fixed costs of $30,000 occurs after 175,000 units of production, the average price drops to $5.25 per unit after 190,000 units are produced, and variable costs drop to an average of $3 after 150,000 units. How are the calculations for break-even affected?

2. Calculate the effect of financial leverage under the following two conditions:

a. Interest rate is 5 percent after taxes; return on net assets is 8 percent after taxes.

b. Interest rate is 6 percent after taxes; return on net assets is 5 percent after taxes.

Develop the effect on return on equity in each case for debt as a percent of capitalization at 0 percent, 25 percent, 50 percent, and 75 percent. Discuss.

3. Develop a five-year financial plan for a company based on the following assumptions:

	Year 1	Year 2	Year 3	Year 4	Year 5
Net assets (000)	$1,500	—	—	—	—
Debt/equity	0.25:1	0.25:1	0.50:1	0.50:1	0.50:1
Return on net assets (after taxes)	8%	9%	10%	10%	10%
Interest rate (after taxes)	4.5	4.5	5.0	5.0	5.0
Dividend payout	⅔	⅔	⅔	½	½
Number of shares	200,000	—	—	—	—

a. Calculate all relevant financial results, such as earnings per share, return on equity, growth in equity, and growth in earnings, and discuss your assumptions and findings.

b. Demonstrate the sensitivity of earnings per share, return on equity, and growth in equity by varying the conditions in Year 5 as follows: debt/equity, 0.75:1; return on net assets, 11 percent; interest rate, 4.5 percent; and dividend payout, two thirds. Discuss your findings.

6 ANALYSIS OF CAPITAL INVESTMENT DECISIONS

In the earlier chapters of this book we focused on the *results* and the *funds implications* of management decisions, but not on the economic *rationale* behind the decisions about business investment, the primary driving force of the financial system. We simply assumed that appropriate analytical methods were used to support business investment decisions and that similar support existed for choosing appropriate financing alternatives to cover the funding of these investments.

In this chapter we will examine in some detail the key *conceptual* and *practical aspects of* capital investment decisions, while Chapters 7 and 8 will similarly address financing costs and the choice of financing alternatives. From time to time it will be useful to provide some of the basic conceptual background by introducing applicable portions of managerial economics and financial theory. In keeping with the scope of this book, however, we will avoid the esoteric in favor of the practical and useful. At the end of each chapter we will summarize, in a separate list, the key conceptual issues underlying the analytical approaches covered, both as a reminder and as a guide for the interested reader in exploring the references listed.

The analysis of decisions about new *capital investments* (as well as *disinvestments*) involves a particularly complex set of issues and choices that must be resolved by management. Because capital investments, in contrast to *operational spending*, are normally relatively long-term commitments, they should be *compatible* with the overall strategy of a company. Therefore, they must first be evaluated from the *strategic perspective* of the business. Further, the financial analysis underlying the decisions must be made within a consistent *framework* of accepted conceptual and practical guidelines and methods that focus on the economic impact of the investment or disinvestment. Finally, there are several key *components of analysis* in the evaluation of capital investment alternatives that must be understood and made explicit as well as comparable for a proper choice.

Our emphasis will be on the latter two areas as we take up the various *methods of analysis* used to choose among capital investments, including the important topic of risk/reward analysis. Building on these methods, we will examine certain *refinements* in the analytical process. Some comments about *specialized topics* will follow, and we will close with a checklist of *key issues* affecting capital investment analysis.

STRATEGIC PERSPECTIVE

Investments in land, productive equipment, buildings, natural resources, research facilities, and other assets deployed for future economic gain are part of a company's strategic direction that management must establish and periodically reevaluate. Investment choices should reflect the *desired direction* the company wishes to take, with due consideration of the expected *economic conditions*, the outlook for the company's specific *industry or business segment*, and the *competitive position* of the company.

An almost infinite variety of business investments are available to most firms. A company may invest in new facilities for *expansion*, with the rationale that the incremental profits from additional volume will make the investment economically desirable. Investments may also be made for upgrading worn or outmoded facilities to improve *cost-effectiveness*. Here savings in operating costs are the justification. Some strategies call for entering *new markets*, which could involve entirely new facilities or even a major *repositioning* of existing facilities through rebuilding or through sale and reinvestment. Other strategic proposals might involve establishing a *research* facility, justified on the basis of its potential for developing new products or processes. Capital investment could also involve significant *promotional* outlays, targeted on raising the company's market share over the long-term and with it the profit contribution from higher volumes of operation.

These and other choices are conceived during the process of strategic planning where they are examined within the context and constraints of corporate and divisional *objectives and goals*. Then the various alternatives are narrowed down to those options that should be given serious analysis, and periodic spending plans are prepared that contain those capital outlays that have been selected and approved. The many steps involved in identifying, analyzing, and selecting capital investment opportunities are collectively known as *capital budgeting*. This process includes everything from broad scoping of ideas to very refined economic analyses. In the end, the company's *capital budget* normally contains an acceptable group of projects that individually and collectively are expected to provide economic returns that meet management's goals.

In a sense, capital budgeting is like managing a personal investment portfolio. In both cases, the basic challenge is to select, within the constraint of available funds, those investments that promise to give the desired level of *economic rewards* in relation to the *degree of risk* that is acceptable. The process thus involves a conscious *economic trade-off* between exposure to potential adverse conditions and the expected profitability of the investment. As a general rule, the higher the profitability, the higher also will be the risk exposure. Moreover, the choice among alternatives in which to invest limited funds invariably involves *opportunity costs*, as committing to one investment means rejecting others, thus giving up the opportunity to earn perhaps higher but more risky returns.

In an investment portfolio, capital commitments are made to receive future inflows of cash in the form of dividends, interest, and eventual recovery of the principal through sale of the investment instrument, which over time may have appreciated or declined in market value. In capital budgeting, the commitment of company funds is made in exchange for future cash inflows from incremental profits and from the potential recovery of a portion of the capital invested.

However, the analogy carries only so far. In a going business, the situation is complicated by the need not only to select a portfolio of investments, but also to *operate* the facilities or other assets deployed. In addition, analyzing potential investments in a business context is far more complex because the outlays often involve *multiple expenditures* spread over a period of time. The construction and equipping of a new factory is an example.

Determining the *economic benefits* derived from the outlay is even more complex. An individual investor generally receives specific contractual interest payments or dividend checks. In contrast, a business investment generates additional profits from higher volume, new products, or cost reduction. The *specific* incremental profit from a business investment may be difficult to identify because it is *intermingled* in the company's reports with other accounting information. As we will see, the analysis of potential capital investments involves a fair degree of *economic* reasoning and projection of *future conditions* that goes beyond merely using normal financial statements.

If we follow the analogy between a capital budget and an investment portfolio to its logical conclusion, capital budgeting would ideally amount to *arraying* all business investment opportunities in the order of their expected economic returns and choosing a combination that would meet the desired portfolio return within the constraints of risk and available funding. The theoretical concepts that have been developed and refined in the last two decades rely heavily on *portfolio theory*, both in terms of *risk evaluation* and in the comparison between *investment returns* and the *cost of capital* incurred in funding the investments. The concepts are highly structured and depend on a series of important underlying assumptions. Not easy to apply in practice, they continue to be the subject of much learned argument. In simple terms, the theory argues that business investments should be accepted up to the point at which incremental benefits equal incremental cost, given appropriate risk levels.

This theory entails several problems in practical application. First, at the time the capital budget is prepared, it is not possible to forecast *all* investment opportunities because management faces a continuously *revolving* planning horizon over which new opportunities keep appearing, while known opportunities may fade as conditions change. Second, capital budgets are prepared only once a year in most companies. As various timing lags are encountered, actual *implementation* may be delayed or even canceled because circumstances often change. Third, economic criteria, such as rate of return and cost of capital, are merely *approximations*, and moreover, they are *not the sole basis* for the investment decision. The broader context of strategy, the competitive environment, the ability of management to implement the investment, organizational considerations, and other factors come into play as management weighs the *risk* of an investment against the potential *economic* gain. Thus, there is nothing automatic or simple in arriving at decisions about the stream of potential investments that are continuously surfaced within a business organization.

Our task in this chapter will be to explore in depth the decisional framework and the analytical techniques that *support* the decision process in capital budgeting. We will not delve into the broader conceptual issues of capital budgeting and portfolio theory except to point out some of the key issues. However, the reader interested further in these topics is directed to the references at the end of the chapter. The important question of the *cost of capital* as related to capital budgeting will be taken up in the next chapter, followed in Chapter 8 by the analytical reasoning behind the *choice among the types of potential funding* of capital investments.

THE DECISIONAL FRAMEWORK

Effective analysis of capital investments requires that the analyst and the decision maker be very conscious of the many dimensions involved. We need to set a series of ground rules to ensure that our results are thorough, consistent, and meaningful. These ground rules cover *problem definition*, the *nature of the investment*, estimates of *future costs and benefits, incremental cash flows, relevant accounting data, sunk costs*, and the *time value of money*.

Problem Definition

We should begin any evaluation by stating explicitly *what* the investment is supposed to accomplish. Careful definition of the problem to be solved (or the opportunity presented) by the investment and identification of any potential *alternatives* to the proposed action are critically important to proper analysis. Unfortunately, this elementary point is often overlooked and even deliberately ignored.

In most cases *at least* two or three alternatives are available for achieving the purpose of an investment, and careful examination of the specific circumstances may reveal an even greater number. For example, the decision of whether to replace a machine nearing the end of its useful life at first appears to be a relatively straightforward "either/or" problem. The most obvious alternative, as in any case, is *to do nothing*, that is, to continue patching up the machine until it falls apart. The ongoing, rising costs likely to be incurred with that option are compared with the expected cost pattern of a new machine to decide on its replacement.

Yet there are some *not-so-obvious* alternatives. Perhaps the company should stop making the product altogether! This "go out of business" option should at least be considered—painful as it may be—before new resources are committed. While the improved efficiency of a new machine or a new facility may raise the product's profit performance from poor to average, there may indeed be alternatives *elsewhere* in the company that would yield greater profit from the funds committed. Thus, an opportunity cost might be incurred by going ahead with the replacement. And even if the decision is to continue making the product, there *still* are several *more* alternatives open to management. Among these are replacement with the same machine, or with a larger, more automated model, or with equipment using an altogether different manufacturing process.

A simple diagram can help us to visualize the key options for a replacement decision, as shown in Figure 6-1. This basic "decision tree," illustrating a relatively simple situation, strongly suggests that we need to think through the many

Figure 6-1
Alternatives for a Replacement Decision

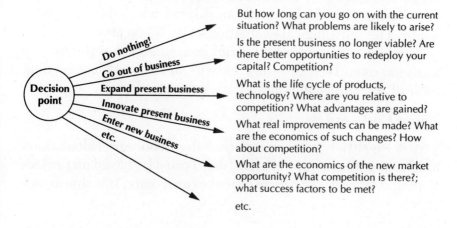

But how long can you go on with the current situation? What problems are likely to arise?

Is the present business no longer viable? Are there better opportunities to redeploy your capital? Competition?

What is the life cycle of products, technology? Where are you relative to competition? What advantages are gained?

What real improvements can be made? What are the economics of such changes? How about competition?

What are the economics of the new market opportunity? What competition is there?; what success factors to be met?

etc.

alternatives usually surrounding a major capital outlay. It is crucial to select the appropriate alternatives for analysis and to structure the problem in such a way that the analytical tools are applied to the real issue to be decided.

Nature of the Investment

Most capital investments tend to be independent of each other; that is, the choice of any one of them does not preclude also choosing any other unless there are insufficient funds available. In that sense they can be viewed as a portfolio of choices, and the analysis and reasoning behind every decision will be relatively unaffected by past and future choices. There are, however, circumstances in which investments compete with each other in their purpose, to the extent that choosing one will preclude the other. Typically, this arises when two alternative ways of solving the same problem are being considered. Such investment projects are called *mutually exclusive*. The significance of this condition will become apparent when we discuss the measures used to judge economic desirability. This condition can, of course, also arise when management sets a strict limit on the amount of spending, often called *capital rationing*, which will preclude investing in some worthy projects once others have been accepted.

Another type of investment involves *sequential* outlays beyond the initial expenditure. Any major capital outlay for plant and equipment usually also entails additional future outlays for major maintenance, upgrading, and partial replacement some years hence, which should be considered when the decision is made. The most logical evaluation of such investments comes from taking into account *all major consequences* at the time of analysis, even though future individual decisions concerning each of the additional outlays are possible.

Future Costs and Benefits

It is essential to recognize that the economic calculations used to justify any capital investment must be based on projections and forecasts of *future revenues and costs*. It is simply not enough to assume that past conditions and experience, such as operating costs or product prices, will continue unchanged and be applicable to a new venture. While this may seem obvious, there is a practical temptation to *extrapolate* past conditions instead of carefully *forecasting* likely develop-ments. The past is at best a rough guide and at worst *irrelevant* for analysis.

The success of investments with time horizons of 2, 5, 10, and even 25 years rests entirely on future events and the *uncertainty* surrounding them. It therefore behooves the ana-lyst to explore as much as possible the likely changes from present conditions in all of the variables relevant to the analy-sis. If potential deviations are great, it may be useful to run the analysis under different assumptions, thus testing the *sen-sitivity* of the quantitative result to changes in particular vari-ables, such as product volumes, prices, key raw material costs, and so on. The reader will recall our references to this type of analysis in the earlier chapters.

The uncertainty of future conditions affecting an investment is the *risk* of not meeting expectations and suffering an eco-nomic loss—the degree of risk being a function of the relative uncertainty of the key variables of the project. Careful esti-mates and research are often warranted to narrow the margin of error in the predicted conditions on which the analysis is based. Since the basic rationale of making investments relies on a conscious *economic trade-off* of risk versus reward, as we established earlier, the importance of explicitly addressing key areas of uncertainty should be obvious.

Incremental Cash Flows

The economic reasoning behind any capital outlay is based strictly on the *incremental* changes resulting from an invest-ment. Moreover, the analysis recognizes only *cash flows*, that is, those funds movements traceable to cash inflows and out-flows. All financial *accounting* transactions related to the deci-sion but not involving cash flows are *irrelevant* for the purpose.

Thus, the first basic question to be asked is: What *additional funds* will be required to carry out the chosen alternative? For example, the investment proposal may, in addition to the outlay for new equipment, entail the sale or other disposal of assets that will no longer be used. The decision thus may *free* some previously committed funds. In such a case it is the *net outlay* that counts, after any applicable additional taxes have been factored in.

Similarly, the next question is: What *additional revenues* will be created over and above any existing ones? If an investment results in *new* revenues, but at the same time causes the loss of some *existing* revenues, only the *net impact*, after applicable taxes, is relevant for economic analysis.

The third question concerns the *costs* that will be *added* or *removed* as a result of the investment. The only relevant items here are those costs, including taxes, that will go up or down *as a consequence* of the investment decision; any cost or expense that is expected to remain the *same* before and after the investment has been made is *not relevant* for the analysis.

The three questions illustrate why we refer to the economic analysis of investments as an *incremental* process. The approach is *relative* rather than absolute and is tied closely to carefully defined alternatives and the differences between them. The only data applicable in any investment analysis are the *differential* funds commitments as well as *differential* revenues and costs caused by the decision, all viewed in terms of aftertax *cash flows*.

Relevant Accounting Data

Investment analysis in large part involves the use of data derived from accounting records, not all of which are *relevant* for the purpose. Accounting conventions not involving cash flows must be viewed with caution. This is true particularly with investments that cause changes in operating costs. There, a clear distinction must be drawn between those items that *do vary* with the operation of the new investment and those that only *appear to vary*. The latter are often *accounting*

allocations, which may change in magnitude but do not necessarily represent a true change in costs incurred.

For example, for accounting purposes, general overhead
costs (administrative costs, insurance, etc.) may be allocated
on the basis of operating volume. Consequently, a new machine with higher output will be charged by the accounting
system with a higher share of overhead than was the machine it
replaces. Yet there has likely been *no actual change* in general
overhead that can be attributed to the substitution of one
machine for the other. Therefore, the reported change in the
allocation is not relevant for purposes of economic analysis.
The analyst must constantly judge as to whether there has
been a change in the *true* cash outlays and revenues—not
whether the accounting system is *redistributing* the existing
costs differently.

Sunk Costs

There is also a very common temptation to include in the
analysis of a new investment all or portions of outlays that
occurred in the *past,* perhaps preparatory to making the new
commitment. Economic analysis does *not* permit backtracking
to expenditures that have already been made and recorded on
the books. Such *sunk costs,* even if they are connected in some
way to the decision at hand, cannot be *altered* by making the
investment *now.*

If, for example, significant amounts had been spent on research and development of a new product, the current decision about whether to invest in facilities to produce the
product should in *no way whatsoever* be affected by those
sunk costs. Perhaps the earlier decision to do research and
development in retrospect was less effective than expected;
the point is that the current investment to exploit the results of
the research now appears economically justified. Economic
decisions are *forward looking* and must involve *only* those
things that can be *changed* by the action being decided. This is
the essential test of relevance for any element to be included in
the analysis.

The Time Value of Money

Given the future orientation of investment analysis, a proper application of economic reasoning requires us to recognize the intimate connection between the *timing* of incremental cash inflows and outflows and the *value* of such cash flows relative to the point of decision. It is a simple axiom that a dollar received today is worth more than a dollar received one year hence because we forgo the opportunity of investing today the future dollar we have to wait for. Thus, the time value of money is related both to the *timing* of a receipt or expenditure and the *opportunity to earn a return* on funds invested. Since the economic analysis of capital investments involves projecting a whole series and pattern of incremental cash flows, both positive and negative, we need a method that will equate the respective values of the future flows into today's terms. Figure 6–2 shows the pattern of cash flows connected with a typical capital investment, consisting of an initial outlay, a series of positive benefits, intermediate additional outlays, and ultimate recovery of part of the resources committed.

Figure 6–2
Typical Cash Flow Pattern for a Capital Investment

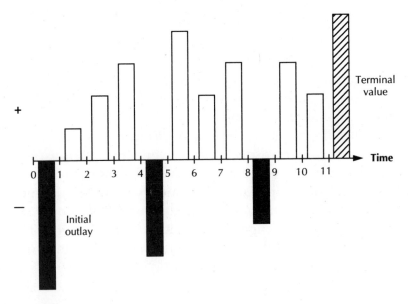

All of these future cash flows have to be "brought back" to the point of decision by a consistent methodology. The formal process of expressing future dollars in equivalent present dollars is called *discounting* and is the basis for all the modern techniques of investment analysis that will be discussed later in this chapter. We will return to describing the key technical aspects of the time value of money shortly.

COMPONENTS OF ANALYSIS

Bearing in mind the strategic perspective and the ground rules just enumerated, we can now turn to the basic components common to all business investment proposals. In essence, capital is invested for one basic reason: to obtain sufficient future economic returns to warrant the original outlay, that is, sufficient cash receipts over the life of the project to justify the cash spent. Analytical methods should take into account in, one way or another, this basic *trade-off* of current cash outflow against expected future cash inflow.

To judge the attractiveness of any investment, we must consider the following elements: (*a*) the amount expended, that is, the *net investment*, (*b*) the potential benefits, that is, the *operating cash inflows*, (*c*) the *economic life* of the investment, which is the time period over which it will provide those benefits, (*d*) any recovery of capital at the termination of the investment, called *terminal value*. A proper economic analysis must relate these four elements to provide an indication whether the investment is worthy of consideration or not.

We can use a simple example to show how this is done. An outlay of $100,000 for equipment needed to manufacture a new product is expected to provide aftertax cash flow benefits of $25,000 over a period of six years, without significant annual fluctuations. Although the equipment will not be fully worn out after six years, it is unlikely that more than scrap value will be realized at that time, due to technical obsolescence. The cost of removal is expected to offset this scrap value. Straight-line depreciation over the six years ($16,667 per year) has been correctly adjusted for in the cash flow figure of $25,000, by being added back to the expected net aftertax improvement in profits of $8,333.

Net Investment

The first element in the analysis, the investment, normally consists of the gross capital requirements for the new assets *reduced by* any capital recovered from the trade or sale of existing assets resulting from the decision. Such recoveries must be adjusted for any change in taxes paid that arises from a recognized gain or loss on the disposal of existing assets. It is the *net amount of outlays* and *recoveries* that will be committed to the decision. Because no old assets were replaced in our simple case, the net investment is the full $100,000.

When an investment is made for new products or for an increased volume of existing products, any increase in *working capital* required to support the additional volume of business must be included in the analysis. Normally, such incremental working capital is added to net investment. For our first example this refinement is ignored, but later in the chapter we will demonstrate how such additional working capital is handled.

Further capital outlays might also be necessary *during* the life of the investment project. This potential consequence of the initial decision must also be considered as part of the investment proposal. We will demonstrate the method of dealing with such sequential elements later on.

Operating Cash Flows

The operational basis for economic benefits over the life of the investment is the period-by-period *net change* in revenues and expenses caused by the investment, after adjusting for applicable income taxes. These incremental changes include such elements as operating savings caused by a machine replacement, the additional profits from a new product line, the increased profits from plant expansion, or the profits created by developing land or other natural resources. Normally these benefits are reflected as an increase in the profit reported in periodic operating statements. From a cash standpoint these changes will improve the company's *aftertax cash flow*, which we know from earlier chapters to consist of aftertax profit plus depreciation.

We will later give numerous examples of how project cash flows are derived, but for our simple case we will assume the annual operating aftertax cash flow to be a *level* $25,000, which we know represents the sum of net profits of $8,333 from the new product and depreciation of $16,667. As we will see, an assumed *variable* pattern of annual or periodic cash flows can significantly influence the analytical results. Level periodic flows are easiest to deal with, but are rare in practice. Uneven cash flows are more common and make the analysis more complex, but can be handled readily, as will be demonstrated later.

Economic Life

The third element, the *time period* selected for the analysis is commonly referred to as the *economic life* of the investment project. For our purposes the only *relevant* time period is the *economic* life, as distinguished from the *physical* life of equipment or the *technological* life of a particular process. Even though a building or a piece of equipment may be perfectly usable from a physical standpoint, the economic life of the investment is finished if the market for the product or service has disappeared. Similarly, the economic life of any given technology is bound up with the economics of the market place—the best process is useless if the resulting product or service can no longer be sold. At that point, any usable resources will have to be repositioned—which requires another investment decision—or they may be disposed of for their recovery value. When management chooses to redeploy resources into another project, the net investment for that decision would, of course, be the estimated recovery value after taxes.

In our simple example, we have assumed a six-year economic life, the period over which the product manufactured with the equipment will be sold. The *depreciation life* used for accounting or tax purposes does not normally reflect an investment's true life span. As we discussed earlier, such write-offs are based on standard accounting and tax guidelines and do not necessarily represent the economic usefulness of the investment.

Terminal Value

Normally, there is a substantial *recovery* of capital from eventual disposal of *physical assets* at the end of the economic life (beyond the minor scrap value assumed in our example), as well as the release of any *working capital* associated with the investment. Such amounts have to be made part of the analysis. Again we will demonstrate the handling of these elements later on.

To summarize, up to this point in the chapter we have laid the groundwork for analyzing any capital investment by describing the *strategic perspective*, the *decisional framework*, and the four essential *components* of the analysis. This background was necessary because the analyst or manager must be aware that analyzing a capital investment is not the simple matter that may appear to be. The points covered so far in the chapter establish *what* must be analyzed. We now turn to the question of *how* this is done—the methods and criteria of analysis that will help us judge the economics of the decision.

METHODS OF ANALYSIS

How do we relate the four basic components—net investment, operating cash flow, economic life, and terminal value—to determine the project's attractiveness? We will first deal briefly with *simple methods* of analysis, which are merely *rules of thumb* that intuitively grapple with the trade-off between investment and operating cash flows. We will describe the *payback* and the *simple rate of return*, both of which occasionally are still used in practice despite their demonstrable shortcomings. Discussion of these shortcomings,

however, will provide important insights into economic reasoning, thus building a transition to *modern investment analysis*. Our major emphasis in this section will be on measures
employing the *time value of money*, enabling the analyst to
deal with relevant cash flows in *equivalent* terms, that is, regardless of the timing of their incidence. Those key measures
are *net present value*, the *profitability index*, and the *internal
rate of return (yield)*. Next we will turn to basic *risk analysis*,
and discuss the *present value payback, annualized net present
value, ranges of estimates, simulation, probabilistic reasoning*, and *risk-adjusted rates*.

Simple Measures

Payback.   This rule of thumb directly relates an assumed
level annual cash inflow from a project to the net investment
required:

$$\text{Payback} = \frac{\text{Net investment}}{\begin{array}{c}\text{Average annual}\\ \text{operating cash flow}\end{array}} = \frac{\$100,000}{\$25,000} = 4 \text{ years}$$

The result is the number of years required for the original
outlay to be "repaid." It is a crude test of whether the investment will be recovered within its economic life span. For our
simple example this is true, as payback is achieved in only four
years versus the estimated economic life of six years.

While the payback period is easy to calculate—which probably accounts for what popularity remains for this tool—some
difficult questions arise. First, the measure tests the recovery
of the original investment on, so to speak, the installment
basis. The implied query is, how long will it be until I get my
money back? Recovering the capital is not enough, of course,
because from an economic standpoint, one would hope to earn
a profit on the funds while they are invested.

To illustrate, we can picture a savings account in which $100
is deposited and from which $25 is withdrawn at the end of
each year. After four years, the principal will have been repaid
in full. The saver would be very upset, however, if the bank
statement showed that the account was now depleted. The

investment was made with the expectation of earning 5 or 6 percent *every year* on the *declining balance* in the account. The saver would certainly demand payment of the accumulated interest.

In the case of our machine investment, the payback period of four years similarly implies that no economic return has been earned on the funds committed. Four years is just sufficient to recover the *original outlay*. Thus, we must look to the years *beyond* the payback point to provide an economic return. In fact, if the economic life and the payback period were to coincide precisely, an *opportunity loss* would have been suffered, because the same funds invested *elsewhere* would probably have earned some return every year—at least at the level of savings account interest! This point is demonstrated in Table 6–1.

Here we assume that a $100,000 capital investment provides an annual operating cash flow after taxes of $25,000. If our hypothetical company typically earned 10 percent after taxes on its investments, part of every year's cash flow would have to be considered as this normal return, while the remainder would be applied to reducing the outstanding balance.

The first column shows the beginning balance of the investment in every year. Normal earnings of 10 percent are calculated on these balances in the second column. The operating

Table 6–1
Amortization of $100,000 Investment at Ten Percent

Year	(1) Beginning Balance	(2) Normal Earnings at 10 Percent	(3) Operating Cash Flow	(4) Ending Balance to be Recovered
1	$100,000	$10,000	$(25,000)	$85,000
2	85,000	8,500	(25,000)	68,500
3	68,500	6,850	(25,000)	50,350
4	50,350	5,035	(25,000)	30,385 (payback)
5	30,385	3,039	(25,000)	8,424
6	8,424	842	(25,000)	(15,734)

cash flows in the third column, reduced by the normal earnings, are applied against the beginning balances to calculate every year's ending balance. The result is an *amortization schedule* for our simple investment that extends to the *sixth* year—requiring two years more than the payback measure would suggest.

Strictly for simplicity we have assumed that earnings are calculated on the *beginning* balance of the investment, and operating cash flows are received at the *end* of the period. A more precise simulation would not materially affect the result. From the figures in the table, it is quite obvious that a payback of four years would mean an opportunity loss of about $30,400, if the project ended at this point. With an economic life of five years, the opportunity loss vis- à-vis the normal expectation of earning 10 percent would be reduced to about $8,400, while at six years there would be a sizable advantage of $15,700.

This brief illustration points up one of the critical shortcomings of the payback measure. It is relatively *insensitive* to the economic life span and thus not a meaningful criterion of earnings power. The speed with which the initial investment is repaid is neither a convenient nor sufficient way to appraise profitability. All we can say about our example in payback terms is that the project pays out in four years, with two "extra" years for profit. Moreover, the payback measure would also give the same "four years plus something extra" reading on other projects with similar cash flows but with 8- or 10-year economic lives, even though those projects are clearly superior to our example.

Another shortcoming is that payback implicitly assumes *level* annual operating cash flows. Projects with rising or decling cash flow patterns—although very common—cannot properly be evaluated. An investment in a new product, for example, may yield cash flows that slowly rise during the early years, eventually level out and decline sharply in the late stages of the product's economic life. A machine replacement, in contrast, will generate ever-growing improvements in operating costs as the existing machine deteriorates. Moreover, any additional investments made during the period, or capital recoveries at the end of the economic life, are ignored by this simple measure. Table 6–2 illustrates the insensitivity of payback to variations in cash flow.

If we assume similar risks for each of the three projects, we would chose Project 2 over Project 1, because over its economic life it will return $50,000 more than Project 1. But the payback ranking is the *same* for both projects. Project 3, on the other hand, appears to be the most favorable one if judged *only* on the payback period of three years. Yet it is obvious that Project 3 involves an opportunity loss, because the operating cash flows during its three-year economic life are just sufficient to recover the original outlay, without providing any economic return at all.

The difference in the cash flow patterns of Projects 1 and 2 is also masked by the payout criterion. Although both projects do recover the initial investment in four years, the cumulative operating cash flows are higher for Project 2 than for Project 1.

Table 6–2
Payback Results under Varying Conditions

	Project 1	Project 2	Project 3
Net investment	$100,000	$100,000	$100,000
Average annual operating cash flow	$ 25,000	$ 25,000	$ 33,333
Economic life	6 years	8 years	3 years
Payback	4 years	4 years	3 years
Cash flow pattern (years):			
1	$ 25,000	$ 20,000	$ 16,667
2	25,000	30,000	33,333
3	25,000	50,000	50,000
4	25,000	40,000	–0–
5	25,000	30,000	–0–
6	25,000	15,000	–0–
7	–0–	10,000	–0–
8	–0–	5,000	–0–
Total	$150,000	$200,000	$100,000
Cumulative first four years	$100,000	$140,000	n.a.
Average first four years	$ 25,000	$ 35,000	n.a.

n.a. = not applicable.

Average annual cash flows are $35,000 versus $25,000 during the first four years. Thus, Project 2 clearly provides significantly higher operating cash flows early on and is more desirable when time value is considered.

A modification of the payback measure substitutes *average accounting profit after taxes* as the denominator in the formula instead of aftertax cash flow. The rationale is that the net income improvement (in accounting terms) attributable to the investment, calculated *after* the annual depreciation allowance, implicitly provides for *both* the return of principal *and* a periodic profit. The amount of depreciation charged against net income is assumed to roughly simulate the recovery of principal—something we had done more precisely in Table 6–1—while the net profit improvement is thought to represent earnings on the original investment.

In our simple example the average aftertax cash flow is composed of an average accounting profit improvement of $8,333, after depreciation of $16,667 ($100,000 depreciated straight-line over six years). In the revised formula the payback jumps to a clearly misleading 12 years:

$$\frac{\text{Net investment}}{\text{Average annual aftertax profit}} = \frac{\$100,000}{\$8,333} = 12 \text{ years}$$

This crude implied investment amortization simply cannot be substituted for the "cash-in, cash-out" reasoning that underlies economic investment analysis. We must not let changes in accounting profits and associated depreciation write-offs take the place of the *economic cash flows*, because each is designed for a valid but quite different purpose. Table 6–1 demonstrated that the project was desirable if its economic life was only *five years* or better. The degree of distortion introduced by the use of accounting profits will, of course, vary with the circumstances, particularly with different economic lives and earnings rates.

By now it should be obvious that the payback measure must be used with caution, if at all. It is a helpful device for investment choices *only* if applied to an array of projects with *similar* cash flow patterns and *similar* economic lives. For example, payback might be applicable in a company routinely replacing machine tools in large numbers. When cash flows and economic lives are dissimilar, however, a more viable and flexible economic analysis is necessary.

Simple Rate of Return.   Only passing comments are warranted about this rule of thumb, which in fact is the *inverse* of the payback formula. It states the desirability of an investment in terms of a percentage return on the *original* outlay. The method shares all of the shortcomings of the payback because it again relates only two of the four critical aspects of any project, net investment and operating cash flows, and ignores the economic life and any terminal value:

$$\frac{\text{Return on}}{\text{investment}} = \frac{\text{Average annual operating cash flow}}{\text{Net investment}} = \frac{\$25,000}{\$100,000} = 25\%$$

All this result indicates is that \$25,000 happens to be 25 percent of \$100,000. It is the only conclusion we can draw because there is no reference to economic life and no recognition that, as is true with a savings account, regular cash benefits will drawn down the balance of the principal. Note that the calculation will give the *same* answer whether the economic life were 1 year, 10 years, or 100 years. The return indicated would be valid in an economic sense *only* if the investment provided \$25,000 per year *in perpetuity*. It would take this unrealistic condition to be able to say that the return was truly 25 percent.

A slightly more meaningful version of the simple rate of return uses aftertax accounting profit as the numerator. A much more credible result seems to emerge for our example, but not necessarily for others:

$$\frac{\text{Return on}}{\text{investment}} = \frac{\text{Average annual aftertax profit}}{\text{Net investment}} = \frac{\$8,333}{\$100,000} = 8.3\%$$

This version of the simple rate of return happens to simulate the impact the project will have on corporate financial statements. It approximates the resulting changes in the operating statement and the balance sheet, at least for the early part of the project's life, and is consistent with the basic rate of return measures applied to investments in place, as discussed in Chapter 3. But as a decisional criterion, it is still subject to all the other shortcomings we have pointed out.

As mentioned earlier, these rules of thumb are relatively easy to calculate. However, with the availability of computer-based spreadsheets and programmed analytical methods, more sophisticated analyses can be performed with comparative ease. The simple methods were useful here mainly to demonstrate, by their shortcomings, the importance of economic reasoning. We will now turn to a full discussion of the relevant economic measures based on the time value of money.

Economic Investment Analysis

Earlier we described capital investment analysis as the process of weighing the economic *trade-off* between current dollar outlays and future net cash flow benefits expected to be obtained over a relevant period of time. This concept applies to all types of investments, whether made by individuals or businesses. The *time value of money* is used as the underlying methodology.

We will begin this section by discussing in detail how the basic principles of *compounding* and *discounting* can be used to translate cash flows into *equivalent* monetary values irrespective of their timing. Then we will explain and demonstrate the major *measures* of investment analysis that utilize these principles to calculate the quantitative basis for making *economic* choices among investment propositions.

Compounding, Discounting, and Equivalence. We said earlier that common sense tells us a person will not be indifferent between two investment propositions that are exactly alike in all aspects except for a *difference in timing* of the future benefits. An investor will obviously prefer the one providing more immediate benefits. The reason for this preference, of course, is that more immediately available funds offer an individual or a company the *opportunity to invest* these funds at a profit—be it in a savings account, a government bond, a loan, a new facility, or any one of a great variety of other economic possibilities. Thus, having to wait for a period of time until funds become available entails an *opportunity cost* in the form of lost earnings potential.

Conversely, common sense dictates that given a choice between making an expenditure now versus making the same expenditure some time in the future, it is advantageous to *defer the outlay*. Again the reason is the opportunity to earn a profit on the funds in the meantime. Stated another way, the value of money is affected directly by the specific *timing* of its receipt or disbursement, and this in turn is related to the *opportunity* of earning a profit during the timing interval.

A simple example will help illustrate this point. If a person normally uses a savings account to earn interest of 5 percent per year, a deposit of $1,000 made today will grow to $1,050 in one year. (For simplicity we ignore the practice of daily or monthly compounding commonly used by banks and savings institutions.) If for some reason the person had to wait one year to deposit the $1,000, the opportunity to earn $50 in interest would be lost. Without question, a sum of $1,000 offered to a person one year hence has to be worth *less* today than the same amount offered immediately. Specifically, *today's value* of the delayed $1,000 must be related to the person's opportunity to earn 5 percent. Given this rate, we can calculate the *present value* of the $1,000 to be received in one year's time as follows:

$$\text{Present value} = \frac{\$1,000}{(1 + 0.05)} = \$952.38$$

The equation shows that with an assumed rate of return of 5 percent, $1,000 received one year from now is the *equivalent* of $952.38 today. This is so because $952.38 invested at 5 percent today will grow into $1,000 by the end of one year. The calculation clearly reflects the economic trade-off between dollars received today versus a future date, based on the *length of time* involved and the available *earnings opportunity*. If we ignore risk for the moment, it also follows that our investor should be willing to pay $952.38 *today* for a financial contract that will pay $1,000 one year hence.

The longer the waiting period, the lower becomes the present value of a sum of money to be received, because for each additional period of delay the opportunity to earn a return during the period is forgone. Principal and interest left in place would have *compounded* by earning an annual return on the growing balance. Conversely, it will be advantageous to defer an expenditure as long as possible, because this allows the individual to earn a return during every period on the amount *not spent* plus the interest left in place.

The process of calculating this change in the value of receipts or expenditures is quite simple when we know the time period and the earnings opportunity rate. For example, a sum of $1,000 to be received at the end of five years will be worth only $783.53 today, because that amount invested today at 5 percent compounded annually would grow to $1,000 five years hence, if the earnings are left to accumulate and interest is earned on the growing balance each year. The formula for this calculation appears as follows:

$$\text{Present value} = \frac{\$1,000}{(1 + 0.05)^5} = \frac{\$1,000}{1.27628} = \$783.53$$

The result of $783.53 was obtained by relating the *future value* of $1,000 to the *compound earnings factor* at 5 percent over five years, shown in the denominator as 1.27628, which is simply 1.05 raised to the fifth power. When we divide the future value by the compound earnings factor, we have in effect *discounted* the future value into a lower *equivalent present value*.

Note that the mathematics are straightforward in achieving what we described in concept earlier: The value of a future sum is lowered in precise relationship to the earnings opportunity and the timing incidence. The earnings opportunity is our assumed 5 percent compound interest, while the timing incidence of five years is reflected in the number of times the interest is compounded to express the number of years during which earnings were forgone.

We refer to the calculation of present values as *discounting*, while the reverse, the calculation of future values, is called *compounding*. The very basic mathematical relationships allow us to derive the equivalent value of any sum to be received or paid at any point in time, either at the present moment or at any specified future date.

The process of compounding and discounting is as old as money lending and has been used by financial institutions from time immemorial. Even though the application of this methodology to business investments is of more recent vintage, the techniques have become commonplace. The advent of hand-held electronic calculators and ubiquitous computer programs with compounding and discounting capability has made the derivation of equivalent values and time-adjusted investment measures routine.

The discount factors are also published in so-called *present value tables*, which were used in years past by analysts calculating present values before computer-assisted methods were available. Two of these tables are provided at the end of this chapter on pages 278 and 280. Even though they are no longer necessary for making actual calculations, they provide a visual demonstration of the effect of discounting. With their help we can clarify a few points. Table 6–9 on page 278 contains the factors that translate into equivalent present values a *single sum* of money received or disbursed at the end of any period, under different assumptions about the rate of earnings. It is based on this general formula:

$$\text{Present value} = \frac{1}{(1 + i)^n}$$

where i is the applicable earnings rate (discount rate) and n the number of periods over which discounting takes place. The table covers a range from 1 to 60 periods, and discount rates from 1 to 50 percent. The rates are related to the *periods*, however defined. For example, if the periods represent years, the rates are annual, while if months are used, the rates are monthly. The present value of a sum of money therefore can be found by simply multiplying the amount involved by the appropriate factor in the table:

$$\text{Present value} = \text{Factor} \times \text{Amount}$$

Note that the results from our savings account example on page 234 can be found in Table 6–9 in the 5 percent column, lines 1 and 5.

Table 6–10 on page 280 is a variation of Table 6–9 that allows the user to directly calculate the present value of a *series of equal* receipts or payments occurring over a number of periods. Such series are called *annuities*. The same result could be obtained by using Table 6–9 and repetitively multiplying the periodic amount with the appropriate series of successive factors and adding all of the results. Table 6–10 directly provides a set of such *additive* factors, however, which allow the analyst to obtain the present value of an annuity in the *single step* of multiplying the periodic receipt or payment by the appropriate factor:

$$\text{Present value} = \text{Factor} \times \text{Annuity}$$

These basic tables can be used for practically all investment problems normally encountered. There are many possible variations and refinements in timing, such as more frequent discounting (monthly, weekly), or an assumption that the annuity is received or disbursed in weekly or monthly increments rather than at the end of the period. The assumption of a continuous flow of receipts or disbursements more closely approximates the cash incidence from such changes in operations as labor and materials savings and other daily, weekly, or monthly changes. The use of this option introduces a forward shift in timing that leads to slightly higher present values, both for single sums and annuities. Many discounting refinements also relate to financial instruments, such as mortgages, bonds, charge accounts, and so forth, which involve specific practices, such as daily discounting or compounding.

For the practical purpose of analyzing business capital investments, such refinements are not critical because the imprecision of many of the economic estimates about them easily outweighs any incremental numerical precision that might be obtained. The periodic discounting embodied in the formula of the two tables at the end of the chapter is quite adequate for most analytical needs and matches the internal programs of most calculators and computer spreadsheets.

We will now turn to the discussion of the measures employing these compounding and discounting principles. We will cover the basic rationale on which these measures are based and their applicability to economic investment analysis as well as their shortcomings.

Net Present Value. The net present value measure weighs the cash flow trade-off between investment outlays, future benefits, and terminal values in *equivalent* terms. It allows the analyst to determine whether the *net balance* of these equivalent present values is favorable or unfavorable. To use the tool, a rate of discount representing normal earnings opportunities must be specified. Appropriate present value factors are then applied to both inflows and outflows over the economic life of the investment proposal. Finally, the present values of all inflows (positive amounts) and outflows (negative amounts) are summed, and the net amount represents the *net present value*. This amount can be positive or negative, depending on whether there is a discounted net inflow or net outflow over the economic life of the project.

The measure indicates whether an investment, over its economic life, will achieve the earnings rate applied in the calculation. Inasmuch as present value results depend on both timing and earnings opportunity, a *positive* net present value indicates that the cash flows generated by the investment over its life will (*a*) recover the original outlay (as well as any future capital outlays or recoveries considered in the analysis), (*b*) earn the desired return standard on the outstanding balance, and (*c*) *in addition* provide a "cushion" of excess value.

Conversely, a *negative* result indicates that the project is *not* achieving the earnings standard and thus will cause an *opportunity loss*. Obviously, the result will be affected by the *level* of earnings specified, the actual *timing pattern* of the cash flows, and the relative *magnitudes of the amounts* involved.

A word should be said at this point about the rate of discount employed. From an economic standpoint, it should be the rate of return an investor normally enjoys from investments of similar nature and risk. In effect, this is an *opportunity rate of return*. In the corporate setting the choice of a discount rate is complicated both by the variety of investment possibilities and by the types of financing provided by both owners and lenders. The corporate earnings standard used to discount capital investment cash flows should reflect the minimum return requirement that will provide the level of shareholder value normally expected, while taking advantage of financial leverage where appropriate.

The standard most commonly employed is expressed as an overall corporate *cost of capital*, which takes into account shareholder expectations, business risk, and financial leverage. It will also often reflect a specific management objective to achieve returns higher than the minimum cost of capital. Sometimes a corporate earnings standard is separated into a set of multiple discount rates for different lines of business within a company, in order to recognize specific risk differentials. We will deal with these concepts in greater depth in the next chapter. For purposes of this discussion we will assume that management has chosen an appropriate earnings standard with which to discount investment cash flows, and we will focus on how present value measures are used to assess potential investments on an economic basis.

To illustrate, we will return to the simple investment example we used earlier in the chapter. As a first step, it is generally helpful to lay out the pertinent information period by period to give us a time perspective. A horizontal time scale can be used, on which the periods are marked off and the positive and

240

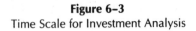

Figure 6–3
Time Scale for Investment Analysis

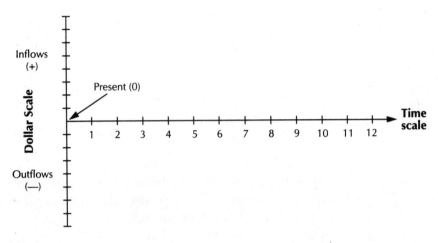

negative cash flows inserted, as shown in Figure 6–3. The information can also be shown in the tabular format as is done in Table 6–3.

When we represent the timing of cash flows on a scale, the present is normally considered the "0" point, with periods marked off in positive increments into the future, and negative increments into the past, as applicable to a particular problem. The table demonstrates that the net investment of $100,000 at point 0 and the six annual benefit inflows of $25,000 each result in a net present value of almost $16,000, on the assumption that our company considers 8 percent after taxes a normal earnings standard. All of the initial outflow will have been recovered over the six-year period, while 8 percent after taxes will have been earned all along on the declining investment balance outstanding during the project life. An additional cushion of $15,575 in equivalent present value dollars can be expected *if* the cash flow estimates are correct and *if* the project does live out its economic life. Note the similarity to the payback concept discussed earlier, where we found the recovery of the investment and "something extra." The critical *difference* between payback and net present value, however, is the fact that net present value has a built-in earnings

Table 6–3
Net Present Value Analysis by Period at 8 Percent

Time Period	Investment (outlays)	Benefits (inflows)	Present Value Factors at 8 Percent*	Present Values	Cumulative Net Present Value
0	$100,000	—	1.000	− $100,000	− $100,000
1	—	$ 25,000	0.926	+ 23,150	− 76,850
2	—	25,000	0.857	+ 21,425	− 55,425
3	—	25,000	0.794	+ 19,850	− 35,575
4	—	25,000	0.735	+ 18,375	− 17,200
5	—	25,000	0.681	+ 17,025	− 175
6	—	25,000	0.630	+ 15,750	+ 15,575
	$100,000	$150,000		+$ 15,575	

*To illustrate the use of Table 6–9, assuming that benefits occur at year-end. We could instead use a factor from Table 6–10: 4.623 times $25,000, because the annual inflows are equal. The result for the total present value of the inflows is identical. (The factors for years 1 through 6 total 4.623.)

requirement *in addition* to the recovery of the investment. Thus, the cushion implicit in a positive net present value is truly an economic gain that goes *beyond* satisfying the required earnings standard.

If a higher earnings standard had been required, say 12 percent, the results would be those shown in Table 6–4. The net present value remains positive, but the size of the cushion has dramatically decreased to only $2,800. We would expect such a decrease, because at a higher discount rate, the present value of the cash flows must decline, with all other circumstances unchanged.

At an assumed earnings standard of 14 percent, the net present value shrinks even further. In fact, it is transformed into a *negative result* ($25,000 × 3.889 − $100,000 = − $2,775). This illustrates the high sensitivity of net present value to the choice of earnings standards.

The importance of the length of the economic life of the investment is demonstrated in the last column of both Tables 6–3 and 6–4. There we can observe that the time required for the cumulative present value to turn positive was lengthened as the earnings standard was raised. At 8 percent, the economic life had to be about five years for the switch to occur (the

Table 6–4
Net Present Value Analysis by Period at 12 Percent

Time Period	Investment (outlays)	Benefits (inflows)	Present Value Factors at 12 Percent*	Present Values	Cumulative Net Present Value
0	$100,000	—	1.000	− $100,000	− $100,000
1	—	$ 25,000	0.893	+ 22,325	− 77,675
2	−	25,000	0.797	+ 19,925	− 57,750
3	—	25,000	0.712	+ 17,800	− 39,950
4	—	25,000	0.636	+ 15,900	− 24,050
5	—	25,000	0.567	+ 14,175	− 9,875
6	—	25,000	0.507	+ 12,675	+ 2,800
	$100,000	$150,000		+ $ 2,800	

*As in Table 6–3, we could use 4.112 times $25,000 from Table 6–10.

net present value after the benefits of year 5 is just about zero), while at 12 percent most of the sixth year of economic life was necessary for a positive turnaround (about $10,000 of negative present value at the end of year 5 has to be recovered from benefits of year 6).

In our example, we assumed a *level* operating cash inflow of $25,000. *Uneven* cash flow patterns will have a notable impact on the results, although the method of calculation remains the same. Net present value can accommodate any combination of cash flow patterns without difficulty. The reader is invited to test this, using a cash inflow pattern that rises from, say, $15,000 to $40,000, and one that falls from $40,000 to $15,000, each totaling $150,000 over six years.

The best use of net present value is as a screening device to indicate whether a stipulated minimum earnings standard can be met over an investment proposal's economic life. When net present value is *positive*, there is potential for earnings in excess of the standard; when net present value is *negative*, the minimum earnings standard and capital recovery cannot be achieved with the projected cash flows. When net present value is close to or exactly *zero*, the earnings standard has just been met, on the assumption that the earnings estimates and the projected life are quite reliable.

While net present value is a useful tool in evaluating investment alternatives, it does not answer all our questions about
the economic attractiveness of capital outlays. For example,
when comparing different projects, how does one evaluate the
respective size of the "cushion" calculated with a given return
standard, particularly if the investment amount differs significantly? Also, to what extent is achieving the expected economic life a factor in such comparisons? Furthermore, how
does one quantify the potential errors and uncertainties inherent in the cash flow estimates, and how does the measure assist
in investment choices if such deviations are significant? Finally, one can ask what *specific return* the project will *yield* if
all estimates are in fact realized? Further measures and analytical methods are necessary to answer these questions, and
we will show how a combination of techniques helps to narrow
the choices to be made.

Profitability Index.   After calculating the net present values of a series of projects, we may be faced with a choice that
involves several alternative investments of *different* size. In
such cases we cannot be indifferent to the fact that even
though the net present values of the alternatives may be close
or even equal, they involve initial funds commitments of
widely varying amounts. In other words, it does make a difference whether an investment proposal promises a net present value of $1,000 for an outlay of $10,000, or whether in
another case a net present value of $1,000 requires an invest-
ment of $25,000—even if we can assume equivalent economic
lives and equivalent risk. In the first case, the cushion (excess
benefit) is a much larger fraction of the net investment than it
is in the second, which makes the first investment clearly more
attractive.

The profitability index is a formal way of expressing this *cost/
benefit* relationship:

$$\text{Profitability index} = \frac{\text{Present value of operating inflows (benefit)}}{\text{Present value of net investment (cost)}}$$

The present values in this formula are the same amounts we used earlier to derive the net present value, although then we *subtracted* inflows from outflows. In the case of the profitability index the question is simply: How much in present value benefits is being created for each dollar of net investment? The two cases we cited above would yield the following results:

$$1.\ \text{Profitability index} = \frac{\$11,000}{\$10,000} = 1.10$$

$$2.\ \text{Profitability index} = \frac{\$26,000}{\$25,000} = 1.04$$

The higher the index, the better the project. As we expected, the first project is much more favorable, given the assumption that all other aspects of the investment are reasonably comparable. If the index is 1.0 or less, the project is just meeting or is even below the minimum earnings standard used to derive the present values. An index of *exactly 1.0* corresponds to a *zero* net present value, based on the mathematical relationship. Our simple machine example has a profitability index of 1.16 at 8 percent in Table 6–3 ($115,575 ÷ $100,000), and 1.03 at 12 percent in Table 6–4 ($102,800 ÷ $100,000).

The profitability index measure does provide additional insight for the analyst or manager. As already mentioned, it allows us to choose between investment alternatives of differing size. But it still leaves several points unanswered, and there are theoretical issues involved that we will point out later in the chapter.

Internal Rate of Return (Yield). The concept of a "true" return yielded by an investment over its economic life (often referred to as the *discounted cash flow return,* or *DCF*) has already been mentioned in the earlier discussion of net present value. This *internal rate of return* is simply that unique discount rate which, when applied to both cash inflows and cash outflows over the investment's economic life, provides a *zero net present value*—that is, the present value of the inflows is exactly equal to the present value of the outflows.

Stated another way, the principal can be amortized over the economic life, while earning the exact return implied by the underlying discount rate. Thus, the project may *yield* the earnings standard desired, but *only if* the underlying rate happens to *coincide* with the standard.

Naturally, the result will vary with changes in economic life and the pattern of cash flows. In fact, the internal rate of return is found by letting it become a *variable* that is dependent on cash flows and economic life. In the case of the net present value and the profitability index, we had employed a *specified* earnings standard to discount the investment's cash flows. For the internal rate of return we turn the problem around to *find the discount rate* that makes cash inflows and outflows *equal*. We can again employ our simple formula (Present value = Factor × Annuity), if the project is simple enough to involve a *single* investment outlay and only *level* annual cash inflows. The formula can then be turned around as follows:

$$\text{Factor} = \frac{\text{Present value (investment)}}{\text{Annuity}}$$

This factor can then be located in the present value table for annuities (Table 6–10 on page 280). Because the economic life is a given, we can find the rate of return by moving along the proper period row to the column containing a factor that approximates the formula result. To illustrate, our earlier investment example has a factor of 4.0 ($100,000 ÷ $25,000). On the line for period 6 in Table 6–10 we find that the factor 4.0 lies almost exactly between 12 percent (4.112) and 14 percent (3.889). Approximate interpolation suggests that the result is about 13 percent. Again, using electronic calculators or computer programs with discounting capability will eliminate the need for the table.

When a project has a more complex cash flow pattern, a trial-and-error approach is needed if the analysis is done with the help of present value tables. Successive application of different discount rates to all cash flows over the investment's economic life must be made until a reasonably close approximation of a zero net present value has been found. With some experience, an analyst will find that usually no more than two trials are necessary, because the first result will show the *direction* of any refinement needed. A positive net present value calls for applying a *higher* discount rate, while a negative one requires a *lower* rate. We observed this effect in our earlier example, when the net present value declined as the discount rate was raised from 8 to 12 percent (see Tables 6–3 and 6–4). Again, programmed calculators and computers will arrive at the result directly.

The internal rate of return is much superior for ranking investments compared to the simple methods (payback and accounting return) discussed earlier. The method is not without problems, however. First, there is the mathematical possibility that a complex project with many varied cash inflows and outflows over its economic life may in fact yield *two different* internal rates of return. This is caused by the specific pattern and timing of the various cash inflows and outflows. While relatively rare, such a result can be an inconvenience.

More important is the practical issue of choosing among alternative projects that involve widely *differing net investments* and have internal rates of return *inverse* to the size of the project (the smaller investment has the higher return). A $10,000 investment with an internal rate of return of 50 percent cannot be directly compared to an outlay of $100,000 with a 30 percent internal rate of return, particularly if the risks are similar and the company normally requires a 15 percent earnings standard. While both exceed the desired return, it may indeed be better to employ the larger sum at 30 percent than the smaller sum at 50 percent, unless *both* projects can be undertaken. If the economic life of alternative projects differs widely, it may similarly be advantageous to employ funds at a lower rate for a longer period of time than to opt for a brief period of higher return, *if* a choice must be made between two investments, both of which *exceed* the corporate standard.

It should be apparent that the internal rate of return, like all other measures, must be used with caution. Inasmuch as it provides the analyst with a *unique* ("true") rate of return inherent to each project, the yield of an investment permits ranking potential alternatives by a single "number." We recall from our earlier discussion of the net present value method that *a specified earnings standard* reflecting the company's expectations from such investments was used there. In contrast, the internal rate of return approach solves for an earnings rate *unique to each project*.

We know, however, that the company's earnings standard usually is an expression of the long-run earnings power of the company, even if only approximate. Thus, a management applying a 15 or 20 percent return standard to investments must realize that a project with its own internal rate of return of, say, 30 percent cannot be assumed to have its cash flows *reinvested* at this unique higher rate. Unless the general earnings standard is quite unrealistic, funds thrown off by capital investments can only be expected to be reemployed over time at this *lower* average rate. This apparent dilemma does not, however, invalidate the internal rate of return measure, because the individual project will certainly yield the higher return if all conditions hold over its economic life.

We will return later in this chapter to a comparative overview of all measures and develop basic rules for their application. The reader is also invited to turn to the references listed at the end of the chapter for more exhaustive discussions of the many theoretical and practical arguments surrounding the use of present value, particularly in the case of the internal rate of return.

Risk Analysis.   The estimates used to analyze capital investments are inevitably uncertain because of their *future orientation*. As we stated before, capital investments involve *risk* because of the uncertainties surrounding the key variables used. Consequently, the analyst who prepares the investment calculations and managers who use these results for decision making must allow for a whole *range* of possible outcomes. Even the best estimates can go wrong as events unfold, yet the decisions have to be made in advance of the actual experience.

As a result, the risk inherent in the variations must be ascertained. Such risk analysis can take many forms. In earlier chapters we mentioned *sensitivity analysis* as a formal means of testing the impact of changes in key assumptions. This can be very informal, back-of-the-envelope reasoning, or it can involve systematically working through the impact of assumed changes in revenues, operating savings, costs, size of outlays, recovery of capital, and so on, either singly or in combination, and testing the impact on the results. We also discussed *ranges of estimates,* either for the total result or for individual key variables. These allow management to examine the most optimistic and pessimistic cases as well as the most likely figures, and are superior to single-point estimating.

In this section we will discuss two time-adjusted measures that help management ascertain how much risk is possible for a project to still meet return standards. These measures, *present value payback* and *annualized net present value,* are technically related to the *net present value* criterion. We will also discuss the use of *ranges of estimates* and their refined application in *probabilistic simulation.* Finally, we will touch on the subject of *risk adjusted rates.* Only the first two measures will be taken up in detail, while the other areas will be covered just enough to indicate to the reader the potential value of further studying these concepts.

Present Value Payback. This measure establishes the *minimum life* necessary for an investment to operate as expected and still meet the earnings standard of the present value analysis. In other words, present value payback is achieved at the point in time when the cumulative amount of the positive present values equals the present value of the outlays. It is the period in the project's life when the original investment has been amortized *and* a return equal to the earnings standard has been achieved on the declining balance—the point at which the project becomes economically attractive.

In Tables 6–3 and 6–4 we included a column for the cumulative net present value of the project. It served as a visual check for determining the point at which net present value turned positive. The present value payback for our example with a discount rate of 8 percent was about five years, while a 12 percent standard required almost six years, just about the full economic life of the investment. The minimum time needed to recover the investment and earn the return standard on the declining balance, when compared to the economic life, is a way of expressing the potential risk of the project. The measure does not specifically address the *nature* of the risk, but rather serves to identify any remaining part of the economic life as a *risk allowance*. Management can then judge whether the risk entailed in the combined elements of the project, or any one key variable in particular, is likely to outweigh the cushion of safety implied in the additional time the project may operate once it has passed the present value payback point. It is important to remember, however, that the measure focuses only on the *life* of the project, with the implicit assumption that the estimated operating *conditions* will continue to be achieved.

If uneven and complicated cash flows are projected, a condition we will examine later, the minimum life test of the present value payback requires a year-by-year accumulation of the negative and positive present values, as was done in simplified form in Tables 6–3 and 6–4. If a project is a straightforward combination of a single outlay at point zero and level annual operating cash inflows, we can make use of the annuity factors of Table 6–10 to quickly identify the present value payback. To illustrate, the following relationship is utilized:

$$\text{Present value} = \text{Factor} \times \text{Annuity}$$

We are looking for the condition under which the present value of the outflows is *exactly equal* to the present value of the inflows. Inasmuch as net investment (outflow) must be recovered by the inflows, we can change the formula to:

$$\text{Net investment} = \text{Factor} \times \text{Annuity}$$

Because we know the level of the annuity, which is represented by the projected annual operating cash inflows, we can find the factor that satisfies the condition:

$$\text{Factor} = \frac{\text{Net investment}}{\text{Annuity}}$$

For our machine example, we can calculate the following results: $100,000 ÷ $25,000 = 4.0. We can look for the closest factor in the 8 percent column of Table 6–10. The answer lies almost exactly on the line for period 5 (3.993), which indicates that the project's minimum life under the assumed operating conditions must be five years to achieve the standard 8 percent return. If the standard were 12 percent, the minimum life has to be approximately 5⅔ years, which is an interpolation between 3.605 and 4.112.

The test for present value payout or minimum life at any given return standard thus becomes one more factor in assessing the margin for error in the project estimates. It sharpens the analyst's understanding of the relationship of economic life and acceptable performance, and it is a much improved version of the simple payback. The measure is a useful companion to the net present value criterion. It does not, however, address specific risk elements and in fact leaves the assessment of any favorable difference between minimum and economic life to the judgment of management.

Annualized Net Present Value.   Another approach to *testing for risk* involves an estimate of how much of an annual shortfall in operating cash inflows is permissible over the *full economic life* of the project while still meeting the minimum return standard. We know that the net present value calculation normally results in either a cumulative excess or deficiency of present value benefits vis-à-vis the net investment. We also know that if the net present value is positive, the amount can be viewed as a "cushion" against any estimating error contained in future cash inflows. Unless a project has highly irregular annual flows, it is often useful to transform this net present value cushion into an *equivalent annuity* over the project's economic life.

Such an annual equivalent, representing the allowable margin of error, can then be *directly compared* to the original estimates of annual operating cash inflow. This is possible because the present value cushion has in effect been "reconstituted" into level cash flows on the *same basis* as the estimates themselves, that is, in terms of annual flows *unadjusted* for time value. To illustrate, we can transform the net present value shown in Table 6–3, $15,575, into an annuity over the six-year life by simply using the familiar present value relationship:

$$\text{Present value} = \text{Factor} \times \text{Annuity}$$

Because we are interested in finding the annuity represented by the net present value, and wish to do so over a known economic life and at a specified discount rate—which is the earnings standard employed in the net present value calculation in the first place—we can transform the annuity formula as follows:

$$\text{Annuity} = \frac{\text{(Net) present value}}{\text{Factor}}$$

Our example has the following result:

$$\text{Annuity} = \frac{\$15,575}{4.623} = \$3,369$$

The annual operating cash inflows were originally *estimated* to be $25,000. Given the result above, the *actual* cash flow experienced could be *lower* by about $3,400 per year, and the project would still meet the *minimum* standard of 8 percent. Note, however, that the investment has to operate over its *full* economic life for this to be true.

In this case, the risk allowance directly translates into a permissible downward adjustment of estimated operating cash inflows by 13 percent. More important, we know that cash flow consists of aftertax operating profit to which depreciation has been added back. In view of the sizable depreciation allowance of $16,667 contained in the cash flow figure, which is *not* subject to uncertainty, the permissible reduction of $3,369 in the *aftertax profit alone* (from $8,333 to $4,964) amounts to a hefty 40 percent! As we can see, this type of analysis represents a *more direct* approach to judging the allowable risk in the key variables than did the present value payback.

Annualization can be more generally applied as a very practical and quick *preliminary scoping* of the attractiveness of an investment project that has not yet been fleshed out in detail. In effect, the method *reverses* the normal investment analysis by finding the *approximate* annual operating cash flow necessary to justify an estimated capital outlay when *specific* operating benefits have yet to be estimated. Given an estimate of the economic life and an earnings standard, we can employ the formula

$$\text{Operating cash flow} = \frac{\text{Net investment}}{\text{Factor}}$$

to find the annual cash flow equivalent that, on average, will be the *minimum target benefit*. The analyst must be careful, however, to interpret this figure properly. Because by definition it is an aftertax cash flow, the result has to be properly adjusted for the assumed annual depreciation in order to transform it into the minimum *pretax operating improvement* necessary to justify the outlay. The process simply involves working "backward" through the analysis, with the knowledge that cash flow consists of the sum of aftertax operating profit and annual depreciation. We can apply this to our example from Table 6–3 as follows:

First, we find the target cash flow benefits over six years at 8 percent, using the appropriate factor from Table 6–10:

$$\frac{\$100,000}{4.623} = \$21,631$$

Next we transform this aftertax cash flow into its equivalent pretax operating improvement:

Aftertax cash flow	$21,631
Less: Depreciation	16,667
Aftertax profit	$ 4,964
Tax at 34% of pretax profit	2,557
Pretax profit	$ 7,521
Add back depreciation	16,667
Minimum pretax operating improvement	$24,188

Thus, our investment has to provide a minimum of about $24,200 in direct operating improvements such as lower costs, incremental revenues, and so on. Clearly, this method results in a quick estimate of the magnitude of pretax profit improvement required and the likely potential of the investment to bring it about. Annualization applied in this way is a useful tool for making a first assessment of the chances that an investment "will be in the ballpark."

Needless to say, annualization is quickly performed on a programmed calculator or computer, and present value tables are unnecessary. Yet, even though electronic assists make the process "automatic," working the calculation as we have just done will give the reader a feeling for the rationale.

Ranges of Estimates.   Risk can be defined as the *degree of variation* in the actual versus estimated cash benefit levels of an investment. The wider the possible deviations, the greater the risk. Therefore, using a *range* of estimates is a more direct approach to investment risk analysis. It may not be necessary to do this for all types of investments, however, because degrees of risk vary widely among business and financial investments, as do the relative importance and magnitude of the investments themselves.

The risk involved in holding a U.S. government bond, for example, is very small indeed, because default on the interest payments is extremely unlikely. Therefore, the range of possible benefits from the bond investment is narrowly focused on the contractual payments—in effect, no range at all. In contrast, the risk of a business investment for a product or service is a function of the whole range of possible benefit levels that may go from very positive cash flows to negative loss conditions. The uncertainty surrounding these outcomes poses a challenge to the analyst and the decision maker.

The "single point" estimates of annual cash flow projections we have used so far are the *expected* results based on the best judgment of the analyst and the information available. In effect, they are the *average* of the possible outcomes, implicitly weighed by their respective probabilities. By introducing a range of "high," "low," and "expected" levels of annual cash inflows and outflows, the analyst can employ a form of *sensitivity analysis* to indicate the consequences of expected fluctuations in the annual results—and thus, the degree of risk. At times, past experience can provide clues to the range of future outcomes, but essentially the projection of future conditions has to be judgmental and based on specific forward-looking estimates.

The decision maker must assess the likelihood that the range of estimated outcomes fairly expresses the characteristics of the project, and decide whether the expected outcome is sufficiently attractive to compensate for the possibility that the actual results may vary as defined. Risk assessment in essence comes down to how comfortable the decision maker is with the possibility of experiencing adverse results—that is, a very personal *risk preference or aversion*. Stipulating a range helps the responsible person or group to visualize the possible extremes in the expected results.

Probabilistic Simulation. A more refined approach to risk assessment consists of estimating ranges not only for the total annual cash flows, but also for the *individual key variables* that make up these cash flows. Probability distributions are then assigned to the likelihood of the outcomes for each of the variables; any interdependencies between variables are defined; and the outcomes of the project can then be *simulated* by running many iterations on the computer. The method is an extension of sensitivity analysis in that the potential changes in many variables are evaluated both *simultaneously* and in *relation to each other*.

The result is a range of possible annual cash inflows in the form of a probability distribution, or even a range of net present values or internal rates of return arrayed by probability. Such a "risk profile" allows the decision maker to think about the relative attractiveness of a project in terms of statements such as "chances are 9 out of 10 that the project will meet the minimum standard of 10 percent," or "there is a probability of 60 percent that the net present value of the project will be at least $1 million or better." Cumulative probability distributions such as those shown in Figure 6–4 can be drawn up as an assist.

The relative ease with which computer simulation can be carried out does not eliminate the many *practical* issues involved in assigning specific probability distributions to the individual variables in the first place or ease the problem of

Figure 6–4
Cumulative Probability Distribution for Two Projects

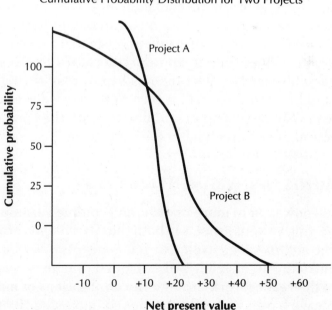

interpreting the final results. As we said before, judging both the likelihood of an event and one's own attitude toward the risk expressed in this fashion is a highly personal response that often defies precise quantification. The amount of risk a decision maker will accept is largely a matter of personal experience and preference. In addition, investment decisions in a business setting are as much a function of complex personal and group dynamics as they are dependent on the pure analytical results, the quality of presentation, and examination of specific economic data.

Risk-Adjusted Return Standards. Another way of adjusting for risk is to *modify* the return standard itself to include a *risk premium* where warranted. In a sense, the concept is quite simple—the greater the risk, the higher the return desired from the investment. Also, this reasoning is intuitively attractive to business decision makers, because the process parallels the way we think about personal investments. Investments in businesses subject to wide profit swings and competitive pressures would command a premium above the return standard, while fairly predictable businesses might find a less-than-average return acceptable. When multiple return standards are employed, it is done on the assumption that a diversified company can use different standards, which, in combination, will ensure an appropriate return to the shareholders and also fairly reflect the risk exposure of the individual lines of business. We will return to the basis for earnings standards in the next chapter and discuss both the conceptual and practical issues involved in deriving them.

REFINEMENTS OF INVESTMENT ANALYSIS

We will now turn to more realistic and complex examples in order to refine various aspects of both the *components* of analysis and the *methodology* itself. No *new* concepts or techniques will be introduced; instead, two expanded practical examples will help the reader work through the implications of many of the points we have so far only mentioned in passing. By going through the projects step by step, the essentials of economic investment analysis should become firmly implanted in the reader's mind. At this point, we stress again the need to fully *define the problem,* as well as to clearly understand the rationale for deriving the *net investment, operating cash flows,* the *economic life,* and *any terminal values.* Once these are properly established, the actual calculation of the appropriate yardsticks becomes almost automatic.

Example One: A Machine Replacement

A company is analyzing whether to replace an existing five-year-old machine with a more automatic and faster model. Acquiring a new machine of some sort is considered as the only reasonable alternative under the circumstances, because the product fabricated on the equipment is expected to continue to be profitable for at least 10 years. Moreover, the markets served could absorb additional output beyond the current capacity, as much as one-third more than the present volume. The old machine is estimated to have at most 5 years' life left before it becomes physically worn out, while the new machine will operate acceptably for 10 years before it has to be scrapped. The old machine originally cost $25,000 and has a current book value of $12,500, having been depreciated straight-line at $2,500 per year. It can be sold for $14,000 in cash to a ready buyer.

The new machine will cost $40,000 installed. Also to be depreciated straight-line over 10 years, it will likely be salable at book value if disposed of before the end of its physical life. It has an annual capacity of 125,000 units, compared to the 100,000 unit ceiling of the present equipment, and it will produce at lower *unit* costs for both labor and materials. In fact, the new machine will involve lower *total* labor costs because it will require fewer setups, releasing the time of the skilled mechanics performing the setups for other productive tasks in the plant. Two operators are required as before. Materials usage will be more efficient due to a lower level of rejects. The company expects no difficulty in selling the additional volume at the current price of $1.50 and will only incur modest incremental selling and promotional expense in the process.

Such a set of conditions is both common and realistic, with the possible exception of the stable long-term market conditions assumed. As we analyze this project, we will expand on several aspects of economic capital investment analysis and draw generalized conclusions where appropriate.

Net Investment Refined. We recall that net investment was defined as the *net change* in funds committed to a project as a result of the decision. Two specific changes in funds must be considered in this case: First, there is the *outlay* of $40,000 for the new machine, which is a straightforward cash commitment. Second, there is the *recovery* of cash from the sale of the old machine. Since it is a *direct consequence* of the decision to replace, this release of funds is *relevant* to the analysis. The amount received for the old machine will be *less* than its $14,000 cash value, however, because the gain from the sale is a *taxable* event. (We recall that the book value was only $12,500; thus the company will be taxed on the difference of $1,500.) For simplicity we will assume that the applicable tax rate is the top corporate income tax rate of 34 percent, resulting in an incremental tax outlay of $510.

We now have all the components of the initial net investment figure relevant for this example, as shown below:

Cost of the new machine	$40,000
Cash from sale of old machine	(14,000)
Tax payable on capital gain of $1,500	510
Net investment	$26,510

In economic analysis we do not recognize the remaining *book value* on the old machine, *except for its impact on income tax* outlays. As we observed before, funds expended in the *past* are irrelevant because they represent a *sunk cost*. We are interested only in the *changes* that are caused by the *current decision*. As a consequence, the proceeds from the equipment sale as well as the tax outlay for the capital gain resulting from the transaction are the relevant elements. Had the old machine been unsalable despite its stated book value of $12,500, the only item of relevance would be the tax *savings* from the capital *loss* under that assumption. Yet some analysts are tempted to confuse accounting practice with economic analysis and will include book values even though they are irrelevant.

The net investment shown represents a net balance of cash movements, both in and out, of all consequences of the investment decision. Were one to assume that the decision might also cause working *capital* to rise, supporting the higher product volume expected to be sold, such an increase in funds committed to receivables and inventories, less increased payables, would also become relevant for our analysis. Similarly, if *further capital outlays* in later years were a direct consequence of this decision, such amounts would have to be recognized in the analysis. Later we will demonstrate in our second example how incremental working capital and sequential investments are handled.

Operating Cash Flows Refined.   As we established before, operating cash flows are the net *cash changes after taxes* in revenue and cost elements resulting from the investment decision. In our replacement example, we must first carefully sort out the relevant conditions to identify relevant *differential revenues and costs*. Each element should be tested whether the decision to replace will make a *cash* difference in operating conditions.

The decision to replace has three significant effects: First, the new machine will bring about greater efficiency, which should result in *operating savings*. Second, the additional volume of product produced will provide additional *profit contribution*, if we assume the sales efforts are successful. Third, we must allow for the *tax* impact of the *change* in the level of *depreciation*. The calculations in Table 6–5 illustrate how to deal with these elements in clearly labeled successive stages.

Stage One: Operating Savings.   Operating savings for the *existing* level of output (100,000 units) are determined by simply comparing the *annual* costs of operating the two machines at that rate. Each requires two operators, but the new machine will incur $1,000 less in setup costs. We were also told earlier that the new machine uses materials more efficiently, and this attribute will save about $2,000.

Table 6–5
Differential Cost and Revenue Analysis

	Old Machine	New Machine	Relevant Annual Differences
1. Operating savings from current volume of 100,000 units:			
Labor (2 operators plus setup)	$ 31,000	$ 30,000	$ 1,000
Material	38,000	36,000	2,000
Overhead (120% of direct labor)	37,200	36,000	—*
	$106,200	$102,000	3,000
2. Contribution from additional volume of 25,000 units:			
25,000 units sold at $1.50 per unit		$ 37,500	
Less:			
Labor (no additional operators)		—	
Material cost at 36¢/unit		(9,000)	
Additional selling expense		(11,500)	
Additional promotional expense		(13,000)	$ 4,000
Total savings and additional contribution .			$ 7,000
3. Differential depreciation (additional expense; for tax purposes only)	$ 2,500	$ 4,000	$(1,500)
Taxable operating improvements			5,500
Income tax at 34%			1,870
Aftertax profit improvement			3,630
Add back depreciation			1,500
Aftertax operating cash flow			$ 5,130

*Not relevant, because it represents an allocation only.

Overhead changes, in contrast, are *not relevant* for this comparison, because the figures represent *allocations* at the rate of 120 percent of direct labor. The fact that labor cost has declined does not mean that *spending* on overhead has changed. What *has* changed is the *basis* of allocation, which in this case happens to be a rate related to the cost of labor. The plant manager and the office staff still receive the same salaries, and other overhead costs are not affected. Only if the decision to replace *directly* caused an actual change in overhead *spending*, such as higher property taxes, insurance premiums, additional maintenance, technical support, etc., would a change have to be reflected in the calculation. Under those conditions, we would estimate the annual overhead expenditures before and after the installation of the new machine, and develop the *differential* cost to be included in the analysis, just as we did for the other differential operating cash flows.

Whenever we are comparing operating costs, it is usually more appropriate to use *annual* costs or revenues rather than *per unit* figures. The latter may cause the analyst to inadvertently apply *accounting allocations*, which as a rule are irrelevant for economic analysis, even though they are necessary and appropriate for cost accounting (determining cost of goods sold, inventory values, price estimating, etc.) in line with generally accepted accounting principles.

Stage Two: Contribution from Additional Volume. Now we are ready to determine the *incremental contribution* from the increased output. This change must be counted as an additional benefit from the decision to replace because the old machine had a ceiling of 100,000 units of production. The additional *sales revenue* from the extra 25,000 units available for sale at $1.50 each is relevant, as are any additional *costs* that can be attributed to the higher volume. We know that the two existing operators are able to produce the higher output, and thus there will be *no* additional *labor* cost. The higher volume will require additional *materials*, however, which are charged at the usage rate of the more efficient machine, that is, 36 cents per unit. We have also been told that additional *selling and promotional* expenses will be incurred to move the higher volume, and these are relevant as well. The combination of savings and incremental profit totals $7,000.

Stage Three: Tax Effect. The only remaining relevant item is the *tax impact of differential depreciation*. As we discussed in Chapters 1 and 2, depreciation *as such* is not relevant to funds flows. For purposes of our analysis, it merits attention only because depreciation is tax deductible. Inasmuch as depreciation charges normally reduce income tax payments, they are called a "tax shield." If an investment decision causes higher or lower depreciation charges, such a difference must be reflected as a *change in the tax shield*.

For our replacement example, the *differential* depreciation for the next five years will be $1,500, an increase due to the higher cost basis of the new machine. We are assuming straight-line depreciation is used for tax purposes, to keep the calculations simple.

As shown in Table 6–5, the analysis results in taxable operating improvements of $7,000, an incremental tax of $1,870 and a change in aftertax profit of $3,630. The applicable tax rate is normally the rate a company would be paying on any incremental profit. As the final step, the differential depreciation is *added back* to arrive at the aftertax operating cash flow of $5,130. In doing this we have correctly reflected a tax reduction due to the differential depreciation, but we then *removed* depreciation itself from the picture to leave us with the *economic cash effect* of the investment. We could have obtained the same result by doing the analysis in two steps: (1) determining the tax on the operating improvement *before* depreciation, and (2) directly determining the tax shield effect of the differential depreciation. This would appear as shown below, and as we might expect, the result is exactly the same.

Taxable operating improvement	$7,000
Tax at 34 percent	2,380
Aftertax operating improvement	$4,620
Tax shield at 34%* of depreciation of $1,500	510
Aftertax operating cash flow	$5,130

Economic Life Refined.   Earlier we defined economic life as the length of time over which an investment yields economic benefits. Now we find that a complication has been introduced because of the expected *difference* in the physical lives of the two machines. Inasmuch as the old machine is assumed to wear out in 5 years while the new will last for 10, the two investments are *comparable only* over the next 5 *years*. After that, the original alternative no longer exists, and

---

* Each dollar of depreciation provides a tax shield of $1 times the applicable tax rate.

Figure 6–5
Overlapping Economic Life Spans

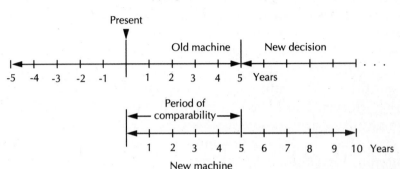

a decision would *have* to be made at that point in any case. The situation is illustrated in Figure 6–5. Differential revenues and costs can be defined *only* as long as both alternatives exist *together*. After five years, the old machine will be gone, which means that we *cannot* analyze the situation *beyond* five years without making some assumptions about the remaining life of the new machine. While we have assumed the product is likely to be salable for at least the total 10-year life of the new machine, the economic comparison for the replacement decision can be made only over 5 years.

There are two ways of handling this problem. First, we can *cut off* the analysis at the end of year 5 and assign an assumed recovery value to the new machine at that point, because the machine should be able to operate well for another five years. This "terminal value" estimate must be counted as a *capital recovery* in year 5; that is, its present value should be counted as a benefit. The approach is widely used in practice, and usually the amount of terminal value is estimated as *at least* the book value. If the value of the asset is quite predictable, however, as is the case with automobiles or trucks, an estimated sales value is stipulated and entered in the present value analysis as a benefit.

An alternative way of dealing with the problem is to assume that the old machine would be *replaced* by a new one in year 5, and a similar replacement would be made in year 10 when the current new machine wears out. This approach involves a great deal of guessing about replacement conditions 5 and 10 years hence. Yet in spite of this analytical effort, the economic lives of the two machines would still not be the same. Admittedly, the power of discounting would make the estimates of the later years almost immaterial. On balance, unless there are compelling reasons to develop such a series of replacement assumptions, the cutoff analysis described earlier is far more straightforward and less fraught with judgmental traps.

Capital Additions and Recoveries. The treatment of terminal values deserves a few more comments here. It is quite common for larger projects to require a series of additional capital outlays. Later on there are likely recoveries of at least part of these funds. As a practical matter, any increments of capital committed or recovered should be entered as *cash outflows or cash inflows* in the present value framework at the point in time when they occur. This also applies to incremental *working capital* commitments, which should be shown as a present outflow and can be assumed to be recovered in total or in part at the end of the economic life of the project.

In our replacement example we have made no provision for additional working capital in order to keep the problem focused on other basic refinements. The assumed terminal value of the new machine after five years, however, would be treated as a *capital recovery* and entered as a positive cash inflow at the end of year 5. For simplicity we will assume that its economic value (realizable through sale or trade) will be equal to its book value. This would amount to $20,000 ($40,000 less five years' depreciation at $4,000 per year), with no taxable capital gain or loss expected. We would have to modify this amount, of course, if circumstances indicated a higher or lower value due to changes in technology or other conditions. Book value is frequently used because it is easy to do, causes no taxable gains or losses, and also because the need for precision in terminal values is diminished by the exponential impact of discounting in later years.

Analytical Framework for Example One. With all the basic data at hand, we can now lay out the framework for a present value analysis. We will assume a 10 percent return standard and again set up the figures in a tabular format. The result in Table 6–6 indicates a sizable net present value of $5,353—that is, if all of our assumptions are borne out in fact. It would suggest that the replacement is desirable, at least on a numerical basis.

Note that the analysis is significantly affected by the assumed recovery of the book value of $20,000 in year 5, which amounts to a present value inflow of $12,420. In effect, this inflow reduces the net investment to only $14,090 in present value terms. For purposes of economic analysis, this value has to be considered an *inflow* at the end of year 5, even though there is no intention of actually selling the machine at that point. The relevance for today's decision is that the company would have the *option* of selling at the end of year 5 and thereby realizing this economic value. After the five years are over, the alternative of selling could, of course, be compared with the alternative of recommitting the realizable value of $20,000 in order to preserve the profitable business at the level of 125,000 units. But these latter considerations deal with a *future* set of decisions and therefore are not relevant today.

Table 6–6
Present Value Analysis of Machine Replacement

Time Period	Investment	Operating Cash Inflows	Present Value Factors at 10 Percent*	Present Value of Net Investment	Present Value of Operating Inflows
0	− $26,510	—	1.000	− $26,510	—
1	—	+$ 5,130	0.909	—	+$ 4,663
2	—	+ 5,130	0.826	—	+ 4,237
3	—	+ 5,130	0.751	—	+ 3,853
4	—	+ 5,130	0.683	—	+ 3,504
5	—	+ 5,130	0.621	—	+ 3,186
5 (end)	+ 20,000	—	0.621	+ 12,420	—
	− $ 6,510	+$25,650		− $14,090	+$19,443
				Net present value	+$ 5,353

*For years 1 to 5, we could use 3.791 from Table 6–10.

The *profitability index* of the project is positive, as we might expect from the sizable net present value of about $5,400. Dividing $14,090 (net investment less recovery) into the operating benefits of $19,443 results in an index of 1.38, which should give the project a favorable ranking if the average return from the company's investment opportunities is only 10 percent. Some analysts prefer to express the profitability index by relating the *original net investment* to the total of *all inflows*, including capital recoveries. In our example the result would be $31,863 ÷ $26,510 = 1.20, again a very favorable showing when this more stringent test is applied. While we could argue for and against either method, consistent application of one of them will be satisfactory.

The *internal rate of return* has to be found by trial and error using the present value tables, because the capital recovery at the end of year 5 complicates an otherwise straightforward annuity. The problem can be handled as shown in Table 6–7. The trial at 15 percent indicates a positive net present value of $626, but at 16 percent it is reduced to a negative $194. Thus, the precise result is slightly under 16 percent.

A *risk analysis* can be made by calculating the *present value payback* (minimum life) and the *annualized net present value*.

Table 6–7
Present Value Analysis to Find Internal Rate of Return

Time Period	Cash Flows	Present Value Factors at 15 Percent	Present Values at 15 Percent	Present Value Factors at 16 Percent	Present Values at 16 Percent
0	− $26,510	1.000	− $26,510	1.000	− $26,510
1					
2					
3	+ 5,130/yr.	3.352*	+ 17,196	3.274*	+ 16,796
4					
5					
5 (end)	+ 20,000	0.497	+ 9,940	0.476	+ 9,520
	+ $19,140		+ $ 626		− $ 194

*From Table 6–10.

For the former we must cumulate the present values of the operating cash inflows until they approximate the present value of the net investment of $14,090. A quick addition shows that this will happen after slightly more than 3 years, which leaves a cushion of almost 2 years against uncertainty.

A technical question arises here as to whether we should bring the assumed recovery amount at the end of year 5 *forward in time* to obtain a more precise calculation of minimum life. This would involve a process of *iteration*, because not only would the present value of the recovery rise, but the sales value of the machine would also be higher in earlier years. Such a refinement is normally not called for, even though it can be handled through computer simulation.

The *annualized net present value* can be found when we divide the net present value in Table 6–6 by the 10 percent annuity factor in year 5 from Table 6–10, or $5,353 ÷ 3.791, which is $1,412 per year. All other aspects being equal, the project would still be acceptable if the annual operating cash inflows over the five years dropped from $5,130 to only $3,718, a possible shrinkage of almost 30 percent. If we remove the tax shield of $510 from this test, (see page 262) the allowable drop in the pure aftertax operating improvement could be better than 30 percent ($1,412 against $4,620).

Another way of looking at the net present value cushion would be to ask how sensitive the result would be to a *reduction* in the expected capital recovery at the end of year 5. This answer can be readily found by *reconstituting* at the *end of year 5* a dollar amount that has the equivalent present value of the cushion of $5,130. To find this *future* dollar amount, we simply divide the present value of $5,130 by the single sum factor given in Table 6–9 for 10 percent in period 5, which is 0.621, an amount of $8,261. We see that if the expected recovery of $20,000 were reduced by about $8,300, the project would still be acceptable, given that all other conditions hold.

While perhaps a little complex, the step-by-step process we have just completed has exposed most of the practical issues encountered in investment analysis. Let us turn to one more illustration that additionally shows the handling of working capital and successive investments.

Example Two: A Business Expansion

The cash flow patterns in Table 6–8 show the kinds of commitments and recoveries normally associated with a major business expansion. In the early life of the project, we find not only an outlay for facilities but also a buildup of working capital during the first and second years. Additional equipment outlays are required at the end of years 4 and 6, while recoveries of equipment and working capital are made as the economic life comes to an end. All cash flows are assumed to have been adjusted for tax consequences along the lines we discussed in our first example. The operating cash flows show a growth stage, peak in the middle years, and decline towards the end.

Nothing new is required to deal with this investment example. *Working capital* (additional inventories and receivables, less new trade obligations) represents a commitment of capital just as definite as an expenditure for buildings and equipment, except that no depreciation write-off is involved. If all inventories and receivables can be expected to be liquidated at the end of the economic life, this capital (net of payables) will be an inflow at that point, a *capital recovery*. If we assume some fraction of this investment to be unsalable or uncollectible, the figure must be lowered.

Additional capital expenditures for equipment during the life of the project are simply recognized as cash outflows when incurred. Care must be taken, however, to reflect the additional *depreciation* pattern in each case as a tax shield during future operating periods. Uneven cash flows present no problems when programmed calculators are used to find the present value of each period's flows. But to demonstrate how the calculations are made, we have employed the present value tables to find the factors, including those for *partial annuities*.

As was shown in Table 6–8, the expected result of the project is a positive *net present value* of almost $12 million. The *profitability index* is 1.07, while the *internal rate of return*

Table 6-8

Present Value Analysis of a Complex Expansion Project
($000)

Time Period	Investments	Operating Cash Inflows (all tax adjustments made)	Present Value Factors at 12 Percent	Present Value of Investments	Present Value of Operating Inflows
0	−$130,000 (facilities)		1.000	−$130,000	
1	− 25,000 (working capital)	+$ 20,000	0.893*	− 22,325	+$ 17,860
2	− 20,000 (working capital)	+ 40,000	0.797*	− 15,940	—
3		+ 40,000 }			
4		+ 40,000 }	2.144†	—	+ 85,760
4 (end)	− 15,000 (additional equipment)‡		0.636*	− 9,540	—
5		+ 50,000 }			
6		+ 50,000 }	1.075†	—	+ 53,750
6 (end)	− 10,000 (equipment overhaul)‡		0.507*	− 5,070	—
7		+ 20,000	0.452*	—	+ 9,040
8		+ 10,000	0.404*	—	+ 4,040
8 (end)	+ 25,000 (equipment recovery)§		0.404*	+ 24,240	—
	+ 35,000 (working capital recovery)§	—			
	−$140,000	+$270,000		−$158,635	+$170,450
			Net present value		+$ 11,815

*From Table 6-9.

†From Table 6-10, representing the difference between the annuity factors applicable: 3.037–0.893, and 4.112–3.037, respectively.

‡Additional depreciation has been reflected in cash inflows.

§Assume loss in liquidation of $10,000.

269

is approximately 13 percent. This finding leaves little margin for error, indeed. The annualized net present value suggests that the annual operating cash inflows can be reduced by $11,815 ÷ 4.968, or at most by about $2.4 million per year. The minimum life (present value payback) is about six years, when all capital recoveries are included.

This is as far as we can carry the analysis with the data at hand. The various judgments leading to the final decision call for much more insight into the nature of the product, the technology, the requirements, and outlook of the marketplace, the competitive setting, and so forth, as we outlined in the first section of this chapter.

When to Use the Investment Measures

During our discussion of the various investment analysis measures, we cautioned the reader about shortcomings and issues of interpretation. We will now review and expand some of these caveats.

Basically, investment analysis measures exist to help analysts and managers determine whether a project meets the earnings standard established for the business. Also, they assist them in ranking the relative desirability of a group of proposals during the capital budgeting process. If the projects being considered are *independent of each other*, the time-adjusted measures of *net present value, profitability index,* and *internal rate of return* will singly or in combination properly reflect the projects' relative economic attractiveness and result in an appropriate ranking sequence. In contrast, the simple measures, *payback* and *simple rate of return,* are quite limited in their use as indicators of economic desirability. They will give a proper ranking *only* if the cash flow patterns and economic lives of the projects are quite similar, a very restrictive assumption.

Uneven lives of capital investments pose complications that are handled by adjusting the analysis to equalize the time spans for purposes of comparison. This can be achieved by truncating the life of a project with an assumed recovery of funds from disposal at an earlier point, as we did in the replacement example, or by extending the shorter alternative by assuming repeated investment. Competing alternative projects with different lives can be compared by annualizing their net present values over their respective economic lives to determine their respective annual equivalent benefits or cost. This process simply calls for dividing the net present value by the relevant annuity factor or using an appropriate computer program.

Mutually exclusive projects, such as those that represent two or three ways of achieving the same objective but require different levels of investments, and which have different operating cash flow patterns or economic lives, pose a special problem. In every case, only one of the alternatives can be undertaken. The various investment measures may show somewhat different rankings, and the analyst is faced with deciding how to optimize the value to the company. Normally, the *profitability index* will give a fair assessment, but the choice has to be considered in terms of the relative size and length of the commitment as well—the risk/reward trade-off. As only one alternative can be chosen, a large investment with a somewhat lower profitability index and yield may be preferable to a smaller investment, if both alternatives show benefits *well above* normal. In other words, it may be better to earn 20 percent on a $10 million investment for 12 years than to earn 22 percent on $6 million for a shorter period, if normal returns are 15 percent, assuming that other conditions including risk are supportive.

Another way of analyzing mutually exclusive alternatives with different levels of investment outlays is the use of *incremental* analysis. The analyst starts with the least costly option to establish the desirability of the investment per se and successively tests the economic attractiveness of each increment of investment against the specific increment of benefits it provides. Again, the results have to be viewed in the broader context of alternate opportunities for earning returns on these funds.

If a company's projects exceed the limits of its funding potential, a fairly common condition, management has to apply *capital rationing*. This involves choosing among projects that might all be acceptable if funds were unconstrained. The investment measures used here have to provide an economic ranking. Essentially, the company should choose that group of projects within the budget limit that will generate the *highest aggregate net present value*. Projects can be ranked in declining order of their profitability index until the budgeted amount has been exhausted. This amounts to maximizing the present value benefits achieved per dollar of investment, because investment funds are the limiting factor. The concept ties closely to the principles of shareholder value, as will be discussed in Chapter 9. In practice, capital budgets are rarely so precise that truly attractive projects initially rejected for lack of funds could not at least be reconsidered.

Let us remember that there should be nothing automatic about the use of investment measures. Yet the seemingly precise results achieved with present value calculations can tempt us to "let the numbers decide." Many more elements have to be weighed in even in fairly straightforward projects, as we observed at the beginning of the chapter. Besides the obvious constraints imposed by uncertainty in the economic estimates, management must also consider competitive, technical, human, societal, and other constraints within the company's strategic context before significant investment or divestment decisions are made.

SOME FURTHER CONSIDERATIONS

Several specialized aspects of capital investment analysis have been mentioned only briefly so far. A detailed treatment would go beyond the scope of this book; yet, for completeness, we will add some further comments on the topics of *leasing*, the impact of *accelerated depreciation* on present value analysis, and the impact of *inflation*. Finally, we will once more put into perspective the degree of accuracy warranted in the calculations.

Leasing

Leasing is a popular means of obtaining a wide variety of capital assets for businesses as well as individuals. For our purposes, the most important point to consider is that leasing represents one *form of financing* that should be considered *only after* economic investment analysis has shown that a project is acceptable. This is consistent with the business systems approach we have taken, where we are separating decisions on investment, operations, and financing. The funding for capital investments should come from appropriate sources, of course, matching their long-term nature. But the specific alternatives of financing, including leasing, are independent of the justification of the investment itself.

When leasing is used to fund an investment, the periodic charges paid by the lessee compensate the lessor for elements such as interest on the capital advanced, risk, obsolescence, maintenance costs, and profit to the legal owner of the asset. The pattern of the lease payments can vary widely among competing offerings. Lease payments are generally tax-deductible outlays for the lessee, but they differ from the economic cash flows we have discussed in this chapter because they include elements of compensation to the lessor. All along, we have viewed investment analysis as a cash flow trade-off that is *independent* of the compensation paid for the funds that finance the asset. Therefore, the analysis of lease patterns would require separation of the implicit financing costs in the cash payments made by the lessee. It is much more direct to test the economic desirability of an investment on the basis of the benefits expected and to make a *separate economic test* whether the company is better off leasing or owning the assets involved, which would involve comparing various funding methods. A number of specialized software programs exist that permit analysts and managers to make the tests necessary for comparing financing alternatives. The question is clearly "lease versus buy," not "invest versus not invest." Because of the special complexities involved in these analytical methods, the reader is directed to the references at the end of the chapter for detailed discussion and illustration.

Accelerated Depreciation

For simplicity, we have used straight-line depreciation in this chapter to derive the tax shield effect of depreciation charges as they affect economic analysis. However, we also referred to the accelerated write-offs allowed under the Internal Revenue Code (see Chapter 3), which are periodically modified by Congress. Rather than focus on any one of the several methods permitted, we will make only a few generally applicable comments.

We are interested in depreciation, *whatever* pattern it may take, *only* insofar as it changes the *tax expenditures* of the company undertaking the investment analysis. From a present value standpoint, accelerated depreciation is an advantage because it moves the tax impact of the write-offs forward in time. In other words, in the early years of a project the tax shield effect will be greater than under straight-line conditions. Similarly, shorter lives permitted by the ever-changing Revenue Code will also place more tax benefits into the early stages of a project. Therefore, project benefits will be *increased* in the present value context, assuming, of course, that the company has sufficient taxable profits to take advantage of higher early write-offs. The calculations required to take account of accelerated depreciation in economic investment analysis can be easily handled with computer spreadsheets, just as any other uneven cash flow pattern can be accommodated.

The reader is encouraged to seek out the most current information published by the IRS to ascertain the proper depreciation class and write-off patterns for the assets being analyzed, and also to be aware of the particular tax management circumstances of the company that may affect its election of write-off patterns for tax purposes.

Accuracy

At all times we must remember that the *precision* implied by the mathematical basis of capital investment tools should be viewed with extreme caution. As we have pointed out before, the very nature of cash flow estimates is uncertain because they are based on expectations, forecasts, projections, and sometimes plain guesses. Only rarely does the analyst deal with contractual sums, such as interest or lease payments—and even these are subject to a degree of uncertainty. It therefore makes no sense to generate deceptively precise results or to allow highly specific numerical rankings to take on undue importance. In our examples we have been more precise than we needed to be; the main intention was to give the reader enough specific details to be able to follow the various methods step by step. In practice, liberal rounding of calculations, and certainly of the final results, is highly advisable to keep the mathematical process from overwhelming the realistic business judgments required.

Keeping accuracy in proper perspective is even more important when we realize that the power of discounting is such that even widely different estimates for distant time periods can be so severely reduced in present value terms that they have relatively minor effects on the final result. A glance at the present value tables will confirm the rapid shrinkage of factors as discount rates rise and periods are more remote.

KEY ISSUES

The following is a recap of the key issues raised directly or indirectly in this chapter. They are enumerated here to help the reader keep the analysis techniques within the perspective of financial theory and business practice.

1. Business investment decisions are made continuously in the larger context of business strategy. This context evolves over time, and the portfolio of potential investments never remains constant.

2. The trade-off between outlays and benefits must be made with the objective of increasing shareholder wealth; that is, the return standards employed in measuring this trade-off must reflect the earnings potential and risks expected from a given business.

3. Shareholder expectations are incorporated into relevant earnings yardsticks through the concept of a weighted cost of capital, which reflects the appropriate level of future compensation to all providers of capital.

4. For an economic judgment, investment measures must take into account the timing of inflows and outflows of an investment and relate economic attractiveness to defined return expectations.

5. Economic analysis of investment decisions must be based on differential revenues and costs in the form of cash flows and not on changes merely due to accounting conventions.

6. Risk is inherent in all estimates of future conditions because of the uncertainty about most variables affecting an investment project. It must be expressed consistently in cash flows and investment measures alike.

7. Inflation and specific price changes in revenues and costs can complicate both the estimating process and the use of investment measures, and they must be handled consistently in both.

8. Capital budgets in practice are neither absolute ceilings on the amount of investments for a company, nor are they automatically affected by purely quantitative project ranking.

9. Financing patterns affect the capability to invest and management's risk tolerance because of the impact of leverage and the need to cover fixed obligations.

10. Analytical techniques can provide ranges of results and quantitative insights of considerable sophistication, but cannot supplant qualitative business judgments that reflect the broader context of strategy and risk assessment.

SUMMARY

In this chapter we have presented the basic analytical framework for investment analysis in the broad context of capital budgeting. The *strategic* backdrop of this activity was highlighted before the techniques themselves were discussed. We put our emphasis on *time-adjusted* concepts and measures because they reflect the economic nature of the analysis and decisions, and we relegated simple rules of thumb to the limited situations where they can be useful. All along, we stressed, however, that the critical aspect of the process was *thoughtful analysis before* the techniques themselves are applied. We emphasized the need to *define the problem*, including development of relevant *alternatives*, and the careful preparation of *relevant data* about the investment, operating differentials, and capital recoveries in an economic *cash flow* context. We found conceptual problems in all of these aspects, particularly in the use and meaning of the investment measures themselves. Working through increasingly complex examples, we provided the reader with a basic ability to perform investment analysis. But we cautioned that numerical results were only inputs to the broader management task of strategic positioning of the business—the selection and matching of appropriate long-term capital commitments with appropriate funding sources, in the framework of defined corporate objectives and goals and with the ultimate achievement of increasing shareholder value.

SELECTED REFERENCES

Analytical Process

Anthony, Robert N. and James S. Reece. *Accounting: Text and Cases.* 8th ed. Homewood, Ill.: Richard D. Irwin, 1988.

Garrison, Raymond H. *Managerial Accounting: Concepts for Planning, Control, Decision Making.* 5th ed. Homewood, Ill: Richard D. Irwin, 1988.

Grant, Eugene L.; W. Grant Ireson; and Richard S. Leavenworth. *Principles of Engineering Economy.* 6th ed. New York: Ronald Press, 1976. A classic.

Rosen, Lawrence R. *Dow Jones-Irwin Guide to Interest: What You Should Know about the Time Value of Money.* Rev. ed. Homewood, Ill.: Dow Jones-Irwin, 1981.

TABLE 6–9

Present Value of Single Sum of $1.00 Received or Paid at End of Period

Period of Receipt or Payment	1%	2%	4%	5%	6%	8%	10%	12%	14%	15%	16%	18%	20%	22%	24%	25%	26%	28%	30%	35%	40%	45%	50%
1	0.990	0.980	0.962	0.952	0.943	0.926	0.909	0.893	0.877	0.870	0.862	0.847	0.833	0.820	0.806	0.800	0.794	0.781	0.769	0.741	0.714	0.690	0.667
2	0.980	0.961	0.925	0.907	0.890	0.857	0.826	0.797	0.769	0.756	0.743	0.718	0.694	0.672	0.650	0.640	0.630	0.610	0.592	0.549	0.510	0.476	0.444
3	0.971	0.942	0.889	0.863	0.840	0.794	0.751	0.712	0.675	0.658	0.641	0.609	0.579	0.551	0.524	0.512	0.500	0.477	0.455	0.406	0.364	0.328	0.296
4	0.961	0.924	0.855	0.823	0.792	0.735	0.683	0.636	0.592	0.572	0.552	0.516	0.482	0.451	0.423	0.410	0.397	0.373	0.350	0.301	0.260	0.226	0.198
5	0.951	0.906	0.822	0.784	0.747	0.681	0.621	0.567	0.519	0.497	0.476	0.437	0.402	0.370	0.341	0.328	0.315	0.291	0.269	0.223	0.186	0.156	0.132
6	0.942	0.888	0.790	0.746	0.705	0.630	0.564	0.507	0.456	0.432	0.410	0.370	0.335	0.303	0.275	0.262	0.250	0.227	0.207	0.165	0.133	0.108	0.088
7	0.933	0.871	0.760	0.711	0.665	0.583	0.513	0.452	0.400	0.376	0.354	0.314	0.279	0.249	0.222	0.210	0.198	0.178	0.159	0.122	0.095	0.074	0.059
8	0.923	0.853	0.731	0.677	0.627	0.540	0.467	0.404	0.351	0.327	0.305	0.266	0.233	0.204	0.179	0.168	0.157	0.139	0.123	0.091	0.068	0.051	0.039
9	0.914	0.837	0.703	0.645	0.592	0.500	0.424	0.361	0.308	0.284	0.263	0.225	0.194	0.167	0.144	0.134	0.125	0.108	0.094	0.067	0.048	0.035	0.026
10	0.905	0.820	0.676	0.614	0.558	0.463	0.386	0.322	0.270	0.247	0.227	0.191	0.162	0.137	0.116	0.107	0.099	0.085	0.073	0.050	0.035	0.024	0.017
11	0.896	0.804	0.650	0.585	0.527	0.429	0.350	0.287	0.237	0.215	0.195	0.162	0.135	0.112	0.094	0.086	0.079	0.066	0.056	0.037	0.025	0.017	0.012
12	0.887	0.788	0.625	0.557	0.497	0.397	0.319	0.257	0.208	0.187	0.168	0.137	0.112	0.092	0.076	0.069	0.062	0.052	0.043	0.027	0.018	0.012	0.008
13	0.879	0.773	0.601	0.530	0.469	0.368	0.290	0.229	0.182	0.163	0.145	0.116	0.093	0.075	0.061	0.055	0.050	0.040	0.033	0.020	0.013	0.008	0.005
14	0.870	0.758	0.577	0.505	0.442	0.340	0.263	0.205	0.160	0.141	0.125	0.099	0.078	0.062	0.049	0.044	0.039	0.032	0.025	0.015	0.009	0.006	0.003
15	0.861	0.743	0.555	0.481	0.417	0.315	0.239	0.183	0.140	0.123	0.108	0.084	0.065	0.051	0.040	0.035	0.031	0.025	0.020	0.011	0.006	0.004	0.002

Period																							
16	0.853	0.728	0.534	0.458	0.394	0.292	0.218	0.163	0.123	0.107	0.093	0.071	0.054	0.042	0.032	0.028	0.025	0.019	0.015	0.008	0.005	0.003	0.002
17	0.844	0.714	0.513	0.436	0.371	0.270	0.198	0.146	0.108	0.093	0.080	0.060	0.045	0.034	0.026	0.023	0.020	0.015	0.012	0.006	0.003	0.002	0.001
18	0.836	0.700	0.494	0.416	0.350	0.250	0.180	0.130	0.095	0.081	0.069	0.051	0.038	0.028	0.021	0.018	0.016	0.012	0.009	0.005	0.002	0.001	0.001
19	0.828	0.686	0.475	0.396	0.331	0.232	0.164	0.116	0.083	0.070	0.060	0.043	0.031	0.023	0.017	0.014	0.012	0.009	0.007	0.003	0.002	0.001	0.001
20	0.820	0.673	0.456	0.377	0.312	0.215	0.149	0.104	0.073	0.061	0.051	0.037	0.026	0.019	0.014	0.012	0.010	0.007	0.005	0.002	0.001	0.001	
21	0.811	0.660	0.439	0.359	0.294	0.199	0.135	0.093	0.064	0.053	0.044	0.031	0.022	0.015	0.011	0.009	0.008	0.006	0.004	0.002	0.001		
22	0.803	0.647	0.422	0.342	0.278	0.184	0.123	0.083	0.056	0.046	0.038	0.026	0.018	0.013	0.009	0.007	0.006	0.006	0.003	0.001	0.001		
23	0.795	0.634	0.406	0.326	0.262	0.170	0.112	0.074	0.049	0.040	0.033	0.022	0.015	0.010	0.007	0.006	0.005	0.003	0.002	0.001			
24	0.788	0.622	0.390	0.310	0.247	0.158	0.102	0.066	0.043	0.035	0.028	0.019	0.013	0.008	0.006	0.005	0.004	0.003	0.002	0.001			
25	0.780	0.610	0.375	0.295	0.233	0.146	0.092	0.059	0.038	0.030	0.024	0.016	0.010	0.007	0.005	0.004	0.003	0.002	0.001	0.001			
26	0.772	0.598	0.361	0.281	0.220	0.135	0.084	0.053	0.033	0.026	0.021	0.014	0.009	0.006	0.004	0.003	0.002	0.002	0.001				
27	0.764	0.586	0.347	0.268	0.207	0.125	0.076	0.047	0.029	0.023	0.018	0.011	0.007	0.005	0.003	0.002	0.002	0.001	0.001				
28	0.757	0.574	0.333	0.255	0.196	0.116	0.069	0.042	0.026	0.020	0.016	0.010	0.006	0.004	0.002	0.002	0.002	0.001	0.001				
29	0.749	0.563	0.321	0.243	0.185	0.107	0.063	0.037	0.022	0.017	0.014	0.008	0.005	0.003	0.002	0.002	0.001	0.001	0.001				
30	0.742	0.552	0.308	0.231	0.174	0.099	0.057	0.033	0.020	0.015	0.012	0.007	0.004	0.003	0.002	0.001	0.001	0.001	0.001				
35	0.706	0.500	0.253	0.181	0.130	0.066	0.036	0.019	0.010	0.008	0.006	0.003	0.002	0.001									
40	0.672	0.453	0.208	0.142	0.097	0.046	0.022	0.011	0.005	0.004	0.003	0.001	0.001										
45	0.639	0.410	0.171	0.111	0.073	0.031	0.014	0.006	0.003	0.002	0.001	0.001											
50	0.608	0.372	0.141	0.087	0.054	0.021	0.009	0.003	0.001	0.001	0.001												
60	0.550	0.305	0.095	0.054	0.030	0.010	0.002	0.001															

1. To find present value (PV) of future amount:
   PV = Factor × Amount

2. To find future amount representing given PV:
   Amount = PV/Factor

3. To find period given future amount, PV and yield:
   Factor = PV/Amount; locate in column

4. To find yield given future amount, PV and period:
   Factor = PV/Amount; locate in row

TABLE 6-10

Present Value of $1.00 per Period Received or Paid at End of Period (Annuity)

Number of Periods	1%	2%	4%	5%	6%	8%	10%	12%	14%	15%	16%	18%	20%	22%	24%	25%	26%	28%	30%	35%	40%	45%	50%
1	0.990	0.980	0.962	0.952	0.943	0.926	0.909	0.893	0.877	0.870	0.862	0.847	0.833	0.820	0.806	0.800	0.794	0.781	0.769	0.741	0.714	0.690	0.667
2	1.970	1.942	1.886	1.859	1.833	1.783	1.736	1.690	1.647	1.626	1.605	1.566	1.528	1.492	1.457	1.440	1.424	1.392	1.361	1.289	1.224	1.165	1.111
3	2.941	2.884	2.775	2.722	2.673	2.577	2.487	2.402	2.322	2.283	2.246	2.174	2.106	2.042	1.981	1.952	1.923	1.868	1.816	1.696	1.589	1.493	1.407
4	3.902	3.808	3.630	3.545	3.465	3.312	3.170	3.037	2.914	2.855	2.798	2.690	2.589	2.494	2.404	2.362	2.320	2.241	2.166	1.997	1.849	1.720	1.605
5	4.853	4.713	4.452	4.329	4.212	3.993	3.791	3.605	3.433	3.352	3.274	3.127	2.991	2.864	2.745	2.689	2.635	2.532	2.436	2.220	2.035	1.876	1.737
6	5.795	5.601	5.242	5.075	4.917	4.623	4.355	4.112	3.889	3.784	3.685	3.498	3.326	3.167	3.020	2.951	2.885	2.759	2.643	2.385	2.168	1.983	1.824
7	6.728	6.472	6.002	5.786	5.582	5.206	4.868	4.564	4.288	4.160	4.039	3.812	3.605	3.416	3.242	3.161	3.083	2.937	2.802	2.508	2.263	2.057	1.883
8	7.652	7.325	6.733	6.463	6.210	5.747	5.335	4.968	4.639	4.487	4.344	4.078	3.837	3.619	3.421	3.329	3.241	3.076	2.925	2.598	2.331	2.108	1.922
9	8.566	8.162	7.435	7.108	6.802	6.247	5.759	5.328	4.946	4.772	4.607	4.303	4.031	3.786	3.566	3.463	3.366	3.184	3.019	2.665	2.379	2.144	1.948
10	9.471	8.983	8.111	7.722	7.360	6.710	6.145	5.650	5.216	5.019	4.833	4.494	4.192	3.923	3.682	3.571	3.465	3.269	3.092	2.715	2.414	2.168	1.965
11	10.368	9.787	8.760	8.307	7.887	7.139	6.495	5.937	5.453	5.234	5.029	4.656	4.327	4.035	3.776	3.656	3.544	3.335	3.147	2.752	2.438	2.185	1.977
12	11.255	10.575	9.385	8.863	8.384	7.536	6.814	6.194	5.660	5.421	5.197	4.793	4.439	4.127	3.851	3.725	3.606	3.387	3.190	2.779	2.456	2.196	1.985
13	12.134	11.343	9.986	9.393	8.853	7.904	7.103	6.424	5.842	5.583	5.342	4.910	4.533	4.203	3.912	3.780	3.656	3.427	3.223	2.799	2.468	2.204	1.990
14	13.004	12.106	10.563	9.898	9.295	8.244	7.367	6.628	6.002	5.724	5.468	5.008	4.611	4.265	3.962	3.824	3.695	3.459	3.249	2.814	2.477	2.210	1.993
15	13.865	12.849	11.118	10.379	9.712	8.559	7.606	6.811	6.142	5.847	5.575	5.092	4.675	4.315	4.001	3.859	3.726	3.483	3.268	2.825	2.484	2.214	1.995

n																							
16	14.718	13.578	11.652	10.838	10.106	8.851	7.824	6.974	6.265	5.954	5.669	5.162	4.730	4.357	4.033	3.887	3.751	3.503	3.283	2.834	2.489	2.216	1.997
17	15.562	14.292	12.116	11.274	10.477	9.122	8.022	7.120	6.373	6.047	5.749	5.222	4.775	4.391	4.059	3.910	3.771	3.518	3.295	2.840	2.492	2.218	1.998
18	16.398	14.992	12.659	11.690	10.828	9.372	8.201	7.250	6.467	6.128	5.818	5.273	4.812	4.419	4.080	3.928	3.786	3.529	3.304	2.844	2.494	2.219	1.999
19	17.226	15.678	13.134	12.086	11.158	9.604	8.365	7.366	6.550	6.198	5.877	5.316	4.844	4.442	4.097	3.942	3.799	3.539	3.311	2.848	2.496	2.220	1.999
20	18.046	16.351	13.590	12.463	11.470	9.818	8.514	7.469	6.623	6.259	5.929	5.353	4.870	4.460	4.110	3.954	3.808	3.546	3.316	2.850	2.497	2.221	1.999
21	18.857	17.011	14.029	12.821	11.764	10.017	8.649	7.562	6.687	6.312	5.973	5.384	4.891	4.476	4.121	3.963	3.816	3.551	3.320	2.852	2.498	2.221	2.000
22	19.660	17.658	14.451	13.163	12.042	10.201	8.772	7.645	6.743	6.359	6.011	5.410	4.909	4.488	4.130	3.970	3.822	3.556	3.323	2.853	2.498	2.222	2.000
23	20.456	18.292	14.857	13.489	12.303	10.371	8.883	7.718	6.792	6.399	6.044	5.432	4.925	4.499	4.137	3.976	3.827	3.559	3.325	2.854	2.499	2.222	2.000
24	21.243	18.914	15.247	13.799	12.550	10.529	8.985	7.784	6.835	6.434	6.073	5.451	4.937	4.507	4.143	3.981	3.831	3.562	3.327	2.855	2.499	2.222	2.000
25	22.023	19.523	15.622	14.094	12.783	10.675	9.077	7.843	6.873	6.464	6.097	5.467	4.948	4.514	4.147	3.985	3.834	3.564	3.329	2.856	2.499	2.222	2.000
26	22.795	20.121	15.983	14.375	13.003	10.810	9.161	7.896	6.906	6.491	6.118	5.480	4.956	4.520	4.151	3.988	3.837	3.566	3.330	2.856	2.500	2.222	2.000
27	23.560	20.707	16.330	14.643	13.211	10.935	9.237	7.943	6.935	6.514	6.136	5.492	4.964	4.524	4.154	3.990	3.839	3.567	3.331	2.856	2.500	2.222	2.000
28	24.316	21.281	16.663	14.898	13.406	11.051	9.307	7.984	6.961	6.534	6.152	5.502	4.970	4.528	4.157	3.992	3.840	3.568	3.331	2.857	2.500	2.222	2.000
29	25.066	21.844	16.984	15.141	13.591	11.158	9.370	8.022	6.983	6.551	6.166	5.510	4.975	4.531	4.159	3.994	3.841	3.569	3.332	2.857	2.500	2.222	2.000
30	25.808	22.396	17.292	15.372	13.765	11.258	9.427	8.055	7.003	6.566	6.177	5.517	4.979	4.534	4.160	3.995	3.842	3.569	3.332	2.857	2.500	2.222	2.000
35	29.408	24.999	18.665	16.374	14.498	11.654	9.664	8.176	7.070	6.617	6.215	5.539	4.992	4.541	4.164	3.998	3.845	3.571	3.333	2.857	2.500	2.222	2.000
40	32.835	27.355	19.793	17.159	15.046	11.925	9.779	8.244	7.105	6.642	6.234	5.548	4.997	4.544	4.166	3.999	3.846	3.571	3.333	2.857	2.500	2.222	2.000
45	36.094	29.490	20.720	17.774	15.456	12.108	9.863	8.282	7.123	6.654	6.242	5.552	4.998	4.545	4.166	4.000	3.846	3.571	3.333	1.857	2.500	2.222	2.000
50	39.196	31.424	21.482	18.256	15.762	12.234	9.915	8.304	7.133	6.661	6.246	5.554	4.999	4.545	4.167	4.000	3.846	3.571	3.333	2.857	2.500	2.222	2.000
60	44.955	34.761	22.623	18.929	16.161	12.376	9.967	8.324	7.140	6.665	6.249	5.555	5.000	4.545	4.167	4.000	3.846	3.571	3.333	2.857	2.500	2.222	2.000

1. To find present value (PV) of series of equal receipts or payments:
   PV = Factor × Annuity
2. To find annuity representing given P.V.:
   Annuity = PV/Factor
3. To find number of periods to recover investment:
   Factor = Investment/Annuity; locate in column
4. To find yield of annuity given investment:
   Factor = Investment/Annuity; locate in row

Broader Framework of Capital Budgeting

Bierman, Harold Jr., and Seymour Smidt. *The Capital Budgeting Decision.* 6th ed. New York: Macmillan, 1984.

Hull, J.C. *The Evaluation of Risk in Business Investment.* Elmsford, N.Y.: Pergamon Press, 1980.

Kaufman, Mike, ed. *The Capital Budgeting Handbook.* Homewood, Ill.: Dow Jones-Irwin, 1985.

Van Horne, James C. *Financial Management and Policy.* 8th ed. Englewood Cliffs, N.J.: Prentice Hall, 1989.

Weston, J. Fred, and Thomas E. Copeland. *Managerial Finance.* 9th ed. Hinsdale, Ill.: Dryden Press, 1989.

Specialized Areas

Present Value Tables

Gushee, Charles II., ed. *Financial Compound Interest and Annuity Tables.* 6th ed. Boston: Financial Publishing, 1980.

Thorndike, David. *The Thorndike Encyclopedia of Banking and Financial Tables, 1980 Yearbook.* Boston: Warren, Gorham & Lamset.

MAPI Method

Terborgh, George. *Business Investment Management.* Washington, D.C.: Machinery and Allied Products Institute, 1967.

Risk Analysis

Brealey, Richard, and Stewart Myers. *Principles of Corporate Finance.* 3rd ed. New York: McGraw-Hill, 1988.

Hertz, David B. "Risk Analysis in Capital Investment." *Harvard Business Review,* September–December 1979, pp. 42-49.

Holder, James E., and Henry E. Riggs. "Pitfalls in Evaluating Risk Projects." *Harvard Business Review,* (January–February, 1985), pp. 128–35.

Levy, Haim, and Sarnat, Marshall. *Capital Investment and Financial Decisions.* 4th ed. Englewood Cliffs, N.J.: Prentice Hall, 1990.

Ross, Stephen; Randolph Westerfield; and Jeffrey Jaffe. *Corporate Finance.* 2nd ed. Homewood, Ill: Richard D. Irwin, 1990.

Leasing

Prichard, Robert E., and Thomas J. Hindelang. *The Lease/Buy Decision.* New York: AMACOM, 1980.

SELF-STUDY EXERCISES AND PROBLEMS

(Solutions Are Provided in Appendix III)

1. An investment proposition costing $60,000 is expected to result in the following aftertax cash flows over seven years:

Year	
1	$10,000
2	15,000
3	15,000
4	20,000
5	15,000
6	10,000
7	5,000

   a. Calculate the net present value at 10 percent and at 16 percent.
   b. Determine the internal rate of return (yield) of the proposition.
   c. If the annual cash flows were an even $13,000 per year for seven years, what would be the net present value at 10 percent?
   d. What level annual cash flows would be required to yield a 16 percent return?
   e. How would the results of (a) and (b) change if there were a capital recovery of $10,000 at the end of year 7?
   f. How would the result of (d) change if there were a capital recovery of $10,000 at the end of year 7?

2. After having spent and written off against expenses of past periods an estimated $1,150,000 of research and development funds on a new product, the ABC Company is faced with the decision of whether to invest a total of $1,500,000 in a large-scale initial promotional and advertising campaign to bring the product to market. The campaign will be conducted over a six-month period, and all costs will be charged off as expenses in the current year. The effect of the campaign is an estimated average incremental profit of $400,000 per year for at least the next five years, before taxes and without the initial promotional costs. The likely pattern of profits is estimated to be $200,000 in the first year, $300,000 in the second, $600,000 in the third, $500,000 in the fourth, and $400,000 in the fifth year.

   Assume that income taxes on incremental profits are paid at the rate of 36 percent and that the company normally has the opportunity to earn 14 percent after taxes. Calculate the various measures of investment desirability, first on the average profit and then on the annual pattern expected. Determine the simple payback and return on investment, average return, net present value, present value index, present value payback, annualized net present value, and internal rate of return (yield).

What is the effect of the research and development expenditures on these results? Discuss your findings.

3. After careful analysis of a number of possible investments, a trustee of a major estate is weighing the choice between two $100,000 investments considered to be of equal risk. The first (a) will provide a series of eight year-end payments to the estate of $16,500 each, while the second (b) will provide a single lump sum of $233,000 at the end of 11 years. Which proposition provides the higher yield? If the normal return experienced by the estate for investments of this risk category is 6 percent, which investment is preferable? Should the pattern of cash flows be a consideration here, and how would this affect the choice? Ignore taxes and discuss your findings.

4. In an effort to replace a manual operation with a more efficient and reliable automatic process, the DEF Company is considering the purchase of a machine that will cost $52,800 installed and has an expected economic life of eight years. It will be depreciated over this period on a straight-line basis for both book and tax purposes, with no salvage value foreseen. The main benefit expected is a true reduction in costs due to the elimination of two operator positions and less materials spoilage. There will be some additional costs such as power, supplies, and repairs. The net annual savings are estimated to be $12,100, and the machine will be scrapped at the end of its life.

   Assume that income taxes on incremental profits are paid at the rate of 36 percent and that normal opportunities return 12 percent after taxes. Calculate the simple payback and return on investment, average return, net present value, present value index, present value payback, annualized net present value, and internal rate of return (yield). Discuss your findings.

5. The strategy of the XYZ Corporation includes the periodic introduction of a new product line, which involves investments in research and development, promotion, plant, equipment, and working capital. Now the company has readied a new product after an expenditure of $3.75 million on research and development during the past 12 months. The decision to be made is whether to invest $6.3 million for the production of the new line. The economic life of the product is estimated at 12 years, while straight-line depreciation will be taken over 15 years. At the end of 12 years, the book value of the equipment is expected to be recovered through sale of the machinery. Working capital of $1.5 million will have to be committed to the project during the first year, and $1.25 million of this amount is expected to be recovered at the end of the 12 years. An expenditure of $1 million for promotion will have to be made and expensed in the first year as well.

The best estimate of profits before depreciation, promotion expenses, and income taxes is $1.9 million per year for the first three years, $2.2 million per year for the fourth through eighth years, and $1.3 million per year for years 9 through 12. Assume that income taxes on incremental profits are paid at the rate of 36 percent and that the company normally earns 12 percent after taxes on its investments. Calculate the various measures of investment desirability. Which of these best indicates the attractiveness of the project? Should the company plan to develop similar opportunities by spending research and development funds? How much margin for error exists in this project? Discuss your findings.

6. The ZYX Company has found that after only two years of using a new machine for a semiautomatic production process, a more advanced and faster model has arrived on the market, which not only will turn out the current volume of products more efficiently but will allow an increased output of the item. The original machine had cost $32,000 and was being depreciated straight-line over a 10-year period, at the end of which it would be scrapped. The market value of this machine currently is $15,000, and a buyer is interested in acquiring it.

The advanced model now available costs $55,500 installed, and because of its more complex mechanism is expected to last eight years. A scrap value of $1,500 is considered reasonable.

The current level of output of the old machine, now running at capacity, is 200,000 units per year, which the new machine would boost by 15 percent. There is no question in the minds of the sales management that this additional output could be sold. The current machine produces the product at a unit cost of 12 cents for labor, 48 cents for materials, and 24 cents for allocated overhead (at the rate of 200 percent of direct labor). At the higher level of output, the new machine would turn out the product at a unit cost of 8 cents for labor (because one less operator is needed), 46 cents for materials (because of less spoilage), and 16 cents for allocated overhead. Differences in other operating costs, such as power, repairs, and supplies, are negligible at both volume levels.

If the new machine were run at the old 200,000-unit level, the operators would be freed for a proportionate period of time for reassignment in other operations of the company.

The additional output is expected to be sold at the normal price of $0.95 per unit, but additional selling and promotional costs are expected to amount to $5,500 per year.

Assume that income taxes are paid at the rate of 36 percent and that the company normally earns 16 percent after taxes on its investments. Calculate the various measures of investment desirability and select those that are most meaningful for this analysis. What major considerations should be taken into account in this decision? Discuss your findings.

7. The UVW Company, a small but growing oil company, was about to invest $275,000 in drilling development wells on a lease near a major oil field with proven reserves. Since other companies were also drilling in the vicinity, the volume of the flow of oil expected could not be predicted except within wide limits. Nevertheless, some oil would be obtained for a period of 12 years, in the best judgment of the geologists. After careful evaluation of the market and distribution aspects, company management decided that the major uncertainty lay in the physical yield, with lesser risk in the other areas. Consequently, an assessment was made of the range of aftertax cash flows (after considering depletion, depreciation, etc.) at various levels of production and the likelihood of occurrence of these levels was estimated. There was believed to be a 5 percent chance that the cash flow would be $15,000 yearly over the life of the project, a 15 percent chance that it would be $35,000 yearly, a 40 percent chance that it would be $45,000 yearly, a 25 percent chance that it would be $50,000, and a 15 percent chance that it would be $60,000 per year. It was expected that oil would flow at any given level for the full life of the project, although there was the risk that the wells could run dry sooner. Would this be a worthwhile project if the company normally earned 10 percent after taxes? What considerations are critical? Discuss your findings.

7 ASSESSMENT OF THE COST OF CAPITAL

As we have pointed out repeatedly, the economic nature of business decisions amounts to a cost/benefit trade-off. Up to this point we have focused mainly on the economic *benefits* from investing in and operating a business. Yet there are also economic *costs* incurred with every business decision. For example, in Chapter 5, during our discussion of financial leverage, we encountered the special profit impact caused by the cost of long-term debt funds. We demonstrated how such fixed obligations introduce magnified earnings fluctuations at different levels of profitability. In Chapter 6 we referred to the overall cost of long-term capital as a criterion by which to judge the desirability of business investments, because projects that provide a time-adjusted cash flow return at or above the cost of capital will leave shareholders at least as well off as before.

In this chapter we will discuss in greater detail the cost of various types of capital employed in a business, examine how this cost is measured, and in what form and for which purposes this economic reality affects business decision making. We will begin by sketching out the *types of decisions* for which cost of capital considerations are important. Then we will discuss the cost of the different types of capital, including *operating funds, long-term debt,* and *owners' equity (preferred stock* and *common equity).* Given the specific costs of each of these types of capital, we will derive an approach to determining the overall corporate *weighted cost of capital,* and discuss the use of this cost of capital in relation to the various *return standards* for business investments. The chapter will end with a list of *key issues.*

COST OF CAPITAL AND FINANCIAL DECISIONS

The *decisional* context we used in the first five chapters stressed the interrelationship of investment, operations, and financing. We observed that, over time, most management decisions cause *funds movements.* However, we did not deal directly with the *sources* of these funds and their respective *costs.* The dynamics of the business system are such that at any time there is temporary and/or permanent utilization of funds from a variety of sources, either *external* (e.g., borrowing or raising new equity), or *internal* (e.g., retained earnings from profitable operations or shifts in existing uses of funds). We also stated that the basic purpose of investing in, operating, and funding a business was to increase the economic value of the owners' stake over time. Thus management decisions should create economic value for the shareholders that is *higher* than the cost of the inputs. Among these is the cost of capital obtained from various sources.

Investment Decisions

In Chapter 6 we discussed various measures used to ascertain the desirability of an investment, most of which were based on the requirement that the project provide an *economic return.* We did not address the cost of the *specific* funds to be used for financing the investments, although an economic return standard implies that *all costs* must be re-covered, including compensation to the providers of all types of funds. We also said that minimum standards for investments had to be set high enough to compensate *both* for the specific risk of the project *and* for the opportunity loss of forgoing the returns from *alternative uses* of the funds invested. Such alter-native investments in the company's normal activities were assumed to adequately compensate *both* shareholders *and* lenders for providing their capital. We then suggested that the company's *overall cost of capital*, when used to measure the economic desirability of investments, implicitly embodied all of these requirements.

The *analytical* methods in Chapter 6 did not *directly* in-clude financing costs; rather, the cash outflows and inflows as defined represented only capital outlays on the one hand, and incremental aftertax *operating* benefits and capital recoveries on the other. These cash flows were then discounted at a return standard that *implicitly* allowed for recovery of all ac-tual costs and opportunity costs combined.

The economic results from an investment had to be suffi-ciently attractive to justify allocation of part of the long-term funds available to the company. Normally, investment funds come from a *pool* of different sources, none of which can or should be specifically identified with the particular project under review. Instead, investment funds should reflect the *overall* cost of the company's pool of funds. Capital expendi-tures are normally backed by the long-term capital structure of a company, which may include different degrees of leverage and a whole range of financial instruments. Thus the *weighted* cost of capital measure, which we will discuss shortly, is an important criterion in the capital budgeting context.

Operational Decisions

The time horizon for *operational* decisions involving funds movements is generally *shorter* than that of the typical capital investment. Nonetheless, operational finance aspects of a business, such as increases or decreases in trade credit—both used and extended—and swings in cash balances and accruals do involve *costs,* in the form of out-of-pocket charges and opportunity costs. Near-term decisions on taking purchase discounts, for example, may involve significant economic benefits when weighed against any incremental borrowing necessary to take advantage of the discount. Cash management decisions to minimize bank balances can eliminate the opportunity costs of tying up idle funds. In fact, there are myriad circumstances in which near-term decisions cause or eliminate the cost of employing funds, as these decisions are often directly connected with incremental sources that entail *specific* costs. We will discuss some of these shortly.

Financing Decisions

There are costs connected with obtaining and compensating for various sources of funds, both short-term and long-term, which must be considered by management in making any financing decisions. Clearly, all types of funds entail an economic cost to the company in one form or another. One of management's obligations is to develop a pattern of funding that both matches the risk/reward profile of the business and is sufficiently adapted to meeting the evolving needs of the company. We will discuss the financing choices and the framework of analyzing them in the next chapter.

COST OF OPERATING FUNDS

In the course of its operations, a business commonly employs many types of debt, including trade obligations (in the form of accounts and notes payable), intermediate-term credit, notes payable to banks or individuals, tax payments due various government agencies, wages due, payments due on installment purchases, and lease obligations. For all types of debt, including long-term obligations in the company's capital structure, the *specific cost* of borrowing can be determined rather easily. Normally, debt arrangements carry stated interest provisions that call for interest payments during the debt period, at its end, or as an advance deduction from principal. The last of these provisions is called discounting. In all of the cases, the *specific cost* of debt is simply the direct cost of this interest commitment.

We must also remember that under current IRS guidelines, interest payments of all kinds are *tax deductible* for corporations. Because of this feature, the *net* cost of interest to corporations (at least for those with sufficient profits to be liable for taxes or able to apply tax-averaging provisions) is the annual interest multiplied by a factor (f) of one minus the applicable tax rate. For example, if a corporation pays 9 percent interest per year on the principal of a note and its effective tax rate (t) for any incremental revenue or cost is 34 percent, the net annual effective interest cost (i) of this note will be:

$$f = 1 - t$$
$$f = 1 - 0.34 = 0.66$$
$$i = 9\% \times 0.66 = 5.94\% \text{ (after taxes)}$$

Tax deductibility effectively *reduces* the cost of debt to a *net amount* after the prevailing tax rate is applied, *if* the company is in a position where changes in net income affect the amount of taxes due. This tax advantage may also be enjoyed by individuals in some circumstances, such as home mortgage interest deductions. Deductibility of the specific cost does *not* apply to other forms of capital at this time, however, as we will see later.

We can define operating debt as short- or intermediate-term *revolving* obligations incurred in the ordinary daily operations of most businesses. Some of these debt funds are provided by creditors *free of charge* for short periods, under trade terms generally accepted in the industry or service in which the company operates. Foremost in this category are *accounts payable*, which are the amounts owed vendors for goods or services purchased. Depending on the terms of the purchase agreement, the company being billed for goods and services can hold off payment for 10 or 15 days, or as long as 45 or even

60 days. In the interim, it can make use of the funds without incurring any specific cost. We recall from Chapter 2 that such trade credit is in fact a significant funds source that is *rolled over continuously*, and which grows or declines with the volume of operations.

In most cases suppliers offer a discount for early payment. For example, the terms may provide for a 2 percent reduction in the invoice amount if payment is received within 10 days (2/10), or 3 percent within 15 days (3/15) of the date of the invoice. This practice, common in many business sectors, allows the customer effectively to *reduce* the original cost of the goods or service by the specified discount. The incentive is designed to speed up the vendor's collections and thus to reduce the level of the vendor's funds tied up in credit extended.

If the buyer lets the discount period lapse, however, the invoice amount becomes due and payable in full at the end of the period specified (n/30, n/45. etc.). Failure to take advantage of the trade discount, and thereby prolonging the time during which the buyer can make alternative use of the funds, results in a very definite *opportunity cost*. While often ignored, this cost can be *quite sizable*. For instance, if the credit terms are 2/10, n/30, the cost of using the funds for the extra 20 days amounts to 2 percent of lost cash discount, or an annual rate of 36 percent!

$$\frac{360 \text{ days}}{20 \text{ days}} \times 2\% = 36\% \text{ (before taxes)}$$

In effect, the company loses, as taxable income, the cash discount it would otherwise have earned. To arrive at the net cost, the cash discount must be reduced by the taxes that would have been paid on the lost income. If we assume taxes to be 34 percent, the *net cost* for using the creditor's funds for the extra 20 days amounts to:

$$1 - 0.34 = 0.66$$
$$2\% \times 0.66 = 1.32\% \text{ (after taxes)}$$

On an *annualized* basis this cost is still sizable, especially when compared to the prime interest rate, which is the rate normally charged large corporations of impeccable credit rating—or even to the higher interest rates smaller companies pay to borrow operating funds. The annualization is calculated as follows:

$$\frac{360 \text{ days}}{20 \text{ days}} \times 1.32\% = 23.76\% \text{ (after taxes)}$$

Some companies, especially small and rapidly growing enterprises, make it a practice to use accounts payable as a convenient source of credit, often unilaterally *exceeding* the outside limits of credit terms by extended periods. The longer the funds are kept, of course, the lower the specific cost of accounts payable becomes, as trade creditors normally do not charge interest unless the receivable has to be renegotiated. In extreme cases, unpaid accounts may be converted into notes payable due on specific dates, with or without interest. This is usually done at the request of a trade creditor who wishes to establish a somewhat stronger claim against the debtor's resources.

It is clearly a poor practice for a customer to violate stipulated trade credit agreements, both from the standpoint of business reputation and for continuing creditworthiness. Prospective creditors will take such tardy performance into account when evaluating the customer's creditworthiness, as such information is readily available from the data bases of credit-rating agencies. This implicit economic cost must be considered in addition to the specific monetary cost incurred with trade credit.

Another form of operating debt includes *short-term notes* and *installment contracts*, in which interest is either charged ahead of time or is added to the amount of principal stated in the contract. For example, a one-year, $1,000 note that carries an interest rate of 9 percent will provide the debtor with only $910 in ready cash if the note is "discounted" by deducting the interest in advance. The *effective cost* before taxes now becomes *higher* than the stated interest, because the company is in effect paying $90 for the privilege of borrowing $910 for one year:

$$\frac{\$90}{\$910} = 9.89\% \text{ (before taxes)}$$

The adjustment for income taxes is handled exactly as shown in the last example. In the case of an installment contract for, say, $1,000 payable in four equal quarterly installments, with annual interest of 10 percent on the original balance, the effective cost of interest is far higher than stated, because *decreasing* amounts of principal will be outstanding over the term of the contract as the quarterly payments amortize the principal while providing interest on the declining balance. The precise cost of 15.7 percent can be easily determined with a pre-programmed calculator or microcomputer, using the present value approach discussed in Chapter 6.

We can use an *averaging* process as a quick method of determining the *approximate* effective cost. Over the term of the contract, the amount of principal will decline from $1,000 to zero, with an average outstanding of roughly one half of this range, or $500. The contractual interest was 10 percent on $1,000, or $100, one quarter of which was added to each of the four payments. When we relate the *total* interest paid to the *average* amount of funds used by the borrowing company during the term of the contract, the *approximate* cost doubles, as follows:

$$\frac{\$100}{\$500} = 20\% \text{ (before taxes)}$$

The actual result of 15.7 percent was lower because in our example the interest is in effect paid on the installment basis. (The adjustment for income taxes is the same as before.) If the contract ran for more than one year, the interest cost must be *annualized;* that is, the amount of interest must be allocated to the specific time period involved to derive the true cost *per year*, which is the normal period of comparison.

More complex financial arrangements are normally handled using present value techniques. Banks and other lending institutions use computers to precisely calculate the payments and charges, and are legally bound to disclose the effective cost of the arrangement on an annualized basis. The simple averaging technique is useful as a quick check in many circumstances, including personal finance, for approximating the effective cost of credit with which to make initial comparisons.

The discussion so far has focused on the *specific cost* of operational debt, which can range from zero to substantial annual rates of interest. This specific cost is not the only aspect of debt, however. As already mentioned in earlier chapters, *repayment of principal* has to be made, which commits part of the company's future *cash flows*. The obligation to repay the principal in a timely fashion forces the financial manager to forecast and plan *cash receipts and disbursements* with care. The outlook could be such that a *refinancing* may be desirable when the principal becomes due. The basic techniques of making cash flow projections, discussed in Chapter 4, are applicable here.

Another element of the debt burden, as already mentioned, is the impact of various forms of debt obligations on the *creditworthiness* of a company reviewing current and future funding requirements. In other words, the balance between owners' equity and "other people's money" may become precarious and forestall borrowing of any kind for some time until the company has worked itself out from under its debt obligations. Having "closed off the top," as debt-heavy operations are often described, can be costly, both in terms of the risk of not meeting obligations as they fall due, and in having to turn to much more expensive sources of credit or equity funds as additional needs arise.

COST OF LONG-TERM DEBT

Most companies employ at least some type of long-term debt obligations to support part of their permanent financing needs arising from major capital outlays, growth of operations, or replacement of other types of capital. This type of debt, exemplified by bonds of various types issued by a company and traded in the financial markets, or long-term borrowing arrangements with banks and other financial institutions, becomes *integral to the capital structure* of the company. Management must make well-planned decisions, weighing the *cost, risk, and debt service* involved in relation to the prospective uses of the funds. Commitments to long-term debt, by their very nature, have a much more lasting impact on a company's situation than do short-term working capital financing or intermediate-term loans.

The *specific cost* of long-term debt is expressed in the stated annual interest rate of the financial instrument involved. For example, a 12 percent "debenture" bond, which is an unsecured (no specific assets are pledged) general debt obligation of the company, has a specific aftertax cost of:

$$12\% \times (1 - .34) = 7.92\%$$

if we assume that the company is able to take advantage of the interest deductibility. An incremental tax rate of 34 percent was used. In addition, we will assume that the bond had been sold at a price that *nets* the company its *par value* (face value). The *stated annual interest rate (coupon rate)* of a bond is based on the par value, or 100 percent of the principal due at a specified future date, regardless of the *actual proceeds* received by the issuing company. Proceeds vary because marketable debt securities are generally sold at the best possible price obtainable in the market through underwriters who take some or all of the risk of marketing the issue for a small percentage of the gross receipts. Legal and registration expenses are also borne by the company. Therefore, depending on the *issue price*, which is related to prevailing interest yields and to the quality of the company's credit rating, the company may actually receive net proceeds *below* par value, or it may receive a small *premium* over par.

In either case, the specific cost has to be *adjusted* to allow for the actual proceeds. The effect is similar to the short-term loan discussed earlier, on which the interest was due in advance and which therefore entailed a specific cost somewhat *higher* than the stated rate. If we assume that instead of 100 percent of par value, the company received 95 percent for its debentures after all expenses and commissions, the *effective cost* with a 12 percent *coupon rate* is as follows:

$$0.12(1 - .34) \times \frac{1}{.95} = 8.34\%$$

Apart from the specific cost of interest, long-term debt also involves repayment of the principal. There are many types of repayment provisions, generally structured to fit the nature of the company and the type of risks the debt holder visualizes. Periodic repayment requirements may be met through a *sinking fund* set aside for that purpose and held in trust by a depository institution. Partial or full principal payments due at the end of the lending period are called *balloon payments*. The point to remember, however, is that debt instruments, even if long term, must in some form and at some time be *repaid*. The cost of this repayment is implicit in the need to carefully plan future cash flows and also to consider the company's ability to achieve future *refinancing* if the funds needs are likely to continue or even grow. The reader will recall the discussion of funds projections in Chapter 4.

Another implicit cost of long-term debt involves the nature and degree of *restrictions* normally embodied in the debt agreement (*indenture*). Such provisions may limit management's ability to use *other forms* of credit, e.g., leasing; or they may specify *minimum levels* of some financial ratios, e.g., working capital proportions or debt service coverage; or they may *limit* the amount of dividends that can be paid to shareholders. At times, specific assets may have to be *pledged* as security. Any set of such provisions carries an *implicit cost* in that they limit management's freedom of choice in making decisions. The greater the perceived risk of the indebtedness, the greater the restrictions are likely to be.

The rationale for these restrictions was presented in the discussion of financial ratios from the point of view of lenders

(Chapter 3). Not to be overlooked is the introduction of *financial leverage* into the capital structure, as discussed in Chapter 5. The implicit cost of this condition again depends on the degree of risk exposure caused by specific company and industry conditions.

COST OF OWNERS' EQUITY

Preferred Stock

This form of equity ownership is conceptually at the "midway point" between debt and common stock. Although subordinated to the various creditors of the corporation, the preferred shareholder has a claim on corporate *earnings* that ranks *ahead* of the common shareholders' position up to the amount of the stated preferred dividend. In liquidation, the preferred shareholder's claims are satisfied prior to the residual claims of the holders of common stock.

The *specific cost* of preferred stock is normally higher than that of debt with a similar quality rating. Because of the near-equity status of preferred stock, preferred dividends at this writing are not tax deductible for the issuing corporation and are therefore an outflow of *aftertax* funds. For instance, a 14 percent preferred stock, issued at par (net of expenses), costs the corporation 14 percent after taxes. For each dollar of dividends to be paid on this preferred stock, the corporation must therefore earn, before taxes:

$$\$1.00 \times \frac{1}{1 - .34} = \$1.52$$

as compared to $1 for every dollar of interest paid on a long-term debt obligation. Where the 12 percent bond in the previous section had an aftertax cost of 7.92 percent, the 14 percent preferred has an aftertax cost of 14 percent. The *stated* dividend rate of a preferred stock is therefore directly comparable to the *tax-adjusted* interest rate of a bond.

We can easily compare the cost to the company of long-term debt and preferred stock if we assume that they were issued at prices that result in proceeds exactly equal to the par (face) value. When proceeds do *not* equal par value, as often happens because of market conditions, the cost must be based on the *proceeds* to obtain the *effective* cost as discussed above.

The additional *implicit* cost of preferred stock lies in the fact that it is a security *senior* to common stock, and the dividend claims of its holders rank *ahead* of common dividends. In addition, the essentially *fixed* nature of preferred dividends (they can be omitted only under serious circumstances) introduces a degree of *financial leverage* with varying earnings levels. Preferred stock being closer in concept to owners' equity than to debt, however, makes the implicit costs of its encumbrances far less serious than those of debt.

Common Equity

The holder of common shares as the *residual* owner of the corporation (the claims of common stock extend to all assets and earnings not subject to *prior* claims) provides long-term funds with the expectation of being rewarded with an increase in the economic value of the shares. This value accretion is composed of the interlocking effects of, hopefully, growing *earnings* and growing *dividends* received on the market *valuation* of the shares, which in turn is impacted by the *risks* specific to the industry and to the individual company. In other words, we are dealing with more variables, but the *contractual* provisions for compensation, such as coupon interest or the stated preferred dividend rate, are absent. As a result, the *specific cost* of common equity calls for a more complex evaluation than was the case with debt or preferred stock.

In the case of common equity, cost has to be viewed in an *opportunity framework*. The investor has provided funds to the corporation, expecting to receive the *combined* economic return of dividends declared by the board of directors and future appreciation in market value. The investment was made—presumably on a logical basis—because the type of *risk* embodied in the company and its business reasonably matched the investor's *own risk preference*, and because *expectations* about earnings, dividends, and market appreciation are considered satisfactory. The investor made this choice by *forgoing* other investment opportunities, however. The investment was made under conditions of uncertainty about *future* results, in that the only hard data available to the new investor are *past* performance statistics. The challenge of measuring the cost of the shareholder's funds to the corporation arises from the need to meet the investor's expectations about the risk/reward trade-off involved in investing in this opportunity. In other words, the company must compensate the shareholder with the economic return *implicit* in its past performance *and* future outlook.

Several approaches to measuring the cost of common equity are used in practice; all involve many assumptions and a great deal of judgment. The greatest difficulty lies in finding a specific link with the *risk versus value* judgments in the security markets that affect the market value of the common shares. We will discuss three major methods: an *earnings* approach, a *dividend* approach, and a *risk assessment* approach based on the *capital asset pricing model*. The earnings and dividend approaches are fairly straightforward; in effect they directly value future streams of earnings or dividends. But they also use highly simplifying assumptions and thus are very *limited* in their effectiveness. The third method, in contrast, approximates shareholder return expectations by adding to a *"normalized" rate of return* on securities in general a calculated numerical *risk premium* that is *company* specific. As we will see, it is the only approach that arrives at an economic return for the *specific* security *relative* to average yields experienced in the securities markets.

Earnings Approach to Cost of Common Equity.   In Chapter 2 we discussed the *price/earnings ratio* as a rough indicator of market valuation. This relationship is the simplest way of approximating the cost of common equity. Because we are interested in a measure of the opportunity cost of common equity, we will use *projected* earnings per share as related to the *current* market price of the stock:

$$\text{Cost of equity} = \frac{\text{Projected earnings per share}}{\text{Current market price per share}}$$

$$k_e = \frac{EPS}{p}$$

or

$$\text{Cost of equity} = \frac{1}{\text{Price/earnings ratio}}$$

$$k_e = \frac{1}{P/E}$$

This result is based on the implicit assumption that *all* of the earnings of the company will be paid out to the shareholders, which is *not realistic*. At the same time, the measure does not allow for the effect of any *reinvested* earnings creating further value for the shareholders. Finally, the result is static in that future *growth* in earnings is *ignored*. If the first assumption about a 100 percent payout holds, an alternative way of estimating the cost of equity would be to project, year by year, the expected earnings pattern and to find the discount rate that would equate these aftertax earnings with the current market value, adjusted for a terminal value at the time the analysis is cut off. Clearly, the number of assumptions we must make for the analysis to be valid multiplies rapidly under these conditions. This simple measure therefore is at best a rough approximation.

Dividend Approach to Cost of Common Equity.   A more direct way of dealing with at least one of the measurable benefits obtained by the shareholder is to use annual dividends to estimate the cost of common equity. Yet the approach also suffers from the liability of serious oversimplification, because companies vary greatly in their rate of dividend payout, and again the effect of reinvestment of retained earnings is ignored. In its simplest form the dividend approach is the same as the *dividend yield* we discussed as one of the market indicators in Chapter 3:

$$\text{Cost of common equity} = \frac{\text{Projected dividends per share}}{\text{Current market price per share}}$$

$$k_e = \frac{DPS}{P}$$

Introducing *growth* in dividends into the formula is an improvement that partially accounts for the *reinvestment* portion of the value received by shareholders. The assumption here is that successful reinvestment of retained earnings will lead to growing earnings and thus growing dividends. The mathematics of the formula allow us simply to add the *assumed rate of growth in dividends* to the equation shown above. We again begin with the dividend yield and add a *stable percentage* rate of dividend growth (g) to simulate the economic expectations of the shareholders:

$$k_e = \frac{DPS}{P} + g$$

The difficulty, however, lies in determining the dividend growth rate, which must be based on our best assumptions about future performance, tempered by past experience. Many estimating processes can be used. In Chapter 5 we discussed the concept of *sustainable growth*, given stable investment, payout, and financing policies. This may yield clues to the growth rate that can be applied with the dividend approach, but again a great deal of judgment must be exercised in projecting expected *future dividend policies*. If significant changes in policies are forecast, the analyst may want to modify the approach, making a series of year-by-year assumptions and in effect calculating a composite of future dividend growth patterns from these yearly forecasts.

A word about taxes is necessary here. In both the earnings and the dividend approaches, we are dealing with *aftertax values* from the point of view of the company. Earnings per share are stated after taxes, while common dividends, like preferred dividends, are *not* deductible and are paid out of aftertax earnings. *No adjustment* is therefore necessary in the results to make them comparable with the aftertax cost of debt and preferred stock. The *investor* likewise is judging the opportunity to earn an economic return in these terms. However, interest and dividends *received* are taxable income to the recipient. Therefore, because personal tax conditions vary greatly, one more adjustment is necessary from the *investor's point of view* to assess investment options objectively. Yet the business analyst cannot perform the precise calculation without knowledge of the individual's tax status. Consequently, the only working assumption we can make in this context is that *most investors* are subject to *some taxation;* we can arrive at financial results that are consistent *up to the point* the individual investor must calculate the personal tax impact.

Risk Assessment Approach to Cost of Common Equity. As we said earlier, the risk assessment method does not rely on specific estimations of present and future earnings or dividends. Instead, a *normal market return* is developed from published data on financial returns and yields, which is adjusted by a *company-specific risk premium or discount*. The rationale is the assumption that a company's cost of equity in terms of shareholder return expectations is related to the *relative riskiness* of its common stock. The greater this relative risk, the greater the premium—in the form of an additional economic return over and above a normalized return—that should be expected by an investor. This approach makes intuitive sense and can also be demonstrated statistically.

At any time, the securities markets yield a *spread* of rates of return ranging from those on essentially *risk-free* government securities at the low end of the scale to the sizable returns from *highly speculative* securities, including so-called junk bonds. The risk/return trade-off inherent in the many classes of security investments is reflected in this spread. *Risk* is defined as the *variability of returns* inherent in the type of security, while *return* is defined as the total *economic return* obtained from it, including both interest or dividends and changes in market value.

A number of specific approaches have been developed over the years to express the *risk premium* concept of return on common equity—which reflects the *cost* of common equity to the corporation—as a methodology both theoretically acceptable and practically usable. While no individual method is totally satisfactory in these terms, the most widely accepted is the *capital asset pricing model (CAPM)*. We will discuss some of its salient features here, but the conceptual and theoretical underpinnings are extensive and far beyond the scope of this book. The reader is encouraged to study the references at the end of the chapter for more exhaustive treatments of the evolution, theory, and validation of the CAPM.

Three elements are required in applying the capital asset pricing model approach, and each must be carefully estimated. The first is an expression of the level of return from a *risk-free security*. The purpose is to find the *lowest part* of the range of yields currently experienced in the security markets as the starting point from which to build up the higher, risk-adjusted return specific to the particular common stock. Long-term U.S. government obligations are commonly used as a surrogate for such a risk-free return. The yields on U.S. government obligations are widely quoted and accessible, both for the present and for historical periods. For purposes of analysis, *current* yields can be used, possibly adjusted for expected changes, such as the inflation outlook during the next several years. Precision is not possible here, and reasonable approximations supported by the analyst's judgment are quite workable.

The second element is an estimate of the return from a comparable type of security of *average risk*. This is needed because the CAPM method develops a specific adjustment for the *relative* riskiness of the particular security *as compared* to an average or base line. For our common equity problem, we can use an estimate of the total expected return for the Standard & Poor's 500 Index, a broad-based measure of the price levels of the common stocks of 500 widely traded companies. Such projections of the *total return—both* dividends and market appreciation—expected from the companies represented in the index, are frequently made by security analysts and published in financial services and newsletters. (See Appendix II.) While the S & P 500 index provides a broad-based estimate of return, more specific indexes could be chosen. Again, the analyst must exercise judgment in using projections of future economic returns. The main point is to obtain a reasonable approximation of the *average return* from *average investments* of the type being evaluated.

The third element required is an expression of relative *risk*, which is based on the *variability of returns* of the particular security being analyzed. The definition of risk is *very specific* in the CAPM method, and this has caused some controversy. Rick is *not* defined as *total variability* of returns, but rather, as the *covariance* of the particular stock's returns with those of assets of *average* risk. The assumption here is that an investor does not focus on the *total variability* of return experienced with each *individual* security, but rather on how each security affects the variability of the *total return* from the *portfolio* held.

Risk, therefore, is a *very relative* concept in CAPM, and its specific definition may not be acceptable to everyone. We will ignore the arguments pro and con about this risk definition in our discussion and concentrate instead on *how* it is used in CAPM to arrive at a company-specific return. The risk measure, in the form of the covariance of an individual stock's return with that of the portfolio of stocks of average risk, is called beta (β). It is found by linear regression of *past* monthly total returns of the *particular* security against a *base line* such as the S&P 500 Index. Services like Value Line provide the beta for publicly traded securities as a matter of course.

How are the three elements combined to arrive at the expected return and, thus, the company's *cost of capital* for a particular equity security? The CAPM method defines the cost of common equity as the combination of the *risk-free return* and a *risk premium* that has been adjusted for the *specific company risk*.

The CAPM formula appears as follows:

$$k_e = R_f + \beta(R_m - R_f)$$

where
k_e is the cost of capital,
R_f is the risk-free return,
β is the company's covariance of returns against the total portfolio,
R_m is the average returns on common stocks.

β is expressed as a simple factor that is used to multiply the *difference* between the expected return on the average portfolio and the expected risk-free return. This difference, of course, is the risk premium inherent in the *portfolio*. The β factor *adjusts* this *average* risk premium to reflect the *individual* stock's higher or lower relative riskiness. β goes above 1.0 as the relative risk of the stock exceeds the average, and drops below 1.0 when the relative risk is below average.

The calculation itself is quite simple, while deriving the *inputs* is not, as we observed. To illustrate, we will arbitrarily choose a risk-free rate of return of 9 percent, an S&P 500 return estimate of 13.5 percent, and a company with a fairly "risky" β of 1.4. The cost of equity in this hypothetical example would be

$$k_e = 9.0 + 1.4(13.5 - 9.0) = 15.3\%$$

composed of the risk-free return of 9 percent plus the calculated company-specific risk premium of 6.3 percent, for a total of 15.3 percent.

There are a large number of issues that surface when the CAPM or related measures are used to derive the cost of securities. One of these, already mentioned, is the estimate of both the risk-free return and the average return on a portfolio of common stocks. While the return on long-term U.S. government securities is a reasonable surrogate for the former, estimating an average portfolio return is fraught with conceptual problems. If β is the indicator of relative risk, the nature of the portfolio against which covariance is measured is clearly important. Broad averages such as the S&P 500 may or may not be appropriate under the circumstances. Also, there is the problem of using *past* data, particularly for *variability* of returns, in estimating the *future* relationships that indicate shareholder expectations.

Consequently, the results of these calculations, as with most types of financial analysis, should be used with caution and a great deal of commonsense judgment.

Inflation.   We have been talking about the cost of capital so far without specific reference to the impact of inflation. This is because *no* adjustment is in fact needed. The risk-free return on a government bond does *implicitly allow* for the expected level of inflation, inasmuch as expectations about future inflationary conditions *affect the yield* from such securities. When inflation abates, the yields decline—as dramatically occurred in the mid-1980s. When inflation expectations rise, so do bond yields. The same is true of the yields from other financial instruments. If no inflation existed, risk-free returns would probably be in the range of 3 to 4 percent. In fact, not just the CAPM but all of the measures of costs of capital we have been discussing include expected inflationary effects in that estimates of future returns take these expectations into account. The spectrum of returns ranging from risk-free bonds to those on speculative securities is also consistent in reflecting the effects of inflation.

To *summarize,* it should be obvious by now that the cost of common equity, apart from the specific method of calculation, is generally *higher* than the cost of interest-bearing securities or preferred stocks. As we said at the beginning of this section, the residual claim represented by common shares involves the *highest risk/reward trade-off.* Thus, returns expected of common shares are higher, which in turn must translate into the *highest cost of capital* from the corporation's standpoint. This fact will become even more important when we examine the alternative choices of financing *new* funds requirements, the subject of the next chapter.

WEIGHTED COST OF CAPITAL

Having determined the specific costs of the various types of capital individually, we now have all the specific cost inputs needed to make some of the *funding decisions* listed earlier. But because most companies use more than one form of long-term capital in funding investments and operations, and because over time the *mix* of sources used for long-term financing may change, it is necessary to examine the cost of the company's *capital structure* as a whole. The result we are looking for is a cost of capital figure that is *weighted* to reflect the cost differences in the various sources used. It encompasses the cost of compensating long-term creditors and preferred shareholders in terms of the specific provisions applicable to them and rewarding the holders of common stock in terms of the expected risk-adjusted return.

Several issues have to be resolved in determining an overall corporate cost of capital. The first is generating appropriate *costs* for the different types of long-term capital employed, which we have already done conceptually. The second is a decision about the weights, or *proportions* of each type of capital in the structure to be analyzed. The third is the question of whether to apply *market values* versus *book values* of the various categories of capital in arriving at the weighting. It is only then that we can calculate a weighted cost of capital that is meaningful for the intended purpose.

Costs

First to be resolved is the question of whether it is relevant to consider the *past* costs of existing securities in a company's capital structure, or alternatively, the *incremental* costs involved in adding newly issued securities. Quite often the *debt and preferred stock* section of the balance sheet lists a whole array of past issues, many of which carry interest or dividend rates that differ *significantly* from current experience. Obligations that are 10, 15, or 20 years old likely carry stated costs that are no longer relevant today. Moreover, the various methods of arriving at the cost of *common equity* were based on *future* expectations, which are not necessarily consistent with past debt or preferred costs. To solve this dilemma, we must remember the principle established early in this book: The *purpose* of the analysis always determines the choice of data and methodology.

Normally, the key purpose of calculating a weighted cost of capital is for use in making decisions about new capital investments that are judged against a standard of return that will adequately compensate all providers of capital. Unless a company undergoes significant restructuring, the funds for new capital commitments are likely to come from current internal cash flow, augmented by new debt or new equity or both. This is an *incremental* condition, in that the choices for *adding* new investments are still being made. Past decisions on investments and financing are *sunk costs*, as we know. Consequently, the cost of capital measure most appropriate here is based on the expected *incremental costs* of the various forms of capital employed by the company.

Weighting

As mentioned earlier, we are deriving a weighted cost that reflects the *proportions* of the different types of capital in a company's capital structure. Again, significant issues arise. The current capital structure as reflected on the balance sheet is the result of *past* management decisions on funding both investments and operations. The question to be asked here is whether the types and proportions of capital in this capital structure are likely to hold in the *future*, that is, whether they match the strategic plans of management. The intended capital budget supporting the company's future strategy, particularly when calling for sizable outlays, may indeed cause significant changes in the long-term financing pattern of a company. Also, management may choose to make gradual modifications to its financial polices that, over time, can cause sizable shifts in the capital structure. (The reader will recall our discussion of the impact of policy changes in Chapter 5.)

In other cases, management may well be satisfied with the current proportions of the company's capital structure as a long-term objective. Yet raising of the incremental capital required from time to time is normally done in *blocks* limited to *one* form of security, that is, debt, preferred stock, or common equity. Therefore, in the near term, any one type of capital may be emphasized *more* than the *long-term proportions* desired would suggest. Capital must be raised in response to *market conditions,* and the choice of which type is appropriate at any given point is based on a series of considerations that we will explore in the next chapter.

The analyst has to resolve the dilemma caused by such divergences *judgmentally*. Given the fact that a company never remains static in the long run, the choice of proportions has to be a compromise intended to approximate the conditions relevant for purposes of analysis, and precision becomes secondary to common sense. Current proportions are a good starting point, but should normally be modified by specific assumptions about the future direction of the company's long-term financing. It may also be useful to generate a range of assumptions to bracket the findings, which is a form of sensitivity analysis.

Market versus Book Values

The weights to be assigned to different types of capital are clearly going to be *different* if we choose to apply current market values as contrasted with the stated values on the right-hand side of the balance sheet. Again we must be guided by the *purpose* of the analysis to decide which value is relevant. If we are deriving a criterion against which to judge expected returns from *future* investments, we should use the *current market values* of the various types of capital of the company, because these values reflect the expectations of *both* creditors and shareholders. The latter certainly did not invest in the *book* value of common equity, which may differ significantly from the current *share* value as traded on the market. Further, it is the obligation of management to meet the expectations of the shareholders in terms of the future *economic value* to be created by investments and operations and to compensate creditors out of future earnings. Stated book values, as we observed before, are static and not responsive to changing performance.

The choice of market values also complements the use of *incremental* funding in that both are expressed in current market terms. The market value of common equity automatically (and implicitly) includes *retained earnings* as reported on the balance sheet. Although many people feel that retained earnings bear no cost, this is a misconception. In fact, retained earnings represent part of the residual claim of the shareholders, even if they are imperfectly valued on the balance sheet because of accounting conventions.

Calculation of Weighted Cost of Capital

Let us now turn to a simplified example of calculating a weighted cost of capital for a hypothetical company. This will allow us to demonstrate the basic mechanics of what we now understand to be a process that involves a great deal of judgment. We will use the condensed balance sheet of ABC Corporation (Figure 7–1), augmented by some additional data and assumptions.

The company has three types of long-term capital. We assume that it could issue new bonds at an effective cost of 12 percent and new preferred stock at an effective cost of

Figure 7–1
ABC CORPORATION
Condensed Balance Sheet
($000)

Assets		Liabilities and Net Worth	
Current assets	$27,500	Current liabilities	$ 9,500
Fixed assets (net)	35,000	Bonds (10%)	12,000
Other assets	1,500	Preferred stock (12%)	6,000
Total assets	$64,000	Common stock (1.0 million shares)	10,000
		Retained earnings	26,500
		Total liabilities and net worth	$64,000

13 percent, based on proceeds from expected pricing in the market and after applicable underwriting and legal expenses. Note that these current costs are above the rates the company has been paying on its long-term capital as stated in the balance sheet. ABC's common stock is currently trading between $63 and $67, and the most recent earnings per share were $4.72. Dividends per share last year were $2.50. The company's beta, as calculated by security analysts, is 1.1, a fairly average risk. We further assume that the estimated risk-free return is 8.5 percent, and the best available forecast for the total return from the S&P 500 is 15 percent.

Overall company prospects are assumed to be satisfactory, and security analysts are forecasting normal growth in earnings at about 6 percent. Given this background, it is possible to calculate a weighted cost of capital. As we proceed, the choices to be made will be highlighted.

The respective *costs* of the three types of capital employed can be derived as shown below. Note that we are employing the *incremental* cost of funds in each case, rather than the *past* costs as reflected in the balance sheet, where outstanding bonds carry a rate of 10 percent and preferred stock a dividend rate of 12 percent. The calculations for each type of capital appear as follows, using the methods discussed earlier:

Long-term debt: $k_a = 12.0 \times (1 - .34) = 7.92\%$ after taxes
Preferred stock: $k_p = 13.0\%$ after taxes
Common equity: $k_e = 8.5 + 1.1 (15.0 - 8.5) = 15.65\%$ after taxes

The cost of debt was based on the effective cost of 12 percent, adjusted for taxes, while the effective cost of preferred stock provided required no tax adjustment. The CAPM was used for the common equity calculation. The result for common equity should be compared to the less satisfactory answers obtained using the earnings or dividend approaches. The *earnings approach* provides the following cost of common equity when we employ the average current market price of $65 {1/2($63 + $67)}:

Common equity: $k = \dfrac{1}{\$65/\$4.72} = 7.26\%$ after taxes

If we were to modify the formula to include expected growth in earnings, (g), in this case, where g = 6 percent, the result would come closer to the 15.65% cost derived using the CAPM:

Common equity: k_e = 7.26% + 6.0% = 13.26% after taxes

The *dividend approach* provides another alternative result, which is a function of the dividend rate and the expected growth rate:

Common equity: $k_e = \dfrac{\$2.50}{\$65} + 6.0\% = 9.85\%$ after taxes

It is not uncommon to find that the three approaches to determining the cost of equity provide rather *different results*, as the data and assumptions going into the calculations are not the same. We highlighted the most significant issues when we discussed each measure earlier.

The *weights* to be used in calculating the corporate cost of capital depend both on the relative stability of the current capital structure and the relevance of market values to the results. Let us assume that management is satisfied with the current capital structure and is likely to raise funds in the same proportions over time. Let us also assume that the existing bonds of the company are currently trading at 83⅜ (a $1,000 bond with a coupon rate of 10 percent is worth a discounted price of about $837.50, in view of the increase in bond yields), while the existing preferred stock with a $12 dividend rate is trading at 92¼ because of the increase in yields (each share with a nominal value of $100 is currently worth about $92.25). As Table 7–1 shows, different proportions result when we list

Table 7–1
CAPITAL STRUCTURE OF ABC CORPORATION

	Book Value	Proportion	Market Value	Proportion
Bonds	$12,000	22.0%	$10,050	12.5%
Preferred stock	6,000	11.0	5,535	6.9
Common equity	36,500	67.0	65,000	80.6
Totals	$54,500	100.0%	$80,585	100.0%

Table 7–2
WEIGHTED COST OF CAPITAL FOR ABC CORPORATION

	Book Value Weighting			Market Value Weighting		
	Cost	Weight	Composite	Cost	Weight	Composite
Bonds	7.92%	.22	1.74%	7.92%	.12	0.95%
Preferred stock	13.00	.11	1.43	13.00	.07	0.91
Common stock	15.65	.67	10.48	15.65	.81	12.68
Totals		1.00	13.65%		1.00	14.54%

both book value and market value for each type of capital.

Depending on the way management assesses its future needs, the proportions could remain as shown in the table, or they could be altogether different in terms of a "target capital structure." Assuming that no significant change is foreseen, we can calculate the weighted cost of capital for *both* the market and book value, as shown in Table 7–2 above.

The results do not differ materially in this case. Differences would become significant only after much more than one percentage point. Given that the assumptions and choices needed to make the calculations all involved a margin of error, the results should be liberally rounded off before the measure is used as a decision criterion. We can say that in the case of ABC Corporation, under the stipulated conditions, the weighted cost of incremental capital is *approximately* 15 percent. If the measure is used to judge the expected return from new investments, it would represent a minimum standard of return from investments with *comparable risk characteristics*. Under these conditions, the weighted cost of capital could be used as the discount rate to determine net present values as discussed in Chapter 6.

COST OF CAPITAL AND RETURN STANDARDS

We stated all along that the basic purpose of deriving a weighed cost of capital was to find a reasonable *criterion* for measuring new investments. This amounts to establishing a level of returns high enough to compensate all providers of funds according to their expectations. By implication, projects considered acceptable when their cash flows are *discounted* at this return standard would create *economic value* for the shareholder in the form of growing dividends and market appreciation. However, using weighted cost of capital for this purpose warrants further discussion. In this section we will examine more closely the notion of this measure as a *cutoff rate* and then discuss the question of projects in different *risk categories*. We will also review the problem of the *multibusiness firm* in which a variety of *business risks* are combined. Finally, we will touch on the issue of modified standards using *multiple discount rates*. In all of these areas, a balance has to be found between the theoretically desirable and the practically doable.

Cost of Capital as a Cutoff Rate

In a *single-business company* with fairly definable risk characteristics, the weighted cost of capital as we have calculated it can well serve as a cutoff rate in assessing capital investment projects ranked in declining order of economic desirability. If *consistent* analytical methods and judgments are applied to projecting the cash flows, and if the *risks* inherent in the projects are *similar* and have been consistently estimated and tested through sensitivity analysis, then acceptance or rejection can be decided with this minimum return standard. We are assuming that the company can finance all of the projects being considered at the same incremental cost of capital and without significantly changing the capital structure.

The weighted cost of capital works well in this idealized condition because the risk premium built into the measure, the proportions of the sources of new funds, and the range of risks embodied in the projects are all *consistent* with each other and with the business risk inherent in the company. When some of these conditions *change*, however, managerial judgment must be exercised to modify the cost of capital and its application.

One common problem, even in the single business firm, is the real possibility that the *amount* of potential capital spending will *exceed* the readily available financing to some degree. If the list of projects contains many proposals that just meet or are somewhat above the standard, they may be attractive enough for management to *modify* the company's capital structure to accommodate them. Then the weighted cost of capital will likely change. Increasing leverage may introduce *additional risk*, thus exerting upward pressure on the cost of both debt and equity. Increasing the equity base significantly will result in near-term *dilution* of earnings per share, thus affecting the market value of the stock and possibly the β of the company's common stock as judged by security analysts. While the changes may be manageable, the point is that the process of business investment and the selection of appropriate standards is never a *static* exercise.

Another practical issue is management's attitude towards taking *business risks*. Knowing that the analyses underlying capital investment projects contain many uncertainties, management may wish to set the cutoff rate arbitrarily *higher* than the weighted cost of capital, to allow for *estimating error* and even for *deliberate bias* in the preparation of the estimates— not at all uncommon in most organizations as managers compete for funds—and also to play it a little safer in view of the degree of reliability of the *return standard itself*. From a theoretical standpoint, this approach may cause opportunity losses in that potentially worthwhile projects are likely to be rejected. From a practical standpoint, however, it may be deemed prudent to leave a margin for error. It is still possible, of course, at any time to reach *below* the higher standard if a project entails many other strategic or operational advantages that mitigate the effects of marginal economic performance.

Finally, we must reiterate that capital budgeting and project selection are *not merely numerical processes*. Even in the most tightly focused single-product company, where all levels of management have firsthand knowledge about the business setting, the decision process is always a *combination of judgments* affected by personal preferences, group dynamics, and the pressures of organizational realities.

Risk Categories

By definition, the weighted cost of capital represents a company's unique relative risk and particular capital structure. Yet in a sense this is misleading because even in the single-business company, different capital investment projects will involve different *degrees of risk*. Normally, a company encounters a variety of classes of investments, ranging from *replacement* of equipment and facilities to *expansion* in existing markets, and beyond that to *ventures* into new products or services and new markets. The degrees of risk inherent in these classes of investments will differ, sometimes materially, even though the products and services involved are within the scope of a *single industry* with a definable overall risk. Replacement of physical assets to continue serving a proven market where the company holds a strong position clearly is far less risky and permits more reliable estimates of cash flow benefits than entering a new domestic or even international market.

A common way of handling such divergences is to set a *higher discount standard* for projects that are perceived to be riskier. A hierarchy of minimum rates of return can be established, somewhat arbitrarily, that ranges upward from the weighted cost of capital cutoff point. For example, if the weighted cost of capital is, say, 15 percent, that standard may be applied to ordinary replacements and expansion in markets where the company has a position. A standard of 16 or 17 percent may be applied to entering related markets, while a new venture may be measured at a premium standard of even 20 percent or higher. As we have demonstrated earlier in discussing the power of discounting, particularly at the higher rates, the chances of riskier projects being acceptable will be severely tested under such conditions. Yet such a demanding risk/reward trade-off standard may be appropriate if management's risk preferences are modest.

On the other hand, it is often argued, particularly in a single-business company, that the weighted cost of capital *implicitly embodies* the whole range of risks normally encountered while participating and growing in that business. Consequently, the concept is advanced that the range of discount standards should be grouped *around* the weighted cost of capital. In effect, this allows the less risky projects to be discounted at a return standard *below* the weighted cost of capital, while riskier ones would be tested at or above that level. When all projects are combined, the result should be an *average* return at or above the weighted cost of capital. This would require, however, that the proportions of projects being approved in the various risk classes be carefully monitored to ensure that over time the overall average will achieve the desired result. Otherwise, the company could encounter significant deviations from expected performance.

An additional practical issue tends to support *raising the return standards* for the different classes of capital projects. Every company faces a certain percentage of capital expenditures that yield *no definable* cash flow benefits. Among these are mandated outlays for environmental protection, investments for improved infrastructure of facilities, expenditures for office space and equipment, and so forth. A strong argument can be made that funds required for these purposes must in fact be economically "carried along" by the expected cash flow benefits obtained from all other productive investments. By definition, therefore, the *total* amount of capital invested should provide a return sufficient to meet or exceed the weighted cost of capital. If some *part* of the capital budget is economically *neutral,* the returns from the economically positive projects will have to be *higher* to make up for such "nonproductive" investment. If management chooses to adjust its return standards for this condition, the modification will likely again involve a fair degree of judgment.

Our discussion has gone beyond the purely analytical aspects of the subject, and we have pointed out many *practical* issues involved in choosing and using economic measures for business decisions, of which discount standards are only one form. It is important to remember that the actual procedures employed by a company are likely to allow for a fair degree of *judgmental override* of the quantitative results of any financial analysis. This includes the *specific* return standards for capital investments, which are likely to be modified from time to time, to assist not only in *project-specific* economic assessment, but also in shifting the strategic emphasis *between classes* of investments. Senior management must, of course, continuously monitor and guide the pattern of investments they wish to undertake so that shareholder expectations are met. The pattern of investments suggested by the economic analyses and the return standards can and should be modified to fit the changing strategic direction of a company.

Cost of Capital in Multibusiness Companies

The issues involved in setting appropriate return standards become even more complex when a company has several divisions or subsidiaries engaged in rather *different businesses* and markets that vary greatly in their risk characteristics. While it is possible to calculate an overall cost of capital for the company, with the help of a β that reflects the company's covariance of *consolidated* returns with the market return, it is far more difficult to derive equivalent cost of capital standards for the *individual* operating divisions. Most commonly, a multibusiness company has a single capital structure that supplies funds for the various businesses. Therefore, capital cannot be apportioned to the different risk categories on the basis of individual cost of capital standards that employ specific *betas* and debt ratings. These would be available only if the divisions were *autonomous* companies whose shares are traded in the securities markets.

The approach often used under such conditions is to estimate a series of *surrogate* costs of capital based on costs for comparable *independent* companies, if this is at all possible. In this way a group of individual standards can be developed for the multibusiness company—modified with a great deal of judgment—that are similar to the array of risk categories in a single-business company.

Obviously, the apportionment of capital in a multibusiness setting is also complicated by the practical issue of divisional management competing for limited funds while having to meet *different* standards. Corporate management must be very careful first to establish *broad allocations* of funds to the various operating divisions that match the desired corporate strategic emphasis. Then projects can be ranked *within* those individual blocks of allocated funds according to the different discount rates, and decisions can be made to accept or reject specific investments. A predictable consequence of such an approach, however, is the dilemma of having to refuse specific higher return (and higher risk) opportunities in one division, whose overall allocation is exhausted, in favor of lower return (and lower risk) opportunities in another division. This dilemma has to be resolved at the corporate management level where the strategic direction of the *total* company is developed and monitored. The main point to remember is that top management needs to shape the company's overall capital investment portfolio in line with shareholder expectations, so that the sum of the parts can be expected to meet or exceed the corporate weighted cost of capital standard.

As we will discuss in Chapter 9, the cost of capital is also used to determine whether individual lines of business in a diversified company are contributing or detracting from shareholder value. The point in this application is to test past and prospective overall cash flows from each business unit as a whole in relation to a minimum cash flow return standard based on the cost of capital.

Multiple Rate Analysis

One additional *technical* observation should be made here. Some practioners argue for applying *different* discount rates to different *portions* of the cash flow pattern of a *single project* when calculating the measures of economic desirability, in order to reflect the relative riskiness of the various elements of the project. In effect, this is one more risk adjustment beyond the risk premium already *inherent* in a particular discount standard. There are many variations of this approach, although it is not widely used in practice.

It should be apparent that the uncertainties inherent in project analysis and complexities of establishing standards for multiple rate analysis may not be warranted in most *normal* business investment situations. At the same time, it may be necessary to do so in assessing *specialized* projects, such as real estate investments, complex leasing proposals, and other uniquely structured cash flow proposals. There some of the financial contracts *integral* to the projects may warrant discounting their portion of the cash flows at lower rates that reflect their *contractual* nature, as compared with other parts of the cash flow pattern that are subject to the uncertainties of *operating* in the business environment. These analytical refinements are too specific to be covered here, but are dealt with in the reference materials listed at the end of the chapter.

KEY ISSUES

The following is a recap of the key issues raised directly or indirectly in this chapter. They are enumerated here to help the reader keep the techniques discussed within the perspective of financial theory and business practice:

1. The specific costs to a company of various types of indebtedness and preferred securities are readily apparent in the tax-adjusted cash obligations involved, but it is difficult to measure the secondary costs implicit in debt service, credit rating, and market assessment.

2. Determining the cost of equity capital is intricately linked to the risk/reward expectations of the financial markets because the cost must be expressed in terms of an expected economic return for the shareholders of the company.

3. Simple surrogates for the cost of equity capital, such as earnings and dividend models, suffer from both variability of underlying conditions, which can distort their results, and from conceptual shortcomings.

4. The link established by modern financial theory between general financial market expectations and the value of an individual company's equity securities remains an approximation based on a series of simplifying assumptions.

5. The use of a company-specific risk factor (β) to adjust average return expectations is a valid theoretical concept, but both definition and measurement of this factor remain open to disagreement and continue to pose practical problems.

6. The development of a weighted cost of capital raises significant questions regarding not only the elements comprising the various costs, but also regarding the weights to be used and the concept of measuring incremental funding.

7. The use of a weighted cost of capital in setting capital investment return standards is conceptually useful for projects within a company's normal range of risk, but the measure may need modification for business investments of dissimilar risk.

8. The theory of finance continues to evolve, but as concepts generated are introduced and refined in the decision-making process, careful linkages to both data sources and to the organizational climate have to be established in order to make practical application both understandable and feasible.

9. Objective analytical approaches to capital investment assessment are only one important input in the choices management must make. Individual and group attitudes, preferences, and judgments exert significant influences over interpretation and decision processes in the areas of investment, operations, and financing.

10. The precision implied in the calculations of economic measures like cost of capital or net present value must be tempered by the knowledge that the data and assumptions underlying them are potentially subject to a wide range of error.

SUMMARY

In this chapter we have sketched out the rationale for determining the *costs* of various forms of financing as an input in making different types of financial decisions. We found that the specific *cost of debt*, both short-term and long-term, was relatively easy to calculate, given the nature of the contracts underlying it in most cases. The same was true for *preferred stock*. We also found that the fixed nature of the obligations incurred with debt and preferred stock raised a host of secondary considerations that exact an *economic cost* from the company in terms of debt service and restrictive covenants. Establishing the *cost of common equity* was particularly challenging because of the residual claim common shareholders have on the company, and because of their risk/reward expectations that are reflected in the market's valuation of the shares.

Once we discussed techniques for calculating the respective costs of the three basic types of financing and pointed out the theoretical and practical caveats, we developed the *weighted cost of capital* as an input in investment analysis. Here we found that the application of the weighted cost of capital as a *minimum standard* for discounting investment cash flows is affected by the way project and business risks are interpreted within the corporate portfolio and by the attitudes of corporate decision makers. At the same time, we found the approximate incremental weighted cost of capital to be a conceptually appropriate *target* around which to build a series of return standards befitting a particular company's range of businesses and the investments and risks connected with them.

SELECTED REFERENCES

Brealey, Richard, and Stewart Myers. *Principles of Corporate Finance*. 3rd ed. New York: McGraw-Hill, 1988.

Harrington, Diana R. *Modern Portfolio Theory. The Capital Asset Pricing Model and Arbitrage Pricing Theory: A Users' Guide*. 2nd ed. Englewood Cliffs, N.J.: Prentice Hall, 1986.

Mullins, David W., Jr. "Does the Capital Asset Pricing Model Work?" *Harvard Business Review*, January–February 1982, pp. 105-114.

Ross, Stephen, Randolph Westerfield, and Jeffrey Jaffe. *Corporate Finance*. 2nd ed. Homewood, Ill: Richard D. Irwin, 1990.

Solomon, Ezra, and John J. Pringle. *An Introduction to Financial Management*. 2nd ed. Santa Monica, Cal.: Goodyear Publishing, 1980.

Van Horne, James C. *Financial Management and Policy*. 8th ed. Englewood Cliffs, N.J.: Prentice Hall, 1989.

Weston, J. Fred, and Thomas E. Copeland. *Managerial Finance*. 9th ed. Hinsdale, Ill.: The Dryden Press, 1989.

SELF-STUDY EXERCISES AND PROBLEMS

(Solutions Are Provided in Appendix III)

1. The GHI company has the following three types of capital in its capital structure:

   Long-term debt at 12% (current yield is 10%)

   14% preferred stock (current yield is 12%)

   Common stock with a book value of $67.50 per share

   Currently, the company's common stock is trading in the range of $75 to $82, and the most recent closing price was $77. The most recent annual earnings per share were $9.50, while dividends paid over the last year were at the rate of $4.50. The company's earnings have been growing on average about 7 percent per year. *Value Line* lists the company's β at 1.25, while the risk-free return is estimated to be 9 percent. Forecasts for returns from the S&P 500 are currently about 15 percent. Calculate the specific cost of capital for each type of capital of GHI Company. Assume a tax rate of 34 percent, and discuss your findings.

2. The KLN Company has the folowing capital structure:

	Proportion	Existing Conditions	Current (incremental)
Long-term debt	$250.0	7% average rate	11% yield
Preferred stock	50.0	6% stated rate	9% yield
Common equity	400.0	—	Price range $45–$60
(10 million shares)			(Recent price $50)
Total capitalization	$700.0		

The company's β is currently estimated at 1.2, while the risk-free return is considered to be 7.5 percent. The most recent estimate of the return from the S&P 500 is 13.5 percent. Develop the weighted corporate cost of capital for KLN Company, both for the existing conditions (original costs) and incremental conditions. Also use both a book value and a market value weighting for each case. Assume a tax rate of 34 percent, and discuss your finds and the range of results achieved.

8 ANALYSIS OF FINANCING CHOICES

It is now time to turn to the analysis of the third portion of the decisional context first developed in Chapter 1—investment, operations, and *financing*. We will concentrate on analyzing the choices available in *long-term* financing, as contrasted to the incremental operational funds sources that are used fairly routinely as part of the way business is done in a particular industry or service. We choose this focus because, as we observed in earlier chapters, the nature and pattern of long-term sources is intricately connected with the types of investments made and is critical to the growth, stability, or decline of operations. As we said before, management must fund its *strategic design* with an *appropriate mix of capital sources* that will assist in bringing about the desired increase in shareholder value.

This chapter will deal with the main considerations in assessing the basic financing options open to management. Even though the choice among debt, preferred, and common equity is blurred by the bewildering array of modifications and specialized instruments in each category, we will only focus on the main characteristics of the basic types of securities. While the emphasis of this material is on *quantitative analysis*, it is important for the reader to realize that the specific types of business and the industry in which a company operates will affect the particular long-term capital structure chosen at various stages of a company's development, as will the preferences and experiences of senior management and the board of directors. These considerations cannot be adequately covered within the scope of this book.

We will begin with a *framework of analysis* that defines the key areas to be analyzed and weighed in choosing sources of long-term financing. Next we will look at the *techniques of calculating* the impact of a company's financial performance brought about by introducing new capital from each of the three basic sources. Then we will turn to one form of graphic representation, the *EBIT break-even chart,* to demonstrate the dynamic impact of funds choices on changing company conditions. After touching on *leasing* as a special source, we will list the *key issues* involved in the area of funds choices.

FRAMEWORK OF ANALYSIS

Several key elements must be considered and weighed when a company is faced with raising additional (incremental) long-term funds. We will take up five of these in some detail: *cost, risk, exposure, flexibility, timing, and control*. The analyst can use this framework as a conceptual checklist to ensure that the most important considerations have been covered.

Cost of Incremental Funds

One of the main criteria for choosing from among alternative sources of additional long-term capital is the cost involved in obtaining and servicing the funds. In Chapter 7 we discussed in detail the specific and implicit costs a company incurs in using debt, preferred stock, or common equity. As a general rule we found that *debt* funds are *least costly* in specific terms, in part because the interest paid by the borrowing company is tax deductible under current laws. The actual rate of interest charged on incremental debt will depend, of course, on the credit rating of the company and on the degree of change introduced into the capital structure by the new debt. In other words, the specific cost will be affected not only by *current market conditions* for all long-term debt instruments, but also by the *company-specific risk* as perceived by the underwriters and investors. As mentioned, other costs are also implicit in the raising of long-term debt, including legal and underwriting expenses at the time of issue, and the nature and severity of any restrictions imposed by the creditors.

The stated cost of *preferred stock* is generally higher than debt, partly because preferred dividends paid are not tax deductible, and partly because preferred stock has a somewhat weaker position on the risk/reward hierarchy, so that holders of these shares expect a higher return. The comparative specific cost of preferred stock was relatively easy to calculate. The dividend level is clearly defined, and legal and underwriting costs incurred at the time of the issue are reflected in the net proceeds to the company. However, a variety of specific provisions could involve *implicit* costs to the company.

Finding the cost of *common equity* turned out to be fairly complex and involved the construction of a theoretical framework within which to assess the *risk/reward expectations* of the shareholder. Direct approaches (shortcuts) to measuring the specific cost of common equity were found wanting because they did not address the company's *relative risk* as reflected in common share values. Therefore, we had to use a more complex framework involving some surrogates and approximations to arrive at a practical result based on the theoretical model.

The approximate cost of common equity we determined through the CAPM approach could be *directly* compared to the specific costs of debt and preferred stock, and it also could be used to arrive at a weighted overall cost of the company's capital structure. As we will see shortly, however, increasing common equity in the capital structure by issuing new shares involves additional considerations. The incremental shares *dilute* earnings per share, require additional and even growing dividends where these are paid, and, of course, cause change in the capital structure itself. Such effects amount to *implicit* economic costs or advantages in the funding picture.

Risk Exposure

If we use *variability of earnings* as a working definition of risk, we find that a company's risk is affected by the specific cost commitments—such as interest on debt, or dividends on preferred shares—that each funding source entails. These fixed charges introduce *financial leverage* effects in the company's earnings performance, or heighten any financial leverage already existing. As we discussed in Chapter 5, the use of instruments involving fixed financial charges will *widen the swings* in earnings as economic and operating conditions change. Management, being responsible for creating growing economic value for holders of common shares, must therefore expend much thought and care in determining the *appropriate mix* of debt and equity in their company's capital structure. This balance involves providing enough lower-cost debt to boost the shareholders' returns, but not so much debt as to endanger shareholder value during periods of low earnings.

The *ultimate risk*, of course, is that a company will not be able to fulfill its debt service obligations. The proportion of debt in the capital structure, and similarly the proportion of preferred stock, *affects the degree* of risk of partial or total default. The analysis of risk exposure is based on establishing a historical pattern of *earnings variability* and *cash flows* from which future conditions are projected. These must take into account the extent to which a company's strategy is *changing*, any shifts in exposure to the business cycle, shifting competitive pressures, and potential operating inefficiencies.

Clearly, the company-specific risk in terms of earnings variability and the company's ability to service its debt obligations is intimately related to the *characteristics* of the business or businesses in which the company operates, and to *general economic conditions*—apart from management's ability to generate satisfactory *operating performance*. The degree of financial leverage advisable and prudent will therefore *differ greatly* for different industries and services and will also depend on the *relative* competitive position and maturity of the company. A business just starting up entails far different risk patterns for the creditor than does the established industry leader, apart from the specific industry situation.

Flexibility

The third area that must be considered is the question of flexibility, defined here as the *range of future funding options* remaining once a specific alternative has been chosen. As each increment of financing is raised, the choice among future alternatives may be *more limited* on the next round. For example, if long-term debt obligations are chosen as a funding source, restrictive covenants, encumbered assets, and other constraints that impose minimum financial ratios may mean that the company can only use common equity as a future source of capital.

Flexibility essentially involves *forward planning*. Consideration must be given to strategic plans and to matching corporate financial policies. Potential acquisitions, expansion, and diversification all are affected by the degree of flexibility management has in choosing proper funding and by the funds drain resulting from servicing debt commitments. To the extent possible, management must match its planned future funds flows and investment patterns to the pattern of *successive rounds of financing* that will support them. Having future funds sources limited to one option because of present commitments poses an additional problem in that *changing conditions* in the financial markets for different types of

securities may make this single option less appealing or even
infeasible when needed.

Timing

The fourth element in choosing long-term funding is the
timing of the transaction. This relates to the *movement of
prices and yields* in the securities markets. The *specific cost* a
company will incur with each option, both in terms of the
stated interest or the preferred dividend rate carried by the
new debt or preferred stock, and in terms of the proceeds to be
received from each of the alternatives, will be affected by
movements in the overall securities market. The timing of the
issue will therefore affect the *cost spread* between the several
funding alternatives. At times, market conditions may in fact
either preclude or distinctly favor particular choices. For instance, in times of depressed stock prices, bonds may prove to
be the most suitable alternative from the standpoint of both
cost and market demand. Inasmuch as the proceeds from any
issue depend on the *success of the placement*—public or private—of the securities, the conditions in the stock or bond
markets at the moment may seriously affect the choice. Uncertainty in financial markets is therefore a strong argument for
always maintaining *some* degree of flexibility in the capital
structure.

Control

Finally, from a funding standpoint, the degree of control
over the company exerted by *existing shareholders* is an
important factor. As should be obvious, if new shares of common stock are issued to others, the effect is *dilution* of both
earnings per share and the *proportion of ownership* of the
existing shareholders. In recent years, the issue of control has
been raised to new heights in the many battles of the corporate
takeover boom.

Even if debt or preferred stock is used as the source of long-
term funding, it may indirectly affect existing shareholders

because restrictive provisions and covenants are necessary to obtain bond financing, or because concessions must be made to protect the rights of these "more senior" preferred shareholders.

Dilution of ownership is a very important problem in *closely held* corporations, particularly new ventures. In such situations, founders of the company or majority shareholders may exercise full effective control over the company. Issuing new shares will dilute both control over the direction of the company and the key shareholders' ability to enjoy the major share of the appreciation of economic value from successful performance. The dilution of earnings and the possible retardation of growth in earnings per share brought about by diluting common equity ownership is, of course, *not limited* to closely held companies. Rather it is a general phenomenon that we will discuss shortly.

Finally, dilution of control and earnings is a consideration in *convertibility*, a very common feature found in certain bonds and preferred stocks. This provision allows conversion of the security into *common stock* under specified conditions of timing and price. In effect, such instruments are hybrid securities, as they represent *delayed* issues of common stock at a price higher than the market value of the common stock at the time the convertible bond or preferred stock is issued. We mentioned this feature in earlier chapters in terms of the effect on financial ratios, particularly the concept of fully diluted earnings per share.

Control becomes a consideration when convertible financing options are being considered, because the eventual conversion of the bond or preferred stock will add *new common shares* to the capital structure and thus cause dilution; the effect is just like a direct issue of common stock. Normally, convertibility makes the bond or preferred stock *more attractive* to the investor, particularly if issued by a company that is growing rapidly. The investor can enjoy a stated rate of interest or preferred dividend until the market price of the common stock surpasses the stipulated conversion price, making conversion advantageous. At the same time, the company is obtaining an *effective price* for the common shares represented by the bond or preferred stock that is *higher* than what it could achieve when the convertible securities are issued. Also, the company usually pays a somewhat lower rate of interest or preferred dividend on these instruments. Finally, the company can usually force conversion once the market price of common stock has reached the conversion price by exercising the *call provision* included in most convertible issues. At any rate, there is an eventual impact on control, earnings per share, and the amount of future common dividends.

The Choice

It should be clear from this brief résumé of the considerations involved that any decision about alternative sources of long-term funding *cannot* be based on *cost* alone, even though this is a most important factor and must be analyzed early in the decision-making process. Unfortunately, there are no hard-and-fast rules spelling out precisely how the final decision should be made because the choice depends so much on the *circumstances* prevailing in the company and in the securities markets at the time. The best approach is to consider carefully the five areas we have presented above and to examine the pros and cons of each *as an input*. Needless to say, a very significant consideration is the effect of each funding source on a company's future earnings performance. In the section that follows, we will examine methods of calculating this effect.

TECHNIQUES OF CALCULATION

For purposes of illustration, we will employ the basic statements of a hypothetical company, ABC Corporation. After analyzing the corporation's *current performance*, we will successively discuss the impact on that performance of introducing *long-term debt*, *preferred stock*, and *common equity* in

Figure 8-1
ABC CORPORATION
Balance Sheet
($ millions)

Assets		Liabilities and Net Worth	
Current assets	$15	Current liabilities	$ 7
Fixed assets (net)	29	Common stock	10
Other assets	1	Retained earnings	28
Total assets	$45	Total liabilities and net worth	$45

equal amounts of $10 million each. These funds are being raised to support the introduction of a new product.

Shown in Figure 8-1 above is ABC's abbreviated balance sheet. The company currently has 1 million shares of common stock outstanding, with a par value of $10 per share. From the company's operating statement (not shown), we learned that ABC Corporation has earned $9 million before taxes on sales of $115 million in the most recent year. Income taxes paid amounted to $3.06 million at the effective rate of 34 percent.

Current Performance

We begin our appraisal of the current performance of ABC Corporation by calculating the *earnings per share (EPS)* of common stock. Throughout the chapter, this format of calculating EPS and related measures will be used. It is a step-by-step analysis of the earnings impact of each type of long-term capital.

First we state the earnings before interest and taxes (EBIT), a measure which was discussed in Chapter 3. From that figure we subtract a variety of charges applicable to different long-term funds. The first of these is *interest charges* on long-term debt. Normally short-term interest is ignored unless it is a significant amount, because we assume, given the temporary nature of short-term obligations that arise from ongoing operations, that the related interest charges have been properly deducted from income *before* arriving at the EBIT figure. The calculations of earnings per share are shown in Figure 8–2.

Provision is made for both long-term interest and preferred dividends. No amounts are shown, however, because our hypothetical company at this point has neither long-term debt nor preferred stock outstanding. The calculations in Figure 8–2 result in earnings available to common stock of $5.94 per share. From that figure, $2.50 has been subtracted, which represents a cash dividend voted by the board of directors. We assume that this level of dividend payout (between 40 and 50 percent of earnings) has been maintained for many years. We further assume that earnings have steadily grown by about 4 percent on average over the past decade.

The stock is widely held and traded, and currently commands a market price ranging from about $38 to $47, which means it is trading at roughly seven to eight times earnings. The latest security analyst's report suggests a β of 0.9, while the risk-free rate of return is judged to be 6.5 percent, and the average expected return from the S&P 500 is forecast at 14.0 percent.

Figure 8–2
ABC CORPORATION
Earnings per Share Calculation
($000, except per share figures)

Earnings before interest and taxes (EBIT)	$9,000
Less: Interest charges on long-term debt	–0–
Earnings before income taxes	9,000
Less: Federal income taxes at 34%	3,060
Earnings after income taxes	5,940
Less: Preferred dividends	–0–
Earnings available for common stock	$5,950
Common shares outstanding (number)	1 million
Earnings per share (EPS)	$ 5.94
Less: Common dividends per share	2.50
Retained earnings per share	$ 3.44
Retained earnings in total	$3,440

Long-Term Debt in the Capital Structure

As debt is introduced into this structure, both the financial condition and the earnings performance of ABC Corporation are significantly affected. To raise the $10 million needed to fund the new product, management has found that it is possible to issue debenture bonds, unsecured by any specific assets of the company but based on the company's general credit standing. These bonds, under current market conditions, will carry an interest (coupon) rate of 11.5 percent, will become due 20 years from date of issue, and entail a sinking fund provision of $400,000 per year beginning at the end of the fifth year. The balance outstanding at the end of 20 years will be repaid as a balloon payment of $4 million. The company expects to raise the full $10 million from the bond issue after all expenses, in effect, receiving the par value.

Once the new product financed with the proceeds has been successfully introduced, the company projects incremental earnings of at least $2 million before taxes. Little risk of product obsolescence or major competitive inroads are expected by management for the next 5 to 10 years because the company has developed a unique process protected by careful patent coverage.

We can now trace the impact of long-term debt both in terms of the change in earnings and dividends and of the specific cost of the newly created debt itself. We will analyze two contrasting conditions: first, the *immediate* impact of the $10 million debt without any offsetting benefits from the new product; and second, the *improved conditions* expected once the investment has become operative and the new product has begun to generate earnings, probably after one year.

The results of the two calculations are shown in Figure 8–3. The instant effect of adding debt is a reduction of the earnings available for common stock. This is caused by the *stated* interest cost of 11.5 percent on $10 million of bonds, or $1,150,000 before taxes. Earnings after interest and taxes dropped by $759,000 as compared to the conditions in Figure 8–2. This

Figure 8–3
ABC CORPORATION
Earnings per Share with New Bond Issue
($000, except per share figures)

	Before New Product	With New Product
Earnings before interest and taxes (EBIT)	$9,000	$11,000
Less: Interest charges on long-term debt	1,150	1,150
Earnings before income taxes	7,850	9,850
Less: Federal income taxes at 34%	2,669	3,349
Earnings after income taxes	5,181	6,501
Less: Preferred dividends	–0–	–0–
Earnings available for common stock	$5,181	$ 6,501
Common shares outstanding (number)	1 million	1 million
Earnings per share (EPS)	$ 5.18	$ 6.50
Less: Common dividends per share	2.50	2.50
Retained earnings per share	$ 2.68	$ 4.00
Retained earnings in total	$2,681	$ 4,001
Original EPS (Figure 8–2)	$ 5.94	$ 5.94
Change in EPS	–0.76	+0.56
Percent change in EPS	–12.8%	+9.4%

drop represents, of course, the aftertax cost of the bond interest, or $1,150,000 times $(1 - .34)$. As a consequence, earnings per share were reduced to $5.18, a drop of 76 cents, or an *immediate dilution* of 12.8 percent from the prior level. This was purely due to the effect of the incremental interest, which on a per share basis amounts to the same 76 cents, that is, the aftertax cost of $759,000 divided by one million shares.

In Chapter 7 we discussed the *stated* annual cost of the incremental debt funds, which is the *tax-adjusted* rate of interest carried by the debt instrument. Assuming a tax rate of 34 percent in our example, the stated cost for ABC Corporation is therefore 7.59 percent. We also explained in Chapter 7 that the *specific* annual cost of debt is developed by relating the stated annual cost to the *proceeds* received. If these proceeds were different from the par value of the debt instrument, the specific annual cost of the debt will, of course, be higher or lower than the stated rate. In the case of ABC Corporation, we assumed that the net proceeds were effectively at par, and therefore the *specific cost* of ABC's new debt is also 7.59 *percent*, a figure which will be compared with the specific cost of the other alternatives for raising capital.

When we turn to the second column of Figure 8–3, we find that the successful introduction of the new product will *more than compensate* ABC Company for the *earnings impact* of the interest paid on the bonds. In other words, the investment project is earning more than the specific cost of the debt employed to fund it. Aftertax earnings have risen to $6,501,000, a net increase of $561,000 over the original $5,940,000 in Figure 8–2. As a consequence, earnings per share rose 56 cents above the original $5.94, an increase of almost 10 percent. By more than offsetting the total aftertax interest cost of the debentures of $759,000, the successful new investment is expected to *boost* the common shares' earnings. Incremental earnings of $1,320,000 ($2,000,000 pretax earnings less tax at 34 percent) considerably exceed the incremental cost of $759,000. Therefore, the investment—if our earnings assumptions prove realistic—has made possible an increment of economic value. In effect, the *financial leverage* introduced by this financing decision is positive.

Yet several questions might be asked: For example, suppose the investment earned just $759,000 after taxes, exactly covering the cost of the debt supporting it and maintaining the shareholders' position just as before in terms of earnings per share. Would the investment still be justified? Would this mean that the investment was made at *no cost* to the shareholders? At first glance, one might believe this, but a number of issues must be considered here. First of all, no mention has been made of the *sinking fund obligations* which will begin five years hence and which represent a cash outlay of $400,000 per year. Such principal payments are not tax deductible and must be paid out of the *aftertax cash flow* generated by the company. Thus the debt service will amount to 40 cents per share over and above the interest cost. This amount is therefore no longer available for dividends or other corporate purposes, because it is committed to the repayment of principal. If we suppose that earnings from the investment exactly equaled the interest cost of the debt, how would the company repay the principal? At what point are the shareholders better off than they were before?

There is an obvious fallacy in this line of discussion. It stems from the use of *accounting earnings* to represent the benefits of the project and comparing these to the *aftertax cost* of the debt capital used to finance it. This is *not* a proper economic comparison, as we pointed out in Chapter 7. Only a time-adjusted cash flow analysis can determine the cost/benefit trade-off. We could say that the project was exactly yielding the *specific cost* of the debt capital associated with it *only* if the net present value of the project were *exactly zero* when we discount the *incremental annual cash flows* at 7.59 percent. This would then represent an internal rate of return of 7.59 percent, a level of economic performance that would scarcely be acceptable to management. Yet even under that condition, the project's *cash flows* (as contrasted to the accounting profit registered in the operating statement) would have to be *higher* than the $759,000 aftertax earnings required to pay only the interest on the bonds. This must be so because under the present value framework of investment analysis, the incremental *cash flows* associated with a project must be sufficient to not only provide the specified return but also to *amortize* the investment itself. We demonstrated this fact earlier in Chapter 6.

Let us now return to the *purpose* of the framework we are using here. This analysis is *not* made to judge the *desirability of the investment*—we must assume that this has been adequately done by management. Instead, we are interested only in which *form of financing* is most advantageous for the company under the circumstances presented. In this context, the impact of each alternative on the company's earnings is only one aspect in deciding on new funding. In the case of debt, which under normal conditions is the lowest cost alternative, we would indeed expect a *financial leverage effect* in favor of the shareholder. When the project was chosen, it must have met a standard based approximately on the weighted cost of capital—a return level that *far exceeds* the cost of debt capital alone.

The introduction of debt, in summary, *immediately dilutes* earnings per share, and this is followed by a *boost* in earnings per share as the project's reported accounting earnings *exceed* the interest cost reflected in the company's income statement. The company must allow for the future sinking fund payments from a *cash planning* standpoint, because beginning with the end of the fifth year, 40 cents per share of the company's cash flow will be committed annually to repayment of principal. It will be useful to examine the implications of these facts under a variety of conditions, that is, the risk posed by *earnings fluctuations* in both the basic business and in the incremental profit contribution of the new product, which we have assumed to be successful. We will take such variations into account later.

Preferred Stock in the Capital Structure

ABC Corporation could also meet its long-term financing needs with an issue of $10 million of preferred stock, at $100 per share, carrying a stated dividend rate of 12.5 percent. For simplicity we will again assume that the net proceeds to the company will be equivalent to the nominal price of $100, after legal and issuing expenses. The analysis of the conditions before and after the introduction of the new product project is shown in Figure 8–4.

This time we find a *more severe* drop in the earnings available for common stock, due to the impact of the preferred dividends of $1.25 million per year. Not only is the stated cost (as well as the specific cost, given that the net proceeds were again at par) of the new preferred stock *higher* by one percentage point than the stated cost of the bonds, but also the dividends paid on the preferred stock are *not tax deductible* under current laws. In fact, we are dealing with an alternative that costs, in comparable terms, *12.5 percent* after taxes versus *7.59 percent* after taxes for the debt alternative. Therefore, the

Figure 8–4

ABC CORPORATION

Earnings per Share with New Preferred Stock Issue

($000, except per share figures)

	Before New Product	With New Product
Earnings before interest and taxes (EBIT)	$9,000	$11,000
Less: Interest charges on long-term debt	–0–	–0–
Earnings before income taxes	9,000	11,000
Less: Federal income taxes at 34%	3,060	3,740
Earnings after income taxes	5,940	7,260
Less Preferred dividends	1,250	1,250
Earnings available for common stock	$4,690	$ 6,010
Common shares outstanding (number)	1 million	1 million
Earnings per share (EPS)	$ 4.69	$ 6.01
Less: Common dividends per share	2.50	2.50
Retained earnings per share	$ 2.19	$ 3.51
Retained earnings in total	$2,190	$ 3,510
Original EPS (Figure 8–2)	$ 5.94	$ 5.94
Change in EPS	– 1.25	+ 0.07
Percent change in EPS	– 21.0%	+ 1.2%

immediate dilution in earnings with the preferred issue is $1.25 per share, or 21 percent, when compared to the starting position. Over time, as the earnings from the new product are realized, the eventual increase in earnings per share amounts to only 7 cents, or a slight improvement of 1.2 percent. The $1.25 million annual commitment of aftertax funds for dividends leaves very little room for any *net gain* in reported profit from the earnings generated by the investment—which we know are estimated as $2 million before taxes and $1,320 after taxes.

In this situation, the assumed conditions allow for very limited financial leverage. Only little more than a 1 percent rise in earnings per share is achieved over the starting level, inasmuch as the fixed aftertax financing costs introduced have nearly doubled when compared to the bond alternative. Earnings per share would be *unchanged* if the new product project were to achieve minimum earnings that represent the pretax cost of the preferred dividends:

$$\frac{\$1,250,000}{(1 - .34)} = \$1,894,000$$

At that level, the incremental earnings from the new product would just *offset* the incremental financing cost—a breakeven situation. Note that this sizable earnings requirement is more than 50 percent larger than the $1,150,000 pretax interest cost with the bond alternative.

Common Stock in the Capital Structure

When ABC considers a new issue of common stock as the third alternative for raising $10 million, the impact on earnings is even *more severe*. Let us assume that ABC Corporation will issue 275,000 new shares at a net price to the company of $36.36 after underwriters' fees and legal expenses are met. Such a discount from the current market price of $40 should ensure successful placement of the issue. The number of shares outstanding thus increases by 27.5 percent over the current 1 million shares. In Figure 8–5 we have shown the impact on earnings in the same way as we did for the other two alternatives.

We observe that immediate dilution is a full $1.28 per share, a drop of 21.5 percent, which is the *highest* impact of the three choices analyzed. Common stock, in terms of this comparison, is the *costliest form* of capital—if only because it results in the greatest immediate dilution in the earnings of current shareholders. Moreover, there will also be an annual cash drain of at least $687,500 in aftertax earnings from the 275,000 new shares, if the current $2.50 annual dividend on common stock is maintained. Further, we can project that this cash drain could *grow* at the historical earnings growth rate of 4 percent per year. This assumption will hold if the directors continue their policy of declaring regular cash dividends at a fairly constant payout rate from future earnings that continue growing.

344

Figure 8–5
ABC CORPORATION
Earnings per Share with New Common Stock Issue
($000, except per share figures)

	Before New Product	With New Product
Earnings before interest and taxes (EBIT)	$9,000	$11,000
Less: Interest charges on long-term debt	–0–	–0–
Earnings before income taxes	9,000	11,000
Less: Federal income taxes at 34%	3,060	3,740
Earnings after income taxes	5,940	7,260
Less: Preferred dividends	–0–	–0–
Earnings available for common stock	$5,940	$ 7,260
Common shares outstanding (number) . . . . 1.275 million		1.275 million
Earnings per share (EPS)	$ 4.66	$ 5.69
Less: Common dividends per share	2.50	2.50
Retained earnings per share	$ 2.16	$ 3.19
Retained earnings in total	$2,752	$ 4,072
Original EPS (Figure 8–2)	$ 5.94	$ 5.94
Change in EPS	– 1.28	– 0.25
Percent change in EPS	– 21.5%	– 4.2%

For the present, the pretax earnings requirement to *cover* the
$2.50 per share dividend is:

$$\$2.50 \times 275,000 \text{ shares} = \$687,500 \text{ (after taxes)}$$

$$\frac{\$687,500}{(1 - .34)} = \$1,041,667 \text{ (before taxes)}$$

We can directly compare this earnings requirement of about
$1 million for the common stock alternative to the bond re-
quirement of $1,150 million and the preferred stock require-
ment of about $1.9 million. From both an earnings and a cash
planning standpoint, these amounts are clearly significant.

Further, the effect of *immediate dilution* of earnings is only
part of the consideration. There will be the second-stage effect
of *continuing dilution,* because the new shares created, in
contrast to the other two types of capital, represent an *ongoing
claim* on corporate earnings equal to that of the existing shares.
Thus, the rate of growth in earnings per share experienced to

date will be *slowed* in the future, merely because more shares will be outstanding—unless, of course, the earnings provided by the investment of the proceeds are *superior* in level and growth to the existing earnings performance.

When we turn to the second column of Figure 8–5, it is quite apparent that despite the incremental earnings contributed by the new product, *net dilution* of earnings per share in the amount of 25 cents, or 4.2 percent, will, in fact, *continue*. The contribution to reported earnings of the new product was not sufficient to meet the earnings claims of the new shareholders and maintain the old per share earnings level. The impact on earnings of the common stock alternative thus is greater than the earnings generated by the new capital raised.

Up to this point we have dealt with the *earnings impact* of common stock financing. To find a first rough approximation of the *specific cost* of this alternative, we can establish as a minimum condition the maintenance of the *old earnings per share level* and relate this to the proceeds from each new share of common stock. The current EPS of $5.94 and the proceeds of $36.36 result in a cost of about 16 percent:

$$\frac{\$5.94}{\$36.36} = 16.34\% \text{ (after taxes)}$$

We know from the discussion in Chapter 7, however, that the *earnings approach* to measuring the *cost of common equity*, for many reasons, has very limited usefulness, even if an allowance is made in the formulation for expected growth in earnings.

If we employ the *dividend approach* to find a specific cost of the incremental common stock, as discussed in Chapter 7, we must relate the current dividend per share to the net price received, and add prospective dividend growth. We know that the company has experienced fairly consistent growth in earnings of 4 percent per year, and we will assume that, given a constant rate of dividend payout, common dividends will continue to grow at the same rate. The result is:

$$\frac{\$2.50}{\$36.36} + 4.0 = 10.9\%$$

As we stated in Chapter 7, however, the dividend approach is similarly lacking in both concept and practical use. Therefore, let us now use the background data provided to test the specific cost of capital for ABC's common equity with the CAPM approach explained in Chapter 7. The resulting cost of common equity, k_e, is approximately 13.25 percent when we put into the CAPM formula the risk-free return, R_f, of 6.5 percent, the β of 0.9, and the expected average return, R_m, represented by the S&P 500 estimate of 14 percent:

$$k_e = R_f + \beta(R_m - R_f)$$
$$k_e = 6.5 + 0.9(14.0 - 6.5)$$
$$k_e = 13.25\%$$

This result is the most credible one for judging the specific cost of the common stock. As we already know, it can be compared to the specific cost of the bonds of 7.59 percent and the specific cost of the preferred stock of 12.5 percent. Clearly, the use of common equity is the *most expensive source* of financing, and we have already established that the dilution effect is also serious. In addition, the cash flow requirements for paying the current dividend of $2.50 per share plus any future increases in the common dividend have to be planned for. Because it is difficult to keep all of these aspects visible in our deliberations, let us now turn to a *graphic representation* of the various earnings and dilution effects to compare the *relative position* of the three alternatives.

EBIT BREAK-EVEN CHART

We have referred several times to *changes* in the earnings performance of a company and the *different impact* the three basic financing alternatives have under varying conditions. The *static* format of analysis we have used so far does not readily allow us to explore the *range* of possibilities as earnings change or the *sensitivity* of the alternative funding sources to these changes. It would be quite laborious to calculate earnings per share and other data for a great number of earnings levels and assumptions. Instead, we can exploit the direct linear relationships that exist between the quantitative factors analyzed. A graphic *break-even* approach can be used to compare the alternative souces of financing. In this section, we will show how such a model, keyed to fluctuations in EBIT and resulting EPS levels, can be employed to display for us the most important quantitative aspects of the relative desirability of the options available. As we will see, the break-even model allows us to perform a variety of analytical tests.

To begin with, we have summarized the data for ABC Corporation in Figure 8–6. The framework for graphic display of variations in these data is a basic chart showing earnings per share (EPS) on the vertical axis and EBIT on the horizontal axis. This EBIT *break-even chart* allows us to plot on straight lines the EPS for each alternative under varying conditions. Commonly, one uses as one of the *reference points* the intersection of each line with the horizontal axis, that is, the exact point where *EPS* are *zero*. These points can easily be found by

Figure 8–6
ABC CORPORATION
Recap of EPS Analyses with New Product
($000, except per share figures)

	Original	Debt	Preferred	Common
EBIT	$9,000	$11,000	$11,000	$11,000
Less: Interest	–0–	1,150	–0–	–0–
Earnings before taxes	9,000	9,850	11,000	11,000
Less: Taxes at 34%	3,060	3,349	3,740	3,740
Earnings after taxes	5,940	6,501	7,260	7,260
Less: Preferred dividends	–0–	–0–	1,250	–0–
Earnings available for common stock	$5,940	$ 6,501	$ 6,010	$ 7,260
Common shares outstanding (number)	1 million	1 million	1 million	1.275 million
EPS	$ 5.94	$ 6.50	$ 6.01	$ 5.69
Less: Common dividends	2.50	2.50	2.50	2.50
Retained earnings	$ 3.44	$ 4.00	$ 3.51	$ 3.19
Retained earnings in total	$3,440	$ 4,001	$ 3,510	$ 4,072
Original EPS change		–12.8%	–21.0%	–21.5%
Final EPS change		+9.4%	+1.2%	–4.2%
Specific cost		7.59%	12.5%	13.25%

working EPS calculations *backward*, that is, starting with an assumed EPS of zero and deriving an EBIT that just provides for this condition. This calculation is shown in Figure 8–7 for the original situation and for each of the three alternatives.

The calculations in Figures 8–6 and 8–7 give us sufficient points with which to draw the linear functions of EPS and EBIT for the various alternatives, as shown in Figure 8–8. We can quickly observe that the conclusions about the earnings impact of the alternatives we drew from the two EBIT levels previously analyzed, $9 million and $11 million, hold true over the fairly wide range of earnings presented; that is, every alternative considered causes a significant *reduction* in earnings per share relative to the original condition. There is a major new observation, however. Under the common stock alternative, the slope of the EPS line is *different*, and in fact the line for common stock *intersects* both the debt and the preferred stock lines. The latter two lines are parallel with each other and also with the line representing the original situation, both appearing to the right of that line.

The *lesser slope* of the common stock line is easily explained. The introduction of new shares of common stock results in a *proportional dilution* of earnings per share at all EBIT levels. As a consequence, the incremental shares cause earnings per share to rise *less rapidly* with growth in EBIT. In contrast, the *parallel shift* by the debt and preferred stock lines to the right of the original line is caused by the introduction of *fixed* interest or dividend charges, while at the same time the number of common shares outstanding *remains constant* over the EBIT range studied.

The significance of the *intersections* should now become apparent. These are break-even points at which, for a given EBIT level, the EPS for the common stock alternative and *one* of the other two alternatives are *the same*. Note that the break-even point of common stock line with the bond alternative occurs at about $5.3 million EBIT, while the break-even point of common stock with preferred stock occurs at about $8.8

Figure 8–7
ABC CORPORATION
Zero EPS Calculation
($000, except per share figures)

	Original	Debt	Preferred	Common
EPS	–0–	–0–	–0–	–0–
Common shares	1 million	1 million	1 million	1.275 million
Earnings to common	–0–	–0–	–0–	–0–
Preferred dividends	–0–	–0–	$1,250	–0–
Earnings after taxes	–0–	–0–	1,250	–0–
Taxes at 34%	–0–	–0–	644	–0–
Earnings before taxes	–0–	–0–	1,894	–0–
Interest	–0–	$1,150	–0–	–0–
EBIT or zero EPS	–0–	$1,150	$1,894	–0–

Figure 8–8
ABC CORPORATION
Range of EBIT and EPS Chart

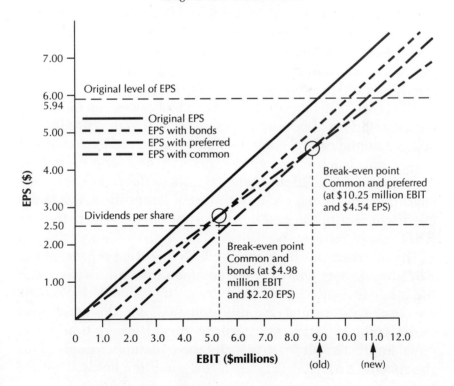

million EBIT. Below $5 million EBIT, therefore, the common stock alternative causes the *least* EPS dilution, while above $9 million EBIT, it causes the *worst* relative dilution in EPS. We recall that ABC's current EBIT level is $9 million and is expected to be at least $11 million once the new product is fully contributing its projected earnings. Both break-even points thus lie *below* the likely future EBIT performance, which makes the common stock alternative the *costliest* in terms of earnings dilution.

Therefore, given that *relative earnings effects* of the three alternatives are *different* over the wide range of EBIT shown, it is not possible to assess the three alternatives without defining a "normal" range of EBIT for the company's expected performance.

If future EBIT levels could, in fact, be expected to move fairly well *within* the two break-even points, common stock looks *more attractive* than preferred stock from the standpoint of EPS *dilution*, but *worse* than debt. If EBIT can be expected to grow and move fairly well to the *right* of the *second* break-even point, as is almost certain in the case of ABC Corporation, new common stock is not only *least attractive* from the standpoint of EPS dilution, but will *remain* so.

All of these considerations are based, of course, on *unchanging assumptions* about the terms under which the three forms of incremental capital could be issued. If we can expect any of these terms, such as the offering price of the common stock or the terms of the bond, to *change significantly*, an entirely new chart must be drawn up, or we must at least reflect any possible discontinuities in cost or proportions of the alternatives as EBIT levels change.

The intersections between the EPS lines that represent the *EBIT break-even points* for the common stock alternative with the other two choices can be quite easily calculated. For this purpose, we formulate simple equations for the conditions underlying any intersecting pair of lines. EPS are then set as equal for the two alternatives, and the equations are solved for the *specific EBIT level* at which this condition holds. To illustrate, let us first establish the following definitions:

E = EBIT level for any break-even point with common stock alternative.

i = Annual interest on bonds in dollars (before taxes).

t = Tax rate applicable to the company.

d = Annual preferred dividends in dollars.

s = Number of common shares outstanding.

The equation for any of the EPS lines can be found by substituting known facts for the symbols in the following generalized equation:

$$EPS = \frac{(E - i)(1 - t) - d}{s}$$

We can now find the EBIT break-even levels for bonds and common stock at the point of EPS equality. For this purpose, we fill in the data for the two expressions and set them as equal:

$$\underset{\text{Bonds}}{\frac{(E - \$1,150,000).66 - 0}{1,000,000}} = \underset{\text{Common}}{\frac{(E - 0).66 - 0}{1,275,000}}$$

When we solve for E, we obtain the following result:

$$0.66E - \$759,000 = \frac{0.66E}{1.275}$$

$$0.842E - \$967,725 = 0.66E$$

$$E = \$5,317,200$$

This result can easily be verified graphically in Figure 8–8. When the same approach is applied to the preferred and common stock alternatives, the following result emerges:

$$\underset{\text{Preferred}}{\frac{(E - 0).66 - \$1,250,000}{1,000,000}} = \underset{\text{Common}}{\frac{(E - 0).66 - 0}{1,275,000}}$$

$$0.66E - \$1,250,000 = \frac{0.66E}{1.275}$$

$$0.842E - \$1,593,750 = 0.66E$$

$$E = \$8,756,900$$

Again, the chart can be used to verify the result.

It is also possible to use the EBIT chart to show the impact of any *dividend assumption* for common stock on the three alternatives. The horizontal line at $2.50 in the chart represents the current annual dividend. Where this line intersects any alternative EPS line, we can read off the minimum level of EBIT required to supply this dividend. Similarly, it is possible to reflect in the chart the earnings requirements for *sinking funds* or other regular repayment provisions. In effect, such annual provisions *commit* a portion of future earnings for this purpose. We develop the effect of these requirements by carrying the calculations one step further and arriving at the so-called *uncommitted earnings per share (UEPS)* for each alternative *after* provision for any repayments. We simply subtract the per share cost of such repayments (which require aftertax dollars) from the respective EPS of the alternative thus affected and redraw the lines in the chart. The result will be a parallel shift of line to the right of its prior position.

For example, the sinking fund requirement of $400,000 per year in the bond alternative would represent 40 cents per share, and the new line would move to the right by this amount over the whole range. Similarly, the intersection at the zero EPS point, currently $1,150,000 EBIT, would move right to a zero UEPS point of $1,756,060. This shift reflects the sinking fund requirement of $400,000 per year, which translates into an incremental pretax earnings requirement of $400,000 ÷ (1 − 0.34), or $606,060. As it turns out in this case, the UEPS line for bonds would move very close to the EPS line for preferred stock in Figure 8–8.

By now, the usefulness of this framework for a dynamic analysis of the various alternatives should be clear. The reader is invited to think through the implications of the variety of tests than can be applied. It is possible, for example, to determine the *minimum EBIT level* under each alternative that would cover the current common dividend of $2.50 per share, while assuming a variety of *different payout ratios*, such as 50 percent or 40 percent. For example, with an assumed 50 percent payout, EPS would have to be $5. A horizontal line would be drawn at the $5 EPS level, and its intersection with the lines of the various alternatives would represent the minimum EBIT levels for the $2.50 dividend. The analyst would have to assess the likelihood of EBIT declining to this level and judge whether this endangers the current dividend payout.

Other tests can be applied, of course, depending on the particular circumstances of the company. The framework can also be used to work through the *cash flow implications* of each of the results, by translating the respective EBIT levels into equivalent cash flow from operations, as discussed in Chapters 2 and 3. This extra step would require determining the *tax shield effect* of depreciation and depletion write-offs. Computer-aided simulation can be used to make the multiple calculations required. Again it must be emphasized, however, that any *specific* EBIT chart works only under *fixed assumptions* about proceeds received and *stable* interest and preferred dividend rates. If there is reason to believe that any of the key assumptions might change, the positions of the EPS lines on the graph must be adjusted.

Obviously, any changes in the *relative* cost of the various alternatives will also have an effect. As the *spread between* the alternatives increases, for example, the differences in earnings impact will widen, and thus the distance between the parallel lines will *increase*. This simply reflects the fact that the imposition of higher fixed obligations depresses EPS. *Enlarging* the new capital issue has an effect also, because the slope of the line is determined by the amount of *leverage* already present in the *existing* capital structure. In other words, if there is already some debt and preferred in the capital structure, the basic EPS would rise and fall much more sharply with changes in EBIT. Any increases in the fixed financing cost alternatives would simply magnify this leverage. At the same time, the *slope* of the EPS line for common equity is governed by the relative number of shares issued, which in turn is related to the degree of *earnings dilution*, as demonstrated in the example.

Financial planning models and computer spreadsheets can be used to enhance the basic analysis demonstrated here. The point to remember, however, is that such a dynamic analysis,

354

in essense, quantifies the relative impact of the alternatives on *reported earnings only*. This effect is only one of the many factors that have to be weighed in making funding choices. As we mentioned in the beginning of this chapter, the conceptual and practical setting for the eventual decision is *far more inclusive* than this graphic expression of respective break-even conditions suggests. Strategic plans for the future, risk expectations, market factors, the specific criteria we listed, and current company conditions all have to enter the final judgment.

LEASING AS A FINANCING CHOICE

We have referred to leasing several times in the course of this book. Leasing is a *special form of financing* that gives a company access to a whole range of assets, from buildings to automobiles, without acquiring these items outright. The lessee pays an agreed-upon periodic fee that covers the lessor's ownership costs and financing and tax expenses, and also provides an economic return. The lessee can use the asset for a specified period, assumes none of the risks of ownership or technical obsolescence, and can replace or upgrade the asset, while the lessor assumes the task of disposing of the old items. The latter provision is particularly appealing in the case of computers or technical equipment. The lessee, in effect, only incurs a tax-deductible periodic expense.

Long-term lease contracts, particularly for buildings, can extend over many years and thus become, in fact, part of a company's financial structure. Current accounting practice requires the disclosure of lease obligations in a company's published financial statements if the leases represent a commitment of material size. While leases are not normally included in the balance sheet itself, footnotes to the balance sheet must disclose the amount of periodic payments and an estimated capitalized value of the lease obligations. This is done in recognition of the fact that lease obligations represent a financial burden that must be serviced just like any other form of financing. Therefore, any company that leases a significant portion of its assets has less flexibility in its financing choices. The effect is the same as that of a large outstanding long-term debt. In effect, fixed leasing charges introduce a *degree of leverage* into the company's operations that is quite comparable to leverage resulting from other sources.

There are many considerations involved in the choice of leasing versus ownership. We will not deal with the techniques of analyzing the cash flow implications of the many types of leasing arrangements because they are too specialized and complex to be covered here. But we must emphasize that there is an economic cost in leasing because the lessor must be compensated for providing, financing, servicing, and replacing the asset. Therefore, leasing charges must be high enough to make leasing attractive for the lessor. At the same time, the lessor is often able to introduce economies of scale to bear that may favorably affect the cost of leasing.

The comparative analysis necessary to make the final choice between leasing and ownership has to weigh such elements as the cost to the lessee, the technological advantages, service, the flexibility of not owning, and the impact of the company's financial position. As in all financial analyses, the choice is based on both quantifiable data and management judgment. In some industries, leasing is part of the normal way of doing business. For example, in wholesaling, warehouses are commonly leased, not purchased; and in the transportation industry, leasing of rolling stock, trucks and aircraft prevails. In other areas, the choice of leasing is wide open and depends on what financing alternative is considered advantageous at the time.

KEY ISSUES

The following is a recap of the key issues raised directly or indirectly in this chapter. They are enumerated here to help the reader keep the analysis techniques discussed within the perspective of financial theory and business practice:

1. The choice among different types of long-term financing is inextricably connected with the business strategy of a company. The choice must match the risk/reward characteristics inherent in both strategy and financing.

2. The cost of different types of capital is only one element on which a decision about new funding is based. While debt is generally the lowest-cost and common equity the highest-cost alternative, the need to build and maintain an appropriate balance in the capital structure often overrides the cost criterion.

3. Noncost elements, such as risk, flexibility, timing, and shareholder control, as well as management preferences, have to be weighed in relation to both changing market conditions and the company's future policies.

4. New financing at times may represent a significant proportion of the existing capital structure. How these funds are raised can cause shifts away from a firm's ideal target capital structure. Because a block of one form of long-term capital was chosen at one point in time, management may be limited in the choices for the next round of financing. To compensate for this imbalance, a compromise mix of funds may have to be used.

5. The specific provisions of a new issue of securities are generally tailor-made for the situation. Investment bankers, underwriters, and management collaborate to negotiate the design and price of a financial instrument that reflects market conditions, the company's credit rating and reputation, risk assessment, the company's strategic plans, and current financial practices.

6. As a company's capital structure changes, so does its weighted cost of capital. However, temporary shifts resulting from blocks of new capital should not affect the return standards based on cost of capital, unless there is a deliberate and permanent change in the company's policies.

7. New common equity has the long-term effect of diluting both ownership and earnings per share. This is true whether the new shares are directly issued or brought about be conversion of other securities. The decision of whether to issue new common shares thus must be closely tied to the expected results from the strategic plans in place. It also involves weighing the advantages of introducing new permanent equity capital into the capital structure.

8. Leasing as a form of financing is based on a series of trade-offs that must be weighed in relation to both the company's capital structure and its business direction.

SUMMARY

In this chapter we reviewed both the *decisional framework* and some of the *techniques* used to analyze the different types of long-term funds. We focused on the three basic alternatives open to management: long-term debt, preferred stock, and common equity, leaving the discussion of the many specialized aspects of funding instruments to be pursued in the reference materials at the end of the chapter.

We found that the choice of financing alternatives is a complex mixture of analysis and judgment. Several areas of consideration were highlighted. We reviewed the *cost* to the company, the relative *risks,* and the issues of *flexibility, timing,* and *control* with respect to the various funding sources. We found that many of the aspects involved in choosing the types of capital require more than quantifiable data.

We also focused on the impact of each financing alternative on the reported earnings of a company, and then developed a *break-even graph* relating EPS and EBIT, which allowed us to test visually the earnings impact of the alternatives over the whole dynamic range of potential earnings levels. This simple model suggested the potential use of broader financial models

358

or computer spreadsheets with which to simulate more fully the impact of alternative financing packages or changing conditions. Last, we briefly examined the key aspects of *leasing* as a specialized form of financing and suggested the kind of analytical considerations applicable to that subject.

SELECTED REFERENCES

Brealey, Richard, and Stewart Myers. *Principles of Corporate Finance.* 3rd ed. New York: McGraw-Hill, 1988.

Donaldson, Gordon. "New Framework for Corporate Debt Policy." *Harvard Business Review,* September–October 1978, pp. 149–64.

Myers, Stewart C. "The Search for Optimal Capital Structures." *Midland Corporate Finance Journal,* Spring 1983, pp. 6–16.

Piper, Thomas R., and Wolf A. Weinhold. "How Much Debt is Right for Your Company?" *Harvard Business Review,* July–August 1982, pp. 106–114.

Pringle, John J., and Robert S. Harris. Essentials of Managerial Finance. Glenview, Ill.: Scott, Foresman, 1984.

Van Horne, James C. *Financial Management and Policy.* 7th ed. Englewood Cliffs, N.J.: Prentice Hall, 1986.

Weston, J. Fred, and Thomas E. Copeland. *Managerial Finance.* 8th ed. Hinsdale, Ill.: Dryden Press, 1986.

SELF-STUDY EXERCISES AND PROBLEMS
(Solutions Are Provided in Appendix III)

1. The ABC Corporation is planning the financing of a major expansion program for late 1990. Common stock has been chosen as the vehicle, and the 50,000 shares to be issued in addition to the 300,000 shares outstanding are to bring estimated proceeds of $5 million. The current price range of common is $120 to $140 per share. The new program is expected to raise current operating profits of $14.7 million by 18 percent. The company's capital structure contains long-term debt of $10 million, with an annual sinking fund provision of $900,000 to begin in 1991 and interest charges of 11 percent. The most recent estimated operating statement of the company, which includes the additional profit, appears as follows:

ABC CORPORATION
Pro Forma Operating Statement
For the Year Ended December 31, 1991
($000)

Net sales	$66,000
Cost of goods sold*	42,000
Gross profit	24,000
Selling and administrative expenses	9,300
Operating profit	14,700
Interest on debt	1,100
Profit before taxes	13,600
Federal income tax (34%)	4,600
Net income	$ 9,000

*Includes depreciation of $2,250.

The company's β was calculated at 1.4, while the risk-free return was estimated to be 8 percent, and the expected return from the stock market 14.5 percent.

a. Develop an analysis of earnings per share, uncommitted earnings per share, and cash flow per share, and show the effects of dilution in earnings.

b. Develop the same analysis for an alternative issue of $5 million of 10 percent preferred stock, and an alternative issue of $5 million of 9 percent debentures due in full after 15 years.

c. Develop the specific comparative cost of capital for all three alternatives and discuss your findings.

2. XYZ Corporation is planning to raise an additional $30 million in capital, either via 240,000 shares of common at $125 per share net proceeds, or via 300,000 shares of 9 percent preferred stock. Current earnings are $12.50 per share on one million shares outstanding, $2.5 million in interest is paid annually on existing long- term debt, and dividends on existing preferred stock amount to $1.5 million per year. The current market price is $140 per share, the β 1.2, and risk-free return is 8 percent. The expected return from the stock market is 13 percent.

a. Develop the specific cost of capital for each alternative and show calculations (long form). Assume income taxes are 36 percent.

b. Develop the point of earnings per share equivalence between the common and preferred alternatives. Assuming a common dividend of $8 per share, calculate the EPS/dividends per share break-even point for the common stock alternative.

    c. Assuming EBIT levels of $10 million, $15 million, $22.5 million, and $33.75 million, demonstrate the effect of leverage with the preferred stock alternative, by graph and calculation. Discuss your findings.

3. The DEF Company was weighing three financing options for a diversification program that would require $50 million and provide greater stability in sales and profits. The options were as follows:

    a. One million common shares at $50 net to the company.

    b. 500,000 shares of 9.5 percent preferred stock.

    c. $50 million of 8.5 percent bonds (entailing a sinking fund provision of $2 million per year).

The current capital structure contained debt on which $1 million per year was paid into a sinking fund and on which interest of $1.2 million was currently paid. Preferred stock obligations were dividends of $1.8 million per year. Common shares outstanding were 2 million, on which $2 per share was paid in dividends. The current market price range was $55 to $60, and the company's β was 1.2. The risk-free rate of return was 7.5 percent, while expectations about the returns from a portfolio of stocks were 14 percent. EBIT levels had fluctuated between $22 million and $57 million, and earnings before interest and taxes from diversification were expected to be about $8 million. The most recent EBIT level of the company had been $34 million.

Assume that proceeds to the company after expenses would equal the par value of the securities in the second and third alternatives; also, disregard the obvious exaggerations in the relationships that were made for better contrast. Income taxes are 36 percent.

Develop a graphic analysis of the data given and establish by calculation the earnings per share, uncommitted earnings per share, dilution, specific costs of capital, break-even points, dividend coverage, and zero earnings per share. Discuss your findings.

9   VALUATION
AND BUSINESS
PERFORMANCE

In this, our final chapter, we will return to the concept of *value* in its various forms and relate it to business performance. Earlier, we discussed such value categories as the stated values reflected in a company's financial statements, the economic values represented by the cash flows generated through capital investments, and the market value of common equity. In each case, value was examined in a specific context of analysis and assessment, but not necessarily against the full dynamics of management's investment, operating, and financing decisions that underlie the performance of any business.

Now we will examine the *meaning of value* as it applies to a variety of common situations in which the issue of valuation arises. In the process, we will not only define the several concepts of value in more precise terms, but also once again use some of the now familiar analytical approaches that can be applied to the *process of valuation*. Among these, of course, is present value and the use of discounting, which was covered in Chapter 6.

We will begin by first discussing some basic *definitions of value* in the business setting. Then we will take the point of view of the *investor* assessing the value of the main forms of securities issued by a company. Finally, we will discuss the main issues involved in *valuing an ongoing business,* as the basis for determining *shareholder value,* which we described earlier as the principal objective of modern management. As we have emphasized throughout this book, the linkage of *cash flows* to creating *economic value* is the ultimate expression of success or failure of business investment, operating, and financing decisions. It is this recognition that spurred the wave of takeovers and restructuring activities of the 1980s—essentially a reassessment of the effectiveness with which *resources* were employed by target companies, and a redeployment of those resources in alternative ways that were expected to generate higher cash flows.

DEFINITIONS OF VALUE

At this point, it will be useful briefly to refresh our memory about the different types of value we have encountered so far and to state as clearly as possible what they represent and for what purposes they may be appropriate.

Economic Value

This concept relates to the basic ability of an asset—or a claim—to provide a stream of aftertax *cash flows* to the holder. These cash flows may be generated through earnings, or contractual payments, and a partial or total liquidation at a future point. As we have discussed in earlier chapters, economic value is essentially a *trade-off concept.* The value of any good is defined as the amount of cash a buyer is willing to give up now—its *present value*—in exchange for a pattern of expected future cash flows. Therefore, economic value is also a *future-oriented concept.* It is determined by assessing potential future cash flows, including proceeds from ultimate disposal of the good itself. We remember that costs and expenditures incurred by *past* decisions are *sunk costs* and thus irrelevant from an economic standpoint.

As we shall see, economic value underlies some of the other common concepts of value because it is based on a trade-off logic that is quite natural to the process of investing funds. Calculating economic value is not without practical difficulties, however. We recall that a representative discount rate (return standard) has to be selected and applied to the expected positive and negative cash flows over a defined period of time, including the terminal value assumption, in order to determine the *equivalence* of amounts occurring in different parts of the time spectrum. We also recall the need for *risk assessment*, both of the cash flow pattern itself and in setting the return standard. In other words, economic value is not absolute, but a criterion based on the *relative risk assessment* of future expectations—in fact, economic value is closely tied to individual risk preferences. Yet economic value is at the core of all business investment, operating and, financing decisions, whether this is recognized or not.

Market Value

Also referred to as *fair market value*, this is the value of any asset, or collection of assets, when it is *traded* in an organized market or between private parties in an unencumbered transaction without duress. The securities and commodity exchanges are examples of organized markets, as are literally thousands of regional and local markets and exchanges that enable buyers and sellers to find mutually acceptable values for all kinds of tangible and intangible assets. Market value is, of course, also established through individual transactions when no convenient organized market is available.

Again, there is nothing *absolute* in market value. Instead, it represents a *momentary consensus* of two or more parties. In a sense, the parties to a transaction *adjust* their respective individual assessments of the economic value of the asset sufficiently to arrive at the concensus. The market value at any one time can therefore be subject to the preferences and even whims of the individuals involved, the psychological climate prevalent in an organized exchange, the heat of a takeover battle, economic variations, industry developments, political conditions, and so forth. Moreover, the current volume of trading in the asset or security will influence the value placed on it by buyers and sellers.

Despite its potential variability, market value is generally regarded as a reasonable criterion to use for estimating the value of balance sheet assets and liabilities. It is also used in inventory valuation, and in capital investment analysis in the form of future recovery values. Mergers and purchases of going concerns are also based on market values established by the parties.

As was the case with economic value, there are practical problems associated with calculating market value. A *true* market value is found only by actually engaging in a transaction. Thus, unless the asset is actually traded, any market value assigned to it is merely an *estimate*, which will tend to shift as conditions change and the perceptions of the parties are altered. But even if market quotations are available, certain judgments apply. For example, popular common stocks traded on the major exchanges have widely quoted market prices, yet there frequently are price *fluctuations* even within a day's trading. Thus, market value based on many similar transactions can be fixed only within a *given range*, which in turn is tied to the trading conditions of the day, week, or month. For assets that are not traded frequently, estimating a realistic transaction value can become even more difficult.

Book Value

We recall from Chapter 3 that the book value of an asset or liability is the stated value on the balance sheet, recorded according to generally accepted accounting principles. While book value is handled *consistently* for accounting purposes, it usually has little relationship to *current economic* value. It is a historical value, which, at one time, may have represented economic value to the company, but the passage of time and changes in economic conditions increasingly distort it. Its usefulness for financial analysis is therefore questionable under most circumstances.

Liquidation Value

This value relates to the special condition when a company has to liquidate part or all of its assets and claims. In essence, this is an *abnormal* situation in that time pressures and even duress serve to distort the value assessments made by buyers and sellers. Under the cloud of impending business failure or intense pressure from creditors, management will find that liquidation values are generally *considerably below* the potential market values. The economic setting is adversely affected by the known disadvantage under which the selling party must act in the transaction. As a consequence, liquidation value is really applicable only for the limited purpose intended. Nevertheless, it is sometimes used in valuing assets of unproven companies to perform ratio analysis in credit assessment.

Breakup Value

A variation of liquidation value, the breakup value concept is related to corporate takeover and restructuring activities, as discussed later in this chapter. On the assumption that the combined economic values of the *individual segments* of a multibusiness company exceed the value of the company as a whole, because of inadequate past management or current opportunities not recognized earlier, the company is broken up into *salable components* for disposal to other buyers. Any redundant assets, such as excess real estate, are also sold for their current values. Note that breakup value is usually realized on business segments with *ongoing operations*, and less frequently through forced liquidation of individual assets supporting these business segments, as would be the case in a bankruptcy sale, for example. Redundant assets may, of course, be liquidated as such. Estimates of breakup value are a critical element in the analysis preceding takeover bids.

Reproduction Value

This is the amount that would be required to replace an existing *fixed* asset in kind. In other words, it is the like-for-like replacement cost of a machine, facility, or other similar asset. Reproduction value is, in fact, one of several yardsticks used in judging the worth of an ongoing business. Determining reproduction value is an estimate largely based on engineering judgments. There are several practical problems involved. The most important of these is whether the fixed asset in question could—or would—in fact be reproduced *exactly* as it was constructed *originally*. Most physical assets are subject to some technological obsolescence with the passage of time, in addition to physical wear and tear. In addition, there is the problem of estimating the currently applicable cost of reproducing the item *in kind*. For purposes of analysis, reproduction value often becomes just one checkpoint in assessing the market value of the assets of a going business.

Collateral Value

This is the value of an asset used as *security* for a loan or other type of credit. The collateral value is generally considered the *maximum amount of credit* that can be extended against a pledge of the asset. With their own position in mind, creditors usually set the collateral value *lower* than the market value of an asset. This is done to provide a cushion of safety in case of default, and the individual risk preference of the individual creditor will determine the size of the often arbitrary downward adjustment. Where no market value can be readily estimated, the collateral value is set on a *purely judgmental* basis, the creditor being in a position to allow for as much of a margin of safety as deemed advisable in the particular circumstances.

Assessed Value

This value concept is established in local legal statute as the *basis for property taxation*. The rules governing assessment vary widely and may or may not take market values into account. The use of assessed values is limited to raising tax revenues, and thus such values bear little relationship to the other value concepts.

Appraised Value

Appraised value is subjectively determined and used when the asset involved has no clearly definable market value. Often used in transactions of considerable size, the value is determined by an *impartial expert* accepted by both sides in the transaction, whose knowledge of the type of asset involved can narrow the gap that may exist between buyer and seller, or at least establish a bargaining range. The quality of the estimate depends on the expertise of the appraiser solicited. Again, individual ability and preference enter into the value equation, and rarely will different appraisals yield exactly the same results.

Going Concern Value

This is an application of economic value, inasmuch as a business viewed as a going concern is expected to produce a series of future cash flows that the potential buyer must value to arrive at a price for the business as a whole. Note that the same concept applies to ongoing businesses in the determination of breakup value, as discussed earlier. Apart from the specific technique of valuation applied here, the concept requires that the business be viewed as an ongoing "living" system of operating parts rather than as a collection of assets and liabilities. The reader will recall the strong emphasis placed in earlier parts of the book on the fact that business value is created by a *positive trade-off* of future cash flows for present commitments and outlays. As we will see later in the chapter, the going concern value is very useful when comparative cash flow analyses, singly and in combination, are considered for acquisitions and mergers. The continuing challenge is to properly weigh this pattern of cash flows.

In summary, we have discussed a number of value definitions. Some were specialized yardsticks designed for specific situations. Many are directly or indirectly related to *economic value*. We defined economic value as the present value of future cash flows, discounted at the investor's risk-adjusted standard. This value concept is *broadly applicable*, and we will exploit it as we examine various decision areas where measures of value are necessary.

VALUE TO THE INVESTOR

As we have done in Chapters 5, 7, and 8, we will concentrate only on the three main types of corporate securities, *bonds*, *preferred stock*, and *common stock* in discussing the techniques involved to assess *value* and *yield*. *Value*, of course, is the current value of the investment to the investor in *present value terms*, while *yield* is the *internal rate of return earned* by the investor on the price paid for the investment. We will discuss major provisions in the basic securities types only insofar as they may affect their value and yield. The techniques should appear quite familiar to the reader because they closely relate to the analytical approaches used in the earlier chapters.

Bond Values

Valuing a bond is normally fairly straightforward. A bond issued by a corporation is a simple debt instrument. Its basic provisions generally entail a series of contractual *semiannual interest* payments, defined as a *fixed* rate based on the stated *par (face) value* of the bond (usually $1,000). The legal contract, or *indenture*, promises repayment of the principal (nominal value) at a specified maturity date a number of years in the future. The basic characteristics of defined interest payments and repayment stipulations are encountered in most normal debt arrangements. Complicating aspects are sometimes found in provisions such as conversion into common stock at a predetermined exchange value or payment of interest only when earned by the issuing company. Such specialized features will not concern us here.

The basic value of a bond rests on the *investor's assessment* of the relative attractiveness of the expected stream of *future interest receipts* and the prospect for eventual *recovery* of the principal at maturity. There is normally, of course, no obligation for the investor to hold the bond until maturity because most bonds can be readily *traded* in the securities markets. Still, the *risk* underlying the bond contract must be considered here, in terms of the issuing company's future ability to generate sufficient cash with which to pay both interest and principal. The *collective judgment* of security analysts and investors about the issuing company's prospects of doing this will influence the price level at which the bond is publicly traded, and the bond is likely to be *rated* in a particular risk category relative to other bonds.

To determine the value of a bond, we must first calculate the *present value* of the *interest* payments received up to the maturity date and add to this the *present value* of the ultimate *principal* repayment. (The reader will recognize this as comparable with the process of calculating the present value of capital expenditures in Chapter 6.) The discount rate applied is the *risk-adjusted rate* that represents the *investor's own standard* of measuring investment opportunities within the range of acceptable risk. For example, an investor with an 8 percent annual return *standard* would value a bond with a *coupon interest rate* of 6 percent annually significantly *lower* than its par value. The calculation is shown in Table 9–1. The investor's annual return standard of 8 percent is equivalent to a semiannual standard of 4 percent, a restatement for purposes of calculation that is necessary to match the semiannual interest payments paid by most bonds.

The resulting value is $832.89, which represents the *maximum* amount our investor should be willing to pay—or the *minimum price* at which the investor should be willing to sell—if the investor normally expects a return, called *yield*, of 8 percent from this type of investment. This particular bond should therefore be acquired *only* at a price considerably below (at a *discount* from) par. Note that the *stated* interest rate

Table 9–1
Bond Valuation

Date of analysis:	July 1, 1990		
Face value (par) of bond:	$1,000		
Maturity date:	July 1, 2004		
Bond interest (coupon rate):	6% per year		
Interest receipts:	$30 semiannually		

	Total Cash Flow	Present Value Factors, 4 Percent*	Present Value
28 receipts of $30 over 14 years (28 periods)	$ 840	16.663 (× $30)	$499.89
Receipt of principal 14 years hence (28 periods)	1,000	0.333	333.00
Totals	$1,840		$832.89

*From Tables 6–10 and 6–9, respectively.

on the bond is relevant only for determining the semiannual *cash receipts* in absolute dollar terms. Actual valuation of the bond and the cash flows it represents depends on the *investor's opportunity rate* (return standard). In other words, the desired yield determines the price, and vice versa. This relationship also applies, of course, to the market quotations for publicly traded bonds. The quoted price, or value, is a function of the yield collectively desired by the many buyers and sellers of these debt instruments.

If our investor were for some unrealistic reason satisfied with the very low annual yield of only *4 percent* from holding the *same* bond (equivalent to 2 percent per six-month period), the value to the investor would rise considerably *above* par, as shown in Table 9–2. Under these assumed conditions, the investor should be willing to pay a *premium* of up to $212.43 for the $1,000 bond, because the personal return standard is *lower* than the stated interest rate. If the investor's own standard and the coupon interest rate were to *coincide* precisely, the value of the bond would, of course, be exactly the par value of $1,000. In fact, the quoted market price of any bond will tend to approach the *par value* as it reaches maturity, because

Table 9–2
Bond Valuation with Lower Return Standard (4 percent per year)

	Total Cash Flow	Present Value Factors, 2 Percent*	Present Value
28 receipts of $30 over 14 years (28 periods) . . .	$ 840	21.281 (× $30)	$ 638.43
Receipt of principal 14 years hence (28 periods) . .	1,000	0.574	574.00
Totals	$1,840		$1,212.43

*From Tables 6–10 and 6–9, respectively.

at that point the only representative value will be the immi-
nent repayment of the principal—assuming, of course, that
the company is *able* to pay as the amount becomes due.

Bond Yields.   A related but common problem for the analyst or investor is the calculation of the *yield* produced by
various bonds, when quoted prices differ from par. The key to
this analysis again is the relationship of value and yield as
discussed above, and the technique used is a present value
calculation that in effect determines the *internal rate of return*
of the cash flow patterns generated by the bond over its remaining life. The method is identical to that used for assessing
the cash flows of any business investment proposal. The key
difference is that the individual investor's calculations are
based on *pretax cash flows* that must be adjusted in each case
by the investor for his or her *personal tax position*. Other
minor differences are the cash incidence in a semiannual pattern and the form in which bond prices (the net investment)
are quoted. Published prices are normally stated as a percentage of par. For example, a bond quoted at 103⅜ has a price of
$1,033.75.

Bond yield tables have long been employed to determine a
bond's internal rate of return, or yield. While, today, personal
computers and calculators have financial routines that allow
direct calculation, we will nevertheless take a quick look at a
yield table, if only to help the reader understand the examples
by *visual* inspection of the relationships. Bond yield tables are

finely graduated *present value tables* that list the whole potential range of stated interest rates, subdivided into fractional progressions of as little as ⅟₃₂ of a point. They are far more detailed than the present value tables we used in Chapter 6.

For example, Table 9–3 is a small segment of such a yield table, in this case for a bond with a coupon interest rate of precisely 6 percent. The columns show the number of *six-month periods* remaining in the life of the bond, while the rows display the *yield to maturity*. The yield to maturity simply refers to the yield obtained by the investor if the bond is actually held *until* its *par value* is repaid at the maturity date. If the investor were to sell at an earlier date, the *market price* of the bond received at that time would be substituted for par value in calculating the return. As a result, the yield achieved for the period up to the date of sale may differ from the yield to maturity if the bond were trading above or below par.

Note that it is possible to quickly find the bond's yield to maturity at any given purchase price in the bond yield tables. Conversely, it is also possible to find the exact *price* (value) that corresponds to any particular desired yield to maturity. Our example of the 6 percent bond used in the previous

Table 9–3
Bond Yield Table (sample section for a 6 percent rate)

	Price Given Years or Periods to Maturity										
Yield to Maturity	13 Years (26 periods)		13½ Years (27 periods)		14 Years (28 periods)		14½ Years (29 periods)		15 Years (30 periods)		15½ Years (31 periods)
3.80%	1.224	043	1.230	661	1.237	155	1.243	528	1.249	782	1.255 919
3.85	1.218	284	1.224	709	1.231	012	1.237	196	1.243	263	1.249 215
3.90	1.212	559	1.218	793	1.224	907	1.230	904	1.236	787	1.242 557
3.95	1.206	868	1.212	913	1.218	841	1.224	654	1.230	354	1.235 944
4.00	1.201	210	1.207	068	1.212	812*	1.218	443	1.223	964	1.229 377
4.05	1.195	585	1.201	260	1.206	821	1.212	273	1.217	616	1.222 853
4.10	1.189	993	1.195	486	1.200	868	1.206	142	1.211	310	1.216 375
4.15	1.184	434	1.189	747	1.194	952	1.200	051	1.205	046	1.209 940
4.20	1.178	908	1.184	043	1.189	073	1.193	999	1.198	823	1.203 549
4.25	1.173	414	1.178	374	1.183	230	1.187	985	1.192	642	1.197 201

*Example used in previous section (slight difference due to rounding of present value factors).

section (Table 9–1) is represented on the 4 percent yield line and in the 28-period column of the bond yield table segment reproduced in Table 9–3. Bond yield tables provide a visual impression of the progression or regression of prices and yields that is, of course, based on their mathematical relationship. The programmed calculator goes through the same steps and formulas used to generate the tables.

Yield to maturity can be *approximated* by using a shortcut method, if neither a programmed calculator nor a bond table is handy. If we assume that our 6 percent bond was quoted at a price of $832.89 on July 1, 1990 (which was the result of our earlier calculation), the *discount* from the par value of $1,000 is $167.11. The investor will thus not only receive the coupon interest of $30 each for 28 periods, but will also earn the discount of $167.11, *if* the bond is held to maturity and *if* the repayment of $1,000 is received. The shortcut method approximates the true yield by adjusting the periodic interest payment with a proportional *amortization* of this discount. The first step reflects the common accounting practice of amortizing discounts or premiums *over the life* of the bond. In our example, the discount of $167.11 is therefore divided by the remaining 28 periods, and the resulting periodic *value increment* of $5.97 is *added* to the periodic interest receipt of $30. The adjusted six-month earnings pattern is now $35.97 per period.

The next step relates the adjusted *periodic earnings* of $35.97 to the *average investment* outstanding during the remaining life of the bond. The price paid by the investor is $832.89, while the investment's value will rise to $1,000 at maturity. The average of the two values is one half of the sum, or $916.44. We can then calculate the *periodic* yield to maturity (based on the six-month interest period) by relating the periodic earnings of $35.97 to the average investment outstanding, or we can find the *annual* yield to maturity by relating *two* six-months earnings amounts of $35.97 each to the average investment:

$$\text{Yield} = \frac{2 \times \$35.97}{\$916.44} = 7.85\% \text{ per year}$$

This result is slightly *below* the precise yield of 8 percent per year on which our original calculation was built. The averaging shortcut will *always* introduce some error, because it imperfectly simulates a progressive present value structure. As yield rates and the number of time periods increase, larger errors will result. Yet the rough calculation provides a satisfactory result for use as an initial analytical check.

Had a *premium* been involved, i.e., had the purchase price been above the par value of the bond, the shortcut calculation would, in contrast, *reduce* the periodic interest earnings by the proportional amortization of the premium. The second example discussed in the previous section (Table 9–2) posed such a condition. The result would appear as follows, again being a close approximation of the true 4 percent solution:

$$\text{Yield} = \frac{(\$30.00 - \$7.59)2}{(\$1,212.43 + \$1,000) \div 2} = 4.052\% \text{ per year}$$

In summary, bond yield calculations involve a fairly straightforward determination of the *internal rate of return* of future cash flows generated by the bond investment at a known present price. As in the case of a business capital investment, a *trade-off* of current outlays for future cash flows under conditions of uncertainty is involved. Yield and value are mathematically related, and this relationship can be utilized to locate either result in preset bond yield tables, or to solve the analysis directly with a programmed calculator or personal computer.

Bond Provisions and Value.   The simple value and yield relationships discussed so far are, of course, affected by the specific conditions surrounding the company and its industry, and also by additional provisions in the specific bond indenture itself. The issuer's *ability to pay* must be assessed through careful analysis of the company's earnings pattern and projections of expected performance. The techniques in the early chapters of this book are helpful in this process. Ability to pay is a function of the projected cash flows and how well these flows cover debt service of both interest and principal.

Sensitivity analysis based on high and low estimates of performance can be useful here.

Variations in the bond indenture agreement will also affect the value and the yield earned. We will refer only to the major types of bond variations here. *Mortgage bonds* are secured by specific assets of the issuing firm. Because of this relationship, the bondholders have a cushion against default on the principal. As a result of the reduced risk, the coupon interest rate offered with mortgage bonds may be slightly lower than that of unsecured debenture bonds and reduce the yield to the investor. *Income bonds* are at the other extreme on the risk spectrum because they are not only unsecured but also pay interest *only if* the earnings of the company reach a specified minimum level. Their yield levels will be correspondingly high.

Convertible bonds, as we already observed, add the attraction of eventual participation in the potential market appreciation of common stock for which they can be exchanged at a set price. Their coupon rate of interest may therefore be somewhat lower than that of a straight bond. The value of these bonds is affected by the market's assessment of the likely performance of the common stock and by the gap between the stipulated conversion price and the current price of the common stock, apart from the coupon interest the bond pays semiannually. Normally, the conversion price is set *higher* than the market value of the common stock at the time of issue, to build in the attraction of expected value growth. Conversion is at the investor's discretion when found advantageous, although the indenture usually stipulates a time limit as well as the right of the issuing company to *call* the bonds for redemption at a slight premium price after a certain date, thus forcing the investor to act. As common share prices approach and surpass the conversion price, the bond's value will rise above par because of the equivalent common shares it represents.

A fairly recent phenomenon in the bond markets is the appearance of so called *junk bonds* extensively promoted by some investment bankers to support company takeovers, using very high levels of debt, or for so-called "leveraged buyouts" by groups of managers or investors that similarly use extremely high financial leverage to finance the purchase of the company involved. These securities are, in effect, *subordinate* to (ranking below) the claims of other creditors in case of default and are sold under often highly risky circumstances, because the amount of indebtedness involved in some of these transactions exceeds what are normally considered prudent levels. The yields provided by these unsecured instruments are usually commensurate with the high risk perceived by investors, and defaults are not uncommon.

Many other modifications and provisions are possible to tailor bonds of various types to the needs of the issuing company and to the prevailing conditions in the securities markets. The possible variations in bond provisions and their impact on value and yield call for careful judgments that go *beyond* the direct analytical techniques we discussed. These calculations are but the starting point. No hard-and-fast rules exist for weighing mechanically all aspects of bond valuation. In the final analysis, value and yield must be adjusted with due regard to the investor's *economic* and *risk preferences*, in line with the *specific objectives* in owning debt instruments. The references at the end of the chapter cover these aspects in greater detail.

Preferred Stock Values

By its very nature, preferred stock represents a *middle ground* between debt and common equity ownership. The obligation provides a series of cash dividend payments, but normally has *no specific provision* (or expectation) for repayment of the par value of the stock. However, at times preferred stock carries a *call provision,* which allows the issuing company to *retire* part or all of the stock during a specific time period by paying a small premium over the stated value of the stock. While the investor enjoys a "preferential" position over common stock with regard to current dividends and also to recovery of principal in the case of liquidation of the enterprise, preferred dividends may *not be paid* if company performance is poor. Such an event will, of course, adversely affect the value of the stock.

Preferred dividends, like common dividends, are declared at the discretion of the board of directors and may *not* be made up if missed, unless the preferred issue carries specific legal requirements to the contrary. Such provisions, for example, may call for *cumulating* past unpaid dividends until the company is in a position to afford declaring dividends of any kind. At other times, particularly in new companies, preferred stocks may carry a *participation* feature, which requires the board of directors to declare preferred dividends *higher* than the stated rate if earnings exceed a stipulated minimum level. But these are two special situations not normally encountered.

The task of valuation, therefore, has to be based on *less definite* conditions than was the case with bonds, because the only reasonably certain element is the stated annual dividend that was set as a *percentage of stated value*. For example, an 8 percent preferred stock usually refers to a $100 share of stock that is expected to pay a dividend of $8 per year, most likely in *quarterly* installments, a pattern normally matching that for common stocks. The investor is faced with valuing this stream of prospective cash dividends. If the price paid for a share of preferred stock was $100 and the stock is held indefinitely, the yield under these circumstances would be 8 percent, assuming that the company is likely to be *able to pay* the dividend regularly. If the price was more or less than the stated value, the yield could be found by relating the amount of the dividend to the *actual* price per share:

$$\text{Yield} = \frac{\text{Annual dividend per share}}{\text{Price paid per share}}$$

If the investor could expect to sell the stock at $110 five years hence, the exact yield can be determined by using either *present value techniques* or the *shortcut methods*, discussed earlier in the section on bonds. However, estimating a *future disposal value* involves a good deal of conjecture. In contrast to bonds, preferred shares have no specific maturity date or par value to be paid at maturity. The actual price of a preferred stock traded in the securities market depends on both company *performance* and on the collective *value* the securities markets place on the given preferred issue. This, in turn, reflects the risk/reward trade-off demanded for the whole spectrum of investments at the time. This value range will depend not only on the respective *risk premiums* assigned to individual securities but also on the *inflationary expectations* underlying the economy, which are reflected in the risk-free rate on which risk premiums are based. Value may be a little earier to estimate if the stock carries a mandatory *call provision* applicable at a specific future date and price, and the date of analysis is close to that time.

When we look at preferred stock values from the viewpoint of investing, we should use the *investor's own* return (or yield) standard to arrive at the *maximum price* the investor should be willing to pay for the stock, or the *minimum price* at which the investor should be willing to sell. We simply relate the stipulated dividend rate to our investor's required return—relevant for the level of risk implicit in the preferred issue—to arrive at the answer. If the standard were 9 percent against which to test the 8 percent preferred, we would determine the investor-specific value as follows:

$$\text{Value per share} = \frac{\text{Stated dividend rate}}{\text{Required return}} = \frac{0.08}{0.09} = \$88.89$$

If the investor were satisfied with only a 7 percent return, the value would be:

$$\text{Value per share} = \frac{0.08}{0.07} = \$114.29$$

The judgments that *remain* to be made, of course, relate to any *uncertainty* in the future dividend pattern and any material *change* in the future value of the stock, either because of changing market conditions or because of a call for redemption at a premium price.

Preferred Stock Provisions and Value. As in the case of bonds, there are many modifications in the provisions of preferred stocks that may affect their value in the market. We mentioned earlier that some preferred stocks, particularly in newly established companies, contain a *participation* feature, which entitles the preferred holder to *higher* dividends, if corporate earnings exceed a set level. This feature can favorably affect the potential yield, and thus the valuation of the stock, depending on how likely it is that the company will reach this higher earnings level. Similar to bonds, a much more common feature is *convertibility*, the possibility of changing the preferred ownership position into that of *common* stock. As in the case of bonds, however, the value of this feature cannot be calculated precisely. Yet, as the price of common stock reaches and exceeds the stated conversion price, the price of the convertible preferred stock will tend to reflect the market value of the equivalent number of common shares. Before this point is reached, the convertible preferred stock's value will be largely considered the same as a regular preferred and based essentially on the stated dividend. Again, convertibility is generally accompanied by a *call provision*, at a premium price, which enables the company to force conversion when conditions are right.

In summary, the challenge of preferred stock valuation also goes *beyond* the simple techniques we have shown. In the end, decisions should be made after careful assessment of the relative attractiveness of the specific features of the particular class of stock and of the conditions surrounding a particular company's preferred stock.

Common Stock Values

The most complex valuation problem is encountered when we turn to common stock, because by definition common stock represents the residual claim of owners to the total performance and outlook of the issuing corporation. We found this to be true when we examined the *relative cost of capital* from the point of view of the corporation in Chapter 7.

Common stock valuation is especially difficult because it involves full ownership risks, yet permits claims on both assets and earnings only after all other claims have been satisfied. An investment in common stock thus involves a *sharing* of both the risks and rewards. This heightens the uncertainty about potential dividend receipts and the amount of "principal" recovered. Consequently, measurement techniques have to deal with variables subject to a high degree of judgment.

The rewards of successful common stock ownership are several: *Cash dividends* (and sometimes additional stock *distributions* in lieu of cash), *growth in recorded equity* through growing earnings, which in part are reinvested by management, and the resulting potential *appreciation of the market price* of the stock. As we observed in Chapter 7, there are many practical and theoretical issues surrounding the interpretation and measurement of these elements. Here we will focus on ways of developing reasonable approximations of *share value*, and similarly, approximations of the *yield* an investor derives from a common stock investment.

Earnings and Common Stock Value.   The most direct way to approach the valuation of a share of common stock is to estimate the likely future level of *earnings per share,* and to *capitalize* these earnings at an appropriate discount rate that reflects *return expectations* within the scope of the investor's personal risk preference. The simple formulation appears as follows:

$$\text{Value per share} = \frac{\text{Earnings per share (projected)}}{\text{Discount rate (investor's expectation of return)}}$$

We recall from our discussion of the cost of capital that there are serious practical shortcomings in using projected *earnings* to measure shareholder expectations. Unless a company continually pays out *all* of its earnings in the form of dividends—which we know from Chapters 2 and 3 to be quite unlikely, especially for a growing company requiring reinvestment of at least some of its earnings—the stream of projected earnings is not at all representative of the benefits *in fact received* by the shareholder. Moreover, the formula is *static* unless any potential *growth* or *decline* in earnings is built in. Finally, there is the basic problem of forecasting the *earnings pattern* itself, both for the company and its industry.

A more useful approach to estimating common share value is to capitalize expected *dividends*. The size, regularity, and trend in dividend payout to shareholders has quite an important effect on the value of a share of common stock. Yet there is also a degree of uncertainty about the receipt of any series of *future* dividends. Not only will such dividends depend on the ability of the company to perform successfully, but dividends are also declared at the *discretion* of the corporate board of directors. No general rule applies—dividend policies can range from *no cash* payment at all to *regular* payments of 75 percent or more of current earnings. At times, dividends paid may even *exceed* current earnings, because the company is unwilling to cut the current dividend per share. Most boards of directors see some value in the *consistency* with which dividends are paid, and major adjustments in the size of the dividend, up or down, are only made very reluctantly.

The approach to valuation via dividends involves *projecting* the expected dividends per share and *discounting* them by the return standard appropriate for the investor. Several issues arise here. First, the current level of dividends paid is likely to *change* over time. For example, in a successful, growing company, the dividend is likely to grow as well. The problem is to make the projection of future dividends *realistic*, even though past performance is the only guide. If a company has been paying a steadily growing dividend over many years, an extrapolation of this past trend may be reasonable, but must be tempered by subjective judgments about the outlook for the company and its industry. Companies with more erratic patterns of earnings and dividends, however, pose a greater challenge.

The second issue involved in valuing common stock via future dividends is the *method* of calculation. The most common format is the so-called *dividend discount model*, or *dividend growth model,* which appears below in its simplest form. The formula is a restatement of the dividend approach we used as one way of calculating the cost of equity in Chapter 7. In that approach we defined the cost of common equity as the ratio of the current dividend to the current market price *plus* the expected rate of growth of future dividends. Here, instead of solving for the cost of equity—which is the investor's expectation of return—we solve for the *value,* or price of the stock:

$$\text{Value per share} = \frac{\text{Current dividend}}{\text{Discount rate (Investor's expectation of return)} - \text{Dividend growth rate}}$$

This particular formula is based on the idea that the value of a share of stock is the sum of the present values of a series of growing annual dividend payments, discounted at the investor's return expectation for this class of risk. But it implies an *ongoing* series of payments, in perpetuity, and it also implies a *constant* annual rate of growth in the dividend payment. The formula also permits using the less realistic assumption of a constantly *declining* dividend. However, it is very important to note that the model would give an *invalid answer* for a company paying dividends that will grow *as fast or faster* than the discount rate, because then the denominator would become zero or even negative. Clearly, under such a happy condition, the investor's return expectation should be reexamined and raised, or the stock should be considered outside the investor's risk/reward spectrum.

The dividend discount model is related mathematically to an annuity formula that assumes a constant growth rate and constant discount rate. The valuation it provides *implicitly includes* any appreciation in the future market value of the stock that is due to management's *reinvestment* of the retained portion of the growing earnings that made the increase in dividends possible. This condition holds because in the model, the market value of the stock at any *future* time is defined as the present value *at that point* of the *ensuing* stream of growing dividends.

The simplifying assumption of a *constant* rate of growth in dividends can be modified if a more erratic pattern of future dividends is expected. The calculation then becomes a present value analysis of *uneven annual cash flows* up to a selected point in the future. If the analyst wishes to assume that the dividend growth rate will become *stable* at some future time, the basic formula can then be inserted and its result discounted to the present. We must realize, of course, that forecasting a precise pattern of dividends is problematic under most circumstances; therefore, the analyst should look for reasonable approximations.

The two measures just discussed do not take into account the general trends and specific fluctuations in the securities markets. However, the values of specific shares certainly are *not* independent of movements in the securities markets, which are affected by economic, industry, political, and myriad other factors. These considerations are beyond the scope of this book. We can merely point out that the *economic returns* a company achieves on the resources invested and managed tend to be recognized in the market value of its shares, relative to those of its competitors, but within the context of *overall* market movements. The value of a company's shares reflects the collective performance assessments by security analysts and institutional investors, and the resulting demand for, or lack of interest in, those shares.

Common Stock Yield and Investor Expectations. In Chapter 3 we presented two simple yardsticks for measuring the owners' return on investment in common stock. One of these was the *earnings yield,* a simple ratio of current or projected earnings per share to the current market price. The other was an inverse relationship, the so-called *price/earnings ratio*. As we pointed out, these simple ratios are static expressions based on some readily available data and should only serve as temporary rough indicators of the real investor's yield created by a company's economic performance, that is, the *cash flow* pattern generated and projected. They are useful mainly for comparative analysis of companies or industry groupings, but must be supplemented by more insights if the analyst wishes to approximate the actual economic yield of a stock. Any serious examination of value or yield relative to the expectations of the shareholder should use more sophisticated techniques, such as the capital asset pricing model (*CAPM*), discussed in Chapter 7, which take into account market risk, specific company risk, portfolio considerations, and investors' risk preferences.

A great deal of research has improved our understanding of the relative performance of common stocks within the movements of the security markets. This has resulted in refined definitions of the *systematic risk* underlying a diversified portfolio of stocks traded and the *unsystematic (avoidable) risk* of a particular security. As we discussed in Chapter 7, the CAPM relates the relative risk of a security to the risk of the market portfolio through a calculated factor, β, which indicates the *difference* in the risk characteristics of the stock versus the risk characteristics of the portfolio. These are defined in terms of the historical trend in returns earned over and above the *risk-free return* from the safest type of investment, such as long-term U.S. government bonds.

Thus the expected yield of a particular common stock is the sum of the risk-free return plus a risk premium, which is the risk premium earned in the total portfolio of stocks, adjusted by the inherent riskiness of the particular security. We described the formula in Chapter 7:

$$\text{Yield} = R_f + \beta(R_m - R_f)$$

where

R_f is the risk-free return
β is the particular stock's covariance of variability in returns (the specific measure of riskiness)
R_m is the average return expected on common stocks.

Fortunately, the β for publicly traded companies is readily available in financial services such as *Value Line*. Indications of the risk-free rate prevalent at the time and estimates of the return from groups of common stocks are also available in published sources.

We have only touched on some of the techniques used to determine value and yield for common stocks. Much more practical and theoretical insight is needed to deal confidently with the complex issues involved. The references listed at the end of this chapter provide greater depth.

Other Considerations in Valuing Common Stock. The *book value* per share of common stock is often quoted in financial references and company reviews. This figure is the *recorded* residual claim of the shareholder as stated on the balance sheet. As we observed before, book value is an accumulation of past values and does not reflect *economic* value in the form of potential earnings or dividends. Only under unusual circumstances will book value per share be reasonably representative of anything approximating the economic value of a share of common stock. This might be true, for example, if a company has just been started or is about to be liquidated. Under normal conditions, however, book value per share will become increasingly remote from current values, because changes in the values of existing assets are rarely, if ever, reflected in an adjustment to the books of account. The *market to book* ratio discussed in Chapter 3 is used as a rough indicator of this divergence, and a book value that is close to or even exceeding market value may suggest the issuing company is underperforming, a situation that could invite takeover attempts by aggressive investors or corporations.

Market values of common stocks have been treated very lightly in our discussion, because a book on techniques of financial analysis is not the place in which to explore the workings of the securities markets. Suffice it to say here that if the following several basic conditions are met, quotations of a stock in the securities markets can reasonably be assumed to represent the underlying economic value based on the current and prospective performance of a company. First, a stock should be *traded frequently* and in fairly sizable volume. Second, share ownership should ideally be *widespread* so that trading does not involve moving large blocks of shares between a small number of concerned parties. Third, the stock should be publicly traded on one or more *exchange*, or be part of the increasingly important *over-the-counter* market.

Even if all of these conditions are met, the market value of a stock at any point may not necessarily reflect the true potential of the company, because external factors, such as changes in the economy, market conditions, publicity about the company and its industry, or takeover attempts may affect the price at which the stock is traded. To help them understand this context, analysts will study the *range* within which market values have moved, preferably over at least one year, and will chart the behavior of prices relative to market averages and composite averages for the industry grouping. One example is the historical and projected charting found in the *Value Line* company analyses.

VALUING AN ONGOING BUSINESS

It is frequently necessary to find the total value of a business as an ongoing entity when its purchase or sale is being considered. The wave of *acquisitions, mergers, and hostile takeovers* in the 1980s involved thousands upon thousands of such valuations. A similar type of valuation may be used when a company, for purposes of internal *restructuring*, disposes of certain product lines or operating divisions. The buyers may be other companies, groups of investors, or even the existing management who may want to acquire the division financed through a "leveraged buyout," employing high proportions of unsecured debt. Regardless of the form of the purchase, sale, or restructuring, both the buyer and the seller need to arrive at a reasonable approximation of the *economic value* of the business as a going concern.

At the same time, both owners and managers have a continuing interest in the current and expected value of the business even if no sale or merger is contemplated. Managing for economic value has become a critical focus in recent years.

We will first discuss the basic concepts of *valuing business cash flows,* which apply to most valuation situations. Next we will turn to the more specialized cases of *restructuring* and the values driving corporate takeovers, and end the chapter with a review of the ultimate management obligation of creating *shareholder value,* the concept with which we started the book.

Valuing Business Cash Flows

In essence, an ongoing business represents a series of future cash flows. Thus the *present value methods* discussed in Chapter 6 are applicable here, just as if the analyst were calculating the desirability of a capital investment project. This calls for a transformation of past and projected earnings performance into a net cash flow framework.

To begin with, the *operating earnings* of the business must be *forecast* for a reasonable number of years in the future. The relevant definition of operating earnings for this purpose is earnings *before* interest, but *after* taxes, that is, EBIT times (1 − tax rate), as discussed in Chapter 8. The reason for using tax-adjusted EBIT is that we are looking for the cash flows generated *before* any financing considerations—just as we did in the case of capital expenditures in Chapter 6.

The projection of the expected earnings pattern calls for a variety of assumptions and judgments. The simplest way to project, of course, would be to consider the current level of earnings as constant. Under most circumstances, however, such a simplification would not be realistic. If operating earnings can be expected to grow or decline or to follow a pronounced cyclical pattern, it is necessary to make a year-by-year projection for as far in the future as possible. Any significant *nonoperating* earnings after applicable taxes, such as investment income, should be recognized and added in every period, as they represent part of the value of the total company.

The second step is to *convert* the operating earnings pattern into *cash flows,* by adjusting the aftertax earnings result for depreciation and amortization write-offs, and for deferred taxes, as we discussed in Chapters 3 and 6.

The third step is to determine the future *capital outlays* expected to be made to support both the present level of earnings and any anticipated changes in operations. These include outlays for property, plant, and equipment, major spending programs such as research and development projects, and incremental working capital requirements.

To some extent, such estimates are quite speculative, yet it is normally unrealistic to assume that earnings of an ongoing business will continue even at present levels *without* the periodic infusion of capital for replacement and upgrading of existing equipment, not to mention the requirements to support growth expectations, as discussed in Chapter 2. A simplifying assumption commonly used to project these capital expenditures is that in order to maintain the present level of earnings, an amount close or equal to *annual depreciation* must be *reinvested* each year. The estimated amount of outlays for expansion and their effect on earnings are dealt with as separate, distinct capital outlays and ensuing cash inflows in the years in which they are expected to occur. We made such an assumption in the business models in Chapters 1 and 5.

The final step in valuing an ongoing business involves *truncating* the analysis after an appropriate number of years and deriving a *terminal value* (market value) for the business at that point. By definition, that terminal value would be the sum of the present values of all future cash flows from that point on. But the difficulty of forecasting operations *beyond* the end of the chosen analysis period calls for finding a shortcut answer for the terminal value. A common way of dealing with the problem is to use a simple *earnings multiple* at that point, that is, to set the value of the business in year 6 or 10, or whatever cutoff point is desired, at 8, 10, or 15 times the aftertax earnings in that year. The multiple chosen will depend on the nature of the business and the trends in the industry it represents. Because of the power of discounting, such an approximation of terminal value will generally suffice.

The approach appears as follows in a generalized format:

Cash flow element	Year 1	Year 2	Year 3	Year i	Year j
Aftertax operating earnings*	+	+	+	+	+
Add: write-offs and other non-cash items	+	+	+	+	+
Less: capital investments (including working capital)	−	−	−	−	−
Plus terminal value					+
Net cash flows	Y_1	Y_2	Y_3	Y_i	Y_j

*Before interest and plus any significant *nonoperating* earnings after taxes.

The resulting annual net cash flows, also referred to as *free cash flow*, represent the cash available to the company to support its obligations to the providers of the long-term funds, that is, the payment of interest, dividends, and potential repayment of debt or even repurchase of its own shares. Once the annual pattern plus the terminal value has been *discounted* at the appropriate return standard, normally the weighted cost of capital, the resulting present value represents a fair approximation of the value of the total business. The quality of the result depends, of course, on the quality of the estimates that were used in deriving it. The analyst should employ *sensitivity analysis* to test the likely range of outcomes.

It will be useful to demonstrate visually how this present value relates to a company's capital structure. What we have developed by discounting the net cash flow stream and the assumed terminal value is the approximate fair market value of the company's *capitalization*. Figure 9–1 demonstrates that the total value of a business is the sum of its working capital, fixed assets, and other assets, which are financed by the combination of long-term debt and equity. The present value approach has enabled us to express this value in *current economic* terms—quite apart from the recorded values on the balance sheet.

It should be evident that to arrive at the market value of the shareholders' equity requires that we *subtract* the value of the long-term debt from the present value result, which was the total market value of the business, also called *value of the*

Figure 9–1
Present Value of Business Cash Flows and the Capital Structure

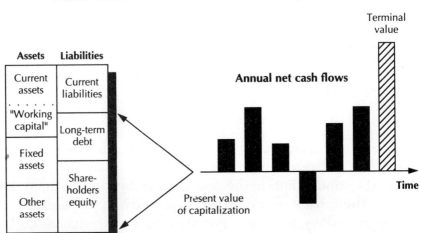

firm or *enterprise value*. We must be careful to determine the value of long-term debt, *not* in terms of the *recorded* values on the balance sheet, but rather in terms of the current yields prevailing for debt of similar risk, as we discussed earlier in this chapter. Thus, if current interest rates are higher than the stated rates for the company's debt, the value of the debt will be lower than recorded, and vice versa. By observing this principle, we remain consistent with the weighted average cost of capital yardstick applied in discounting the cash flow pattern, a measure which contains the cost of *incremental* debt, as we recall from Chapter 7. A similar deduction must be made for any preferred stock contained in the capital structure.

We now have achieved a *direct* valuation of the company's *common equity* by means of an economic approach that is superior to the simpler devices discussed in the common stock section of this chapter. This concept is the basis for much of the analytical work underlying modern security analysis, where the importance of cash flow analysis has overshadowed most other methodologies.

In a *multibusiness company*, the approach can be refined by developing operating cash flow patterns for *each* of the business units, and discounting these individual patterns at the corporate cost of capital or, if the businesses differ widely in their risk/reward conditions, by applying different discount standards that reflect these differences. In recent years, the concept of testing the present value of individual business units to determine the relative contribution to the total value of the corporation has become widely accepted.

Yet, given the nature of the estimates underlying the analysis, there is nothing automatic about the application of such values in an actual transaction involving the sale of a company or any of its parts. Different analysts, and certainly buyers and sellers, will use their own sets of assumptions in developing their respective results. There will also be efforts to test the analytical results against *comparable transactions*, to the extent these are available and relevant. The *actual value* finally agreed upon in any transaction between a buyer and a seller will depend on many more factors, not the least of which is the difference in the return expectations of the parties involved, and the negotiating stance and skills used.

Shortcuts in Valuing an Ongoing Business.   In the previous example, an *earnings multiple* was used to derive the terminal value for the business. This multiple simply indicated what a particular level of current or projected earnings was "worth" at the end point of the analysis. Closely related to the *price/earnings ratio*, this rule of thumb is often applied to quickly value the company, and the result can be an "opener" in initial negotiations. Never precise, the earnings multiple is derived from rough statistical comparisons of similar transactions and from a comparative evaluation of the performance of the price/earnings ratios of companies in the industry.

When the measure is turned into a ratio of estimated *earnings to value*, it provides a rough estimate of the *rate of return* on the purchase or selling price, assuming that the earnings chosen are representative of what the future will bring. When taken as only one of the indicators of value within a whole array of negotiating data, an earnings multiple (or a cash flow multiple) and the related crude rate of return have some merit.

Other shortcuts in valuing an ongoing business involve determining the total *market value* of common and preferred equity from market quotations—in itself somewhat of a challenge in view of stock market fluctuations—and adjusting this total for any long-term debt to be assumed in the transaction. One issue involved in this approach is the question of how representative the market quotations are depending on the trading pattern and volume of the particular stock. At times, when no publicly traded securities are involved, the *book value* of the business is examined as an indicator of value. Needless to say, the fact that recorded values do not necessarily reflect economic values can be a significant problem.

All of these results may at one time or another be entered into the deliberations, but considerable judgment must be exercised to determine their relevance in the particular case. In most situations, the discounted cash flow approach will be the conceptually most convincing measure.

Value in Restructuring and Combinations

This section will apply the concepts of cash flow analysis of an ongoing business and related measures to the specific issue of restructuring a company for higher value, or for seeking higher value in a combination of two or more companies.

Restructuring and Value. The opportunity to restructure arises from the recognition by management or by interested outside parties that a *value gap* exists between the value actually being created by a company and the potential value achievable under changed circumstances. This value gap, in simple terms, is the difference between the present value of the projected cash flows under existing conditions and the present value of a different and usually higher cash flow pattern from the restructured company. The attraction of a corporate takeover is for the acquirer to realize the potential benefits implicit in the value gap, and depending on the circumstances, the value gap supports very sizable premiums in the price bidding encountered in takeover situations—even though the actual results may, in fact, fall short of the premiums paid in the heat of the contest.

It is beyond the scope of this book to develop all aspects of the rationale and the special considerations and techniques employed by corporate takeover specialists, leveraged buyout consultants, and investment bankers using instruments such as junk bonds to achieve the restructuring of companies large and small. Instead, we will briefly discuss the economic rationale and basic analytical approach to determining the value gap. For this purpose, the most common reasons that explain the value gap should be listed first.

Underperformance by parts or all of a company is likely to be the most important cause of lowered values. In thousands of situations, the historical record and projected performance by existing managements using existing strategies and policies was demonstrated to be inferior to comparable businesses. Such a record is usually directly reflected in relative share price levels. Whether restructuring is initiated by the board of directors from within, or through friendly or hostile initiatives by outsiders, the aim is to raise lagging performance and cash flow expectations. Revision of business strategies, improved cost-effectiveness and technology, reduction of unnecessary expenses, and more aggressive management of resources are commonly used to achieve such results.

Disposal of selected lines of business is an extension of the improvement strategies mentioned above. Here the considerations may involve the sale of poor performers and reinvesting the proceeds in more promising parts of the company, distributing the cash to owners in the form of special dividends, or even repurchasing shares. Successful businesses may also be sold with the idea of realizing the economic gains from such a "star," and using the proceeds to fund remaining potential successes. Another consideration is to more sharply focus the attention of management on lines of activity it can competently manage for long-term success. Not to be overlooked is the fact that proceeds from the sale of part of a company can help the acquirer finance a takeover situation.

Eliminating redundant assets is often used as a means of freeing economic value that tends to remain hidden, such as unused real estate, investments, and even excessive amounts of cash bearing only minimal returns. The restructuring analysis, in effect, focuses on separating those economic values that are necessary to carry on the desired activities, while "cashing in" on all resources not relevant to the core purposes of the new company—the repositioning concept of Chapter 1.

It should be clear that the point of view of restructuring is to develop in essence a *breakup value* of the company under study, carefully examining each business unit and all major assets held, and looking for ways of not only improving operating cash flows but also realizing the economic values of resources that can be stripped away without affecting the chosen direction.

From an analytical standpoint, the approach is quite similar to the cash flow valuation discussed earlier. The main difference is that a set of estimates is used that identifies specific *enhancements* in the cash flow pattern, as well as disposal values from businesses or redundant resources. If our earlier analysis can be stated as

$$\text{Value} = \text{PV(Free cash flow} + \text{terminal value)}$$

the restructuring approach can be stated as

$$\text{Value} = \text{PV(Free cash flow} + \text{terminal value)} + \text{PV(Enhancements)}$$
$$+ \text{PV(Disposal proceeds} - \text{cash flow lost from disposals)}$$

and the value gap will be the difference between the two results. A key attraction to the restructurer is, of course, obtaining control of the higher cash flows involved.

It should be noted that two other aspects enter the picture. If a company *changes hands* in a restructuring, the *depreciation basis* for the assets involved is usually increased because of the higher values recorded in the transaction. The resulting increase in the tax shields from depreciation will enhance cash flow because income taxes paid are reduced. Also, if the restructuring introduces higher *financial leverage,* as is usually the case, the impact on return on shareholders' equity should be favorable, even though the cash flow *valuation* may be adversely affected—because as the risk exposure increases, the cost of debt in the company's weighted cost of capital will rise, causing the discount standard to rise, thereby lowering the present value.

Combinations and Synergy.   Another form of restructuring is found in the combination of two or more hitherto independent companies. The rationale often claimed for acquisitions and mergers is that significant economic benefits from *synergy* are expected to occur. While many empirical studies have cast doubt on whether business combinations are always as mutually beneficial as hoped, it is logical to assume that joining two separate businesses, particularly in the same industry, will tend to bring about some *operating efficiencies*. These might include the potential to fully utilize partially utilized manufacturing facilities or warehousing space, eliminating duplicate railway tracks or delivery routes, or consolidating certain activities, such as marketing and selling, support staffs, and administration. Many of these benefits can also be expected when complementary companies or even those in different businesses are combined.

The impact of synergy can be felt in two major ways: The more *direct benefits* are identifiable cash flow improvements, i.e., lower expenses that result from consolidation and reduction of facilities and staffs, and higher contribution from improved market position and coverage. The specific levels of such cash flow benefits must be estimated when an acquisition or merger is considered. Such estimates will, of course, vary in quality depending on how quantifiable the opportunities for improvements are. There are also likely to be tax shield and leverage effects as we discussed in the previous section.

A *more direct benefit* is that the stock of the combined company may become more attractive to investors and will achieve a higher market price, reflecting improved cash flows.

Securities analysts and the investment community generally expect combinations considered as synergistic to result not only in a more *profitable* company, but possibly in one poised for faster *growth,* one with a stronger market position, or one subject to lesser earnings *fluctuations* as the cycles of the individual businesses could offset each other. This reassessment may in time lower the company's *risk premium,* its cost of capital, and also improve the expected price/earnings ratio.

Possible profit improvements resulting from a business combination can be displayed to the extent they are quantifiable. To do this the analyst uses two sets of *pro forma income statements.* One set shows the projected net profits and cash flows from each company *separately,* while the other reflects the *combined* company and includes the envisioned *improvements.* These statements then become the basis for comparative ratio analysis, for calculating value with various methods, including present value analysis, and for highlighting the estimated annual amount of synergistic effect included in the second set of statements.

At times it may be useful to determine *separately* the *present value* of all the synergistic cash flow benefits contained in the combined pro forma statements. This present value can then be used as a rough guide in negotiating the terms of the merger, as the value of these benefits may have to be considered in setting the value *premium* the acquirer has to pay. In the end, the basis for valuation is likely to be a combination of present value analysis, rules of thumb, and the effect of large variety of conditions both tangible and intangible.

Combinations and Share Values. When an *exchange of common stock* is involved in an acquisition or merger agreement, the valuation challenge is extended beyond the economic valuation of the cash flow patterns themselves. The issue of valuing *two different securities* arises, as well as having to find an appropriate *ratio of exchange* that reflects the respective values of the shares. Moreover, in most cases the acquirer has to pay a *significant premium* (between 15 and

25 percent is the common range) over the objective value of the acquired company. This premium will, of course, affect the actual ratio of exchange of shares agreed on. While, in the end, a numerical solution is applied, the underlying values and the premium will be the result of extensive negotiation and a certain amount of "horse trading."

As the two stocks are valued, any differences in the quality and breadth of *trading* in the securities markets can be an important factor. If, for example, a large, well-established company acquires a new and fast-growing company, the market value assessment of the acquirer's stock is likely to be more reliable than that of the candidate, whose stock may be thinly traded and unproven. But even if they had *comparable* market exposure, the *inherent* difference in the nature and performance of the two companies may exhibit itself in, among other indicators, a pronounced difference in *price/earnings ratios*. In effect, this means one company's performance is valued *less* highly in the market than the other. This difference will influence valuation of the stocks and the final price negotiated.

We will demonstrate just a few key calculations needed to arrive at the basis of exchange, using a simplified example. Let us assume that Acquirer Corporation and Candidate, Inc. have the following key dimensions and performance data at the time of their merger negotiations:

Key data	Acquirer Corporation	Candidate, Inc.
Current earnings	$50,000,000	$10,000,000
Number of shares	10 million	10 million
Earnings per share	$5.00	$1.00
Current market price	$60.00	$15.00
Price/earnings ratio	12X	15X

Negotiations between the management teams have reached a point where, after Candidate had rejected several offers, Acquirer now considers a price *premium* of about 20 percent *over* the current market value of Candidate's stock necessary to make a deal. This would call for an *exchange ratio* of $18/$60, or about 0.3 shares of Acquirer stock for each share of

Candidate stock. The impact on Acquirer would be as follows, at the combined *current* levels of earnings that include *no synergistic benefits:*

	Acquirer Corporation
Combined earnings	$60,000,000
Number of shares (10.0 + 3.0 million)	13 million
New earnings per share	$4.62
Old earnings per share	$5.00
Immediate dilution	$0.38

Under these conditions, Acquirer would suffer an *immediate dilution* of 38 cents per share from the combination. Yet the fact that the stock of Candidate had a *higher price/earnings ratio* suggests that the smaller company enjoys desirable attributes that may include high growth in earnings, a technologically protected position, and so on. Acquirer must consider two points: first, whether the earnings of Candidate are likely to *grow* at a rate that will *close the gap* in earnings per share relatively quickly, aided by any *synergistic* benefits available now. Second, Acquirer must judge whether the inclusion of Candidate is likely to *change the risk/reward characteristics* of the *combined* company so as to improve the price/earnings ratio—and thus help overcome the dilution.

In our example, the earnings gap to be filled is 13 million shares times 38 cents, or almost $5 million in annual earnings, just to *return* to the current level of Acquirer's earnings per share. How much in synergistic benefits can be expected? Perhaps the *ratio* of exchange has to be reconsidered in this light? But would the smaller company even be interested in being acquired at less than a 20 percent premium over market, a not uncommon inducement?

Note that a *reversal* of the price/earnings ratios in the example would dramatically change *both* the terms of the offer and the reported performance of the combined companies. At 15 times earnings, the price of Acquirer would be $75 per share, while at 12 times earnings, Candidate would sell at $12 per share. Given a 20 percent acquisition premium for Candidate's stock, the exchange ratio would be $14.40/$75.00, or

0.192 shares of Acquirer for each share of Candidate. This would call for 1.92 million new shares of Acquirer and the new earnings per share would amount to $60,000,000 ÷ 11,920,000, or $5.03 per share, a slight net *improvement* even *before* realizing any synergistic benefits. In this changed situation, *both* parties would be better off immediately, simply because we assumed the price/earnings ratios to be reversed. It is possible, of course, that a company acquired at a premium, which has caused the combined earnings per share to drop initially, may *more* than offset the gap with higher growth and synergistic benefits later. This would depend on the *relative size* of the two companies as well as on the value and exchange considerations discussed.

This is but one simplified example, and thus only a quick glimpse of the nature of the deliberations involved in exchanges of stock. At the same time we have attempted to alert the reader to the many issues underlying the valuation process in mergers and acquisitions. Analysis of such transactions always involves *careful projections* of the separate and combined earnings and cash flow patterns, the calculation of *dilution*, and an assessment of the likely *risk/reward market response* (in effect, a potential change in the β) as an input to the negotiation process.

Managing for Shareholder Value

We now return to the primary concept we established at the beginning of this book, namely, that the basic obligation of the management of a company is to make investment, operating, and financing decisions that will *enhance shareholder value* over the long term. Our discussion of valuing business cash flows and the issues of restructuring strongly suggest that any management should periodically reexamine the policies and strategies followed to test whether its basic obligation of creating shareholder value is being met. Despite the upheavals caused by the takeover boom of recent years, its most beneficial aspect has been the rediscovery of management fundamentals—even if under threat of dismissal by hostile raiders.

In fact, testing the efficiency with which all resources are employed and the relative contribution from various business segments—with an objective "outside" orientation—has become commonplace in many companies. One could argue that this should have been commonplace all along, because the economic basis of all business decisions should have been recognized.

Shown in Figure 9–2 is a diagram which will be useful in tying together the various concepts we have discussed and assist the reader in visualizing the linkage between management decisions and shareholder value. The diagram shows the three basic types of decisions on the left and identifies their key impacts. The combination of investment and operating decisions generates cash flow from operations after taxes, while the financing decisions will influence the capital structure and the development of the weighted cost of capital of the company.

Applying this cost of capital as a discount rate to the cash flow from operations, or free cash flow, determines the shareholder value, as we discussed earlier. At the same time, product life cycles, competition, and many other influences will affect the size and variability of the cash flow from operations.

The result of the discounting of the cash flows (including a terminal value) is shareholder value. The last part of the dia-

Figure 9–2
An Overview of Shareholder Value Creation

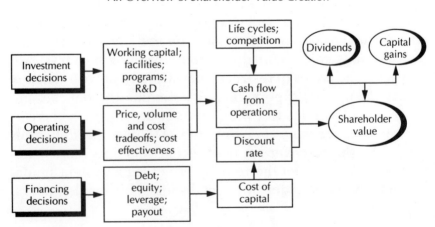

gram recognizes that shareholder value is also the result of a combination of cash dividends and realized capital gains, when seen through the eyes of the shareholder. This alternative view, however, cannot be divorced from the basic driving forces of the business, the cash flow patterns, for it is positive free cash flow that will permit the company to pay dividends in the first place, and that will also boost the market value of the shares, enabling the investor to realize capital gains.

What are the implications of this overview? Note that we have once more returned to a systems view of the corporation, driven by the same basic management decisions, but stressing the cash flow patterns that are the economic underpinning of performance and value. All financial analysis techniques and methodologies in the end are related to the business system as viewed here and in Chapter 1.

The basic message of managing for shareholder value is nothing more than the obligation management has to base all of its investment, operating, and financing decisions on an economic, that is, cash flow, rationale, and to manage all resources entrusted to its care for superior economic returns. Over time, consistency in this approach will generate growing shareholder value, and relative growth in share price performance.

If this sounds fundamental, it is intended to be, for the challenge of the 1990s will be competitive survival by managing better in a world arena—where economic fundamentals are gaining dominance over ideology. Financial analysis in its many forms, as it was introduced in Chapter 1 and more specifically explained in the remainder of this book, is an essential tool kit for analytically oriented persons of any viewpoint, as they judge the performance and outlook of any business.

KEY ISSUES

The following is a recap of the key issues raised directly or indirectly in this chapter. They are enumerated here to help the reader keep the techniques discussed within the perspective of financial theory and business practice:

1. The challenge of valuation involves the dual problems of forecasting economic benefits derived from an asset, and of selecting an economic standard with which to measure these benefits.

2. Value takes many forms, but in the end valuation in business must rest on an attempt to express an economic risk/reward trade-off in the form of cash flows committed and cash flows generated.

3. Investors approach the valuation of an investment proposition in terms of their individual risk preferences; thus, market values are a function of individual and collective risk assessments.

4. Valuation techniques are essentially assessment tools that attempt to quantify the available objective data. Yet such quantification will always remain in part subjective, and in part open to forces beyond individual parties' control.

5. While securities markets provide momentary indications, the value of a common stock at any time is a combination of residual claims, future expectations, and assessments of general and specific risk, subject to economic and business conditions and the decisions of management and the board of directors.

6. Valuation is distorted by the same elements that distort other types of financial analysis: price-level changes, accounting conventions, economic conditions, market fluctuations, and many subjective intangible factors.

7. Valuing a business for sale or purchase is one of the most complex tasks an analyst can undertake. It calls for skills in projection of earnings and cash flows, assessment of risk, and interpretation of the impact of combining management styles, operations, and resources.

8. Shareholder value is the ultimate result of a successful investments, operations, and financing carried out by management within an economic framework. However, the link between a company's current and prospective performance in these areas and the market value of its

common stock at a particular time is not necessarily direct or directly measurable, because of the combination of forces acting on the stock market.

SUMMARY

In this final chapter we have brought together a whole range of concepts and techniques to provide the reader with an overview of how to value assets, securities, and business operations. To set the stage, we discussed key *definitions of value*, and then took the viewpoint of the *investor assessing* the *value* of the three main forms of securities issued by a company. After covering both value and yield in these situations, we expanded our view to encompass the value of an *ongoing business*. Our purpose was to find ways of setting the value in transactions such as sale of a business, *restructuring*, or the *combination* of companies in the form of a merger or acquisition. We found that methods were available for deriving such values, but that the specific assumptions and the background of the transaction added many dimensions to the basic calculations. Finally, we reviewed the concept of *managing for shareholder value*, returning to a systems overview that linked management decisions on investment, operations, and financing to the present value of a business, and in turn linked shareholder value to dividends and capital gains. Ultimately, value will always remain partially subjective and be settled in an exchange between interested parties, but managing for economic performance and value was seen as the basic and most important obligation of management.

SELECTED REFERENCES

Brealey, Richard, and Stewart Myers. *Principles of Corporate Finance*. 3rd ed. New York: McGraw-Hill, 1988.

Copeland, Tom; Tim Koller; and Jack Murrin. *Measuring and Managing the Value of Companies*. McKinsey & Company, Inc. New York: John Wiley & Sons, 1990.

Pratt, Shannon P. *Valuing a Business: The Analysis and Appraisal of Closely Held Companies.* 2nd ed. Homewood, Ill.: Dow Jones-Irwin, 1989.

Rappaport, Alfred. *Creating Shareholder Value.* New York: Free Press, 1986.

Rock, Milon R. *The Merger and Acquisition Handbook.* New York: McGraw-Hill, 1987.

Rosen, Lawrence R. *The Dow Jones-Irwin Guide to Calculating Yields.* Homewood, Ill.: Dow Jones-Irwin, 1985.

Van Horne, James C. *Financial Management and Policy.* 7th ed. Englewood Cliffs, N.J.: Prentice Hall, 1986.

Weston, J. F., and Eugene Brigham. *Essentials of Managerial Finance.* 8th ed. Hinsdale, Ill.: Dryden Press, 1987.

SELF-STUDY EXERCISES AND PROBLEMS

(Solutions Provided in Appendix III)

1. Using the present value tables in Chapter 6, develop the value (price) of bonds with the following characteristics:

   a. A bond with a face value of $1,000 carries interest of 8 percent per year, paid semiannually. It will be redeemed for $1,075 at the end of 14 years. At what price would the bond yield a return of 6 percent? A yield of 10 percent?

   b. A bond with a face value of $1,000 carries interest of 8.5 percent per year, paid semiannually. It is callable at 110 percent of face value beginning October 1, 1999, and will be redeemed (unless called) on October 1, 2009. What price on October 1, 1990, would yield a prospective investor a return of 6 percent? What price would yield 9 percent? (Use interpolation.)

2. Develop the approximate yield (return) of bonds with the following characteristics:

   a. A bond with a face value of $1,000 carries interest at 7 percent per year, paid semiannually on January 15 and July 15. It will be redeemed at 110 on July 15, 2001. The market quotation on July 15, 1990, is 124⅛. What is the approximate yield to an investor who purchases the bond on this date? What is the exact yield given in an appropriate bond table?

   b. The same bond is quoted at 122½ on September 1, 1990. In addition to the market price, accrued interest is paid by the purchaser if the trade takes place between interest dates. What is the exact yield given in an appropriate bond table?

c. A bond with a face value of $500 carries interest at 8 percent per year, paid annually. It will be redeemed at par on March 1, 2011. The bond was purchased on August 20, 1990, for $487.50, including accrued interest. What is the approximate yield? What is the exact yield, using an appropriate bond table or a preprogrammed computer or calculator?

3. The following information is available about two different common stocks, Company A and Company B:

	Company A	Company B
Earnings per share	$2.50	$7.25
Dividends per share	1.00	5.00
Growth in earnings	8%	4%
Price range	$26–$20	$60–$56
Beta	1.3	0.8
Risk-free return	7.0%	7.0%
Expected return, S&P500	13.5%	13.5%

On the assumption that the companies' growth rates will continue, develop an estimate of the value of the common stock and its yield for each. Discuss.

4. The following estimates about the next five years' performance of GHI Company have been provided to you. Based on this information and the current data available to you, calculate the value of the company as a going business, assuming that the expected return from such a business investment would be 12 percent after taxes. Test the present value calculation against other yardsticks of value. Discuss.

GHI Company Projections ($ millions)					
	Year 1	Year 2	Year 3	Year 4	Year 5
Projected earnings (A.T.)	$2.7	$2.9	$3.2	$3.6	$4.0
Projected investments (including working capital)	$0.5	$2.5	$1.5	$1.5	$2.0
Projected depreciation	$1.0	$1.1	$1.4	$1.6	$1.8

The terminal value at the end of the period can be estimated at between 10 and 12 times earnings. The company's earnings for the past year were $2.5 million, and the price/earnings ratio for its industry is currently 11.0.

5. The MNO Company's stock was closely held, and the volume of stock traded over the counter represented only a small fraction of the total shares outstanding. You have been asked to develop as many valuation approaches as possible in preparation for the disposition of a 25 percent block of common stock held by the estate of one of the founders. The executor of the estate will be interested in the possible viewpoints to be

taken in arriving at a fair value. The following data have been made available for the purpose:

MNO COMPANY
Balance Sheet, December 31, 1990
($000)

Assets

Current assets:

Cash	$ 230	(working balance, $150)
Marketable securities	415	(held for payment of taxes and investment in equipment)
Accounts receivable	525	(94% collectible, net of expenses)
Inventories	815	(quick disposal value two thirds of book, normal sale 95%)
Total current assets	1,985	
Fixed assets	1,715	(quick sale value $225, replacement value $2,500)
Less: Accumulated depreciation	820	
Net fixed assets	895	
Prepaid expenses	40	(insurance, licenses, etc.)
Goodwill	175	(based on previous acquisitions)
Organization expense	20	(legal fees, taxes)
Total assets	$3,115	

Liabilities and Net Worth

Current liabilities:

Accounts payable	$ 370	($350 current, $20 overdue)
Notes payable	125	(due 60 days hence)
Accrued liabilities	290	(wages, interest, etc.)
Accrued taxes	150	(income taxes, withholding)
Total current liabilities	935	
Mortgage payable	175	(80% of fixed assets as security)
Bonds, net of sinking fund	520	(unsecured)
Deferred income taxes	55	
Reserve for self-insurance	110	(contingency surplus reserve)
Preferred stock	300	(7% preferred, 3,000 shares)
Common stock	525	(52,500 shares, $10 par)
Capital surplus	110	(excess paid in for common)
Earned surplus	385	(accumulated earnings)
Total liabilities and net worth	$3,115	

The company's β is estimated at 1.2 while the spread between risk-free return of 7 percent and S&P 500 returns is expected to be about 6 percent.

MNO COMPANY
Operating History

	1986	1987	1988	1989	1990	3-31-91*
Profit after taxes (000)	$92	$110	$126	$139	$118	$34
Earnings per share	1.75	2.10	2.40	2.65	2.25	0.65
Dividends per share	1.20	1.60	1.60	1.80	1.80	0.45
Market price, high	31⅜	33¼	37⅞	34⅛	29¾	30⅞
Market price, low	13⅞	19¾	23⅝	22⅛	19¼	19⅜
Market price, average	22⅝	26½	31¾	28⅛	24½	25⅛
Industry price-earnings ratio	14x	15x	16x	12x	11x	—

*Quarter.

Develop valuation approaches based on book values, market values, past trends, and projections (no significant changes are expected in the operations of the company and the industry), taking into account redundant assets and limited trading of the stock. Stipulate your assumptions and list additional information you would consider necessary for a recommendation. Discuss your findings.

6. Two companies are discussing a potential merger. Company A has a price/earnings ratio of 12 × , with current EPS of $8, a dividend of $2, and a market price range of $90 to $100, with a recent price of $98. Ten million shares are outstanding. Company B has a price/earnings ratio of 20 × , and is growing at twice the 6 percent rate of Company A. Its current EPS are $3, it pays no dividend, and its market price is ranging between $45 and $70. One million shares are outstanding. Company A is assessing the impact of a potential offer to Company B at a price of $65, as compared to Company B's current price of $54. Calculate the appropriate measures to assess the impact of these terms, and discuss potential implications.

APPENDIX I
BASIC INFLATION
CONCEPTS

Thoughout this book we have referred to the distorting effects of inflation on financial decisions and analysis. In this appendix we will offer a brief commentary on the basic nature of the often misunderstood phenomenon of inflation. Financial transactions are carried out and recorded with the help of a common medium of exchange, such as United States dollars. Variations in this medium will affect the numerical meaning of these transactions. But we know that underlying the transactions are *economic trade-offs*; that is, values are given and received. We must be careful not to confuse changes in economic *values* with changes in the *medium* used to effect and account for these transactions. We will examine the ramifications of this statement in several contexts below.

PRICE LEVEL CHANGES

The *economic values* of goods and services invariably *change* over time. The reason for this is as basic as human nature: The law of supply and demand operates, in an uncontrolled market environment, to *increase* the value of goods and services that are in *short supply*, and to *decrease* the value of those available in *abundance*. This shift in *relative* values takes place even in a primitive barter economy that does not utilize any currency at all. The ratio of exchange of coconuts for beans, for example, will move in favor of coconuts when they are scarce, and in favor of beans when these are out of season. Many seasonal agricultural products go through a familiar price cycle, reflecting their temporary unavailability, on to the first arrivals in the market place, and eventually to an abundance before they become unavailable again. The phenomenon is not limited to seasonal goods, however. Natural resources go through cycles of availability, be it from the need to set up the infrastructure to exploit new sources as old ones expire, or from extreme concerted actions such as those of OPEC in the 1970s and '80s that upset world oil prices through the cartel's power of control of over half the world's oil production.

We know that the economic value of manufactured goods is similarly subject to the law of supply and demand. For example, as a new technology emerges in the market, such as the first digital watches or compact disk players, the price commanded by the early units will be well above the prices charged later on, after many suppliers have entered the market and competed for a share of consumer demand. The same is true of all goods and services for which there are present or potential alternative suppliers, domestic or international.

The point we are making here is that the economic value underlying personal, commercial, and financial transactions is determined by forces that are largely *independent* of the monetary expression in which they are recorded. As we will see, an analysis of price level changes ideally should *separate* the change in price levels caused by shifts in economic value from those caused by changes in the currency itself. Accurate separation of the two is difficult in practice, but the concept is necessary for understanding the meaning of financial projections.

MONETARY INFLATION

Another phenomenon affecting transaction values is any basic change in the *purchasing power of the curency*. There are many reasons underlying the decline or strengthening of a currency's value as a medium of exchange. One of the most important factors causing inflationary declines in purchasing power is the *amount of currency* in circulation relative to *economic activity*. If the government raises the money supply *faster* than required to accommodate the growth in economic activity, there will literally be more dollars chasing relatively fewer goods and services, and thus the stated dollar prices for all goods or services will rise—even though the *basic demand* for any specific item may be unchanged.

This description is oversimplified, of course. A great many more factors affect currency values. One of these is the impact of government deficits and the way they are financed. Another is the value of the dollar relative to other currencies and the impact of exchange rates on international trade. In addition, international money flows and investment in response to more attractive investment opportunities cause shifts in the values of national currencies over and above the effects of the individual countries' fiscal and economic conditions. Union negotiations, wage settlements, and cost of living adjustments in wages, pensions, and social security are also related to changing currency values. Every nation's central bank—the Federal Reserve bank in the case of the United States—is of critical importance in the process, because its policies affect both the size of the national money supply and the level of interest rates. These, in turn, affect government fiscal policies, business activity, international trade, and money flows, and so forth. And ultimately, serious declines in the value of a currency can also affect the basic supply and demand of goods and services, as, for example, customers and businesses "buy ahead" to beat anticipated price increases.

The point here is not to systematically analyze inflation and its causes, but rather to make the *basic distinction* between *economic* and monetary changes influencing price levels. Suffice it to say that price level changes due to monetary effects are largely the ones that distort economic values of personal and commercial transactions. If monetary conditions remained *stable,* that is, the amount of currency in circulation always matched the level of economic activity, price level changes would only reflect changes in economic values—something we have agreed is at the core of management's efforts to improve the owners' economic condition. Because monetary stability is an unrealistic expectation, however, the challenge remains to make the analysis of the actual conditions affecting prices and economic values more meaningful.

NOMINAL AND REAL DOLLARS

Business and personal transactions are expressed in terms of *nominal* dollars, also called *current* dollars, that reflect today's prices, unadjusted or altered in any way. For accounting purposes, nominal dollars are used every day to record transactions. However, when dollar prices change over time, the amounts recorded in the past no longer reflect current prices, either in terms of the underlying economic values or in terms of the value of the currency at the moment.

To deal with changes in the value of the currency, economists have devised *price indexes* intended to separate, at least in part, monetary distortions from fluctuations in economic value. Such an index is constructed by measuring the aggregate *change* in the prices of a representative group of products and services as a *surrogate* for the change in the value of the currency. Yet we already know that any goods and services chosen for this purpose are themselves also subject to changes in supply and demand, *apart* from mere currency fluctuations. But there is no *direct* way of measuring changes in currency values as such. Inevitably, therefore, the price index approach involves *mixing* demand/supply conditions and currency values, and the only hope is that the selection of goods and services employed in a given index is broad enough to compensate somewhat for the underlying demand/supply conditions.

The *consumer price index*, a popular index of inflation, is calculated in this fashion. It is based on frequent sampling of the prices of a "market basket" of goods and services purchased by U.S. consumers, including food, housing, clothing, transportation and so forth. The composition and weighting of this basket is changed gradually to reflect changing habits and tastes, although there is much room for argument about how representative the selection is. Another popular index, applicable to business, is the *producer price index*, based on a representative weighted sampling of the wholesale prices of goods produced. Other indexes deal with wholesale *commodity* prices and a variety of specialized groupings of products and services. The broadest index in common use is applied to the gross national product as a whole, the so-called *GNP deflator*, which expresses the price changes experienced in the total range of goods and services produced in the U.S. economy. Based on broad statistical sampling, the current level of the GNP deflator is announced frequently thoughout the year in connection with other economic statistics about business and government activity. All of these indexes are prepared by calculating the changes in prices from those of a selected *base year*, which is changed only infrequently in order to avoid having to adjust comparative statistical series whenever the base year is changed.

The price indexes are used to translate nominal dollar values in government statistics and business reports into *real dollar values*. This involves converting nominal dollar values to a chosen standard, so that past and present dollar transactions can be compared in *equivalent* terms. For example, to compare this year's performance of the economy to that of last year, we may choose to express *current* economic statistics using *last year's* dollars as the standard. Last year's dollars are then called *real*, and today's data are expressed in these "real" terms. To do this, we simply adjust today's dollars by the amount of inflation experienced since last year. If inflation this year was 4.5 percent over last year, as expressed in the GNP deflator, every nominal dollar figure for this year would be adjusted *downward* by 4.5 percent. The result would be an expression of this year's results in terms of *real dollars*, which are based on the *prior year*.

A real dollar is thus simply a nominal dollar that has been *adjusted* to the price level of a particular stated base year, using one of the applicable price indexes. The base chosen can be *any* year, as long as past or future years are consistently stated in terms of the currency value for the base year. In fact, real dollars are often called *constant dollars*, a name that simply recognizes that they are derived from *a constant base*. The process of adjustment has the following effect: during inflationary periods, the real dollars for the years *preceding* the base year will be adjusted *upward*, while the real dollars of *future* years will be adjusted *downward*. The reverse would be true, of course, if the period under analysis had involved *deflation* instead.

To illustrate, let us assume that the following price developments took place during a five-year period. We are using the producer price index (PPI). This index was constructed on the basis of Year 0. In the following table, we have set Year 3 as the base year for our analysis:

	Year 1	Year 2	Year 3	Year 4	Year 5
Producer Price Index (Year 0)	1.09	1.15	1.21	1.25	1.33
Producer Price Index (Year 3)	0.90	0.95	1.00	1.03	1.10
Real Value of $100 (Base Year 3)	$111	$105	$100	$97	$91

Note that two steps were involved. First, the producer price index had to be adjusted for our chosen base Year 3; that is, the index had to be set at 1.00 for Year 3, and all index numbers were divided by the value of the index for the base year, which is 1.21. (However, the index could have been constructed on any other year, because an index measures price changes year by year from *whatever* starting point is chosen.) The next step was to divide the adjusted index values on the second line into the nominal dollars of each year. We chose to use the amount of $100 for all years, but the process applies, of course, *to any amount* of nominal dollars in *any one* of the years. Using a single round figure permitted us to illustrate the shifts in value with the same dollar amount.

The example clearly shows that the purchasing power of a dollar in Year 4 versus Year 3 *declined* by 3 percent. The implication from a business point of view is that a company must increase its nominal earnings power by 3 percent in order to keep up with inflation in the prices it must pay for goods and services. Anything less than that will leave the owners worse off.

The simple process allows us to convert *nominal* dollars into inflation-adjusted *real dollars*. Problems arise in choosing the proper index for a business situation, and also from the fact that the index embodies changes in economic value as well as in currency value, as we discussed earlier. Much thought has been expended on refining the process of inflation adjustment, but in the end the judgment about its usefulness depends on the purpose of the analysis and the degree of accuracy desired.

APPLICATIONS OF INFLATION ADJUSTMENT IN FINANCIAL ANALYSIS

Restatement of company data or projections in real dollar terms is at times a useful device to assess whether the company's performance has kept up with shifts in currency values. Such restatement may be used to revalue a company's assets and liabilities, or to show the real growth or decline in sales and earnings. As we observed, publicly traded companies are obligated to include an annual inflation-adjusted restatement of key data in their published shareholder reports.

Much effort goes into adjusting financial projections for inflation, particularly in the area of capital investment analysis. There are no truly satisfactory general rules for this process, however. When an analyst needs to project cash flows from a major capital investment, the easiest approach continues to be projection in nominal dollars, taking into account expected cost and price increases of the key variables involved, tailored specifically to the conditions of the business. The discount standard applied against the projection is also based on nominal return expectations that, of course, embody the inflationary outlook.

To refine the analysis, many companies prepare projections in *real dollars*, attempting to forecast the *true economic* increases or decreases in costs and prices. Then an appropriate inflation index is applied to the figures to convert them into nominal dollars. The problem is, however, that the *margin* between revenues and costs may widen unduly, simply because the same inflation index is applied to the larger revenue numbers and to the smaller cost numbers. Often, arbitrary adjustments have to be made to keep the margin spread manageable.

Another approach involves developing projections expressed in real dollars and discounting these with a return standard that has also been converted into *real returns*. The result will be internally consistent as far as the project is concerned. However, the result is *not* readily *comparable* with the current overall performance of the business—recorded and expressed in *nominal dollar* terms—unless the company has also found a way to convert and measure ongoing performance in real dollar terms. Some companies are beginning to experiment with such restated reports and measures, but the approach involves a massive effort, both in terms of data preparation and education of personnel generating and using the projections and performance data. It is instinctively easier to think about business in nominal dollars than real dollars, and progress in this area is being made only gradually. The complexities are such that the financial and planning staffs of companies wishing to use this approach face a lengthy conceptual and practical conversion problem.

IMPACT OF INFLATION

To restate quickly, the basic impact of inflation—and the much less common opposite situation, deflation—is a growing distortion of recorded values on a company's financial statements and an ongoing partial distortion of operating results. Accounting methods discussed in Chapters 1 and 2 are designed to make the effect of the inflationary distortion at least consistent. In terms of cash flows, inflation distorts a company's tax payments, if the taxes due are based on low historical cost apportionment, and results in a cash drain if dividends are higher than they would be if real-dollar earnings were considered, to name two examples. Inflation also affects financing conditions and particularly the repayment of principal on long-term debt obligations. As we observed before, however, the mediating influence of interest rates—which respond to inflation expectations—will tend to prevent windfalls for the borrower looking to repay debt with "cheap" dollars. Normally, over the long run, distortions from inflation affect lenders and borrowers alike. Relative advantages gained by one over the other are only temporary.

Overall, the subject of inflation adjustments continues to evolve in financial analysis, and it is unlikely that totally consistent methods that are generally applicable will be found.

APPENDIX II
SOURCES OF
FINANCIAL
INFORMATION

While the orientation of the book is techniques of financial analysis, many of the applications we discussed implied the use of information beyond that stipulated or available directly. The reader therefore needed to be familiar with at least the main sources of financial information to obtain the necessary input for analysis. For this reason we have devoted this appendix to a brief review of common data sources, and given guidelines, where required, for the interpretation of the financial data presented. The information provided will give the reader the background needed to make more sophisticated decisions about company performance, new financing, temporary borrowing, investments, credit, capital budgeting, and so on.

Again, in keeping with the nature of this book, this appendix is meant only as an introduction to sources of *current financial, periodic financial,* and *background company and business information.* A number of additional references for further study and data are provided at the end of this appendix.

CURRENT FINANCIAL INFORMATION

The most common and convenient way to keep abreast of financial developments is through the daily financial pages of national, metropolitan, and regional newspapers. The most complete and widely read financial coverage

417

is found in the pages of *The Wall Street Journal* and *The New York Times*, which contain detailed information on securities and commodity markets; news, feature articles, and statistics on economic and business conditions; news and earnings reports for individual companies; dividend announcements; currency, commodity, and trading data; and a great deal of coverage of international business and economic conditions. The major dailies in the United States and Canada also carry key financial and economic data, but the coverage and emphasis vary greatly. Smaller and regional papers will often provide only selected highlights tailored to the area and the readership.

The bulk of the materials shown in the financial pages involve securities transactions and current financial data. This information is not entirely self-explanatory. We will describe the meaning of some of the abbreviations and symbols used in *The Wall Street Journal* listings for stock transactions (traded on exchanges and over the counter), bond transactions, and other key financial data. Other newspapers generally present data in a fairly comparable fashion, but in less detail.

Stock Quotations

Exchange Quotations. Transactions made on organized exchanges (The New York Stock Exchange, the American Stock Exchange, several regional exchanges) and the electronic network of the National Association of Securities Dealers (NASDAQ) generally include the kind of information shown in Figure II–I. It shows the day's transactions in 10 stocks out of the 1,982 individual stocks traded on the New York Stock Exchange on Monday, April 23, 1990, as reported in *The Wall Street Journal* on Tuesday, April 24, 1990. The total volume of shares traded for the day was about 136 million, an average volume in a year when daily volumes well over 175 million were quite common, and in which a "slow day" involved trading volumes under 100 million shares. Daily trading statistics for the NYSE, the AMEX, and the NASDAQ are summarized in *The Wall Street Journal* under an overall heading "Stock Market Data Bank" and "The Dow Jones Averages."

The first stock listed in Figure II–I, Abitibi, had a high value of 17¼ and a low of 11¼ over the previous 52 weeks. (This is the range in which transactions took place in the last 12 months.) The quotations are given in dollars per share and fractions of a dollar not smaller than ⅛ ($0.125). Abitibi paid dividends at the annual rate of $.50 during the period (based on the last quarterly declaration). The special symbol "g" indicates that Abitibi, a major paper company headquartered in Canada, paid its dividends in Canadian dollars.

The next column shows the company's symbol used in the electronic stock quotations that are flashed all over the world. Next is listed the dividend yield based on the current market quotations, while the following column

Figure II–1

NEW YORK STOCK EXCHANGE—SAMPLE OF STOCK TRANSACTIONS

Monday, April 23, 1990

52 Weeks							Sales				
High	*Low*	*Stocks*	*Sym.*	*Div.*	*Yield %*	*P/E Ratio*	*in 100s*	*High*	*Low*	*Close*	*Net Change*
17¼	11¼	Abitibi g	ABY	.50	—	—	2	12¾	12¾	12¾	− ⅛
66	52½	Caterpillar	CAT	1.20	2.0	12	6783	61¼	60⅜	60⅝	+ ⅛
▼40⅜	32	ComwEd pf		1.42	4.5	—	3	32⅛	31¾	31¾	− ¼
n 45¼	31	Fiat	FIA	.78e	1.8	8	5	42½	42½	42½	− ½
s 35⅞	24⅝	Heinz	HNZ	.84	2.6	18	1954	33	32¼	32¼	− ¾
5¼	⅛	vj Southmark pf		—	—	—	50	⅜	⅜	⅜	+ 1/16
16	8½	RoyalOptical	RIO	.20a	2.2	12	173	9⅜	9¼	9¼	—
sx 33⅛	22¼	SyscoCp	SYY	.20	.7	22	x868	30¼	29¼	29⅜	− ¾
13½	3¼	TranscoExpl	EXP	9.85c	—	4	244	3⅛	3¼	3⅜	—
40½	31½	US West wi			—	—	12	35¾	35¾	35¾	− ¼

reports the price/earnings ratio based on current reported earnings (12-month period) and current price levels. Abitibi's yield and P/E were not shown on that day because very few shares were traded, but they were listed for most of the other companies.

The day's transactions in Abitibi stock totaled only 200 shares as indicated in the eighth column, where sales are listed in multiples of 100 shares. This is done because stocks are ordinarily traded in round lots of 100 shares, while less than 100 shares is considered an odd lot, and brokers usually charge a premium for trading in the latter.

The next four columns indicate price movements of the stock based on actual transactions during April 23, 1990. Trades in Abitibi stock reached a high for the day of $12.75 and a low of $12.75. They are the same because there may have been only one or two transactions. Note that there were spreads between highs and lows in the other, more heavily traded stocks. The net change of − $.125 in Abitibi's last column indicates the difference between its price at the close of trading on April 23 and the price at the close of the previous trading day.

Unless otherwise indicated, the transactions listed involve common stocks. If a preferred stock were traded, the symbol "pf" would be added right after the name. In our example, Commonwealth Edison and South-mark are preferred stocks. The dividend quoted for preferred stock is the annual rate, as was the case with common stock. Thus, Commonwealth Edison has a dividend rate of $1.42, yielding about 4.5 percent. The symbol ahead of the 52-week high/low range (▼) indicates that the stock has reached a new 52-week low. (The inverse of this arrow (▲) would indicate a new 52-week high.) Southmark, where the symbol "vj" ahead of the name indicates a state of bankruptcy, is not paying any dividends at all. The 52-week price range of Southmark and the day's high and low are indicative of its severe difficulties.

A number of additional symbols and abbreviations are commonly used and explained briefly in footnotes on the financial pages of most papers. A number of these are used in our sample listing. For example, an "n" ahead of Fiat's 52-week high/low range indicates that this is a new issue on the exchange. An "s" in the same place, as in the case of Heinz, denotes a stock dividend or stock split of more than 25 percent within the past 52 weeks. An "x" in that position, as is shown with Sysco Corporation, indicates that the stock is trading ex-dividends or ex-rights, that is, a very recently declared dividend or rights issue will no longer accrue to the purchaser at this date. An "e" with the dividend rate, as in the case of Fiat, signals that a cash dividend was paid but that no regular dividend rate exists (it is a new issue), while the "c" with Transco Exploration stands for liquidating dividend. Other symbols are used to show dividends in arrears ("k"), and the annual rate of cash dividends plus a stock dividend ("b").

Apart from notations for dividend exceptions, symbols are also used to show a company's calling for redemption of a particular stock ("cld"), various conditions of rights and warrants, which represent options to purchase additional shares, anticipatory quotations of a new issue on a when-issued basis" ("wi") —the last company in our example, US West represents such advance trading. Also, a "z" indicates that total sales transactions for the day involved fewer than 100 shares.

The individual listings of stock transactions in *The Wall Street Journal* are supplemented by various summaries of overall trading figures in the so-called "Stock Market Data Bank." One of these is the list of the day's most active stocks. On April 23, 1990, the stock with the highest turnover of shares among the 15 stocks listed for the NYSE was Merrill Lynch (2.85 million shares), closing at 22½, off (down) ¾.

Another market summary, the "Diary" for the past two trading days and for trading one week ago, covering the NYSE, NASDAQ, and AMEX, showed that on April 23, 1990, 1,982 different issues were traded on the NYSE, of which 328 advanced and 1,229 declined, leaving 425 issues unchanged. The number of new highs achieved was 4, while the number of new lows was 137—reflecting the downtrend in the market in late April 1990. The volume of declining issues outpaced advancing issues by 104 million to 20 million in the total trading volume of 136 million shares. The diary also lists price percentage gainers and losers for the day, which on April 23, 1990, were Todd Shipyard (up 10.5 percent) and Pansophic Systems (down 32.8 percent), and volume percentage leaders, with Pansophic taking first place at 1.76 million shares, which represented a surging 5,298 percent increase over its average trading volume during the past 65 days.

Also shown are graphic displays of four months of the movements of the Dow Jones Averages for industrials, transportation, and utilities, and a table of the opening, closing, and hourly values of the averages for five trading days. For example, on Monday, April 23, 1990, the Dow Jones Industrial Average closed at 2,666.67, down 29.28 from Friday, April 20. Briefer listings of the other major market indicators, such as the Standard & Poor's 500 Index, the NASDAQ Composite Index, and the London and Tokyo indexes are shown in an overview table. These and other indicators collectively provide an impression of the "mood" and direction of the market.

Quotations of transactions on the American Stock Exchange are similar. Transactions on regional exchanges, such as the Pacific Stock Exchange in San Francisco and the Midwest Stock Exchange in Chicago, are often listed together with the most important quotations on the major Canadian stock exchanges in Toronto and Montreal. These transactions are quoted in less detail. Normally, only the number of shares traded, the high and low prices, and the closing prices with changes from the previous close are listed. At times the quotations are limited to volume and closing prices only.

Reference was made earlier to the various stock price averages, which are popular and important clues to the behavior of the stock market in general. These averages are calculated daily and in some cases continuously from on-line data bases. The averages are followed closely by analysts, investors, and financial managers who interpret market movements to decide on purchase or sale of securities, or to assess various types of new securities. Because the various averages involve a selected and relatively small number of stocks, their upward or downward movement over time is not necessarily a predictor of the likely movement of any particular stock or of the overall market.

As discussed earlier, there are many factors underlying the value and market position of a particular security, the most important of which are the current and prospective operating circumstances of the company. The atmosphere of the market and general economic conditions will certainly influence the behavior of a particular stock, but we must caution against the adage that a "rising tide lifts all ships in the harbor," which is a gross oversimplification of the behavior of the stock market. The limitations of stock indexes are those of averages in general which can only be broad indicators of a likely trend against which all particulars of a security have to be compared.

The most commonly quoted and publicized stock price averages are the Dow Jones averages of 30 industrial, 20 railroad and 15 utility stocks, and the composite average of all 65 securities. The Dow Jones Industrial Average contains most well-known companies in the United States, such as IBM, General Motors, General Electric, U.S. Steel, Du Pont, Procter & Gamble, and so on. Because it is heavily weighted toward these "blue-chip" securities, the Dow Jones average is less applicable for analysis of the securities of lesser known companies, specialized "growth situations," or conglomerate corporations.

The *New York Times* average of 50 stocks includes 25 railroad and 25 industrial stocks. This average is also weighted somewhat in favor of blue chips. The Standard & Poor's averages (composite indexes of 425 industrial stocks, 50 utilities and 25 railroads, and a combination of all these averages in the "S&P 500") are more broadly based and more closely approximate the average price level of all stocks listed on the New York Stock Exchange because the S&P 500 includes about one quarter of the issues actively traded there.

As pointed out before, the various stock averages, including daily ranges and average price levels, are available for each trading day. Because transactions are electronically tracked, the current level of these averages is always available almost instantaneously during the trading day. Continuous adjustments are made for stock splits, stock dividends, and many changes in the corporate structures of the companies in the index. Some of the references listed at the end of the appendix give more details about how the indexes are calculated.

Over-the-Counter (OTC) Transactions.   A huge volume of securities is traded outside of the organized exchanges in an "auction market" consisting of hundreds of security dealers and individuals in all parts of the country who are electronically linked via computer networks. This over-the-counter market is an amazingly flexible arrangement which allows trading between prospective buyers and sellers of such securities as goverment bonds, state and municipal bonds, stocks and bonds of smaller and newer companies, bank stocks, mutual funds, insurance companies, small issues and infrequently traded issues. On Monday, April 23, 1990, 4,312 issues were traded in the OTC market, with a total volume of 129 million shares, about equivalent to the volume of the NYSE. Financial listings for OTC transactions are similar to stock exchange transactions for what are called the *NASDAQ National Market Issues,* except that notations indicating special conditions are incorporated into the four-or-five letter listing symbol. If a fifth letter is used, its special meaning is keyed to a symbol explanation below the NASDAQ listing.

For issues traded over the counter by individual dealers who specialize in particular securities to "maintain a market," quotations are reported in the form of "bid and asked" in a separate listing for the NASDAQ. Unlike the cumulative transactions for the day on organized exchanges, such quotations are only indicative of the prices at which an individual or a dealer would have been willing to buy or sell a particular security during the trading period. In other words, the quotes may not reflect actual transactions. A dealer specializing in the security, and handling both sides of the transaction, may cover expenses and make a profit from the difference between the purchase and sale prices of the issue.

Figure II–2 from *The Wall Street Journal* of April 24, 1990, provides a sample listing of over-the-counter quotations for April 23, 1990. The price at which traders would be willing to *buy* the security is the *bid*, the *asked* price

Figure II–2
NASDAQ—SAMPLE OF STOCK TRANSACTIONS
Monday, April 23, 1990

Stock	Dividend	Sales in 100s	Bid	Asked	Net Change
Aurora	—	579	1¹⁵⁄₁₆	2¹⁵⁄₁₆	− ¹⁄₁₆
Bowater	.33e	x5	7⅞	8	—
vj Bcst pf	3.50	44	9¼	10	—
Millfld un	—	40	6¹⁵⁄₁₆	5¹¹⁄₃₂	+ ¹⁄₁₆
StrtAm s	.02e	5	1⅝	1⅞	—
TideR h	82e	5	10	11½	—
WstR wt	—	30	2⁵⁄₁₆	2⁷⁄₁₆	—

is the amount desired for a *sale*. The format used to list OTC trading begins with the abbreviated name of the company and current dividend, then lists sales in 100s, and provides bid and asked "prices," ending with the net change from the prior trading day. The bid quotations are normally below the asked quotations, as we would expect in an auction market.

In our sample listing we again encounter a series of symbols that are quite comparable to the ones used in the stock exchange listings. For example, the "e" used with the Bowater, StrtAm, and TideR quotations indicates that a dividend was paid in the last 12 months, but that there is no regular dividend rate. The "vj" with the Bcst preferred signals bankruptcy or reorganization, while the "h" with TideR indicates a temporary exception to NASDAQ qualifications. The "un" with Millfield indicates units rather than shares, while the "wt" with WestR identifies this issue as warrants for the purchase of stock. The "x" with Bowater indicates that the issue was trading ex-dividends or ex-rights.

Other Exchange Quotations.   Some of the larger newspapers carry limited quotations from major foreign stock exchanges. Trading of internationally recognized securities on the Paris, London, Tokyo, or Frankfurt stock exchanges is reported in the currency of the country involved. At times, the financial pages may contain current stock averages for foreign countries, supplemented by accounts of major activities there.

Mutual Funds.   Mutual funds are professionally managed investment pools. A share of a mutual fund represents an investment in a portfolio of different securities, which may be oriented towards a variety of investment objectives, such as earnings, or capital appreciation. These funds have gained in importance in recent years, and mutual fund trading is quoted in most newspapers. Price ranges are provided by the National Association of Securities Dealers. The quotes normally show the net asset value per share, an offering price that includes net asset value and the maximum sales charge, and the change in net asset value from the previous day.

Options.   Options, which are essentially contracts to buy or sell a security on a future date and at a stipulated price, are traded on various exchanges and are listed in terms of closing prices for "puts" (sales prices) and "calls" (purchase prices) for three different months in the future. This specialized market has grown rapidly in recent years, as has the market for commodity futures, which similarly represent contracts for future sales and purchases of certain commodities and are quoted in the financial pages.

Bond Quotations

The three major types of bonds—corporate, state, and municipal, and federal government—represent a huge market that involves both the organized exchanges and the OTC market. In fact, the overwhelming majority of government bonds of both types are traded in the over-the-counter market, while the majority of corporate bond issues are traded on the stock exchanges.

It will be useful briefly to discuss how bond transactions are listed. Figure II–3 shows a listing for the NYSE, but trading on other exchanges is handled similarly.

The first line gives not only the name of the issuing company but also the coupon interest rate and the maturity date. Thus, the first line is an American Telephone and Telegraph issue with a stated interest rate of 7 percent and due in the year 2001. Note that the issue is trading at a price to yield 8.5 percent, more in keeping with the long-term interest conditions of 1990.

The most important difference to remember vis-à-vis stock quotations is that bonds are quoted in percentages of par value, expressed in fractions no smaller than one eighth of a percent. For example, the AT&T bonds closed at a price of $826.25 for each $1,000 of par value. Sales volumes are given in thousands of dollars because $1,000 is the most common denomination of a single bond. In contrast to stocks, only the closing price and the change from the prior day's closing price are listing.

The symbols used with the individual bonds parallel those discussed earlier. For example, "vj" with the General Development and Republic Steel bonds indicates these two companies' state of bankruptcy. Note the extremely low quotations in both cases, despite the high coupon interest rate, reflecting the poor outlook for regular payment of interest. No yield is quoted for Republic Steel, while the General Development yield is an amazing 57.2 percent, in keeping with the company's depressed price. The symbol "cv" indicates that the bond is convertible into common stock. Note that the 6 percent Xerox bond is trading at a yield of only 6.7 percent $(6.00 \div 90)$, which signals that the price reflects the underlying value of the

Figure II–3
NEW YORK STOCK EXCHANGE BOND TRANSACTIONS
Monday, April 23, 1990
Volume $34,670,000

Bonds	Current Yield	Volume	Close	Net Change
Am T&T 7s 0l	8.5	117	82⅝	+1¾
Beverly 7⅝s 03	cv	47	59	—
vj GnDev 12⅞s 95	57.2	47	22½	+⅜
MGMUA 12⅝s 93	17.5	17	72	+1
MPac 4¾s 30f	—	20	47	—
vj RepStl 12⅛s 03f	—	10	17½	—
Xerox 6s 95	cv	31	90	—

Xerox common stock into which it is convertible, and not just the low coupon interest. The "f" with the Missouri Pacific and Republic Steel bonds means that these issues are trading "flat," that is, without any claim for current unpaid interest. Their prices reflect this precarious position.

A slightly different method is used to list current quotations for government agency bonds and miscellaneous securities traded over the counter. Again we will use an example from *The Wall Street Journal* for the trading day of Monday, April 23, 1990. Figure II–4 gives quotes for U.S. Treasury bonds, U.S. Treasury bills, Federal Home Loan Bank bonds, World Bank bonds, and some tax-exempt municipal and agency bonds.

As was the case with over-the-counter transactions for stocks, we find bid and asked quotations that represent the price desired for purchase or sale on the trading day and do not denote specific transactions. An important difference reflected in this example is the custom of quoting prices in *percent of par value,* stated in terms of fractions of a percent in *32nds* of a

Figure II–4
GOVERNMENT AGENCY, AND
MISCELLANEOUS SECURITIES QUOTATIONS
Monday, April 23, 1990
(over the counter)

U.S. Treasury bonds:			Bid	Asked	Bid Change	Yield
6.75s, Feb 1993			94-28	95-08	− .02	8.68
12.62s, May 1995			114-11	114-17	− .06	8.98
15.75s, Nov. 2001			147-02	147-08	− .11	9.07
U.S. Treasury bills:						
.00 April 26, 1990			7.96*	7.84*	+ .15	7.96
.00 April 11, 1991			7.90*	7.88*	+ .05	8.48
Federal Home Loan Bank:						
Rate	Maturity					
7.75	5-90	. . . .	99-29	100	—	6.81
12.15	12-93	. . . .	109-05	109-15	—	9.05
World Bank Bonds:						
Rate	Maturity					
16.63	11-91	. . . .	110-04	110-20	—	9.25
5.88	9-93	. . . .	90-09	90-25	—	9.33
Tax Exempt Bonds:						
Agency	Coupon	Maturity	Current price			
L.A.Calif. Wastewtr	6.800	08-01-19	93		− ⅛	7.38
Ohio Hsing Fin Agcy . . .	7.650	03-01-29	97⅝		− ⅛	7.84

*Discount rates.

point. Thus a quote of 99–28 means a price of 99^{28}/$_{32}$ percent, or $998.75 per $1,000 of par value. The final column is yield to maturity, which reflects the return on investment earned at the current price if the bond were held to its maturity date and redeemed at par.

Note that the yield on the 6.75 percent Treasury bonds due in 1993 is well above the coupon rate, while the 12.62 percent bond due in May 1995 and the 15.75 percent bonds due in 2001 are trading at a significant premium to yield around 9 percent. These differentials reflect the interest levels prevailing in 1990, which were far below the inflation-driven conditions of the late 1970s and early 1980s. U.S. government securities as well as other debt instruments are always affected by the general outlook for interest rates. They will tend to yield a lower return than most corporate and other public bonds, because the likelihood of default is extremely remote and the purchaser is normally looking for a safe investment with an assured long-term or short-term yield.

As we found in the case of the stock market quotations, bond market listings are supplemented by a variety of reports on the volume of trading, bonds averages, summaries of advancing and declining conditions, highs and lows for the year, and so on. Again, these provide the investor with a general feel for the daily movements of the bond markets and interest rate conditions. The most commonly used averages are the Dow Jones Bond Averages (20 bonds: 10 public utilities and 10 industrials), Merrill Lynch Corporate Bonds, and Shearson Lehman Hutton Treasury Bonds. Bond averages are calculated in percentages of par, as were the quotations themselves. On Monday, April 23, 1990, the NYSE bond volume was $34,670,000 for all issues, with the 20-bond average falling slightly to 89.46, down .30 from the prior trading day. Issues traded numbered 605, of which 139 staged advances, 336 declined, and 130 remained unchanged. New highs for the year were achieved by 3 issues, and new lows by 41 issues.

Other Financial Data

Most papers list, in one form or another, so-called leading, coincident, and lagging business and economic indicators—such as indexes of industrial production, freight car loadings, prices, output in the automotive industry, steel production—both in feature stories and in tabular form. When supplemented by reports of earnings and dividend declarations of individual corporations, news about corporate management, analysis and announcement of new financing, and industry analysis, this information can provide a broad background for financial analysis.

Among the more specialized data in the financial pages are listings of transactions in the *commodities markets*. Commodities include a great variety of basic raw materials such as cotton, lumber, copper, and rubber; and foods, such as coffee, corn, and wheat. The best-known exchange for commodity trading is the Chicago Board of Trade, while more specialized exchanges include the New York Cotton Exchange or international exchanges such as the London Metal Exchange. Commodities may be traded on a *spot* basis; that is, the commodity is purchased outright at the time. Commodities *futures* are also traded. These are contracts to buy or sell a commodity at a specified price at some point in the future. The commodities market is far too varied to describe here, but we should take a quick look at how commodities are quoted.

The information on commodities trading provided by most sources usually involves opening and closing transactions, as well as highs and also lows for the trading day and the season. Changes from the previous trading day are also often listed. A variety of indexes are available, such as the Dow Jones Spot Index, the Dow Jones Futures Index, or the Reuters United Kingdom Index. A company whose operations depend to a large extent on raw materials traded in a spot or futures market can be severely influenced by fluctuations in spot or futures prices. Because fluctuations in commodities markets can be severe, traders in these markets often *hedge*. This involves arrangements to *both* buy and sell the same commodity, which will "cover" the trader for shifts in prices. References at the end of this appendix provide more detailed information on commodities trading.

Foreign Exchange

Most newspapers list the major currencies of the world in equivalents of U.S. dollars. Normally, the quotations represent selling prices of bank transfers in the United States for payment abroad, and quotations are given for the current trading day as well as for the previous day. Also, prices for foreign bank notes are often quoted in equivalents of U.S. dollars, both on a buying and selling basis.

PERIODIC FINANCIAL INFORMATION

Apart from the financial data contained in daily newspapers, a wealth of information is provided by various financial, economic, and business periodicals. Furthermore, readily available reference works contain periodic listings and analyses of financial information oriented toward the investor and financial analyst. The advent of the computer has made possible the rapid collection and analysis of company and economic data, and collective information can now be obtained on-line through data base access or in hard copy on a very timely basis. The most important sources of periodic financial and business information are listed below.

Magazines

Major Weekly Periodicals. For general business coverage, *Business Week* remains one of the most useful and widely read publications. It covers current developments of interest in business and economics, both national and international. The weekly magazine contains analyses of major events as well as reports on individual companies, the stock markets, labor, business education, and so on, and a selective listing of economic indicators, as well as a special index of business activity.

For more detailed coverage of stock quotations, security offerings, banking developments, and financial, industrial, and commodity trends, the *Commercial and Financial Chronicle* is the most comprehensive source available. The *Wall Street Transcript* contains analyses of the securities of a great variety of individual companies, both on a financial and economic basis, and of the technical basis of stock market charts. It further discusses major corporate presentations to security analysts about past performance and future plans, and features roundtable discussions on industry groups by security analysts.

Barron's covers business trends in terms of individual companies as well as major industries, and provides a great deal of information about corporate securities. The section titled " Stock Market at a Glance" is a very useful and detailed picture of the securities markets. *Fortune* magazine biweekly comments on national economic trends and sketches profiles of major U.S. and international executives, in addition to giving detailed articles on industry, company, or socio-economic trends. The magazine's annual listing and ranking of the "Fortune 500," the best-performing U.S. companies, and similar listings of banks and major foreign companies, are useful references.

Forbes, also a semimonthly magazine, takes the investor's viewpoint, providing detailed and searching analyses of individual companies and their managements. The annual January issue, which reviews the performance of major U.S. industries, is an excellent source of information on industry trends and provides a ranking of companies by a series of criteria.

For an international outlook the British magazine *The Economist* surveys international and United Kingdom developments in politics, economics, and business, and discusses U.S. developments in depth. It can be considered an international *Business Week*, as can *World Business*.

Major Monthly Periodicals. Economic and business trends are covered in considerable detail in publications of major commercial banks, such as the *National City Bank Monthly Letter* and the *New England Letter* of the First National Bank of Boston. The various Federal Reserve banks issue general bulletins and regional bulletins that contain regional economic data of interest.

The *Harvard Business Review* is a highly regarded forum for discussion of management concepts and tools, including financial insights, presented bimonthly by practitioners and academicians to an extensive worldwide readership of business executives. Several other major business schools publish journals of similar orientation.

Dun's Review presents trade indexes, data on business failures, and key financial ratios in addition to articles about industry and commerce. *Nation's Business*, a publication of the United States Chamber of Commerce, presents general articles on business subjects. Statistical information in great depth is provided by the *Federal Reserve Bulletin*, which contains statistical data on business and government finances, both domestic and international, and by the *Survey of Current Business*, which covers business statistics in detail.

Detailed stock exchange quotations and data about many *unlisted securities* (those not traded on a recognized exchange), foreign exchange, and money rates are contained in the *Bank and Quotation Record*. The *Journal of Finance*, a quarterly publication, presents articles on finance, investments, economics, money and credit, and international aspects of these topics.

Other Periodicals.   Many specialized periodicals are published by trade associations and banking, commercial, and trading groups too numerous to mention. Also useful are the great variety of U.S. government surveys and publications, statistical papers provided by the United Nations and its major agencies, and the various analyses and reviews in academic journals. At the end of this appendix, we have listed several books that provide detailed guidelines on and descriptions of the type of information available from various sources.

Listed below are some major periodicals that deal directly with, or relate to, the area of corporate finance. The list is meant only as a guide. Many other relevant publications are available. Some of the publications are specialized and oriented toward a specific community of interest, others deal with financial conditions in foreign countries. The titles are largely self-explanatory:

Banking
Credit and Financial Management
Journal of Commerce
Corporate Financing
Finance
Financial Analysts Journal
Financial Executive
Financial World

Investment Dealers Digest
Mergers and Acquisitions
National Tax Journal
World Financial Markets

Financial Manuals and Services

The most popular and best-known set of financial manuals and services is provided by Moody's, with Standard & Poor's a close second. Moody's publishes five volumes: *Industrials; Banks, Insurance, Real Estate and Investment Funds; Public Utilities; Railroads;* and *Government and Municipals.* These manuals are published each year and contain up-to-date key historical data, financial statements, securities price ranges, and dividend records for a very large number of companies, including practically all publicly held corporations. Helpful summary statistics and industry data are found in the so-called "blue sections" in the middle of the manuals, which are printed on blue paper. Moody's manuals are updated through semiweekly supplements, with detailed cross-references.

Moody's publishes a *Quarterly Handbook,* which gives one-page summaries of key financial and operating data for major publicly held corporations. Furthermore, Moody's publishes weekly stock and bond surveys that analyze market and industry conditions, a semiweekly *Dividend Record,* and a semimonthly *Bond Record* that contains current prices, earnings, and ratings of most important bonds traded in the country.

Standard & Poor's publications include the *Standard Corporation Records.* This financial information about a large number of companies is published in loose-leaf format and is updated through daily supplements. A very useful S&P publication is the *Analysts Handbook;* these industry surveys are compilations of key financial data on individual companies and some industries. Other services of Standard & Poor's include several dealing with the bond market, weekly forecasts of the security markets, securities statistics, and a monthly earnings and stock rating guide.

Other financial services similar to Moody's and Standard & Poor's are provided by *Fitch's Corporation Manuals,* and by more specialized manuals such as *Walker's Manual* of Pacific Coast securities. An almost overwhelming flow of information, judgments, and analyses of individual companies from an investor's standpoint is provided by the major brokerage houses and their research departments. Furthermore, services available to individuals on a subscription basis provide up-to-date financial analyses and evaluations of individual companies and their securities. The most important among these services are *Value Line, United Business Service, Babson's,* and *Investor's Management Sciences.* The *Value Line* investment survey particularly provides ratings and reports on companies, with selections and opinions for

432

the investor, while *Investor's Management Sciences* concentrates on providing a great deal of standardized statistical information as the basis for making analytical judgments. The credit information services of *Dun & Bradstreet* make evaluating small or unlisted companies easier. The advent of on-line data bases has made important information about companies listed on stock exchanges available instantly through various data bases and *time-share services*.

BACKGROUND COMPANY AND BUSINESS INFORMATION

Annual Reports

The most commonly used reference source about the current affairs of publicly held corporations is the annual report furnished to shareholders. The formats used by individual corporations vary widely from detailed coverage that may even go so far as to include current corporate, industry, and national issues, to a bare minimum disclosure of financial results. Nevertheless, the annual report is generally an important direct source of financial information. Because the disclosure requirements of the Securities and Exchange Commission, the recommendations of the accounting profession, and state laws have become more and more demanding over time, the analyst can usually count on annual reports presenting a fairly consistent set of data.

Government Data

More specific details about company operations can often be found in the annual statement that corporations must file with the Securities and Exchange Commission (SEC) in Washington, D.C. This information is filed on Form 10-K and is available upon request for public inspection. Furthermore, when a corporation issues new securities in significant amounts or alters its capital structure in a major way, the detailed proposal that must be filed with the SEC, the *prospectus*, is generally a more complete source of company background data than is the normal annual report. It will cover the history of the company, ownership patterns, directors and top management, financial and operating data, products, facilities, and information regarding the intended use of the new funds.

If a company is closely held, or too small to be listed by the key financial services, information about its financial operations can often be obtained from the corporation records departments of states in which the company does business. Again, these reports are open to the public for inspection.

Trade Associations

Trade associations are a prime source of information about their respective industries. A great deal of statistical information is available annually or more often and covers products, services, finances, and performance criteria applicable to the industry or trade group. Often, the financial and performance data are grouped by types and sizes of firms, to make overall statistics on the industry somewhat more applicable to a particular operation. Trade associations include organizations such as the American Electronics Association, the American Paper Institute, and the National Lumber Manufacturers Association, to name but a few. Sources for listings and addresses of these associations and their publications can be found in the references at the end of the appendix.

Econometric Services

Many forecasts of U.S. and international economic conditions are available to the financial analyst. Based on so-called *econometric* models developed by a variety of academic institutions and economic advisory services, these forecasts of the United States economy, and more recently of economies of other countries as well, can provide valuable clues regarding the likely movement of the country's economy within which financial conditions must be viewed. Among the widely quoted and used econometric models are those developed by the Wharton School at the University of Pennsylvania, Data Resources Inc., and Chase Econometric Associates. Many corporations subscribe to such forecasting services and make use of the projections in their operational and financial planning. Increasingly, corporate and academic economists are testing their own assumptions about economic trends with the help of econometric models. Another feature of these services is the growing variety of on-line data bases containing a vast array of statistical and financial information for immediate access.

While we have merely touched on the major sources of specific or general information on financial business affairs, the reader is encouraged to make use of the sources discussed, as well as the references provided at the end of this appendix. In addition a great deal of information is available from various business libraries in corporations and in colleges and universities, as well as from local institutions. The problem facing a financial analyst, whether student or professional, is not a lack of data; rather, it is selecting what is truly relevant.

SELECTED REFERENCES

Clasing, Henry K., Jr. *The Dow Jones-Irwin Guide to Put and Call Options.* Rev. ed. Homewood, Ill.: Dow Jones-Irwin, 1978.

Daniells, Lorna M. *Business Information Sources.* Rev. ed. Berkeley: University of California Press, 1985.

Gould, Bruce G. *Dow Jones-Irwin Guide to Commodity Trading.* Rev. ed. Homewood, Ill.: Dow Jones-Irwin, 1981.

Kruzas, Anthony T., and John Schnittroth, Jr. *Encyclopedia of Information Systems & Services.* 4th ed. Detroit: Gale Research, 1980.

Lehmann, Michael B. *The Dow Jones-Irwin Guide to Using The Wall Street Journal.* Homewood, Ill.: Dow Jones-Irwin, 1990.

Levine, Sumner N., ed. *Dow Jones-Irwin Business Almanac.* Homewood, Ill.: Dow Jones-Irwin, 1982.

Pierce, Phyllis S., ed. *The Dow Jones Averages 1885–1980.* New York: Dow Jones, 1982.

Ruder, William, and Raymond Nathan. *The Businessman's Guide to Washington.* New York: Collier Books, 1975.

Wasserman, Paul, ed. *Encyclopedia of Business Information Sources.* 4th ed. Detroit: Gale Research, 1980.

APPENDIX III
SOLUTIONS TO
SELF-STUDY PROBLEMS

CHAPTER TWO

Solutions to Problems

1. CBA Company

Changes in Balance Sheet ($000)

Assets		Liabilities	
Cash	$ (12.2)	Accounts payable	$ 11.8
Marketable securites	10.0	Notes payable	90.0
Accounts receivable	(8.8)	Accrued expenses	2.9
Inventories	60.7	Total current liabilities	$104.7
Total current assets	49.7		
Land	–0–	Mortgage payable	$(15.2)
Plant and equipment (net)	19.6	Common stock	5.0
Total fixed assets	19.6	Earned surplus	(17.0)
		Total net worth	$(27.2)
Other assets	8.2	Total liabilities and	
Total assets	$ 77.5	net worth	$ 77.5

435

Funds Flow Statement (Year 1990)

Sources		Uses	
Depreciation	$ 32.2*	Loss from operations	$ 2.0*
Decrease in cash	12.2	Dividends paid	15.0**
Decrease in accounts receivable	8.8	Increase in securities	10.0
Increase in accounts payable	11.8	Increase in inventories	60.7
Increase in note payable	90.0	Investment in plant	51.8†
Increase in accrued expenses	2.9	Increase in other assets	8.2
Increase in common stock	5.0	Decrease in mortgage	15.2
Total	$162.9	Total	$162.9

The results were built up from:

* Taken from 1990 operating statement.

** Change in earned surplus matches the combination of loss from operations ($2,000) on the 1990 operating statement and dividends paid ($15,000), from footnote. No extraordinary items appear and no assumptions are necessary.

† Since net plant and equipment increased by $19,600, and the only known element affecting the account is depreciation ($32,200), the amount of investment must have been the sum of these amounts ($51,800).

Observations:

The biggest single use is a drastic rise in inventories, even though sales volume changed little. Are inventory controls failing? Dividends were wisely cut as profits plummented. The key funds source was borrowing (short term) of $90 which provides more than half of funds needs. Sizable capital investment (almost twice depreciation) points to optimistic future plans—any problems in sight? Is the company beginning to lean on suppliers? (Accounts payable up somewhat.) Is equity capital called for?

2. a. ABC Company:

Beginning balance, earned surplus (12/31/89)		$167,300
Less:		
Net loss for 1990 (incl. loss from aband.)	$14,100	
Common dividends paid	12,000	
Inventory adjustment	24,000	
Amortization of goodwill, patents	15,000	65,100
Ending balance, earned surplus (12/31/90)		$102,200

Funds Flow Items

Sources		Uses	
Depreciation	$21,400	Net operating loss	$ 10,100
Total Sources	$21,400	Loss from abandonment	4,000
		Dividends paid	12,000
		Investment in fixed assets	57,500
		Amortization	15,000
		Inventory adjustment	24,000
		Total Uses	$112,600

Depreciation (noncash) should be reflected as a source as it reduced operating profit/loss; loss conditions do not change in basic character.

Loss from abandonment can be separated from profit/loss; it was offset by reduction in asset. A gain could be shown as a separate source, offset by the increase in cash.

Amortization and inventory adjustments are assumed to have been earned surplus reductions here; can be separated out as shown, as they have been offset by decrease in patents and inventories, or they can be *eliminated* on both sides of the statement.

b. DEF Company:

The layout of the data appears on page 438.

Observations:

Any assumption about a gain or loss on sale and/or abandonment would be handled as in Item 2*a*. Any disposition of partially depreciated assets would cause greater "reductions" in assets than in accumulated depreciation, which in turn would raise the derived asset additions.

c. XYZ Company:

The layout of the data appears as follows:

	Beginning Balance	Additions	Reductions	Ending Balance	Change
Gross fixed assets	$823,700*	$236,100**	$ 2,500*** 110,000*	$947,300	$123,600
Accumulated depreciation	N.A.	78,500*	2,500*** 81,000*	N.A.	(5,000)*
Net fixed assets	$ N.A.	$157,600	$ 29,000**	$ N.A.	$128,600
		(Result)			(Result)

The result was built up from:
* Given information.
** Forced figures.
*** Assumption that fully depreciated assets of $2,500 were written off.

Gain on sales of assets:

Recorded value	$110,000
Accumulated depreciation	81,000
Book value	$ 29,000
Cash received	45,000
Gain on sale	$ 16,000

Funds Flow Items

Sources		Uses	
Depreciation	$ 78,500		
Net write-off of assets	29,500*	Investments	$236,100
	$107,500		

* Could be split into gain ($16,000) and cash received ($45,000).
Note that sources and uses net out to $128,600.

DEF Company (page 437)

	Beginning Balance	Additions	Reductions	Ending Balance	Change
Gross property and fixed assets	$8,431,500*	$1,250,500*	$1,252,000**	$8,430,000*	$(1,500)
Accumulated depreciation	3,513,000**	1,613,000*	1,252,000†	3,874,000*	361,000
Net property and fixed assets	$4,918,500	$ 362,500	$ -0-	$4,556,000	$(362,500)
					(Result)

The result is built up from:

* Given information.

** Forced figures.

† Assumption that fully depreciated assets were abandoned.

3. FED Company

Funds Flow Statement (Year 1990)

Sources			Uses**		
Net income	$	6*	Increase in accounts		
Depreciation		26*	receivable	$	5
Increase in deferred			Increase in notes		
income taxes		2	receivable		20
Gain from sale of asset		4**	Increase in inventories		7
Decrease in cash		12	Investment in plant and		
Overdraft		4	equipment		38**
Decrease in securities		18	Increase in prepaids		2
Increase in accounts payable		24	Decrease in notes payable		30
Increase in accrued expenses		9	Decrease in secured notes		
Increase in preferred stock		4	payable		20
Increase in common stock and			Dividends (preferred and		
capital surplus		20	common)		7
Total		$129	Total		$129

The results were built up from:
* Taken from 1990 operating statement.
** The fixed property conditions are as follows:

	Beginning Balance	Additions	Reductions	Ending Balance	Change
Gross property and expenses	$268	$38	$ 23	$283	$15
Accumulated depreciation	157	26	23	160	3
Net property and expenses	$111	$12	$-0-	$123	$12

The key element is the forced figure of $38, which is based on the stated assumptions. The gain from sale of assets in the earned surplus account should be reflected as a source, just like net income.

*** Patent and other amortization of #3 is adjusted for in the earned surplus account; thus it is not a funds item.

Observations:

Key funds movements revolve around capital investments and financing. Repayments of short- and long-term notes and credit demands from customers make up better than half of the funds uses. Some new equity has come in, but not enough. The company is running out of cash and stretching payables.

A short-term solution only—(working capital items could be lumped in one figure, of course).

A funds flow statement by area of management concern highlights these findings:

Operating inflows:

Net sales	$	1,237
Increase in accounts payable		24
Increase in accrued expenses		9
Increase in deferred income taxes		2
Total operating inflows	$ + 1,272	

Operating outflows:

Cost of goods sold (excluding depreciation)	$	896
Selling and administrative		297
Income taxes		5
Increase in accounts receivable		5
Increase in notes receivable		20
Increase in inventories		7
Increase in prepaids		2
Total operating outflows	$ − 1,232	
Net operating inflows		$ + 40

Financial inflows:

Increase in preferred stock	$	4
Increase in capital stock and surplus		20
Decrease in securities		18
Gain on sale of assets		4
Total financial inflows	$	+ 46

Financial outflows:

Repayment of notes payable	$	30
Repayment of secured notes		20
Interest on debt		7
Total financial outflows	$	− 57
Net financial outflows		$ − 11

Discretionary outflows:

Additions to plant and equipment	$	38
Cash dividends paid		7
Total discretionary outflows		$ − 45
Net outflows from operations, financing and investment		$ − 16

Analysis of cash impact:

Beginning cash balance	+ 12
Ending cash balance	$ − 4

This format shows clearly the important financial and discretionary movements, which leave operations strapped.

4. ZYX Company

A variety of funds flow statements are possible here:

From peak to trough of season (two seasons).

From peak to peak, or trough to trough.

From April to April, or any other month.

Two-year span, July to July, to provide long-term debt.

Samples of these possible funds flow statements appear as follows:

Sources of Funds	1/31/90 to 4/30/90	1/31/91 to 4/30/91	4/30/89 to 1/31/91	1/31/89 to 1/31/91	4/30/89 to 4/30/91	7/31/89 to 7/31/91
Profit from operations	$ 10	$ 17	$ 67	$ 77	$ 84	$172
Depreciation	6	7	21	27	28	54
Decrease in cash	—	—	1	—	—	5
Decrease in receivables	191	237	—	—	—	11
Decrease in inventories	184	253	—	—	33	—
Decrease in other assets	1	—	—	—	—	—
Increase in payables	—	—	85	67	—	16
Increase in notes	—	—	342	48	—	45
Increase in common	—	—	25	25	25	25
Total sources	$392	$514	$541	$244	$170	$328

Uses of Funds	1/31/89 to 4/30/90	1/31/89 to 4/30/91	4/30/89 to 1/31/91	1/31/89 to 1/31/91	4/30/89 to 4/30/91	7/31/89 to 7/31/91
Capital investments	$ 48	$ 50	$—	$ 48	$ 50	$ 98
Increase in cash	17	13	—	16	12	—
Increase in receivables	—	—	260	69	23	79
Increase in inventories	—	—	220	36	—	—
Increase in other assets	—	—	3	2	3	2
Decrease in payables	18	91	—	—	6	—
Decrease in notes	294	342	—	—	—	—
Decrease in mortgage	—	—	10	10	10	20
Dividends paid	15	18	48	63	66	129
Total uses	$392	$514	$541	$244	$170	$328

Observations:

This strong seasonal pattern from January to April shows up vividly in the peak to trough and trough to peak comparisons, where receivables and inventories are matched with payables and sizable short-term notes. There is a lag effect in buildup of inventories and receivables, as expected. Growth shows up in like-to-like comparisons, with no undue strains. Good example to demonstrate effect of careless placement of funds flow analysis over alternative time periods.

Questions for Discussion

1. Differentiate between cash flow and funds flow. What is "cash flow from operations"?

2. In what ways does a funds flow statement correspond to the operating statement for a period? In what ways does it differ? Can the two be readily reconciled?

3. In what ways are the concepts of debit and credit related to funds uses and sources? On the basis of a simple balance sheet, derive the principles of this relationship. Discuss.

4. Does a sizable profit for a period necessarily mean an increase in a company's cash account? If not, why not?

5. Does a company whose operations are shrinking always throw off cash? If not, why not? What assumptions must be made?

6. Why is depreciation a "source of funds" when it is clear that a mere bookkeeping entry is involved?

7. If a company incurred an operating loss for a period, is depreciation still treated as a funds inflow?

8. What is the tax impact of depreciation—are there any funds movements involved?

9. Why is it necessary to "reverse" such transactions as write-down of goodwill, or amortization of patents?

10. What is the funds impact of accelerated depreciation, and why?

11. By what criteria is the selection of the proper time period for funds flow analysis made? Can you derive any rules?

12. What are the major ways in which inflation distorts the funds flow picture? Should adjustments be made?

CHAPTER THREE

Solutions to Problems

1. a. $\dfrac{\text{Net Profit}}{\text{Sales}} = 11.4\%$

$\text{Assets} = \dfrac{\text{Sales}}{1.34}$ (Sales > Assets)

Thus:

$$\frac{\text{Net Profit}}{\text{Assets}} = \frac{\text{Net profit}}{\dfrac{\text{Sales}}{1.34}} = 11.4\%(1.34) = \underline{\underline{15.28\%}}$$

If we assume no debt in the capitalization, then net worth equals capitalization. Thus:

$$\frac{\text{Net Profit}}{\text{Capitalization}} = \frac{\text{Net Profit}}{\text{Net Worth}} = \frac{1}{.67} \times \frac{\text{Net Profit}}{\text{Assets}}$$

Return on net worth:

$$\frac{15.28}{.67} = \underline{\underline{22.8\%}}$$

A faster asset turnover means a smaller asset base and smaller capitalization relative to sales—thus return figures go up.

b.   Gross margin is 31.4%; thus the cost of goods sold of $4,391,300 must represent sales of

$$\frac{\$4,391,300}{1.0 - .314} = \underline{\underline{\$6,400,000}}$$

Net profit must be 9.7% of $6,400,000, or $\underline{\underline{\$621,000}}$.
Total assets must be derived from:

$$\frac{\text{Sales}}{\text{Assets}} = .827; \text{Assets} = \frac{\text{Sales}}{.827} = \frac{\$6,400,000}{.827} = \underline{\underline{\$7,740,000}}$$

Return on capitalization must be:

$$\frac{\text{Net Profit}}{\text{Assets} - \text{Current Liabilities}} = \frac{\text{Net Profit}}{.79 \text{ (Assets)}} = \frac{\$621,000}{6,115,000} = \underline{\underline{10.15\%}}$$

c.   Changes in current ratio and effect on working capital:

$$\text{Current Ratio: 2.2 to 1} = \frac{\$573,100}{\$260,500*}$$

Working Capital: $573,100 - $260,500 = $\underline{\underline{\$312,600}}$

1.   Payment of accounts payable:

Decrease in cash $67,500
Decrease in payables $67,500

Both current assets and current liabilities *reduced* by same amount; this *improves* current ratio but leaves working capital unaffected:

$$\frac{\$573,100 - \$67,500}{\$260,500 - \$67,500} = \frac{\$505,600}{\$193,000} = \underline{\underline{2.62 \text{ to } 1}}$$

This is a common action taken by small companies at year-end to improve their ratio.

2.   Collection of note:

Increase in cash $33,000
Decrease in notes receivable $33,000

---

* Derived from relationship.

Both elements are within current assets; thus there is no net effect on either the ratio or the working capital.

3. Purchase on account:

    Increase in inventory $41,300
    Increase in payables $41,300

    Both current assets and current liabilities are *increased*; thus the opposite effect of (1), with working capital unaffected:

    $$\frac{\$573,100\ +\ \$41,300}{\$260,500\ +\ \$41,300} = \frac{\$614,400}{\$301,800} = \underline{\underline{2.04\ \text{to}\ 1}}$$

4. Dividend payment:

    Decrease in cash $60,000
    Decrease in accrued dividends $42,000
    Decrease in earned surplus . . . . $18,000 (no effect)

    Uneven effect on the two elements; thus change in both the ratio and working capital:

    $$\frac{\$573,100\ -\ \$60,000}{\$260,500\ -\ \$42,000} = \frac{\$513,100}{\$218,500} = \underline{\underline{2.35\ \text{to}\ 1}}$$

    The current ratio is slightly improved, while working capital drops by $\underline{\$18,000}$.

5. Machine sale:

    Increase in cash . . . . $ 80,000
    Decrease in fixed assets . . . . $202,000 (no effect)
    Decrease in accumulated depreciation . . . . . . $112,000 (no effect)
    Loss on sale of assets $ 10,000 (no effect)

    The only effect is an increase in current assets, which changes both the ratio and working capital:

    $$\frac{\$573,100\ +\ \$80,000}{\$260,500} = \frac{\$653,100}{\$260,500} = \underline{\underline{2.51\ \text{to}\ 1}}$$

    The current ratio rises to 2.51, while working capital improves by $\underline{\$80,000}$.

6. Sale of merchandise:

    Increase in receivables $109,700*
    Decrease in inventory . . . . $ 73,500
    Increase in retained earnings . . . . $ 36,200 (no effect)

    ---

    * Derived from $\dfrac{\$73,500}{1.0\ -\ .33} = \underline{\underline{\$109,700}}$.

There is a net increase in current assets, which improves the ratio and working capital:

$$\frac{\$573,100 + \$109,700 - \$73,500}{\$260,500} = \frac{\$609,300}{\$260,500} = \underline{2.34 \text{ to } 1}$$

The current ratio rises to 2.34, while working capital improves by $\underline{\$36,200}$.

7. Write-offs:

Decrease in inventory . . . . $ 20,000
Decrease in goodwill $ 15,000 (no effect)
Decrease in retained earnings . . . . $ 35,000 (no effect)

There is a reduction of current assets, which affects both the ratio and working capital:

$$\frac{\$573,100 - \$20,000}{\$260,500} = \frac{\$553,100}{\$260,500} = \underline{2.12 \text{ to } 1}$$

Slight drop to 2.12, while working capital is reduced by $\underline{\$20,000}$.

d. Days' receivables and payables:

$$\frac{\text{Net sales}}{\text{Days}} = \frac{\$437,500}{90} = \underline{\$4,861 \text{ per day}}$$

$$\frac{\text{Purchases}}{\text{Days}} = \frac{\$143,500}{90} = \underline{\$1,594 \text{ per day}}$$

$$\text{Days' receivables} = \frac{\text{Accounts receivable}}{\text{Daily sales}}$$

$$= \frac{\$156,800}{\$4,861} = \underline{32.3 \text{ days}}$$

$$\text{Days' payables} = \frac{\text{Accounts payable}}{\text{Daily purchases}}$$

$$= \frac{\$69,300}{\$1,594} = \underline{43.5 \text{ days}}$$

The company's collections are fairly slow, in view of the discount period of 10 days, while its payments are slightly faster than needed against the 45-day terms.

Inventory turnover:

$$\text{Average inventory: } \frac{(\$382,200 + \$227,300)}{2} = \underline{\$304,750}$$

Turnover on sales:

$$\frac{\text{Average inventory}}{\text{Sales for quarter}} = \frac{\$304,750}{\$437,500} = \underline{\underline{69.6\%}} \text{ (quarterly)}$$

or

$$\frac{\text{Average inventory}}{\text{Annual sales}} = \frac{\$304,750}{4(\$437,500)} = \underline{\underline{17.4\%}} \text{ (annualized)}$$

or

$$\frac{\text{Sales for quarter}}{\text{Average inventory}} = \frac{\$437,500}{\$304,750} = \underline{\underline{1.44 \text{ times}}} \text{ (quarterly)}$$

or

$$\frac{\text{Annual sales}}{\text{Average inventory}} = \frac{4(\$437,500)}{\$304,750} = \underline{\underline{5.74}} \text{ (annualized)}$$

Turnover on cost of sales:

$$\frac{\text{Average inventory}}{\text{Cost of sales for quarter}} = \frac{\$304,750}{\$298,400} = \underline{\underline{102.1\%}} \text{ (quarterly)}$$

$$\frac{\text{Average inventory}}{\text{Annual cost of sales}} = \frac{\$304,750}{4(\$298,400)} = \underline{\underline{25.5\%}} \text{ (annualized)}$$

or

$$\frac{\text{Cost of sales for quarter}}{\text{Average inventory}} = \frac{\$298,400}{\$304,750} = \underline{\underline{.98 \text{ times}}} \text{ (quarterly)}$$

or

$$\frac{\text{Annual cost of sales}}{\text{Average inventory}} = \frac{4(\$298,400)}{\$304,750} = \underline{\underline{3.92 \text{ times}}} \text{ (annualized)}$$

Turnover on ending inventory:

$$\frac{\text{Ending inventory}}{\text{Cost of sales for quarter}} = \frac{\$227,300}{\$298,400} = \underline{\underline{76.2\%}} \text{ (quarterly)}$$

or

$$\frac{\text{Cost of sales for quarter}}{\text{Ending inventory}} = \frac{\$298,400}{\$227,300} = \underline{\underline{1.31 \text{ times}}} \text{ (quarterly)}$$

The cost of sales figures are more useful as a rule. Ending inventory should be used in relation to the quarterly cost of sales if there are significant seasonal swings. Annualization on a simple "4×" basis is problematic if a strong pattern is suspected.

2. ABC Company
The various ratios are grouped by point of view:
a. Management's view:

	1989	1990
Cost of goods sold	70.4%	70.6%
Gross margin	29.6%	29.4%
Profit margin	5.7%	5.4%
Profit before interest and taxes	10.7%	10.8%
Profit after taxes, before interest	5.8%	5.8%
Selling and administrative expenses	15.0%	14.4%
Employee profit sharing	4.1%	4.4%
Other income	.2%	.2%
Tax rate	46.0%	46.0%
Contribution	N.A.	N.A.
Gross asset turnover $\left(\dfrac{\text{Assets}}{\text{Sales}}\right)$	59.5%	64.6%
Net asset turnover $\left(\dfrac{\text{Assets}}{\text{Sales}}\right)$	39.4%	44.4%
Ending inventory turns $\left(\dfrac{\text{Cost of Sales}}{\text{Inventory}}\right)$	5.2×	4.8×
Days' receivables	51.1 days	60.7 days
Days' payables (cost of sales)	34.0 days	37.0 days
Net profit to total assets	9.6%	8.3%
Net profit to capitalization	14.4%	12.1%
Net profit before interest and tax to total assets	18.0%	16.8%
Net profit before interest and tax to capitalization	27.2%	24.4%
Net profit after tax, before interest, to total assets	9.7%	9.0%
Net profit after tax, before interest, to capitalization	14.6%	13.2%

b. Owner's view

	1989	1990
Net profit to net worth (including deferred tax)	15.1%	16.3%
Net profit to common equity (w/o deferred tax)	15.2%	16.7%
Earnings per share	$3.69	$4.61
Cash flow per share	$6.48	$8.38
Dividends per share	$ .54	$ .59
Dividend coverage—earnings	6.8×	7.8×
Dividend coverage—cash flow	11.9×	14.2×

c. Lender's view

	1989	1990
Current ratio	2.1:1	2.2:1
Acid test (excluding advances)	1.3:1	1.4:1
Total debt to assets	35.7%	48.7%
Long-term debt to capitalization	3.0%	25.3%
Total debt to net worth	55.5%	95.0%
Long-term debt to net worth	3.1%	32.9%
Interest coverage (pretax)	70×	13×
Cash flow before taxes—interest coverage	98×	18×
Full interest coverage ($8.5 million)	—	11×

Observations:

Slight worsening shown in operating performance, at the same effective tax rate, which makes 1989 the better year. More investment has been committed both in working capital and fixed assets—collections are slowing, inventories are up, and profits on assets are down by every measure.

Leverage has improved the profit on net worth, however, and earnings per share are up sharply. No problems exist in covering dividends on interest, even if a full year's interest is assumed.

Comparisons should be made with companies in similar product lines, particularly on capital structure, return on net worth, and coverages. High-low analysis of good and bad years should highlight risk of earnings fluctuations. Two-year static picture not enough.

Questions for Discussion

1. Explain the relationships of the four basic financial statements. Which statement encompasses the results of all decisions? Why?

2. Why does the balance sheet have to balance at all times? What does the statement signify?

3. What are the key factors that allow comparison of industry ratios to the ratios of an individual company?

4. List several accounting practices that can result in changes in the ratios that measure profitability. What is their effect?

5. List several accounting practices that can result in changes in the ratios that measure liquidity and debt exposure. What is their effect?

6. What measurement issues arise when two different divisions of a company are compared on the basis of management ratios, given widely divergent conditions in age, markets, and costs?

7. A commonly used ratio from the standpoint of the lender is "times interest earned." How meaningful is this ratio in assessing the quality of the indebtedness involved?

8. Does operating cash flow represent the majority of funds movements caused by operations? If not, why not?

9. What are the key questions you would ask if you were a banker reviewing a loan request from a small, rapidly growing company?

10. What is the impact of inflation on ratio analysis? What key distortions can be expected, and in which ratios?

11. What are the major problems encountered in the process of adjusting for inflation?

12. If you were general manager of a division, which key ratio would you choose to be evaluated on for your unit's financial performance, and why? What conditions would you stipulate?

CHAPTER FOUR

Solutions to Problems

1. *a.* Change in credit policy:
18 days' sales developed as follows:

$$\text{Daily sales: } \frac{\$9,137,000}{360} = \$25,380/\text{day}$$

18 days' sales: $18 \times \$25,380 = \$\ \ \ 456,800$

40 days' sales: $40 \times \$25,380 = \$1,015,200$

Increase in receivables: $\quad\quad \$\ \ \ 558,400$

60 days' sales: $60 \times \$25,380 = \$1,522,800$

Increase in receivables: $\quad\quad \$1,066,000$

Observations:
Funds need increase is over one-half million dollars. Cash flow per year available from operations is only $305,000—likely the company must secure other funds. Need is doubled if policy is changed to 60 days.

b. Inventory consignment:
Average inventory: $725,000

$$\text{Current turnover: } \frac{\text{Cost of goods sold}}{\text{Average inventory}} = \frac{.83 \times \$9,137,000}{\$725,000} = 10.5 \text{ times}$$

$$\text{Turnover slowdown: } \frac{\text{Cost of goods sold}}{7.0} = \frac{\$7,583,700}{7.0} = \$1,083,400$$

Inventory increases by $1,083,400 less $725,000 = $\ \ \ 358,400$

$$\text{Turnover increase: } \frac{\text{Cost of goods sold}}{11.0} = \frac{\$7,583,700}{11.0} = \$\ \ \ 689,400$$

Inventory decreases by $725,000 less $689,400 = $\ \ \ \ \ 35,600$

Observations:
Funds needs change as indicated. Likely will require increased production operations to achieve higher supply (about 5 percent),

some increased purchases, which will provide some funds through higher payables—but the slowdown must be financed by other funds sources.

c. Change in payment terms:
Company now has 10 days' purchases outstanding:

$$\text{Payables} = \frac{\text{Purchases}}{360} \times 10 = \frac{\$5,316,000}{36} = \underline{\underline{\$147,670}}$$

Change in terms means 5 more days' extension, which provides funds of $\underline{\underline{\$73,835}}$ (1/2 of above) for no additional cost.

Observations:
Company earns 2 percent now to pay 20 days sooner; will earn 2 percent to pay 30 days sooner (from day 15 to day 45). Annual interest thus 12 times 2% = 24%. If company can obtain funds for less, it is desirable to discount. (See Chapter 7.)

d. Capital expenditures and dividends:

```
Funds need . . . . . . . . . . . . . . . . $125,000 for equipment
Plus 60% of $131,000 =  . . . . . . . . .   79,000
      Total . . . . . . . . . . . . . . . . $204,000
```

Against cash from operations:

```
Profits . . . . . . . . . . . . . . . . . . $131,000
Depreciation . . . . . . . . . . . . . . .  174,000
      Total . . . . . . . . . . . . . . . . $305,000
```

Observations:
Can be handled by internal funds unless significant changes in working capital needs occur (such as in earlier examples).

e. Sales growth:
10% increase in sales ($913,700) requires:

```
Funds for receivables: 18 days of increased sales . . . . . . . . . . $ 45,700
Funds for inventories: 10 percent increase  . . . . . . . . . . . . .   72,500
Funds from payables: 10 days of increased purchases  . . . . . . . .  (14,800)
      Total funds need . . . . . . . . . . . . . . . . . . . . . . .  $103,400
Against additional profits of 10% (assume no efficiency of scale):    $ 13,100
```

Observations:
Unless there are significant improvements in profit elements, the increase in sales requires funds of about $90,000. This makes dividends and capital expenditures under d. barely possible from internal funds, and leaves no room for inefficiency.

2.   ABC Company
Pro forma operating statement from data given:

ABC COMPANY
Pro Forma Operating Statement
for the Year Ended October 31, 1992
($000)

	Amount		Percent	
Net Sales		$4,350		100.0
Cost of goods sold:				
Labor $1,044			24.0	
Materials	631		14.5	
Overhead*	862		19.8	
Depreciation	143	2,680	3.3	61.6
Gross profit		$1,670		38.4
Selling expense	430		9.9	
General and administrative	352	782	8.1	18.0
Profit before taxes		$ 888		20.4
Income taxes (46%)		408		9.4
Net Income		$ 480		11.1

* $743 + $45 + $74

Observations:
Slight increase in the rate of profit due to higher efficiency in labor and overhead, which combine to overcome a rise in selling expense.

3.   DEF Company
Pro forma balance sheet developed from data given:

DEF COMPANY
Pro Forma Balance Sheet
December 31, 1992

Cash	$ 150,000	(desired level)
Receivables	348,300	(12 days on $10.45 mil.)
Inventories*	1,044,600	(as calculated below)
Total current assets	$1,542,900	
Land, buildings, etc.	$ 478,500	(plus $57,000)
Accumulated depreciation	248,700	(plus $31,400)
	$ 229,800	
Other assets	21,700	(no change)
Total assets	$1,794,400	
Accounts payable	$ 648,300	(24 days' purchases)
Note payable—bank	468,900	(plug figure—up by $43,900)
Accrued expenses	63,400	(no change)
Total current liabilities	$1,180,600	

DEF COMPANY
Pro Forma Balance Sheet
December 31, 1992 (Continued)

Term loan—properties	$ 110,000	(minus $10,000)
Capital stock	200,000	(no change)
Paid-in surplus	112,000	(no change)
Earned surplus	191,800	($184,400 + $19,900 − $12,500)
Total liabilities and net worth	$1,794,400	

Observations:

Main difference appears to be rise in inventories that requires about $130,000, while receivables drop. Apparently sales are leveling off or dropping (if 12 days' sales are assumed outstanding in 1992, sales for the year must have been $10,836,000, while purchases keep going up). Repayment of note and high dividend payout cause need for extra borrowing (plug figure) of about $44,000, even if cash is drawn down to $150,000.

*Beginning inventory	$ 912,700	
Purchases	9,725,000	
	$10,637,700	
Cost of goods sold	9,593,100	(91.8% of $10,450,000)
Ending inventory	$ 1,044,600	

4. XYZ Company

Cash budget by month developed from data given:

XYZ COMPANY
Cash Budget for Six Months
October 1991 through March 1992
($000)

	Oct.	Nov.	Dec.	Jan.	Feb.	Mar.	Total
Cash receipts:							
Collections from credit	$ 215	$ 245	$ 265	$ 385	$ 345	$ 505	$1,960
Cash sales	385	345	505	325	290	360	2,210
Total receipts . . .	$ 600	$ 590	$ 770	$ 710	$ 635	$ 865	$4,170
Cash disbursements (see breakdown of purchases below):							
Cash purchases . . .	$ 61	$ 54	$ 29	$ 32	$ 45	$ 48	$ 269
Credit purchases —10 days (less 2% discount) . . .	218	220	146	121	160	184	1,049
Credit purchases —45 days	257	266	286	205	153	192	1,359

	Oct.	Nov.	Dec.	Jan.	Feb.	Mar.	Total
Salaries and wages	$ 146	$ 131	$ 192	$ 124	$ 110	$ 137	$ 840
Operating expenses	108	97	141	91	81	101	619
Cash dividend	—	—	40	—	—	—	40
Federal income tax	—	—	—	20	—	—	20
Mortgage payment	7	7	7	7	7	7	42
Total cash disbursements	$ 797	$ 775	$ 841	$ 600	$ 556	$ 669	$4,238
Net cash receipts (disbursements) . . .	$(197)	$(185)	$ (71)	$ 110	$ 79	$ 196	$ (68)
Cumulative net cash flow	$(197)	$(382)	$(453)	$(343)	$(264)	$ (68)	
Analysis of cash requirements:							
Beginning cash balance	$ 95	$(102)	$(287)	$(358)	$(248)	$(169)	
Net cash receipts (disbursements) . .	(197)	(185)	(71)	110	79	196	
Ending cash balance	$(102)	$(287)	$(358)	$(248)	$(169)	$ 27	
Minimum cash balance	75	75	75	75	75	75	
Cash requirements . . .	$ 177	$ 362	$ 433	$ 323	$ 244	$ 48	

Observations:

In spite of sizable cash needs, which reach a peak of $433,000 in December, the pattern of cash movements winds up not far below the minimum cash balance six months hence. Seasonal short-term borrowing indicated here to cover inventory buildup and lag in collection pattern.

5. ZYX Corporation
Pro forma statements developed from data given:

Initial cash	$250,000
Less: Equipment	175,000
	$ 75,000
Organization expenses	15,000
Cash remaining	$ 60,000

Breakdown of Monthly Purchases

Terms	Aug.	Sept.	Oct.	Nov.	Dec.	Jan.	Feb.	Mar.
Cash	N.A.	$ 45	$ 61*	$ 54	$ 29	$ 32	$ 45	$ 48
2/10, n/30	N.A.	60/60/60*	81*/81*/82	71/71/72	38/39/39	42/43/43	60/60/60	64/64/64
n/45	145/145*	112*/113	153/152	134/133	72/73	80/80	112/113	120/120
Total	—	$450	$610	$535	$290	$320	$450	$480

* Due for payment in October (September purchases reconstructed from $60 amount to 2/10, n/30, which must be one third of 40 percent of total purchases).

ZYX CORPORATION
Pro Forma Operating Statement
Six Months Ended July 31, 1991
(thousands of dollars)

Sales revenue		$2,400 (6 × $400,000)
Cost of goods sold:		
Labor	$ 360	(6 × $ 60,000)
Materials purchased	750	(6 × $125,000)
Rent	111	(6 × $ 18,500)
Overhead	456	(6 × $ 76,000)
Depreciation	36	(6 × $ 6,000)
Amortization	3	(6 × $ 500)
Total	$1,716	
Less: Prepaids	$ 12	
Inventories	205	
	$ 217	1,499
Gross margin		$ 901
Selling and administrative expenses		330 (6 × $ 55,000)
Profit before taxes		$ 571
Taxes at 40%		228
After tax profit		343

ZYX CORPORATION
Pro Forma Balance Sheet
July 31, 1991
(thousands of dollars)

Cash		$ 40 (minimum balance)
Accounts receivable		600 (45 days' sales)
Inventories		205 (given)
Total current assets		$ 845
Equipment	$175	
Less: Depreciation	36	139
Prepaid items		12 (given)
Patents		47 (net of amortization)
Organization expense		15 (given)
Total assets		$1,058
Accounts payable		$ 125 (30 days' purchases)
Accrued expenses		15 (1 week's wages)
Accrued taxes		228 (from operating statement)
Total current liabilities		$ 368
Capital stock ($1 par)		300 (given)
Retained earnings		343 (from operating statement)
		$1,011
"Plug" figure		47 (*Funds need 7/31/91*)
Total liabilities and net worth		$1,058

Observations:

Figures appear quite optimistic; no allowance for start-up problems. Profitability thus seems excessive. There are likely to be greater funds needs early in the period, as collections lag and production problems appear. Also, if taxes have to be prepaid, a major funds source will be affected. Moreover, growth will require additional funds:

10% increase in sales requires:
10% increase in receivables, inventories	$80
Less: 10% increase in payables, accruals	34
	$46
10% increase in cash flow from operations	38
Need	$ 8

This need will increase drastically if key assumptions are off.

6. ABC Supermarket

ABC SUPERMARKET
Cash Budget
for Six Months Ended June 30, 1991
($000)

	Jan.	Feb.	Mar.	Apr.	May	June	Total
Receipts:							
Cash sales . . .	$200.0	$190.0	$220.0	$200.0	$230.0	$220.0	$1,260.0
Cash from sale of property . . .	—	—	6.0	6.0	6.0	—	18.0
Rental income .	—	—	.3	.3	.3	.3	1.2
Total receipts .	$200.0	$190.0	$226.3	$206.3	$236.3	$220.3	$1,279.2
Disbursements:							
Purchases recorded . . .	$150.0	$142.5	$165.0	$150.0	$172.5	$165.0	$ 945.0
Payment for pur-chases (15-day lag)	$159.0	$146.3	$153.7	$157.5	$161.3	$168.7	$ 946.5
Salaries (12% of sales)	24.0	22.8	26.4	24.0	27.6	26.4	151.2
Other expenses (9% of sales) .	18.0	17.1	19.8	18.0	20.7	19.8	113.4
Rent	3.5	3.5	3.5	3.5	3.5	3.5	21.0
Income taxes . .	2.0	—	2.0	3.5	—	2.0	9.5
Note payment .	—	3.0	—	—	5.0	—	8.0
Repayment to principals . .	3.0	—	3.0	—	3.0	—	9.0
Payment on fixtures	—	12.0	12.0	12.0	12.0	—	48.0

	Jan.	Feb.	Mar.	Apr.	May	June	Total
Total disburse-ments . .	$209.5	$204.7	$220.4	$218.5	$233.1	$220.4	$1,306.6
Net cash flow .	$ (9.5)	$ (14.7)	$ 5.9	$ (12.2)	$ 3.2	$ (.1)	$ (27.4)
Cumulative net cash	$ (9.5)	$ (24.2)	$ (18.3)	$(30.5)	$ (27.3)	$ (27.4)	

Analysis of cash requirements:

Beginning cash balance	$ 42.5	$ 33.0	$ 18.3	$ 24.2	$ 12.0	$ 15.2	
Net cash flow .	(9.5)	(14.7)	5.9	(12.2)	3.2	(.1)	
Ending cash balance	$ 33.0	$ 18.3	$ 24.2	$ 12.0	$ 15.2	$ 15.1	
Minimum cash balance	20.0	20.0	20.0	20.0	20.0	20.0	
Cash Need (Excess)	$ (13.0)	$ 1.7	$ (14.2)	$ 8.0	$ 4.8	$ 4.9	

Observations:

The cash pattern indicates excess funds needs in four out of the six months, if a $20,000 minimum balance is desired. The greatest funds need is in April 1991, but even by the end of the period no cleanup of required borrowing will have been achieved.

7. XYZ Company

Cash budget developed from data given:

XYZ COMPANY
Cash Budget by Month
Six Months Ended March 31, 1992
($000)

	Oct.	Nov.	Dec.	Jan.	Feb.	Mar.	Total
Cash receipts:							
Collections (see next page)	$2,608	$2,092	$2,983	$2,400	$2,567	$2,708	$15,358
Cash disbursements:							
Payments for purchases (see below)	712	663	650	650	650	650	3,975
Wages	215	215	215	215	215	215	1,290
Other expenses . .	420	420	420	420	420	420	2,520
Selling & adminis-trative expense .	326	345	343	368	330	342	2,054
Note repayments . .	—	750	—	—	750	—	1,500
Interest	—	—	—	300	—	—	300
Dividend payments	25	—	—	25	—	—	50

XYZ COMPANY (Continued)
Cash Budget by Month
Six Months Ended March 31, 1992
($000)

	Oct.	Nov.	Dec.	Jan.	Feb.	Mar.	Total
Tax payment	—	—	—	375	—	—	375
Total disbursements	$1,698	$2,393	$1,628	$2,353	$2,365	$1,627	$12,064
Net cash receipts (disbursements)	$ 910	$ (301)	$1,355	$ 47	$ 202	$1,081	$ 3,294
Cumulative cash flow	$ 910	$ 609	$1,964	$2,011	$2,213	$3,294	

Collection Pattern

				Sales				
Timing	Aug.	Sept.	Oct.	Nov.	Dec.	Jan.	Feb.	Totals
Oct. 1–10	$ 641							
Oct. 11–20	642							$2,608
Oct. 21–31	642	$ 683*						
Nov. 1–10		683						
Nov. 11–20		684						$2,092
Nov. 21–30			$ 725					
Dec. 1–10			725					
Dec. 11–20			725	$ 766*				$2,983
Dec. 21–31				767				
Jan. 1–10				767				
Jan. 11–20					$ 816			$2,400
Jan. 21–31					817			
Feb. 1–10					817			
Feb. 11–20						$ 875		$2,567
Feb. 21–28						875		
Mar. 1–10						875		
Mar. 11–20							$916	$2,708
Mar. 21–31							917	
Totals	$1,925	$2,050	$2,175	$2,300	2,450	$2,625	—	

* Change in collection pattern assumed.

Accounts Receivable

Sept. 30, 1991:

August sales $1,925
September sales 2,050
$3,975 (60 days)

Dec. 31, 1991:

⅓ of November sales . . . . $ 767

December sales $2,450

$3,217 (40 days)

March 31, 1992:   ⅓ of February sales . . . . $ 917

March sales 2,850

$3,767 (40 days)

Purchase Pattern

45 days' payables throughout; thus there is a lag of ½ months.

Pro forma statements developed from data given and calculated:

XYZ COMPANY
Pro Forma Income Statements
Three Months Ended 12/31/91 and Six Months Ended 3/31/92
($000)

	1991	1991/92	
	3 Months	6 Months	
Sales	$6,925	$15,150	(given)
Cost of sales	4,848	10,605	(70 percent of sales)
Gross margin	$2,077	$ 4,545	
Selling and administrative	$1,014	$ 2,054	(from cash budget)
Interest	75	150	(developed)
	$1,089	$ 2,204	
Profit before taxes	$ 988	$ 2,341	
Income taxes	494	1,171	(50 percent of profit)
Net income	$ 494	$ 1,170	(to balance sheet)

XYZ COMPANY
Pro Forma Balance Sheets
December 31, 1991 and March 31, 1992
($000)

	12/31/91	3/31/92
Cash	$ 2,704 (+$1,964)	$ 4,034 (+$3,294)
Accounts receivable	3,217 (see above)	3,767 (see above)
Raw materials	2,200 (see below)	1,675 (see below)
Finished goods	6,081 (see below)	4,833 (see below)
Plant and equipment (net) . .	7,081 (−$129 depr.)	6,952 (−$258 depr.)
Other assets	1,730 (no change)	1,730 (no change)
Total assets	$23,013	$22,991
Accounts payable	$ 975 (45 days)	$ 975 (45 days)
Notes payable	3,370 (−$750)	2,620 (−$1,500)
Accrued liability	3,444 (see below)	3,521 (see below)
Long-term debt	5,250 (no change)	5,250 (no change)

XYZ COMPANY (Continued)
Pro Forma Balance Sheets
December 31, 1991 and March 31, 1992
($000)

	12/31/91	3/31/92
Preferred stock	$ 1,750 (no change)	$ 1,750 (no change)
Common stock	5,000 (no change)	5,000 (no change)
Earned surplus	3,224 (− $25, + $494)	3,875 (− $50, + $1,170)
Total liabilities	$23,013	$22,991

Inventory Analysis

	12/31/91	3/31/92
Raw Materials:		
Beginning balance	$ 2,725	$ 2,725
Purchases @ $650/month	1,950	3,900
	$ 4,675	$ 6,625
Withdrawals @ $825/month	2,475	4,950
Ending balance	$ 2,200	$ 1,675
Finished Goods:		
Beginning balance	$ 6,420	$ 6,420
Materials @ $825/month	2,475	4,950
Wages @ $215/month	645	1,290
Other expenses @ $420/month	1,260	2,520
Depreciation @ $43/month	129	258
	$10,929	$15,438
Cost of goods sold reported	4,848	10,605
Ending balance	$ 6,081	$ 4,833

Accrued Liabilities

Assume interest of $300 covers one year. Thus, by 9/31/91, $225 must have been accrued. Also, assume liabilities to accrue until paid in cash.

	12/31/91	3/31/92
Beginning balance	$ 2,875	$ 2,875
Accrued interest	75	150
Accrued taxes (income statement)	494	1,171
	$ 3,444	$ 4,196
Interest payment	—	(300)
Tax payment	—	(375)
Balance shown	$ 3,444	$ 3,521

Observations:

The key change is the transformation of receivables and inventories into cash, due to the change in policies. Note the dramatic drop in inventories by 3/31/92, *if* the policies work as expected. No funds needs arise during the period, and the main collection impact is felt in October and December. If collections do not come in as expected, $1,833 will be deferred and not available by 3/31/92, and $1,533 by 12/31/91:

Receivables 12/31/91	$3,217
60 days	4,750
Difference	$1,533
Receivables 3/31/92	$3,767
60 days	5,600
Difference	$1,833

Must make sure inventories go down, and this depends on quality and nature of goods on hand.

Questions for Discussion

1. As it is possible to balance a pro forma balance sheet with a "plug" figure representing cash or a loan, is it necessary to be very careful with accounting conventions?

2. Given the freedom to project pro forma balance sheets and "plugging" them in the end, what limitations are there to this freedom? If so, why?

3. Name key assumptions that have to agree for both a pro forma balance sheet and the matching pro forma operating statement.

4. Differentiate between a cash budget and a pro forma operating statement.

5. Should depreciation ever appear on a cash budget? If not, does it have any direct impact?

6. Must a cash budget and a corresponding set of pro forma statements always tie together so that they can be reconciled?

7. Differentiate between an operating budget (sales, manufacturing, service) and a cash budget.

8. Is it permissible to show an increase in finished goods inventories on a pro forma balance sheet, while at the same time reflecting a production level less than current unit sales in the cost of goods sold area of the operating statement?

9. In what ways is a pro forma funds flow statement helpful to understand projected conditions?

CHAPTER FIVE

Solutions to Problems

1. ABC Corporation

    Break-even point calculation:
    Price per unit $5.50

Variable costs per unit $3.25

Contribution $2.25

Fixed costs: $360,000

Units required to recover fixed costs with contribution:

$$\frac{\$360,000}{\$2.25} = 160,000 \text{ units}$$

a. Leverage

Profit Increases (20%)				Profit Decreases (20%)		
Units	Profit	Change		Units	Profit	Change
160,000	$ 0	—		160,000	$ 0	—
192,000	72,000	infinite		128,000	(72,000)	infinite
230,400	158,400	120.0%		102,400	(129,600)	80.0%
276,480	262,080	65.5%		81,920	(175,680)	39.8%
331,776	386,496	47.5%		65,536	(212,544)	21.0%

Note the declining rate of change as we move away from break-even point.

b. Changes in Conditions
Price drop:
Change in contribution from $2.25 to $1.75:

$$\text{Break-even point: } \frac{\$360,000}{\$1.75} = 205,715 \text{ units}$$

Cost increase—variable:
Change in contribution from $2.25 to $2.00:

$$\text{Break-even point: } \frac{\$360,000}{\$2.00} = 180,000 \text{ units}$$

Cost increase—fixed:
Change in fixed cost from $360,000 to $400,000:

$$\text{Break-even point: } \frac{\$400,000}{\$2.25} = 177,778$$

c. Changing Conditions by Operating Level Calculations must be made step by step to take account of changing conditions:

Contribution from first 150,000 units:

Price $5.50

Variable costs 3.25

Contribution . . . . $2.25 × 150,000 = $337,500

Contribution from next 25,000 units:
Price $5.50
Variable costs 3.00
Contribution . . . . $2.50 × 25,000 = $62,500

Break-even point will lie between 150,000 and 175,000 units, since combined contribution of $400,000 exceeds fixed costs by $40,000. Thus: Break-even point is based on fixed cost remaining after 150,000 units, $22,500.

$$\frac{\$22,500}{\$2.50} = 9,000 \text{ units added to } 150,000, \text{ or } 159,000 \text{ units}$$

Contribution from units after 175,000 units and after 190,000 does not come into play unless fixed costs were raised earlier.

Break-Even Chart
ABC Corporation

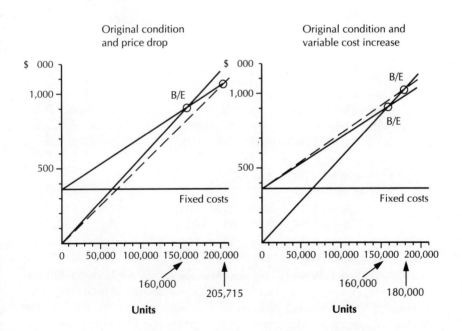

464

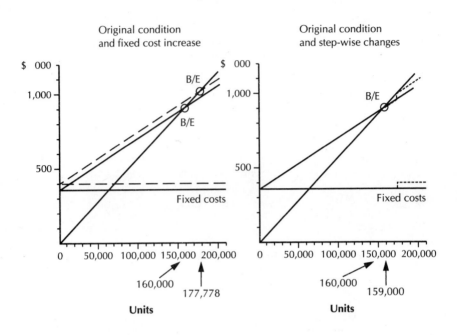

Break-Even Chart
ABC Corporation (continued)

Original condition
and fixed cost increase

Original condition
and step-wise changes

2. Financial Leverage
   a. For $i = 5\%$ and $R = 8\%$:
      —no debt: .... $r = 8\%$
      —25% debt: $0.08 + 25/75(.08 - .05)$; .... $r = 9\%$
      —50% debt: $0.08 + 50/50(.08 - .05)$; .... $r = 11\%$
      —75% debt: $0.08 + 75/25(.08 - .05)$; .... $r = 17\%$
   b. For $i = 6\%$ and $R = 5\%$:
      —no debt: .... $r = 5\%$
      —25% debt: $0.05 + 25/75(.05 - .06)$; .... $r = 4.7\%$
      —50% debt: $0.05 + 50/50(.05 - .06)$; .... $r = 4\%$
      —75% debt: $0.05 + 75/25(.05 - .06)$; .... $r = 2\%$

Observations:
   The leverage effect is less dramatic as the difference between interest rates paid and return on assets earned decreases. Still, at high leverage, a more than proportional push on ROE is achieved, as the graph in the chapter suggested. The negative leverage resulting from poor performance achieved by investing the capital is just as powerful as in the positive case.

3. Five-Year Financial Plan*

	Year 1	Year 2	Year 3	Year 4	Year 5	Revised Year 5
Capitalization:						
Debt-equity ratio	0.25:1	0.25:1	0.50:1	0.50:1	0.50:1	0.75:1
Debt	$ 300	$ 309	$ 638	$ 664	$ 706	$1,059
Equity	1,200	1,235	1,277	1,330	1,413	1,413
Net assets	$1,500	$1,544	$1,915	$1,994	$2,119	$2,472
Profitability:						
Return on net assets	8%	9%	10%	10%	10%	11%
Amount of profit	$120	$139	$192	$199	$212	- $272
Interest rate (after taxes)	4.5%	4.5%	5.0%	5.0%	5.0%	4.5%
Amount of interest	$ 14	$ 14	$ 32	$ 33	$ 35	$ 48
Profit after interest	$106	$125	$160	$166	$177	$224
Earnings disposition:						
Dividend payout	2/3	2/3	2/3	1/2	1/2	2/3
Dividends paid	$ 71	$ 83	$107	$ 83	$ 88	$149
Reinvestment	$ 35	$ 42	$ 53	$ 83	$ 89	$ 75
Financing and Investment:						
New debt, old ratio	9	10	26	42	44	56
New debt, new ratio	—	319	—	—**	—	—
New investment	$ 44	$371	$ 79	$125	$133	$131
Results:						
Net return, net assets	7.1%	8.1%	8.4%	8.3%	8.4%	9.1%
Return on equity	8.8	10.1	12.5	12.5	12.5	15.8
Growth in equity	2.9	3.4	4.2	6.2	6.3	5.3
Growth in earnings	—	17.9	28.0	3.8	6.6	34.9
Earnings per share	$0.53	$0.62	$0.80	$0.83	$0.88	$1.12
Dividends per share	$0.36	$0.42	$0.54	$0.42	$0.44	$0.74

* In thousands of dollars.
** For revised year 5, this item should be $353.

Observations:

The results displayed are self-explanatory and show a rising level as both operating and financial conditions are changed. The higher dividend payout in the revised Year 5 situation causes a drop in equity growth, even though operating conditions are more favorable.

Questions for Discussion

1. Derive a simple formula to express the break-even point in relation to volume and cost.

2. What influence has depreciation, as a fixed cost, on the break-even characteristics of a company?

3. Draw parallels and distinctions between operating and financial leverage, and cite examples from your own experience.

4. Why is it not possible, at the same time, to have high growth in equity and a high dividend payout?

5. What are the key levers management can apply in bringing about high growth in equity?

6. What relevant growth areas can you name as modeling targets, and why are they relevant?

7. Is it realistic to assume a continuous rollover of debt in the growth model? Are there any likely limitations?

8. What are the potential lags involved in attaining sustainable growth targets, such as were discussed in Chapter 2?

9. How does funds flow analysis relate to the business systems diagram in Chapter 1?

10. Which are the most important assumptions in a growth model?

CHAPTER SIX

Solutions to Problems

1. *a.* Net present value at 10 percent and 16 percent (factors from Table 6–9):

Amounts		PV Factors at 10%	Present Value	PV Factors at 16%	Present Value
$10,000	×	.909	$ 9,090	.862	$ 8,620
15,000	×	.826	12,390	.743	11,145
15,000	×	.751	11,265	.641	9,615
20,000	×	.683	13,660	.552	11,040
15,000	×	.621	9,315	.476	7,140
10,000	×	.564	5,640	.410	4,100
5,000	×	.513	2,565	.354	1,770
			$63,925		$53,430
Outlay			60,000		60,000
Net present value			$ 3,925		$ (6,570)

b. Internal Rate of Return (Yield):
Must be between 10 and 16 percent; closer to the lower end.
Trial at 12 percent: (factors from Table 6–9)

Amounts		PV Factors at 12%	Present Value
$10,000	×	.893	$ 8,930
15,000	×	.797	11,955
15,000	×	.712	10,680
20,000	×	.636	12,720

Amounts		PV Factors at 12%	Present Value
$15,000	×	.567	$8,505
10,000	×	.507	5,070
5,000	×	.452	2,260
			$60,120
Outlay			60,000
Net present value			120

The IRR (yield) is approximately <u>12 percent</u>.

c. **Even Cash Flows:**
$13,000 per year at 10 percent (factor from Table 6–10):

$13,000 × 4,868 = $63,284
Net investment   = 60,000
Net present value = $ 3,284

d. **Cash Flows to Yield 16 Percent:**
Annualize the investment of $60,000 at 16 percent:

$$A = \frac{PV}{f}$$

$$A = \frac{\$60,000}{4.039} = \$14,855$$

The required amount over seven years is slightly under <u>$14,900</u>.

e. Net present values at 10 and 16 percent, given recovery of $10,000:
Recovery of $10,000 at end of year 7 (factors from Table 6–9):

at 10 percent: $10,000 × .513 = $5,130
at 16 percent: $10,000 × .354 = $3,540

      Original values in (a):

      at 10 percent: $3,925, plus recovery of $5,130   = <u>$ 9,055</u>

      at 16 percent: $(6,570), plus recovery of $3,540 = <u>$(3,030)</u>

IRR must now be somewhat <u>under 16 percent</u>, since net present value turns negative below that rate.

f. Cash flows to yield 16 percent, given recovery of $10,000:
    Present value of recovery at 16 percent: $3,540 (from e.)
    Present value of investment:

Outlay less present value of recovery
        $60,000 less $3,540 = <u>$56,460</u>

Cash flows required based on annualizing present value of investment: (see *d.*)

$$A = \frac{\$56,460}{4.039} = \underline{\$13,979}$$

Note that the recovery of $10,000 in year 7 reduced required cash flows by about $900 per year. This can, of course, be shown directly by developing the annual equivalent of the recovery:

$$A = \frac{\$3,540}{4.039} = \underline{\$876}$$

2. ABC Company

Net investment: 64% of $1,500,000 = $960,000

Past research and development: Not relevant here.

Profit improvement:

Year 1 64% of $200,000	=	$	128,000
Year 2 64% of $300,000	=		192,000
Year 3 64% of $600,000	=		384,000
Year 4 64% of $500,000	=		320,000
Year 5 64% of $400,000	=		256,000
Total			$1,280,000
Average yearly amount:		$	256,000

Measures calculated: (000 omitted):

a. Payback (on average amount):

$$\frac{\$960}{\$256} = \underline{3.75 \text{ years}} \qquad \text{—Almost 4 years on actual pattern}$$

b. Return on investment:

$$\frac{\$256}{\$960} = \underline{26.7 \text{ percent}} \qquad \text{—Cannot calculate on actual pattern}$$

c. Average return:

$$\frac{\$256}{\$480} = \underline{53.3 \text{ percent}} \qquad \text{—Cannot calculate on actual pattern}$$

d. Net present value (at 12 percent):

—Based on average:	3.605 × $256 (Table 6–10)	= +$922,880
	Outlay	− 960,000
	Net present value	−$ 37,120

—Based on actual pattern: (factors from Table 6–9)

Amounts		PV Factors		Present Value	Cumulative
$128,000	×	.893	=	$114,304	$114,304
192,000	×	.797	=	153,024	267,328
384,000	×	.712	=	273,408	540,736
320,000	×	.636	=	203,520	744,256
256,000	×	.567	=	145,152	889,408

$$+\,\$889,408$$

Outlay . . . . $-\underline{\ 960,000}$

Net present value . . . . $-\underline{\underline{\$\ 70,592}}$

(Note that actual pattern causes worsening of result!)

e. Present value index:

$$\text{—based on average:} \quad \frac{\$922,880}{960,000} = \underline{\underline{.96}}$$

$$\text{—based on pattern:} \quad \frac{\$889,408}{960,000} = \underline{\underline{.93}}$$

f. Internal rate of return:
Due to the closeness of the present value results, the IRR is approximately 12 percent in either case, slightly below on the average basis, and somewhat below on the actual pattern.

g. Present value payback:
Just about five years; a little less on the average basis, a little more on the pattern.

h. Annualized Net Present Value (factors from Table 6–10):

$$\text{Based on average:} \quad \frac{+\$37,120}{3.605} = \underline{\underline{+\$10,297/\text{yr.}}}$$

$$\text{Based on pattern:} \quad \frac{-\$70,592}{3.605} = \underline{\underline{-\$19,582/\text{yr}}}$$

Observations:
The project barely meets current standards. If the data had been available *before* the R&D expenditures were made, the expenditures then and now should not be made. If no other preferable investments are available now, however, the investment is OK since past outlays are *sunk* costs.

3. Trustee of Major Estate
Net investment: $100,000 in a and b.
Yield:

a.
$$\text{Yield factor:} \quad \frac{\$100,000}{\$16,500} = 6.061$$

In Table 6–10, on the eight-year line this corresponds to a yield of about 7 percent if a rough interpolation is made.

b.
$$\text{Yield factor:} \quad \frac{\$100,000}{\$233,000} = .429$$

In Table 6–9, on the 11-year line this corresponds exactly to a yield of 8 percent. Thus, the second proposition is preferable.

4. **DEF Company**

Net investment: $52,800
Life: 8 years, no salvage
Depreciation: $6,600/yr. straight-line

Annual operating cash flow:

Net labor and material savings	$12,100
Less depreciation	6,600
	$ 5,500
Taxes at 46%	2,530
Aftertax savings	$ 2,970
Add back depreciation	6,600
Operating cash flow	$ 9,570

a. Payback:

$$\frac{\$52,800}{\$9,570} = \underline{5.5 \text{ years}}$$

b. Return on Investment:

$$\frac{\$9,570}{\$52,800} = \underline{18.1 \text{ percent}}$$

c. Average Return:

$$\frac{\$9,570}{\$26,400} = \underline{36.2 \text{ percent}}$$

d. Net Present Value (at 10 percent):

Present value of operating cash flow:		
5.335 × $9,570 (Table 6–10):	=	+$51,056
Present value of net investment		− 52,800
Net present value		−$ 1,744

e. Present Value Index:

$$\frac{\$51,056}{\$52,800} = \underline{.97}$$

$f.$ Internal Rate of Return:
Approximately 10 percent.

$g.$ Present Value Payback:
Just about 8 years—very little "cushion" available.

$h.$ Annualized Net Present Value:

$$\frac{-\$1,744}{5.335} = \underline{-\$327/yr.}$$ This shows the annual gap that has to be overcome to meet standard!

Observations:
This example introduces depreciation and its importance as a tax shield. This is an opportunity to demonstrate various ways of calculating tax shield effect. Accelerated depreciation available under the tax laws would tend to boost considerably the benefits of the project in the early years—class should work through different depreciation patterns and develop present values using Tables 6–9 and 6–10.

5. XYZ Corporation
Past investment: $3.75 million (sunk)
Net investment data:
  Original outlay: $6,300,000
  Recovery in 12 years: $1,260,000 (book value)
  Working capital:
    Initial $1,500,000
    Recovery in 12 years $1,250,000
  Promotion expenditure ($1.0 million × .64): $640,000 (after tax)
  Life of proposition: 12 years
  Profit improvements:

	Years 1-3	Years 4-8	Years 9-12	Total
Profit improvement	$1,900	$2,200	$1,300	$21,900
Less: Depreciation	420	420	420	5,040
	1,480	1,780	880	16,860
Tax at 36% (rounded)	533	640	317	6,070
	947	$1,140	563	10,790
Add back depreciation	420	420	420	5,040
Operating cash flow	$1,367	$1,560	$ 983	$15,830

Present Value Analysis at 12 Percent

Time Period	Investments	Operating Cash Flows	PV Factors at 12%	Present Values	PV Factors at 15%	Present Values
0}	−$6,300 −$1,500 −$ 640		1.000	−$8,440	1.000	−$8,440
1 2 3}		+$1,367/yr.	2.402	+ 3,284	2.283	+ 3,120
4 5 6 7 8}		+$1,560/yr.	4.968 −2.402 2.566	+ 4,003	4.487 −2.283 2.204	+ 3,438
9 10 11 12}		+$ 983/yr.	6.194 −4.968 1.226	+ 1,205	5.421 −4.487 .934	+ 918
12}	+$1,260 +$1,250		.257	+ 645	.187	+ 469
	Net present values			+$ 697		−$ 495

Net Present Value at 12 percent is about $700,000, indicating a better-than-standard result. In fact, the recovery of working capital and book values of equipment in year 12 could be foregone and the project would still meet standards.

Present Value Index at 12 percent:
  Based on initial investment

$$\frac{\$9,137}{\$8,440} = \underline{\underline{1.08}}$$

  Based on net investment

$$\frac{\$8,492}{\$7,795} = \underline{\underline{1.09}}$$

Present Value Payback:
  Just about <u>12 years</u> because the recovery represents the excess present value.

IRR:
  By trial and error a little <u>under 15 percent</u>. (See PV analysis above.)

Annualized Net Present Value:

$$\frac{\$697}{6.194} = \underline{\underline{\$112,500/\text{yr.}}} \text{ (narrow margin for error).}$$

Observations:

Project is close to standard; shows problems of handling uneven cash flows. Cannot carry past and sunk R&D—similar future projects are of doubtful value.

6. ZYX Company

Net Investment

Original machine	$32,000	
Current book value	$25,600	
Market value	15,000	(relevant)
Loss on sale	$10,600	
Tax savings on loss @ 36%	3,816	(relevant)
Net loss	$ 6,784	
New investment	$55,500	
Value in eight years	$ 1,500	

Calculation of Net Investment

New machine	$55,500
Less cash on old	15,000
	$40,500
Less tax savings	3,816
Initial investment	$36,684

To be adjusted for recoveries in year 8.

Comparison of Lives

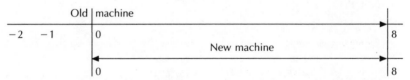

Only eight years are comparable—if new machine lasted longer, its life would have to be cut off for purposes of comparison.

Operating Savings and Benefits

	Old Machine	New Machine	Annual Difference
Operating savings—current volume:			
Labor	$ 24,000	$ 16,000	$ 8,000
Materials	96,000	92,000	4,000
Overhead (200% of labor)	48,000	32,000	(Not Applicable)
	$168,000	$140,000	$12,000

Operating Savings and Benefits (Continued)

	Old Machine	New Machine	Annual Difference
Contribution—additional volume:			
30,000 units @ $.95		$ 28,500	
Less: Labor @ $.08		(2,400)	
Materials @ $.46		(13,800)	
Selling and promotion		(5,500)	6,800
Total savings and contribution			$18,800
Depreciation	$ 3,200	$ 6,750*	(3,550)
Taxable benefits			$15,250
Taxes at 36%			5,490
Aftertax benefits			$ 9,760
Add back depreciation			3,550
Aftertax cash flow			$13,260

* $55,500 New machine
 −1,500 Scrap
 $54,000 ÷ 8 = $6,750/year

Payback:

$$\frac{\$36,684 \; - \; \$1,500}{\$13,260} = 2.65 \text{ years}$$

Return on Investment:

$$\frac{\$13,260}{\$35,184} = 37.7\%$$

Net Present Value:

Time Period	Amounts	PV Factor 16%	Present Values
0	−$36,684	1.00	−$36,684
1–8	+$13,260/yr.	4.344	+$57,601
8	+$ 1,500	.305	+$ 458
	Net present value		+$21,375

Present Value Index:
net investment basis

$$\frac{\$57,601}{\$36,684 \; - \; \$458} = 1.59$$

without terminal value

$$\frac{\$57,601 \; + \; \$458}{\$36,684} = 1.58$$

Present Value Payback:
This is determined through use of the annuity tables.

$$\text{Annuity factor} = \frac{\$36,226}{\$13,260/\text{yr.}} = 2.732$$

Interpolation in the 16 percent column of Table 6–10 indicates a little under four years required. The terminal value can be a problem if significantly larger, because it has been discounted for receipt in year 8. If precision is required, year-by-year trial-and-error approaches can be made.

Annualized Net Present Value:

$$\frac{\$21,375}{4.344} = \$4,920$$

This is a sizable cushion for error in the performance estimates.

Internal Rate of Return:

Trial and error necessary; result about 32%.

Time Period	Amounts	PV Factors at 35%	Present Values	PV Factors at 30%	Present Values
0	− $36,684	1.000	− $36,684	1.000	− $36,684
1–8	+ $13,260/yr.	2.598	+ $34,449	2.925	+ $38,786
8	+ $ 1,500	.091	+ $ 136	.123	+ $ 184
			− $ 2,098		+ $ 2,286

Observations:

This is the best example, among the ones provided, with which to practice your mastery of problem structure, differential costs, different lives, and accounting allocations. Questions could be raised concerning a 10-year life of the new machine, and also whether the product is *worthwhile per se*—which is the assumption on which the differential cost analysis rests. The improvement could merely raise product profitability from *poor to mediocre!*

7. UVW Company

Net investment: $275,000
Life: 12 years
Operating cash flows:

Amount	Probability	Expectation
$15,000	.05	$ 750
35,000	.15	5,250
45,000	.40	18,000
50,000	.25	12,500
60,000	.15	9,000
	1.00	$45,500

Net present value (6 percent):

a. Benefits: 8 × $16,500
    Present value of benefits: 6.210 × $16,500 (Table 6–10) = $102,465
    Net present value: +$2,465

b. Benefits: Lump sum in 11 years, $233,000
    Present value of benefits: .527 × $233,000 (Table 6–9) = $122,791
    Net present value: +$22,791

Observations:

If a higher discount factor were used, the results would be reversed since proposition (A) provides continuous early benefits. The question of risk looms large here—11 years is a long time. Also, some students argue that reinvestment of the cash flows from (A) makes (A) preferable—they must be convinced that the effect has been taken into account in the discount procedure. It is worthwhile to calculate with the class a *compounding* of all cash flows to 11 years to prove this point. The question of changing earnings opportunities over time should be posed.

a. *Net Present Value at 10%* (on expectation):

    Investment outlay . . . . −$275,000
    12 years at $45,500 (6.814) . . . . + 310,040
    Net present value . . . . +$ 34,960

    This is also approximately the same as the net present value based on the most likely outcome ($45,000):

    Investment . . . . −$275,000
    6.814 × $45,000 306,630
    Net present value . . . . +$ 31,630

b. Annualized net present value:
    —on expectation

    $$\frac{\$34,960}{6.814} = \underline{\$5,130}$$

    —on most likely value

    $$\frac{\$31,630}{6.814} = \underline{\$4,640}$$

    In either case there is a sizable cushion against estimating error.

c. Internal rate of return:

    $$\frac{\$275,000}{\$45,500} = 6.044; \text{ or } \frac{\$275,000}{\$45,000} = 6.111$$

Yield over 12 years is about <u>12 percent</u> (12-year life in Table 6–10) in either case.

d. Minimum life at $45,000/yr.:

$$\frac{\$275,000}{\$45,000} = 6.111 \text{ at } 10\%$$

This requires a little under <u>10 years</u> (10 percent column in Table 6–10), a cushion of about 2 years.

e. Minimum cash flow to achieve 10%:

$$\frac{\$275,000}{6.814} = \underline{\$40,360} \text{ per year for 12 years}$$

The chances of achieving this level of cash flow are better than 80 percent—is this good enough?

Observations:

This example serves to point up by elements of probabilistic reasoning, holding a lot of assumptions stable. It appears that the success of the project has a reasonable chance, but the final answer rests on the judgment of the people involved.

Questions for Discussion

1. Define the difference between cash flows, differential costs, and relevant costs.

2. Why is it necessary to study what the various alternatives are before making a capital investment decision?

3. Are sunk costs always to be ignored in capital investment analysis? Cannot such a practice lead to financial difficulties?

4. Do past investments in large support facilities count when considering production investments that will make use of this unused capacity?

5. Do accounting allocations ever become relevant in investment analysis?

6. Define the difference between present value payback and annualized net present value.

7. What is the difference between an annualized net present value and an annuity?

8. Why is it possible that the internal rate of return (yield) can provide two answers at the same time?

9. Why is it necessary to adjust for uneven lives in alternative capital investments when discounting reduces the importance of future cash flows anyway?

10. Is it possible to make an annual charge for working capital in a capital investment proposal, in lieu of specifying an outflow for the amount of

working capital at point zero and an inflow for its recovery at the end of
the last year?

11. Differentiate between capital budgeting and capital investment analysis. Which additional questions need to be resolved in the former?

12. Which aspects of capital investment analysis and capital budgeting lend themselves to modeling?

CHAPTER SEVEN

Solutions to Problems

1. GHI Company

Calculations of Cost of Capital:

Existing debt:	12% × (1 − .36) =	7.7%
Incremental debt:	10% × (1 − .36) =	6.4%
Existing preferred:		14.00%
Incremental preferred		12.00%

Common equity:

earnings basis: $\dfrac{\$\,9.50}{\$77.00} = 12.3\%$

dividend basis: $\dfrac{\$\,4.50}{\$77.00} + 7\% = 12.8\%$

CAPM: $k_e = 9\% + 1.25\,(15.0 - 9.0) = 16.5\%$

Observations:
   There is a need to define the purpose of the analysis, and the figures by themselves are only the beginning. The cost of common equity shows a large differential between the shortcuts and the CAPM approach. It would be useful to be able to review recent company performance. Apparently the risk premium implicit in the β suggests that more volatility can be expected.

2. KLN Company
Weighted Cost of Capital:
Existing conditions

Debt cost 7.0(1 − .46) 3.78%

Preferred cost 6.00%

Common equity cost—(CAPM 7.5 + 1.2 (13.5 − 7.5) 14.7%

Incremental conditions

Debt cost 11.0(1 − .46) 5.94%

Preferred cost 9.00%

Common equity (CAPM) 14.7%

Assignment of weights:
Book value basis:

Debt	$250	35.8%
Preferred	50	7.1
Common equity	400	57.1
	$700	100.0%

Market value basis:

Debt (7.0/11.0 × 250)	$159	23.0%
Preferred (6.0/9.0 × 50)	33	4.8
Common equity $50/share	500	72.2
	$692	100.0%

Weighted Cost (Incremental):

	Book Value			Market Value		
Debt	35.8% ×	5.94 =	2.13%	23.0% ×	5.94 =	1.37%
Preferred	7.1 ×	9.00 =	0.64	4.8 ×	9.00 =	0.43
Common						
equity	57.1 ×	14.70 =	8.39	72.2 ×	14.70 =	10.61
	100.0%		11.16%	100.0%		12.41%

Weighted Cost (Existing):

	Book Value			Market Value		
Debt	35.8% ×	3.78 =	1.35%	23.0% ×	3.78 =	0.87%
Preferred	7.1 ×	6.00 =	0.43	4.8 ×	6.00 =	0.26
Common						
equity	57.1 ×	14.70 =	8.39	72.2 ×	14.70 =	10.61
	100.0%		10.17%	100.0%		11.74%

Observations:

The range of results is narrow, within two percentage points. If we ignore the book value basis as not relevant, the market value results are even closer. If any use is made of the concept for future investments, the existing conditions are not relevant either—thus, the weighted cost is about 12 percent, perhaps a little higher.

Questions for Discussion

1. Why is it not possible to speak of "*the* cost of capital" as an absolute figure?
2. What indirect costs can be ascribed to a long-term loan, or to a convertible debenture?
3. Why are shareholder expectations important in developing the cost of

common equity when the company has no control over the behavior of the stock market?

4. If beta, as defined in the CAPM, is not a fully satisfactory measure of risk, what alternative concepts can you suggest?

5. How important is the choice of weights in developing the weighted cost of capital as a minimum return standard?

6. If weighted cost of capital is a useful standard with which to assess prospective returns from new capital investments, how should the return on existing investments be judged?

7. If a company's financial policies are changing, i.e., the use of leverage increases, does this mean its return requirements must change also?

8. If you were president of a multidivision company with rather different businesses, how would you answer the argument that some divisions should use lower return standards than others?

9. How critical is it that a capital investment project exactly meet the weighted cost of capital standard? What questions would you ask?

10. What are the major elements you would consider in developing a broad allocation of capital to the rather different divisions of a company? Which would be the most important?

CHAPTER EIGHT

Solutions to Problems

1. ABC Corporation

   a. Per Share Analysis
($000, except per share amounts)

	Old Level	New Level
EBIT	$ 14,700	$ 17,400 (118%)
Interest (same)	1,100	1,100
Profit before taxes	$ 13,600	$ 16,300
Taxes at 34%	4,625	5,540
Profit after taxes	$ 8,975	$ 10,760
Number of common shares	300,000	350,000
Earnings per share	$ 29.91	$ 30.74
Sinking fund	$ 900	$ 900
Sinking fund per share	$ 3.00	$ 2.57
Uncommitted earnings per share	$ 26.91	$ 28.17
Depreciation per share	$ 7.50	$ 6.43
Cash flow per share	$ 37.41	$ 37.17

Immediate dilution: $\frac{\$8,975,000}{350,000} - \$29.41 = \underline{(\$3.77) \text{ Dilution } (12.8\%)}$

Net dilution (strengthening) $30.74 - \$29.41 = \underline{\$1.33 \text{ Strengthening } (4.5\%)}$

b. $5.0 million preferred stock (10%)
or $5.0 million debentures (9%), due in 15 years

Per Share Analysis
($000, except per share amounts)

	Preferred		Debentures	
	Old Level	New Level	Old Level	New Level
EBIT	$ 14,700	$ 17,400	$ 14,700	$ 17,400
Interest—old	1,100	1,100	1,100	1,100
Interest—new	—	—	450	450
Profit before taxes	$ 13,600	$ 16,300	$ 13,150	$ 15,850
Taxes at 34%	4,625	5,540	4,475	5,390
Profit after taxes	$ 8,975	$ 10,760	$ 8,675	$ 10,460
Preferred dividends	500	500	—	—
Profits to common	$ 8,475	$ 10,260	$ 8,675	$ 10,460
Number of common shares . . .	300,000	300,000	300,000	300,000
Earnings per share	$ 28.25	$ 34.20	$ 28.92	$ 34.86
Sinking fund	$ 900	$ 900	$ 900	$ 900
Sinking fund per share	$ 3.00	$ 3.00	$ 3.00	$ 3.00
Uncommitted earnings per share	$ 25.25	$ 31.20	$ 25.92	$ 31.86
Depreciation per share	$ 7.50	$ 7.50	$ 7.50	$ 7.50
Cash flow per share	$ 35.75	$ 41.70	$ 36.42	$ 42.36

Immediate dilution:

Preferred: $28.25 − $29.91 = (1.06)

$$\frac{\$\ 1.66}{\$29.91} = \underline{5.9\%\ \text{Dilution}}$$

Debentures: $28.92 − $29.91 = ($.99)

$$\frac{\$\ .99}{\$29.91} = \underline{3.4\%\ \text{Dilution}}$$

Net dilution: (strengthening)
Preferred: $34.20 − $29.91 = $4.29; <u>14.3% Strengthening</u>

Debentures: $34.86 − $29.91 = $4.95; <u>16.5% Strengthening</u>

c. Comparative Cost of Capital:
—Common Stock:
$5 million represents 50,000 shares, or $100 per share, far below the current average price of $130. EPS required to keep stockholders as well off as before: $29.91. Thus, the apparent "cost" of this issue is

$$\frac{\$29.91}{\$100.00} = \underline{29.9\%\ \text{after taxes}}, \text{a very } \textit{low} \text{ P/E ratio, indeed.}$$

Based on the CAPM, the cost of common stock is

$$8.0 + 1.4\ (14.5 − 8.0) = 17.1\%\ \text{after taxes.}$$

Obviously a risky company, from which the market is demanding a high risk premium.

—Preferred stock: <u>10% after taxes</u>

—Debentures: <u>5.9% after taxes</u>

Observations:
Note the apparent attractiveness of the new investments, and the leverage effect of lower-cost preferred or debt. (Example has been *exaggerated*—low P/E—to make differences more apparent.)

2. XYZ Corporation
   a. Comparative cost of capital:
      (1) Determine EBIT level:

EPS (current)	$12.50
Number of common shares	1,000,000
Profit to common	$12,500,000
Preferred dividends (existing)	1,500,000
Profit after taxes	$14,000,000
Taxes (46%)	11,925,000
Profit before taxes	$25,925,000
Bond interest (existing)	2,500,000
EBIT	$28,425,000

      (2) Determine profit to common at current EBIT level:

	Common	Preferred
EBIT	$28,425	$28,425
Interest	2,500	2,500
Profit before taxes	$25,925	$25,925
Taxes (46%)	11,925	11,925
Profit after taxes	$14,000	$14,000
Preferred dividends	1,500	4,200
Profit to common	$12,500	$ 9,800
Number of shares	1,240,000	1,000,000
EPS	$10.08	$ 9.80

      (3) Determine profit to common needed to maintain current eps:

	Common	Preferred
Eps	$12.50	$12.50
Number of shares	1,240,000	1,000,000
Profit to common	$15,500	$12,500
Profit to common—current EBIT	12,500	9,800
Incremental profit (after taxes)	$ 3,000	$ 2,700

	Common	Preferred
Incremental investment	$30,000	$30,000
Specific cost of capital	10.0%	9.0%
Specific cost before taxes	18.5%	16.7%

Preferred stock cost of capital is the same as the stated dividend rate, of course, assuming issue at par.

(4)   Calculation of cost of common equity based on CAPM:

$$k_e = 8.0 + 1.2\,(13.0 - 8.0)$$
$$k_e = 8.0 + 6.0 = \underline{14.0\%}$$

b.   Equivalency between common and preferred alternatives:

Formula: $\dfrac{(E - i)\,.54 - p}{n}$

(Common) (Preferred)

$$\frac{(E - \$2,500)\,.54 - \$1,500}{1,240} = \frac{(E - \$2,500)\,.54 - \$4,200}{1,000}$$

$$540E - 1,350,000 - 1,500,000 = 669.6E - 1,674,000 - 5,208,000$$
$$129.6E = 4,032,000$$
$$E = 31,111$$

Earnings equivalency thus at $\underline{\$31,111,000 \text{ EBIT}}$.

Earnings per share/dividend per share equivalency:

EPS needed for $8.00 dividend	$8.00
Number of common shares	1,240,000
Profit to common	$ 9,920,000
Preferred dividends	1,500,000
Profit after taxes	$11,420,000
Taxes (46%)	9,728,000
Profit before taxes	$21,148,000
Interest	2,500,000
EBIT for $8.00 dividend	$23,648,000

c.   Leverage effect of preferred alternative:

	Level 1	Level 2	Level 3	Level 4
EBIT (current $28,425)	$10,000	$15,000	$22,500	$33,750
Interest	2,500	2,500	2,500	2,500
	$ 7,500	$12,500	$20,000	$31,250
Taxes (46%)	3,450	5,750	9,200	14,375
	$ 4,050	$ 6,750	$10,800	$16,875
Preferred dividend	4,200	4,200	4,200	4,200
Profit to common	$ (150)	$ 2,550	$ 6,600	$12,675

	Level 1	Level 2	Level 3	Level 4
Common shares	1,000,000	1,000,000	1,000,000	1,000,000
Eps (current $ $12.50)	$ (.15)	$ 2.55	$ 6.60	$12.68
Percent increase in EBIT		50%	50%	50%
Percent increase in EPS		Infinite	159%	92%

Highly leveraged situation, but rate of increase drops as earnings move away from EBIT break-even level. (Coverage of fixed charges = zero Eps, or EBIT level of $10.28 million.)

XYZ CORPORATION
EBIT Chart

Break-even point

DPS = $8.00

Zero EPS

Common

Preferred

EPS (dollars)

$5,278 $10,028 $23,648 $31,111

EBIT (millions of dollars)

Observations:
Again, some exaggeration to make the points involved. Should use for good drilling of concepts—work data in both directions.

3. DEF Company

EPS Calculations
($000, except per share amounts)

	Common		Preferred		Debentures	
	Current*	Low	Current*	Low	Current*	Low
EBIT	$42,000	$22,000	$42,000	$22,000	$42,000	$22,000
Interest—old	1,200	1,200	1,200	1,200	1,200	1,200

EPS Calculations (Continued)
($000, except per share amounts)

	Common		Preferred		Debentures	
	Current*	Low	Current*	Low	Current*	Low
Interest–new	—	—	—	—	$ 4,250	$ 4,250
Profit before taxes . . .	$40,800	$20,800	$40,800	$20,800	$36,550	$16,550
Taxes (46%)	18,768	9,568	18,768	9,568	16,813	7,613
Profit after taxes	$22,032	$11,232	$22,032	$11,232	$19,737	$ 8,937
Preferred dividend						
—old	1,800	1,800	1,800	1,800	1,800	1,800
Preferred dividend						
—new	—	—	4,750	4,750	—	—
Profit to common . . .	$20,232	$ 9,432	$15,482	$ 4,682	$17,937	$ 7,137
Number of common						
shares (millions) . . .	3.0	3.0	2.0	2.0	2.0	2.0
EPS	$6.74	$3.14	$7.94	$2.34	$8.97	$3.57
SFPS	$ .33	$ .33	$ .50	$ .50	$1.50	$1.50
UEPS	$6.41	$2.81	$7.24	$1.84	$7.47	$2.07
Dividend coverage						
(EPS)	3.37×	1.57×	3.87×	1.17×	4.49×	.79×

* Current EBIT plus incremental earnings on new capital.

Dilution Data

	Common	Preferred	Debentures
EBIT (old)	$34,000	$34,000	$34,000
Interest	1,200	1,200	5,450
Profit before taxes	$32,800	$32,800	$28,550
Taxes (46%)	15,088	15,088	13,133
Profit after taxes	$17,712	$17,712	$15,417
Preferred dividends	1,800	6,550	1,800
Profit to common	$15,912	$11,162	$13,617
Number of shares (millions)	3.0	2.0	2.0
EPS (old = $7.96)	$ 5.30	$ 5.58	$ 6.81

Immediate Dilution:

Common: $7.96 − $5.30 = $2.66; drop of 33.4%

Preferred: $7.96 − $5.58 = $2.38; drop of 29.9%

Debentures: $7.96 − $6.81 = $1.15; drop of 14.4%

Net Dilution (strengthening):

Common: $7.96 − $6.74 = $1.22; drop of 15.3%

Preferred: $7.96 − $7.74 = $(.22); drop of   2.8%

Debentures: $7.96 − $8.97 = $(1.01); drop of 12.7%

Dilution Data (Continued)

Cost of Capital (after tax):

Common: $7.96 per share for $50.00—apparent "cost" = 15.9%

Preferred: 9.5 percent stated rate   =   9.5%

Debentures: 9.5 percent before tax $(1 - .46) \times 8.5\%$ =   4.6%

* Based on the CAPM, the cost of common is $7.5 + 1.2(14.0 - 7.5) = 15.2\%$.

Break-Even Points:
Common versus preferred:

$$\frac{(E - 1,200).54 - 1,800}{3,000} = \frac{(E - 1,200).54 - 6,550}{2,000}$$
$$\text{(common)} \qquad\qquad\qquad \text{(preferred)}$$

$1,080E - 1,296,000 - 3,600,000 = 1,620E - 1,944,000 - 19,650,000$
$540E = 16,698,000; \; E = 30,922; \; \text{EBIT} = \$30,922,200$

Common versus debentures:

$$\frac{(E - 1,200).54 - 1,800}{3,000} = \frac{(E - 5,450).54 - 1,800}{2,000}$$

$1,080E - 1,296,000 - 3,600,000 = 1,620E - 8,829,000 - 5,400,000$
$540E = 9,333,000; \; E = 17,283; \; \text{EBIT} = \$17,283,300$

Dividend Coverage:
Shown in first set of calculations (EPS).

Zero EPS:
Common:

$(E - 1,200).54 - 1,800 = 0$
$.54E - 648 - 1,800 = 0$
$E = 4,533,300 \text{ EBIT}$

Preferred:

$(E - 1,200).54 - 6,550 = 0$
$.54E - 648 - 6,550 = 0$
$E = \$13,329,600 \text{ EBIT}$

Debentures:

$(E - 5,450).54 - 1,800 = 0$
$.54E - 2,943 - 1,800 = 0$
$E = \$8,783,300 \text{ EBIT}$

DEF Company
EBIT Chart

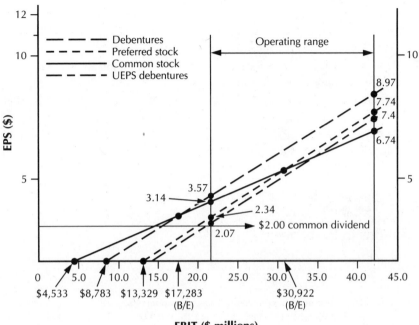

EBIT ($ millions)

Observations:

The example allows full treatment of the technical aspects of the three alternatives, and the display is useful in its exaggeration. Please review the key points beyond those represented by the figures, which are also necessary for choice. Otherwise the data are self-explanatory.

Questions for Discussion

1. List the key conditions that would affect the relative importance of the areas of cost, risk exposure, flexibility, timing, and control.

2. Why is it important to look ahead to the potential next stage of financing when deciding the choice among current alternatives for new funds?

3. Relate the weighted cost of capital of a company to the costs of the respective alternatives for incremental funds. Are they based on the same reasoning?

4. How does the immediate dilution of earnings caused by alternative ways

of raising additional funds relate to the return standards required for new investments?

5. Why are calculations of the comparative cost of alternative financing choices based on the proceeds and not on the face value?

6. What are the key assumptions underlying the EBIT chart, and under what conditions is it necessary to redraw the lines?

7. How does prospective inflation affect the choice among alternative methods of raising additional funds?

8. When leasing is an alternative, what are the key considerations that would make it attractive?

9. Is there such a thing as an ideal long-term capital structure, and should blocks of incremental capital be tailored to fit such a structure?

CHAPTER NINE

Solutions to Problems

1. Bond Price Examples

   a. Price at 6%:

Principal due after 28 periods at 3%, plus premium of $75 (using preprogrammed calculator) $1,075 × 0.437	$ 469.78
PV of 28 semiannual interest payments of $40, at 3% per period (factor from calculator) $40 × 18.764	750.56
Price to yield 6% per annum	$1,220.34

   Price at 10%

$1,075 × 0.255 (Table 6–9)	$ 274.12
$40 × 14.898 (Table 6–10)	595.92
Price to yield 10% per annum	$ 870.04

   b. Price at 6%:

Principal due after 44 periods at 3% if not called: $1,000 × 0.31 (interpolation, Table 6–9)	$ 310.00
44 semiannual interest receipts of $42.50: $42.50 × 24.0 (interpolation, Table 6–10)	1,020.00
Price to yield 6% per annum	$1,330.00

   If called at 110 on 10/1/99:

Principal plus call premium due after 24 periods at 3%: $1,100 × 0.50 (interpolation, Table 6–9)	$ 550.00
24 semiannual interest receipts of $42.50: $42.50 × 16.9 (interpolation, Table 6–10)	718.25
Price to yield 6% per annum	$1,268.25

c. Price at 9%:

$1,000 × 0.13 (interpolation, 4.5%) . . . . $ 130.00
$42.50 × 18.7 (interpolation, 4.5%) 794.75
Price to yield 9% per annum . . . . $ 924.75

If called:
$1,100 × 0.33 (interpolation, 4.5%) . . . . $ 363.00
$42.50 × 14.3 (interpolation, 4.5%) 607.75
Price to yield 9% per annum . . . . $ 970.75

2. Bond Yield Examples:

a. No interest accrued, because interest date coincides with purchase date.

Market price 7/15/90 . . . . $1,241.25
Redemption price 7/15/04 . . . . 1,100.00
                                                       $2,341.25
Average investment (1/2) $1,170.63

Number of periods: 28
Interest per period: $35.00
Amortization of premium: $141.25 ÷ 28 = $5.04
Average periodic income: $35.00 − $5.04 = $29.96, or $59.92 per year

Yield: $\dfrac{\$59.92}{\$1,170.63}$ = 5.12%

Exact yield from bond table: 4.65%

b. Exact yield from bond table: 4.85%

c. Annual interest: $40.00
Accrued interest on August 20, 1990:

$$5 \text{ months} + 20 \text{ days} = 170 \text{ days}$$

or $\dfrac{170}{360} \times \$40 = \underline{\$18.89}$

Net price on August 20:

$$\$487.50 - \$18.89 = \underline{\$468.61}$$

Market price 8/20/90 . . . . $468.61
Redemption price 3/1/02 . . . . 500.00
                                                          $968.61
Average investment (1/2) $484.30

23½ (approximately) periods of interest @ $40.00
Amortization of discount: $31.39 ÷ 23.5 = $1.34
Annual income: $40.00 − $1.34 = $38.66

Approximate yield: $\dfrac{\$38.66}{\$484.30} = \underline{\underline{7.98\%}}$

Exact yield from bond table: $\underline{\underline{8.62\%}}$

3. Calculation of Common Stock Value:

  a. Expected yield using the CAPM:

  Company A: $7.0 + 1.3(13.5 - 7.0) = 7.0 + 8.45 = \underline{\underline{15.45\%}}$

  Company B: $7.0 + 0.8(13.5 - 7.0) = 7.0 + 5.2 = \underline{\underline{12.2\%}}$

  b. Valuation: (Dividend discount model)

  Company A: $P = \dfrac{D}{I - g}; \; P = \dfrac{\$1.00}{.154 - 0.08} = \underline{\underline{\$13.50}}$

  Company B: $P = \dfrac{\$5.00}{0.122 - 0.04}; \dfrac{\$500}{.082} = \underline{\underline{\$61.00}}$

  c. Other yardsticks:

	Company A	Company B
Earnings yield:	$\dfrac{\$2.50}{\frac{1}{2}(26 + 18)} = \underline{\underline{11.4\%}}$	$\dfrac{\$7.25}{\frac{1}{2}(60 + 56)} = \underline{\underline{12.5\%}}$
Dividend yield:	$\dfrac{\$1.00}{\$22.00} = \underline{\underline{4.5\%}}$	$\dfrac{5.00}{\$58.00} = \underline{\underline{8.6\%}}$

Observations:

Company A is the more volatile if faster-growing company. The market is apparently awarding it a premium at the moment. It would be useful to check out public expectations about the company's future performance. Company B seems stable and properly priced; no surprises here.

4. Valuation of GHI Company as an ongoing business

Calculation of Present Values

	Year 1	Year 2	Year 3	Year 4	Year 5	Terminal Value
Earnings after taxes	$2.7	$2.9	$3.2	$3.6	$ 4.0	—
Add: Depreciation	1.0	1.1	1.4	1.6	1.8	—
Aftertax cash flow	$3.7	$4.0	$4.6	$5.2	$ 5.8	—
Less: Investments	0.5	2.5	1.5	1.5	2.0	—
Net cash flow	3.2	1.5	3.1	3.7	3.8	$40.0
Present value factors (from Table 6–9)	.893	.797	.712	636	.567	.567
Present values	$2.86	$1.20	$2.21	$2.35	$ 2.15	$22.68
Cumulative	$2.86	$4.06	$6.27	$8.62	$10.77	$33.45

Based on current P/E ratio, the company is worth about 11 × $2.5 million, or $27.5 million. Building in the projected growth raises the value.

Observations:

Quality of estimates is a question, as is the choice of the discount rate. If the rate is raised, the value drops, of course. Would need to know more about financial condition, debt to be assumed, nature of business, etc. Many more questions must be asked—this is just the start.

5. MNO Company

Book Value
(based on balance sheet)

Common equity:

Common stock	$ 525
Capital surplus	110
Earned surplus	385
Total	$1,020
Number of shares	52,500
Book value per share	$19.43

If we assume surplus reserves and deferred taxes to be part of equity, the total rises to $1,185, and the value per share to $22.57. The redundant cash is minimal in this picture and should probably be applied to accounts payable.

Liquidation Value

Assets	Fast Liquidation	Normal Sale
Cash	$ 230	$ 230
Securities	415	415
Receivables (94%)	494	494
Inventories (2/3; 95%)	543	774
Fixed assets	225	225+
Prepaids (assume 25%)	—	10
Goodwill	—	—
Organization expense	—	—
Total	$1,907	$2,148
Less:		
Current liabilities	$ 935	$ 935
Mortgage payable	175	175
Bonds	520	520
Preferred stock	300	300
Total deduction	$1,930	$1,930
Value of common	$ (23)	$ 218
Per share	$ (.44)	$ 4.15

Market Value

Most recent: $25⅛, but thinly traded.

Based on average of past 3 years: $28⅛.

Based on recent industry P/E of 11: $.65 × 4 × 11 = $28.60.

Based on average P/E of 13: $.65 × 4 × 13 = $33.80.

Based on long-term profit growth, EPS should be about $3.00, and P/E of 11 would be $33.00.

Observations:

Because no forced liquidation is intended, the value should be based on a going concern concept, and the main argument should be on the breadth of the market, the use of industry P/E ratios, etc.

Additional information should be sought about nature of the industry, long-term product trends, profitability of similar companies, dividend policies of other companies, product line changes and threats, competitive abilities, etc.

6. **Potential Merger**

	Company A	Company B
P/E ratio	12X	20X
Earnings per share	$8.00	$3.00
Dividends per share	$2.00	none
Aftertax earnings	$80.0 million	$3.0 million
Price range	$90 to $100	$45 to $70
Current price	$98.00	$54.00 ($65.00 offered)
Growth rate	6% per year	12% per year
Number of shares	10 million	1 million

a. Exchange ratio:

   65 ÷ 98 = ⅔ share of A for 1 share of B = 667,000 shares

b. Impact on earnings:

   $80.0 million plus $3.0 million = $83.0 million
   10.0 million shares plus 667,000 = 10,667,000 shares
   $83.0 ÷ 10,667,000 = $7.78 per share (22¢ dilution)

c. Impact on dividends:

   Each share of Company B now receives the equivalent of $1.33 per share in dividends versus none before.

d. Impact on earnings growth:
   3 years hence the situation is expected to be:
   Company A @ 6% growth will earn $95.3 million ($9.53 eps)

Company B @ 12% growth will earn $ 4.2 million ($4.20 eps)
Total company earnings thus will grow to $99.5 million,
and eps will be $99.5 ÷ 10,667,000 = $9.33.

Observations:

The dilution in earnings of 22 cents immediately is not likely to be overcome in the foreseeable future, inasmuch as in three years the earnings per share of the combined company will be 20 cents *lower* than what Company A alone could have achieved. On the other hand, synergy, if any, has not been considered. In view of the sizable annual dividends now paid them, the holders of Company B stock might perhaps consider a somewhat lower offer.

Questions for Discussion

1. Differentiate between economic value and market value. Are both concepts absolute?

2. Is value in the eye of the beholder or can conditions be quantified sufficiently to allow objective choices?

3. Discuss the relationship between yield and value. Are both concepts based on the same conditions?

4. Is it possible to allow specifically for the effect of such provisions as participation, convertibility, callability, and other special covenants in valuing preferred stocks or bonds?

5. Why should one attempt to value an ongoing business via cash flow analysis when in the end the decision is based on many other factors as well?

6. List major considerations affecting valuation in an inflationary environment?

7. If price/earnings ratios are so important in setting the ratio of exchange in a merger based on a share swap, how can such a volatile measure give reasonable indications of value?

8. Synergy is an argument for business combinations, but hard to measure and achieve. Why?

9. With vast increases in computer capabilities, will valuation likely become more quantified?

10. If there is so much uncertainty in estimates of future cash flows, why does it make sense to apply even more sophisticated valuation formulas?

INDEX